Reality TV

The Work of Being Watched

Mark Andrejevic

ROWMAN & LITTLEFIELD PUBLISHERS, INC.
Lanham • Boulder • New York • Toronto • Oxford

ROWMAN & LITTLEFIELD PUBLISHERS, INC.

Published in the United States of America
by Rowman & Littlefield Publishers, Inc.
A wholly owned subsidiary of The Rowman & Littlefield Publishing Group, Inc.
4501 Forbes Boulevard, Suite 200, Lanham, Maryland 20706
www.rowmanlittlefield.com

P.O. Box 317, Oxford OX2 9RU, United Kingdom

British Library Cataloguing in Publication Information Available

Library of Congress Cataloging-in-Publication Data

Andrejevic, Mark, 1964–
Reality TV : the work of being watched / Mark Andrejevic.
    p. cm. — (Critical media studies)
Includes bibliographical references and index.
    ISBN 0-7425-2747-6 (cloth : alk. paper) — ISBN 0-7425-2748-4 (pbk. :
alk. paper)
 1. Reality television programs.   2. Television broadcasting—Social
aspects. I Title. II. Series.
    PN1992.8.R43A53 2003
    791.45'6—dc21
                                                    2003007441
Printed in the United States of America

♾™ The paper used in this publication meets the minimum requirements of American
National Standard for Information Sciences—Permanence of Paper for Printed Library
Materials, ANSI/NISO Z39.48-1992.

To my mother, Helen, and the memory
of my father, Mileta. Their version of realism
always included the attempt to improve
upon the given reality.

Reality TV

Contents

Acknowledgments

This book is, in large part, an expression of my time at the University of Colorado's School of Journalism and Mass Communication (SJMC) amid the faculty, students, and staff who made that experience so productive and fulfilling. In particular, Janice Peck's boundless intellectual generosity and support, her graceful mentorship and warm friendship, are at the heart of that experience and thus of this book. Andrew Calabrese supported this project from its inception, and his interest, encouragement, feedback, and sage advice have been vital to its development and my own.

Much of the initial work on this book was supported by a Thomas Edwin Devaney Fellowship from the Center for Humanities and the Arts at the University of Colorado. My profound gratitude to the Center and its supporters, as well as to its director, Jeff Cox, and program assistant Paula Anderson. The support of the SJMC and its administrators and staff over the years was similarly invaluable: particular thanks to Stewart Hoover, Trager, and Dave Martinez.

The book benefited greatly from the two summers I spent at the University of Ljubljana's summer program in media literacy, thanks to Zala Volcic and Karmen Erjavec and the wonderful group of students they assembled. My profound gratitude to Zala for her encouragement and perseverance.

The ideas and arguments also took shape under the guidance of the faculty members I was fortunate enough to work with at Colorado, including: Jeff Cox, Robert Craig, David Gross, Jerry Hauser, Michael Tracey, and Eric White. I am indebted to those who introduced me to critical theory over the years: David Fairris, Ralph Bradburd, and Richard Campbell. While writing, I was the beneficiary of the companionship and intellectual community provided by the students at the SJMC, including (but not limited to!): Dean Colby, Eric Berthelette, Scott Webber, Travis Ripley, Helga Tawil, Claudia Maximino, Andrea Roth, Shoba Rajgopal, Tim Schoechle, Jan Fernback, and Lynn Clark. So many people have been generous with their minds: James Martel, Slavko Andrejevic, James McDaniel,

ix

James Hay, Gabe Shapiro, Fred Turner, Greg Elmer, Mick Khoo, Priya Jha, Elenie Opffer, Lisa Guerin, Chris Becker, and many more.

At Fairfield, thanks to Robbin Crabtree for her ongoing support and to Sharon Abbott and Joanna Swyers for their warmth and humor and for repeatedly saving me from late-night revision solitude.

Thanks to editors Brenda Hadenfeldt and Dianne Ewing and editorial assistants Heather Armstrong and Jeska Horgan-Kobelski for their interest, invaluable assistance, and efficiency.

Much of chapter 4 first appeared in *New Media and Society* (Andrejevic, M., "The Kinder, Gentler Gaze of Big Brother," June 2002) and sections of chapter 3 first appeared in *Critical Studies in Media Communication* (Andrejevic, M., "The Work of Being Watched: Interactive Media and the Exploitation of Self-Disclosure," June 2002); http://www.tandf.co.uk. They are reprinted here with permission.

Chapter One

Between the New Medium
and the Old

[I]t is going to be a VERY interesting day indeed when . . . EVERYONE has
a TV show :) I can't wait!

—from the public diary of webcam celebrity Ana Voog

One Saturday afternoon in the summer of 2000, a digital camera uploaded an image to the World Wide Web of Minneapolis-based webcam artist Ana Voog seated on a black leather couch, knees tucked up in front of her, gazing off-screen. The caption above the photo—one that remained onscreen for the next hour or so—said simply, "It's just a lazy Saturday, watching *Big Brother*. The image, perhaps unintentionally, provided a wonderfully succinct description of the relationship to surveillance that characterized the summer television season of the new millennium. Voog was watching the CBS reality series *Big Brother*, which documented the lives of ten people who had agreed to spend part of the summer living their lives in front of a national television audience and competing for a $500,000 grand prize. An average of between eight and ten million people tuned in five nights a week to watch the houseguests and the process whereby they were voted off the show, one by one, until only the winner remained.

Despite drawing a relatively large audience (significantly eclipsing the network's ratings for the time slot the previous year), *Big Brother* was not the most popular surveillance-based reality show of the summer. It trailed in the ratings behind another CBS series, the smash hit *Survivor*, which monitored the daily lives of several contestants enduring a "back-to-basics" existence on a tropical island off the coast of Borneo while competing for a $1 million prize. *Survivor*, of course, became a runaway success, drawing an average of twenty-five million viewers per episode and shattering the record for the most popular summer TV series ever. Like Voog, a significant number of U.S. viewers spent part of their summer watching surveillance—as a form of entertainment. In the wake of *Survivor*'s runaway success, reality TV was rapidly transformed from a cheap form

1

of niche programming to the hot programming trend of the new millennium, and eventually into a genre of its own, spanning two new Emmy categories in the United States.

At the dawn of the era of reality TV, Voog's simple description offered a timely reformulation of George Orwell's famous phrase: no longer was Big Brother simply ominously watching. Rather, millions of people were watching *Big Brother*: surveillance had itself become a mediated spectacle. Voog's webpage was an appropriate site for this observation because it highlighted the way in which the viewers themselves were increasingly *being* watched in the age of interactive media that have ostensibly ushered in the era of the end of privacy.[1] Caught in a seemingly "private" moment, alone in her room, watching TV, Voog doubled as a home-grown version of reality TV, since she documents her life online for her fans (and anyone else with Internet access), by sending photos of her home to the World Wide Web every five minutes, twenty-four hours a day. The grainy digital image of Voog thus traced a somewhat dizzying spiral of surveillance: she was watching *Big Brother* while being watched, staging a scene that could only be viewed by spectators willing to enter into a virtual space—the World Wide Web—that notoriously allows for ever more pervasive forms of personal surveillance.

The image of Voog caught between her television and her camera evokes the central themes of new media convergence that this book sets out to explore. On the one hand is the promise of interactivity—that access to the means of media production will be thrown open to the public at large, so that "everyone can have their own TV show"—or at least a distant chance of becoming a star on one of the dozens of reality formats that have seemingly taken over the airwaves. On the other hand is the reality represented by reality TV—that interactivity functions increasingly as a form of productive surveillance allowing for the commodification of the products generated by what I describe as the work of being watched. This book sets out to explore some of the ways in which the latter version of interactivity (productive surveillance) deploys the promise of the former (participatory interactivity). In the economic realm, the promoters of e-commerce envision an economy of "mass customization" based on ever more precise forms of consumer surveillance that allow for individualized marketing and production. Viewers and consumers are invited to subject themselves to forms of interactivity that monitor their behavior with the promise that this interactivity offers an outlet for creative self-expression. Within the context of an emerging interactive economy, reality TV appears not simply as one more programming trend but as a format uniquely suited to its historical moment insofar as it bridges these two versions of interactivity. The promise deployed by reality TV is that submission to comprehensive surveillance is not merely a character-building challenge and a "growth" experience, but a way to participate in a medium that has long relegated audience members to the role of passive spectators. It therefore works neatly as an advertisement for the benefits of submission to comprehensive surveillance in an era in which such submission is increasingly productive. Its promise—that of access to the real via comprehensive monitoring—lines up alongside those of the interactive revolution generally: spectators shall become participants. The many shall take on the role previously monopolized by the privileged few: power will be shared with the people. This revolution will, moreover, ostensibly result in the overthrow of the rule of the culture industry and replace the homogenized pabulum of mass-produced pop culture with the vital fare of the "real."

Or at least that's the promise. The reality is a bit different. Reality TV formats have multiplied to the point that they have become self-conscious parodies of their original premise of access to the unscripted interactions of people who are not professional entertainers. The genre has done little to follow through on the promise to "share" control with viewers by setting aside hackneyed formulas. Rather, reality shows are becoming the latest and most self-conscious in a string of transparently staged spectacles, complete with their own formulas and increasingly reliant on a cast of demicelebrities culled from the pool of would-be actors who do the rounds of the reality TV casting calls on the advice of their agents. Most recently, faded celebrities are attempting to use reality shows to launch a comeback, or at least to pay the bills. Indeed, the contrived character of reality TV has become an emergent theme in some of the more recent genres, which focus on "behind-the-scenes" glimpses into such products of the culture industry as boy bands and Las Vegas showgirls (and on Bravo, the Cirque du Soleil). As of this writing, there are currently more than fifty recently developed reality-based formats on network and cable television, ranging from expensive and popular formats like *Survivor* and *The Bachelor*, to cheaper formats like *Blind Date* and cable staples like *Cops* and *America's Funniest Home Videos*.

As the formats have proliferated and the novelty has worn thin, new and upcoming formats are developing ever more outrageous and controversial premises. A show called *The Will*, for example, recently announced its search for "someone with a sizable fortune and a substantial sense of humor to be the Benefactor of this program in which his or her family will compete, game show style, to be named the heir to a fortune."[2] Other recent formats poke fun at the genre itself, like a show called *Joe Millionaire*, which sent six women to France to compete for the affections of an "eligible millionaire" who, unbeknownst to them, was actually a construction worker with a salary of less than $20,000 a year. The format is a swipe at the recent spate of marriage reality formats that encourage women to compete for the attentions of a wealthy bachelor (and, in one case, for men to compete for the attentions of an eligible bachelorette). Still other formats have reached the point that often marks the decline of a format: the cannibalization of previous programming successes in a desperate attempt to cobble together "new" content out of old. Plans have already been announced to re-create two popular fictional formats from the 1960s that were canceled when the networks started to compete for so-called quality audiences: *Green Acres* and *The Beverly Hillbillies*. The premises of the two shows complement one another: the former recounts the antics of a wealthy and glamorous couple who move from Manhattan to a farm in the countryside, the latter the antics of a family of "hillbillies" who strike oil and move into an extravagantly wealthy neighborhood. The reality TV remakes will add an empirical/experimental element to the well-known U.S. formats: What would happen if you took a "real" hillbilly family and transported them into a wealthy urban enclave in order to capture the whole thing on film? If the remakes prove popular, we can surely expect a flood of copycat formats and casting calls for, among others, married couples who each have three kids from previous marriages (*The Brady Bunch*), an African American family from Bel-Air who want to take in a teen from the inner city (*Fresh Prince of Bel-Air*), and so on.

One of the marketing advantages of reality TV is that its exercise in envelope pushing generates its own hype. The fact that the genre itself reinvents conventions of prime-time programming provides a ready-made media hook that encourages coverage of the latest and most outrageous formats. The result is that the symbiotic relationship between entertainment coverage and the culture industry has served reality TV well. According to the Lexis-Nexis database, for example, *Survivor* received more than twice the predebut coverage that *ER* received several years earlier (more than 270 articles in "major newspapers" as compared with 131 for *ER*). The runaway success of the genre itself has predictably generated its own publicity. There are behind-the-scenes shows about the making of hit formats, news magazine ruminations on the public fascination with instant celebrity, and endless tabloid and "serious" magazine covers devoted to the latest popular reality format. Indeed, the appeal of the success story of reality TV echoes that of its stars: the rise from low-budget obscurity to people's favorite. Moreover, what started as a cheap programming gimmick has proven surprisingly durable and adaptable. In the wake of the terrorist attacks on 11 September 2001, I was contacted by reporters from two major newspapers who were working on premature predictions of the end of the reality trend. Their stated assumption reflected the instant wisdom of the moment: that in the wake of a dose of brutal reality, people might want less reality, not more. The prediction missed the mark. Not only did reality TV rejuvenate itself in new and sometime surprising forms (*The Osbournes* and *The Anna Nicole Show*), but viewers proved themselves savvy enough to understand that the contrived fare they were watching functioned more as escapist entertainment than immersion in brute reality. Fans were no more duped by the promise of access to an unmediated spectacle than the self-consciously savvy pundits.

What, then, might help explain the resilience of reality programming? Producers and fans alike have a tendency to attribute reality TV's success to its incipiently "democratic" character: its lottery-like ability to make a star out of a "nobody." Indeed, star mimicry has become a subgenre of its own, fueled largely by MTV, which has developed shows that invite viewers to impersonate their favorite pop stars in video remakes (*Becoming*) and which audition viewers for stints as professional wrestlers (*Tough Enough*) and members of a hip-hop group

(*Making the Band*). In keeping with this line of shows, MTV's website features a game called "fantasy music tycoon" that, in imitation of popular baseball and football fantasy leagues, allows viewers to "buy and sell" bands to see whether they can create a successful talent roster (the tag line asks, "Got what it takes to be a music impresario?"[3]). The invitation is to become famous by play-acting the role of the celebrity. However, the form of democracy on offer is an oddly impersonal one. Indeed, one of the results of the reality TV boom has been to focus attention on the *apparatus* of celebrity production rather than the intrinsic qualities of the star. The aura of the individual talent is undermined by the ostensibly demystifying effort to foreground strategies of promotion and manipulation. On shows like *Making the Band*, for example, we see talented singers fall by the wayside because they don't fit the marketing formula. It is hard to watch these shows without getting the message that talent is insignificant compared to the awesome power of the promotional apparatus that can transform a mediocrity into a superstar—and then just as casually drop its latest creation in order to move on to the next. Cultural critic Walter Benjamin got it right—sort of. The apparatus of mechanical reproduction helped contribute to a form of demystification; but the aura, rather than disappearing, has been displaced onto the apparatus itself, which is endowed with the mystical power of creating or negating celebrity, seemingly regardless of the individual talent.

All of which remains a rather distant and distorted echo of the version of media democratization envisioned by webcam artist Ana Voog. To her, the advent of an interactive medium represents a progressive challenge to the top-down, monopolistic mass media. The Internet allows people like her to become content producers, rather than remaining merely media consumers. In so doing, it ostensibly offers them the ability to control the product of their creative labor. In the words of a scholar describing the U.K. reality series *Video Diaries*, which provides members of the public with cameras to tell their own stories, "it brings us that much closer to realizing the Brechtian aspiration that communication technology should one day be able to transform the passive individual consumer of mass media messages into an active and creative producer/consumer."[4] Described in these terms, the era of interactivity provides a political, social, and even economic challenge to monopolistic media (as evidenced, perhaps, by the fact that Voog supports herself with the proceeds from subscriptions to her webcam site). Moreover, the new medium offers to surpass the mass media model whereby a small group of producers frame the stories consumed by the public. The promise of the Internet, in short, is not just that it increases the chances of an obscure outsider to make it big but that it allows everyone to gain greater participation in and control over the mediated version of reality in which they are immersed. When the medium is no longer a mass medium, the mass itself is dissolved into an active body of participants, foreshadowing futurist Howard Rheingold's descriptions of "smart mobs"—distributed activism that coalesces into powerful strategic formations facilitated by new information and communication technologies.[5] This is the anticipated form of empowerment that aligns itself with Voog's version of online reality programming as the translation of the promise of shared control into the realm of media production. If everyone can be a producer, the forms of central-ized, top-down control associated with industrial modernism will allegedly be eroded from within: the system will create the (interactive) tools that guarantee its own obsolescence.

Reality TV, by contrast, offers a somewhat different and more cynical version of democratization, one whereby producers can deploy the offer of participation as a means of enticing viewers to share in the production of a relatively inexpen-sive and profitable entertainment product. In this respect, reality TV anticipates the exploitation of what this book describes as the work of being watched, a form of production wherein consumers are invited to sell access to their personal lives in a way not dissimilar to that in which they sell their labor power.[6] The promise of access to reality lines up with that of access to the means of production. The content of a show like *Big Brother* is purportedly more authentic and less phony than fictional programming in part because real people—not Hollywood scriptwriters—share in its production. This ability of real people—those who are not officially part of the entertainment industry—to participate in a realm from which they have been excluded is offered, at least in part, as compensation to the public for allowing themselves to be watched.

Within the context of prime-time entertainment, the promise of reality as a form of "collaborative" production clearly has its limits. Despite Voog's utopian enthusiasm, not everyone can have their own television show. But, to the extent that they conduct their lives online, they *can* be watched all the time. The prom-ise of the emerging, interactive, mass-customized economy is that consumers can gain control by submitting to comprehensive monitoring of the rhythms of their daily lives. The more details we divulge about our shopping and viewing habits, our lifestyle and even our movements during the day, the more we can have goods and services crafted to meet our individual needs. The possibility of total sur-veillance is portrayed as power sharing: by providing information about our-selves, we supply valuable inputs to the production process and thereby help to shape it.

Against the background of an emerging surveillance-based interactive econ-omy, the logic of reality TV snaps into focus. The incoherent promise of univer-sal access to the apparatus of self-promotion (the fact that it's not possible for everyone to watch everyone else's "TV" shows) doubles as an invitation to com-prehensive self-disclosure. Maybe we won't all be stars, but we'll all be able to gain some form of symbolic participation in the production of the goods and ser-vices we consume by submitting to ever more detailed forms of self-disclosure. This form of participation is democratic in the sense that it doesn't require any special talent or skill; people are not excluded on the basis of their education or training—*anyone* can perform the work of being watched. Seen in this light, the parallel to reality TV becomes a bit clearer: One of the promises of the genre is that you don't have to be a professional actor or entertainer—being on a reality show is work that anyone can do. Indeed, this is precisely what makes it easier for fans to identify with cast members—the fact that the latter are drawn from the viewing public. Here the standard praise for the celebrity who "acts" just like an "average Joe/Jane" is realized: the cast members do not have to *act* like they're no different from audience members; they *are* regular audience members. The viewers have ostensibly taken over the airwaves. Viewed from a slightly different angle, however, the promise of power sharing reveals itself as a ruse of economic rationalization and the promised form of participation comes to look a lot like work. Hence the importance of situating the burgeoning reality TV trend within the context of the "revolutionary" promise of the emerging online, interactive economy, which promises a similar fundamental shift in control toward those who increasingly find themselves participating by being watched. Like Ana Voog, we find ourselves caught between the promise of an empowering form of interactivity and the potential of an increasingly exploitative one.

THE APPEAL OF THE REAL

> Reality shows and amateur video shows dominate TV programming. It is the age of scopophilia, voyeurism, and vicarious living. . . . We like to watch. It is a surveillance culture.
>
> —From James Cameron's screenplay for the movie *Strange Days*[7]

Shortly after the airing of *Who Wants to Marry a Multi-Millionaire*, which featured fifty women competing to marry a millionaire they'd never met, the Fox network's entertainment director was quoted describing reality-based specials as "ratings crack"—a cheap, addictive, short-lived high.[8] He was right about the cheap and addictive part but not about the duration. The summer after the Fox special, CBS broke ratings records with *Survivor*, whose sequel again placed CBS at the top of the ratings charts. Fox's *Temptation Island*, which featured four couples "testing" their relationship by dating other singles on yet another remote tropical island, was also a ratings success for the network and helped spawn a variety of "singles"-oriented reality formats. In the wake of these successes, the rather loosely defined genre of reality TV has continued its rapid growth, as demonstrated by the fact that at the close of 2002, the genre was still going strong: all of the major networks have developed reality formats, and there are more than thirty shows currently in development. By the first month of 2003—more than two years after the stunning success of *Survivor*—reality TV was increasing its hold on the airwaves with hits including *American Idol, Joe Millionaire*, and *The Bachelorette*. No longer an off-season summer phenomenon, reality TV has become a dominant prime-time programming staple, easily dominating the ratings in many of the most coveted time slots.[9] In response to the emergence of the genre, the U.S. Academy of Television Arts and Sciences (which hosts the Emmys each year) created two new categories for reality TV: one that recognizes those formats that include a "game-show" element, and one for those (like *Cops*) that seek to entertain by showing dramatic incidents from "real" life.[10]

Pundits and trend watchers have made much of the decimation of the private sphere, the glorification of celebrity, and the penchant for voyeurism associated with the explosion of reality programming. They have described the longing for a taste of the real as symptomatic of a waning sense of reality in the postmodern era and a symptom of the merging of news and entertainment. My own consideration of reality TV situates it within the broader social context of the deployment of the promise of interactivity. What precisely is the appeal of the real within the current social context and how does it figure in the emerging relationship between interactivity and surveillance that characterizes the development of new information and communication technologies? The goal is to examine the promise of a format that offers not an escape from reality but an escape *into* reality (and away from fictional entertainment that reality TV fans describe as formulaic, predictable, and, hence, boring). The following chapters will trace the preliminary outlines not of a theory of reality TV per se, but of modes of consumption, production, and cultural practice that employ the capabilities of interactive media anticipated by the reality trend. It is perhaps not a coincidence that the emergence of relatively inexpensive highly sophisticated technologies for comprehensive consumer monitoring coincides with a trend in popular culture toward the portrayal of surveillance as a means of self-expression and a shortcut to fame and fortune. At a time when being watched is an increasingly productive activity, we are presented with the spectacle of how fun surveillance can be, how it can help us learn about ourselves and provide access to the reality ostensibly occluded by the advent of the forms of homogenization, abstraction, and media manipulation associated with the culture industry.

As is perhaps abundantly clear, the book does not provide a neutral assessment of the emergence of a new programming trend but rather a critical interpretation of its significance. The reality TV trend offers one way of thinking through broad-reaching societal developments that are reorganizing the division between labor and leisure, consumption and production, shopping and watching TV. The reality TV formats considered in the following chapters—all members of a subgenre that focuses on the comprehensive monitoring of the unscripted rhythms of daily life—anticipate a world in which we will create value for advertisers and marketers by allowing ourselves to be watched as we go about our daily routines, in which the promise of interactive participation serves as a ruse of the rationalization of consumption, and in which the imperative to "get real" reproduces the abstracted relations of mass society. Simply put, I propose to explore how the "digital revolution" fulfills the claim by technology critics Kevin Robins and Frank Webster that "what is commonly taken as . . . 'revolution' is in fact no more—and no less—than the extension and intensification of processes set underway some seventy or so years ago" (with the advent of techniques for the scientific management and rationalization of consumption).[11] The crucial observation that Robins and Webster make, for the purposes of this book, is that this so-called revolution is no *less* than a dramatic intensification of such processes. The transformations envisioned by the proponents of the new economy are real and, if implemented as planned (and we can already discern the beginning of such implementation), will significantly transform the role that the media play in our labor and leisure.

All of which is not to discount some of the very practical reasons for the appeal of reality TV to both fans and producers. A 2001 study commissioned by *American Demographics* determined that 45 percent of all Americans watch reality TV and that a fifth of these (which would amount to one in eleven Americans overall) describe themselves as "die-hard" fans.[12] Particularly appealing to advertisers is the fact that the format is a strong draw for the coveted eighteen- to twenty-four-year-old demographic, which represents the largest single group of reality TV viewers.[13] As I discuss in greater detail in the chapters on *Big Brother* and *Survivor*, viewers describe the appeal of reality TV in some of the same terms deployed by the critics of mass culture. Rightly or wrongly (probably wrongly), it is seen as a genre that is less predictable and thus more authentic than the well-worn formulas of fictional programming. Moreover, the fans whom I interviewed overwhelmingly spoke of the ease with which they could identify with reality TV cast members, precisely because they were not professional actors or well-known celebrities. As one respondent discussing *Survivor* put it, "I like the fact that it's real people—people I can identify with, instead of superstars and Olympians." Another viewer who is part of the predominant demographic to which reality TV caters, women ages eighteen to twenty-five, wrote, "I can see myself or others I know in the actions of those on television." The implicit theme of these responses—and many others—is that the celebrities and scenarios that populate prime-time fictional programming are harder to identify with, perhaps because they are mass-produced artifacts of an ostensibly outdated era.

Once again, the thrust seems to be toward a variant of democratization, one that underwrites the urgent desire to close the gap that has sustained both entertainment programming and the advertising it has supported for more than half a century: the gap between the unfulfilled passive viewer and the impossible fullness of the screen idol/advertising model. Reality shows promise to collapse the distance that separates those on either side of the screen by cultivating the fantasy that "it really could be you up there on that screen—just send in your head shots and a homemade video, or call this number now." A show called *Extreme Makeover* takes this collapse literally, offering to rebuild "real" people via plastic surgery so that they can physically close the gap between themselves and the contrived aesthetic of celebrity they have been taught to revere. The democratized version of the star-making apparatus goes beyond demonstrating its ability to transform real people into celebrities seemingly at will; it literally and physically manufactures celebrity-grade humans. The power that the airbrush once exerted over the image is transposed into the register of reality in the form of the power the scalpel exerts on flesh. *Extreme Makeover* neatly combines the double gesture of transforming members of the audience into real television celebrities *while* rebuilding them to fit the conventional image of celebrity beauty. The logic is circular: the process of watching the cast members as they are made over to look like celebrities becomes the source of their fame. The referent—talent, genius, and so forth—has been eclipsed by this very circularity: one becomes famous by being made, both physically and symbolically, to look famous. The gesture is an appealing one not least because it reflects back upon the fame of "real" celebrities—implicitly bringing them down to the same level as everyone else, at least insofar as anyone can become a product of the star-making apparatus. And who is to say otherwise in this era of the lottery of fame? Did celebrities become famous because of some inherent quality, or were they merely happened upon by the star-making industry? The way in which the celebrity-making apparatus is foregrounded reverses the process described in the Borges fable about a lottery that becomes indistinguishable from the random character of everyday reality. In the reality TV era, the contrived character of the lottery is pushed to the fore in a gesture of democratization. The star-making apparatus can make a celebrity out of *anyone*.

As if to highlight this new, ostensible demystification of celebrity, one of the more popular recent permutations of the genre is the rehabilitation of faded stars who agree to turn their lives into reality shows. In the wake of the success of MTV's *The Osbournes*, second-tier celebrities and former superstars including Cybil Shepherd, Gene Simmons, and David Lee Roth have reportedly expressed interest in having their own reality shows.[14] Shows like *I'm a Celebrity, Get Me out of Here,* and *Surreal Life* ironically parody previous reality formats (*Survivor* and *The Real World*) by stocking the show with real celebrities, who in turn are invited to take on the favorite "role" of the current programming era: that of real people. Such formats represent an extension of the tabloid coverage of the private lives of celebrities with the added appeal to performers that they can capture some of the revenues generated by their self-disclosure.

These formats also, perhaps, reflect the fact that the lives of celebrities are often slightly more sensational than the predictable plots of their fictional vehicles. Consider, for example, the recent remake of *Ocean's Eleven* in which the characters played by superstars Julia Roberts, Brad Pitt, George Clooney, and Matt Damon conspire to split a $150 million payday eleven ways. In actuality, of course, the sum that represents the crowning achievement of their fictional characters' lives is dwarfed by the real salaries earned by the actors. Roberts famously earned $20 million for just one movie: *Erin Brockovich*; the movie itself grossed well over *twice* the value of the supposedly stupendous fictional Vegas heist in *Ocean's Eleven*—almost $412 million worldwide, $300 million more than it cost to make.[15] The fictional fantasies have become inadequate to the reality of a society in which the economic gap between the hyperrich few and the making-ends-meet millions continues to grow ever more extreme. Thus, it seems perfectly logical that when it comes to celebrity, reality shows that showcase the extreme wealth of celebrities (e.g., *Cribs* and *The Osbournes*) stand a good chance of displacing the actual genres in which the characters that populate them became famous. The fascination exerted by individual rap stars promises to be less durable and consistent than that exerted by the extremes of wealth they manage to amass rapidly over the course of often brief careers.

The apparent fascination of viewers with the extremes of wealth should not eclipse the fact that much of what goes on in celebrity-based reality shows is the interest generated by a humanizing glimpse of remote cultural icons. Paradoxically, the success of celebrity reality shows—at least those of *The Osbournes* and *The Anna Nicole Show* variety—seems to reflect the logic of the promise of reality from the other side of the celebrity divide. If reality TV offers to make stars out of real people, its celebrity variant offers to make real people out of stars.

The promise made to fans, of course, is quite different from the appeal of reality TV to producers, who don't seem particularly interested in power sharing and democratization, or even in contesting the hackneyed formulas of prime-time programming, except insofar as it helps keep costs down and generate promotional buzz. As a side benefit, reality-based productions help discipline demanding actors and writers with the threat that they are superfluous in the new, hot programming genre. In the face of threatened strikes by unions representing actors and writers, producers have repeatedly invoked the possibility that reality shows could be used as a hedge against walkouts.[16] More recently, reality TV cast members, cognizant of the high profits that networks and production companies have made on the backs of their private moments, have attempted to sue for a larger piece of the action. However, the fact that there is no shortage of "real" people eager to surrender their privacy for a spot on prime-time television gives the networks bargaining power and the confidence in the face of lawsuits exhibited by an unnamed television executive quoted by the *New York Times*: "These people are not represented by any unions—they have very little power, and there are literally thousands of people behind them waiting for their 15 minutes."[17] Reality programming has, paradoxically, undermined the uniqueness of celebrity. The star quality that commanded large premiums has been rendered fungible.

In part because of their reliance on nonprofessionals, reality TV formats, with the exception of some of the higher-priced variants like *Survivor,* are often more than a third less expensive than comparable prime-time programming—much less in the case of notoriously low-budget formats like *Funniest Home Videos* and *Cops*.[18] In the case of a successful series, like *Big Brother* in Europe, the payoff can be enormous: a top-rated show with relatively low production costs that can serve as the basis of an international franchise. Perhaps one of the more interesting achievements of the genre from the perspective of the global entertainment industry is the way in which it has forced Hollywood producers to take an increasing interest in imported programming formats. Because it can be relatively inexpensive to produce, reality TV is a niche in which producers working in smaller markets with tight budgets can get around barriers to entry into international programming erected by the glossy and expensive production values of Hollywood. Reality TV producer Gary Carter, who worked with the Dutch production company Endemol on the *Big Brother* franchise, noted that after the U.S. success of *Who Wants to Be a Millionaire* and the European success of *Big Brother*, Hollywood started to take note of foreign programming that it had largely overlooked. "Before that, you couldn't get American television executives on the plane to Europe; after, you couldn't keep them off."[19]

In some sense, then, reality TV does seem to mount a challenge to the established "powers that be"—if not on behalf of the viewing audience, at least on behalf of non-U.S. production companies that have enriched themselves thanks to the success of a variety of imported formats including the U.S. versions of *Big Brother*, *Survivor*, *American Idol*, *The Weakest Link*, and *Who Wants to Be a Millionaire*. In some cases—most notably that of *Big Brother* and *Who Wants to Be a Millionaire*—the producers have developed a franchise that can be marketed internationally and adapted to local audiences. Reality TV, in other words, fits well with the dictates of global media production insofar as it combines a local cast and local viewer participation with a customizable transnational format. What is exported is not the content itself but a recipe for creating a local version of an internationally successful TV show. In this sense, reality TV parallels the emergence of the interactive aesthetic of digital media: what becomes important, as we shall see in coming chapters, is not so much the content but the rules for interaction. This relationship between interactivity and the promise of access to the real is a recurring theme of this book, and as such it demands closer inspection.

THE INTERACTIVE REVOLUTION

Gary Carter, one of the producers of the successful *Big Brother* franchise, argues that for a show to meet his definition of reality TV, it must incorporate an element of audience interaction.[20] This is the case not just because of the element of uncertainty it introduces, since, for Carter, "real" reality TV is by its very nature unpredictable, insofar as it documents an evolving situation *as it happens*. Needless to say, much of what passes for reality TV in the U.S. context doesn't meet Carter's definition of the term. But we are still left with the question as to what is added to the unpredictability he favors by the element of audience participation. It is not just the fact that the producers have relinquished some measure of control but that the audience has *gained* it. As I will argue in the following chapters, the notion that collective participation in the creation of cultural commodities salvages their claim to authenticity implicitly invokes a critique of the top-down forms of control associated with the culture industry. The corollary of the claim that mass culture is somehow inauthentic because it is created *for* audiences and not *by* them—that, in short, they are in some sense alienated from the production process itself—is that including their participation might help cultural products reclaim an element of authenticity. In short, that mass culture might regain an element of what media critics Alan O'Connor and John Downing describe as popular culture (as in the sense of "the people's culture"): forms of entertainment created by and for the people that help typify "the essence of a people's way of life."[21]

The equation of participation with an authenticity repressed by the centralized control characteristic of the culture industry recapitulates the current revolutionary claims of the digital revolution. In the 1950s, the mass market was portrayed as that force which stood in opposition to the socialist state: a self-proliferating cornucopia of industrial capitalism and the symbol of Western strength and prosperity. Now the proponents of the digital revolution seem to be aligning themselves with mass society's harshest critics: it turns out the culture industry *was* totalitarian after all. Now it can be told, because the digital revolution is at hand—and like the industrial revolution before it, it is largely driven by technology. The promise of this technology, it should be noted, is described by its supporters not just as dramatically transformative, but as inherently political. As Howard Rheingold, who helped popularize the idea that computer networks can revitalize a functional sense of community in an increasingly atomized society, puts it, "The political significance of computer mediated communication lies in its capacity to challenge the existing political hierarchy's monopoly on powerful communications media, and perhaps thus revitalize citizen-based democracy."[22] Futurist Derrick de Kerckhove has pushed even further, arguing that technological developments succeed where political struggle has failed: "In a networked society, the real powershift is from the producer to the consumer, and there is a redistribution of controls and power. On the Web, Karl Marx's dream has been realized: the tools and the means of production are in the hands of the workers."[23]

Lining up this celebratory rhetoric alongside the claims of reality TV yields the odd result that reality TV is implicitly politicized. If interactivity is a central element of the form of new media, mediated and recorded human interaction have an important role to play in its content. The production of "real" content based on monitoring is the flip side of interactivity, a fact that, as the following chapters suggest, spans the uses of new media in art, commerce, and entertainment. The reality TV trend is part of the same family tree as the popularity of webcam performance artists like Ana Voog, the development of surveillance-based interactive commerce, and the promise of interactive television. Which is not to downplay the differences between the mass medium of television and the interactive medium of the Internet—a difference that, drawing on the surveillance theory of Thomas Mathiesen, we might describe in terms of the (eroding) opposition between panopticism (the few watching the many) and synopticism (the many watching the few).[24] This book's focus is on some of the fundamental similarities between reality programming on television and online, and particularly on the way in which both portray submission to comprehensive forms of monitoring as a form of empowerment and self-expression. As Mathiesen notes, the promise of interactive media, taken to its limit, is to realize an Orwellian synthesis of the two forms of surveillance:

> George Orwell described panopticism and synopticism in their ultimate form as completely merged: through a screen in your living room you saw Big Brother, just as Big Brother saw you. We have not come this far, but we clearly see tendencies for panopticism and synopticism to merge into one. . . . Today it is technologically entirely possible to have a large number of consumers synoptically watch television and order and pay for the commodities advertised . . . while the producers of the commodities panoptically survey everyone.[25]

This version of synoptic panopticism is anticipated by the "training wheels" for interactivity devised by broadcasters: interactive webpages that serve as companion pieces for television programming. The goal is not just to provide viewers with a sense of participation but to keep track of them, to gather information from them, and to monitor their interest in the show.

The kinship between reality TV and the promise of interactivity is highlighted by the fact that the reality genre has proven particularly amenable to this rudimentary form of convergence. According to *American Demographics*, more than a quarter of reality TV viewers read or post messages on sites devoted to reality shows, and 70 percent of self-described "avid fans" go to show-related websites.[26] Similarly, more than a fifth of regular viewers go online to play Internet games based on the shows.[27] Predictably, the article's author, drawing on interviews with reality TV fans, credits a climate of technology-facilitated democratization for both the fascination with shows based on "real" people and the interest of fans in going online: "The popularity of the format with youth also has a lot to do with their growing up in a democratized society, where the Internet, Web cams and other technologies give the average Joe the ability to personalize his entertainment."[28]

This ready equation of customized programming options with democratization is, of course, the latest variant of the collapse of the role of the citizen into that of consumer. It exemplifies the conflation of what legal scholar Cass Sunstein calls "consumer sovereignty"—an increasing spectrum of consumption choices—with democratic participation, which, for him, necessarily includes not only a broad set of choices, but the optimal conditions for forming political preferences through deliberation.[29] As the critique of interactivity developed in the following chapters suggests, one of the pressing challenges of a society inundated with the promise of interactivity is to resuscitate the distinction between the promised democratization deployed by the promoters of the interactive economy and a version of participation more in line with Sunstein's conception of citizen sovereignty. Such a conception would necessarily embrace the three elements that technology critic Darin Barney proposes as necessary components of a democracy in which citizens are provided with the necessary tools to participate *meaningfully* in the decisions that affect them: equality, participation and "a public sphere from which sovereignty emanates."[30] Equality for him is substantive in the sense that it entails not just an equal opportunity to participate (guaranteed by the absence of formal or legal constraints preventing participation), but an equal *ability* to do so (as facilitated perhaps by the role of the welfare state in promoting the knowledge of politics and deliberative skills associated with the notion of "civic competence" outlined by communication scholars Andrew Calabrese and Mark Borchert).[31] Barney's use of the term "meaningful participation" is admittedly vague, but it invokes an informed and active deliberation of the kind envisioned by scholars including James Carey and Cass Sunstein, while preserving the structure of representative democracy.[32] Many of the celebrants of the digital revolution cited in this book implicitly mobilize a definition similar to that put forth by Barney, insofar as they argue that interactive technology will enable "meaningful" participation not only in the sense of enhanced opportunities for gaining relevant information and participating actively in public deliberation, but also in the sense that citizens will gain power over the political and economic systems that help shape the society in which they live.

The so-called revolution envisioned by such writers allegedly goes hand-in-hand with the dismantling, or at least the redistribution, of control over the propaganda apparatus. The assumption is that to the extent that interactivity facilitates the process of redistribution it is inherently subversive and democratizing. However, as Schiller demonstrates, existing corporate power (the same powers to which "the information revolution is *profoundly threatening*," according to Wriston) is placing its money behind the ostensible revolution, not against it.[33] Thus, we are led to ask with Barney, "If network technology is *inherently* revolutionary—it leads one to wonder why existing governmental, bureaucratic, corporate, and financial elites are so enthusiastic about, and so heavily invested in, the success of this technology?"[34] The fact that the revolution is taking place with the blessing of the Crown—that it is being fomented by ruling political and economic elites—suggests heads won't be rolling any time soon.

All of which implies that the challenge faced by a critical evaluation of the ostensibly revolutionary potential of new media is to demonstrate how dramatic transformations are absorbed by existing social relations *without* revolutionizing them. Tracing the thick vein of continuity between the revolutionary utopia of the digital revolution and the era of mass society means understanding the emerging digital economy in terms of the "micro-electronic reorganization of Taylorism."[35] As such, the digital revolution appears not as a remedy for the power imbalances of industrial society, but as an attempt to resolve the contradictions that impaired its efficiency. The genius of the "selling of the Internet" is that the latter is equated with the former: the participation of consumers in the rationalization of their own consumption is sold as empowerment.

RETHINKING REALITY TV

The standard critique of reality TV—one that has come to dominate not just the popular press but the fan response—is that the term itself is a misnomer, perhaps even an oxymoron. Despite the promise of unmediated access to the real, viewers are, according to this account, presented with yet another highly produced product of the culture industry. Producer Gary Carter suggests that one hallmark of authentic reality TV is the attempt to sidestep the standard slick production conventions of Hollywood programming—but, of course, low production values can themselves be deployed as one more strategy for cultivating the illusion of authenticity.[36] In practice, only the "exceptional moment" versions of reality TV, which rely on found footage like commercial surveillance tape and homemade video, embrace gritty production values. Reality shows like *The Real World*, *Survivor*, and even *Big Brother*—despite the fact that it's edited on the fly—are all slickly produced. Moreover, the increasingly contrived and sensationalistic premises of the shows combined with the Los Angeles luster of the cast members contribute to the debunking of any pretensions to "real" reality. Perhaps most intriguingly, the thematization of the apparatus of manipulation in many reality formats serves as an invitation to debunking. A show that focuses on the contrived nature of, for example, professional wrestling, teeters on a fine line: its claim to realism is predicated on the way in which it foregrounds the artifice of the culture industry, of which it remains one more product. The appeal is a reflexively savvy one that offers up a demystifying, behind-the-scenes glimpse of the spectacle as the *latest spectacle*. It is an appeal that incorporates its own self-critique in a seeming concession to the savviness of its spectators. Consequently, the promise of reality TV lends itself to a critique of the ideology of the end of ideology: an exploration of how, as culture critic and philosopher Slavoj Zizek (following Lacan) puts it, the "non-duped err."[37] If reality TV caters to our own skepticism by showing us how mediated appearances are constructed by the apparatus of the culture industry—if it enacts what it displays by simultaneously debunking celebrity and creating new stars—we can concede that the savvy attitude becomes a strategy for protecting artifice by exposing it. As Zizek puts it, "The final deception is [the suggestion that] the social appearance is deceitful: in the social-symbolic reality, things ultimately are what they pretend to be."[38] Reality TV, to the extent that it demonstrates the artificial character of mediated reality, highlights the reality of artifice in the mass media. To the extent that it deploys the work of being watched as a means of generating content, it accurately reflects the emerging reality of the interactive economy.

In this respect, reality TV echoes the logic of deception traced by Lacan in his seminar on "The Purloined Letter," a logic that Zizek describes as deception by means of the truth.[39] By way of explanation, Zizek refers to Lacan's retelling of the joke about two travelers who encounter each other on the street: "One character shouts breathlessly, 'Yes, why do you lie to me saying you're going to Cracow so I should believe you're going to Lemberg, when in reality you *are* going to Cracow?'"[40] We might propose the following paraphrase with respect to reality TV: "Why is reality TV pretending that it's real, so that we may cannily believe it's phony, when it accurately portrays the reality of contrivance in contemporary society?"

If this sounds too facile, consider Rupert Murdoch's latest brainchild: a reality TV show called *The American Candidate* that enlists the talents of the director of the political documentary *The War Room* to film a two-year game show that recruits candidates for president. The show will start with one hundred "real" candidates recruited from the public at large, allowing the audience to call in, question candidates, and eliminate them until one winner remains as the "people's choice."[41] The fascinating aspect of the show is not so much its realization of Reform Party candidate Ross Perot's pseudopopulist fantasy of interactive democracy, but its proximity to the media spectacle that politics has already become. Contrary to its ostensible premise, it doesn't highlight the fact that *anyone* has a chance to become president, as much as the central role of the media machinery in manufacturing candidates: that the media can make almost anyone president. To paraphrase Lacan once again, we might ask, "Why does this show tell us that presidential politics is merely a media marketing spectacle, so that we should believe *real* politics is more serious and legitimate, when in reality campaigns are nothing more than the latest form of mass marketing?"

THE INTERACTIVE CONSUMER

Getting real, within the context of an increasingly interactive media environment, means drawing on viewers themselves to provide programming content. In this respect, reality programming in all its incarnations—including homemade webcasts, viewer-submitted videos, and produced scenarios like *The Real World* and *Survivor*—fits neatly with the emerging interactive paradigm. Indeed, this affinity goes partway toward answering the question as to why reality TV is emerging as the dominant form of programming during the incunabulum of the digital era. Rather than treating the impulse to "get real" as an autonomous cultural formation—one more trend during a period of increasingly rapid turnover—this book treats it as a starting point for thinking about the implications of new media for entertainment as well as for anticipated shifts in the ways we work, consume, and communicate with one another. Viewed as a cultural artifact caught up in the logic of an emerging social formation, reality programming highlights the increasing importance not just of surveillance but of interactive technologies that rearrange the conventional distinctions between work and play and between consumption and production. The Illinois housewife who agrees to move into a house where her every move can be watched by millions of strangers to compete for a cash prize exhibits more than an incidental similarity (albeit on a different scale) to the computer user who allows Yahoo to monitor her web-browsing habits in exchange for access to a free e-mail account. The aspect of reality programming that is truly "real" is not the contrived and sensational aspect that gains the most attention in the media coverage, but the way in which it anticipates real societal changes. Thus, the following chapters examine aspects of the reality TV genre with an eye to developing a critical framework for thinking about the relationship between getting real, the deployment of new media, and a digitally enhanced economy.

Drawing on examples of reality programming ranging from home-made webcam sites like Jennicam to popular reality formats including *Big Brother*, *Temptation Island*, and *Survivor*, the following chapters explore the ways in which interactive media operate as a form of digital enclosure, within which activities previously conducted beyond the scope of market-based monitoring can be subjected to techniques for the scientific management of (the labor of) consumption. Reality programming offers a pop culture example of the extension of the monitoring gaze associated with this digital enclosure. It also anticipates the portrayal of surveillance as a form of self-empowerment by the promoters of the online economy. Finally, it helps reposition surveillance as the guarantor of individualism and self-expression and thereby as a means of overcoming the homogeneity of mass society.

Thus, the relationship of "getting real" to the historical context of mass society is of central concern to this book. The link between reality programming and new media interactivity can be discerned in their respective promises: Just as the former is promoted as an alternative to the hackneyed and predictable storylines of fictional entertainment, so the latter ostensibly provides an alternative to the stultifying uniformity of mass society. In both cases, getting real (by incorporating the input of viewers, consumers, and workers) implies a critical engagement with the legacy of mass society. More precisely, it highlights one of the constitutive contradictions of mass society: its self-propagation via the promise of its self-overcoming.

Describing the contemporary role of mediated interactivity as a form of "getting real" thus requires a particular kind of triangulation: the promise of interactivity must be located in relation to the history it offers to surpass. Such a triangulation provides the basis for the theoretical approach outlined in chapter 2, which explores the configuration of mass society against which the promise of interactivity directs itself in anticipation of the advent of a "mass-customized" society reliant on the widespread deployment of mediated interactivity. The promise of interactive media can be read as an offer to undo the forms of abstraction and hierarchy associated with industrial modernity. Countering the one-way, top-down forms of control and communication associated with the rationalization of production, consumption, and politics is portrayed as a means of undoing the process of abstraction that separated planning from execution, producers from consumers, and elites from the masses. It is in this respect that interactivity aligns itself with a rehabilitation of the real: of authentic forms of democracy and community, rather than the ersatz forms that prevailed in the mass societies of the twentieth century. Understanding the way in which this alignment comes to serve as a marketing strategy for the deployment of interactivity (as an extension of the forms of economic and social control it ostensibly challenges) means developing an alternative framework for thinking about the role of new media in the emerging paradigm of mass customization. The remaining chapters draw on this framework to situate the emergence of reality programming within the context of e-commerce and flexible forms of production and consumption.

Chapter 3 provides some historical and theoretical background for a consideration of reality programming in general, exploring the roots of the genre in documentary film, popular entertainment, and online. To situate the genre within the context of the emerging interactive economy, the chapter explores the relation between new media, webcam celebrity, and reality programming. Chapter 4 turns to a consideration of MTV's *The Real World* and *Road Rules*, which can be considered precursors of the current spate of reality programming based on the comprehensive monitoring of the rhythms of everyday life. Drawing on interviews with cast members and producers, the chapter outlines some of the characteristic elements of the equation of surveillance with self-expression, personal growth, and access to "reality." It likewise explores the emerging form of subjectivity that underwrites the emerging, participatory, online economy.

Chapters 5 and 6 focus on the U.S. version of *Big Brother*, which is the first reality format to incorporate the Internet directly into the show, offering a hybrid combination of twenty-four-hour webcasting and prime-time programming. Drawing on the online fan response to *Big Brother*, these chapters discuss the way in which surveillance is equated with interactivity as a form of democratic participation.

Chapter 7 explores the relationship between voyeurism, understood in psychoanalytic terms, and surveillance-based e-commerce, drawing on the example of *Temptation Island*.

The final chapter on reality TV, chapter 8, draws on fan response to a survey about the hit series *Survivor* to discuss the status of reality in the era of what social theorist Ulrich Beck has termed "The Risk Society." The savvy attitude toward reality exhibited by *Survivor* fans parallels the mistrust of the forms of rationality that served as the guarantor of reality prior to the advent of what Beck terms "reflexive modernization." In an era of savvy reflexivity, the needs served by industrial rationality and the risks it generates become self-referential and thus "removed from their residual mooring in natural factors" that can be measured and determined objectively.[42] Interestingly, the reflexivity of reality TV fans, ever conscious of the contrived nature of TV's promise of access to reality—and thus, implicitly, of the reality of contrivance—neatly parallel the self-referentiality that Beck associates with the risk society.

The latter portion of the book provides evidence for the critique of online interactivity outlined in chapter 2. The consequences of this critique are further developed in the concluding discussion, which explores the lessons about emerging social formations that can be gleaned from an examination of reality TV. Media theory needs to update its assessment of the relationship between mass media and mass society to incorporate the anticipated relationship between *interactive* media and *mass-customized* society. While the continuity between media new and old needs to be understood, the anticipated changes associated with the development of new media are socially significant and must be taken seriously by any attempt to theorize the relationship between the revolutionary promise of new media and its decidedly nonrevolutionary deployment—what Robins and Webster have termed the "revolution of the fixed wheel."[43]

NOTES

1. See, for example, *Simon Garfinkel, Database Nation: The Death of Privacy in the 21st Century* (Cambridge: O'Reilly, 2000), and Reg Whitaker, *The End of Privacy: How Total Surveillance Is Becoming a Reality* (New York: New Press, 1999).

2. *The Will,* at www.thewilltv.com/main.html (accessed 12 January 2003).

3. *Fantasy Music Tycoon,* at www.mtv.com/bands/fantasy_music_tycoon/ (accessed 14 January 2003).

4. John Kilborn, "'How Real Can You Get?': Recent Developments in 'Reality' Television," *European Journal of Communication* 9 (1994): 437.

5. Howard Rheingold, *Smart Mobs: The Next Social Revolution* (Cambridge, Mass.: Perseus, 2002).

6. A Berkeley, California–based company called Lumeria is one of a number of new Internet companies forming to operate as privacy brokers for online consumers. Lester notes that the company will make personal information about its clients available to advertisers for a fee: "The more specific the information stored . . . the more valuable that profile will become to advertisers" (Toby Lester, "The Reinvention of Privacy," *Atlantic Monthly* [March 2001], 36).

7. James Cameron, "Strange Days," at www.hundland.com/scripts/StrangeDays_Scriptment.txt (undated "scriptment" accessed 12 January 2003).

8. Bill Carter, "Fox Network Will End 'Multimillionaire' Marriage," *New York Times*, 22 February 2000, C1. The "crack" trope was recently reiterated by ABC president Susan Lyne, who was widely quoted for her observation that "[t]his reality craze can be like crack for network executives" (Alessandra Stanley, "Forgotten Stars Never Die: They Show Up in Reality TV," *New York Times*, 18 January 2003, A1).

9. Bill Carter, "Reality TV Alters the Way TV Does Business," *New York Times*, 25 January 2003, A1.

10. Jim Rutenberg, "Reality Shows Set Off Fight over Awards," *New York Times*, 12 February 2001, C1.

11. Kevin Robins and Frank Webster, *Times of the Technoculture: From the Information Society to the Virtual Life* (London: Routledge, 2000), 100.

12. Rebecca Gardyn, "The Tribe Has Spoken: Reality TV Is Here to Stay," *American Demographics*, 5 September 2001; at www2.realitytvfans.com/newspub/story.cfm?id=3335.

13. Gardyn, "The Tribe Has Spoken."

14. Alex Kuczynski, "In Hollywood, Everyone Wants to Be Ozzy," *New York Times*, 19 May 2002, 9;1.

15. "The Numbers," at www.the-numbers.com/movies/2001/OCEAN.html (19 August 2002; accessed 12 January 2003).

16. Paul Brownfield and Brian Lowry, "As the Storm Clouds Gather," *New York Times*, 31 December 2000, Calendar, 9; Chris Meyer, "Hollywood Writers' Looming Walkout Could Hurt Films and TV and Lead Actors to Follow Suit," *San Francisco Chronicle*, A1.

17. Lee Bailey, "For Reality Stars, the Reality of a One-Time Payment," *New York Times*, 16 December 2001, 2, 33.

18. Ilana Epstein, "Thanks a Million," *Jerusalem Post*, 1 February 2002, 9; David Zurawik, "Real Deal; Clever Production, True Drama and Low Costs Make an Open-and-Shut Case for a New Breed of Network Reality Shows," *Baltimore Sun*, 4 June 2002, 1E.

19. Gary Carter, telephone interview with the author, 23 December 2002.

20. Carter, telephone interview with the author, 23 December 2002.

21. Alan O'Connor and John Downing, "Culture and Communication," in *Questioning the Media: A Critical Introduction*, ed. John Downing, Ali Mohammadi, and Annabelle Sreberny-Mohammadi (London: Sage, 1995), 3.

22. Howard Rheingold, *Virtual Community* (Reading, Mass.: Addison-Wesley, 1993), 14.

23. As quoted in Darin Barney, *Prometheus Wired: The Hope for Democracy in the Age of Network Technology* (Chicago: University of Chicago Press, 2000), 104.

24. Thomas Mathiesen, "The Viewer Society: Michel Foucault's 'Panopticon' Revisited," *Theoretical Criminology* 1, no. 2 (1997): 215–34.

25. Mathiesen, "The Viewer Society," 223–24.

26. Gardyn, "The Tribe Has Spoken."

27. Gardyn, "The Tribe Has Spoken."

28. Gardyn, "The Tribe Has Spoken."

29. Cass Sunstein, *Republic.Com* (Princeton, N.J.: Princeton University Press, 2002).

30. Barney, *Prometheus Wired*, 22.

31. Andrew Calabrese and Mark Borchert, "Prospects for Electronic Democracy in the United States: Re-thinking Communication and Social Policy," *Media, Culture and Society* 18, no. 2 (1997): 249–68.

32. James Carey, "The Press, Public Opinion, and Public Discourse," in *Public Opinion and the Communication of Consent*, ed. Theodore L. Glasser and Charles T. Salmon (New York: Guilford, 1995), 373–402; Sunstein, *Republic.Com*.

33. Dan Schiller, *Digital Capitalism* (Cambridge, Mass.: MIT Press, 1999); William Wriston, *The Twilight of Sovereignty: How the Information Revolution Is Transforming Our World* (New York: Macmillan, 1992), 2; emphasis in the original.

34. Barney, *Prometheus Wired*, 19; emphasis in the original.

35. Joachim Hirsch, quoted in Kevin Robins and Frank Webster, *Times of the Technoculture: From the Information Society to the Virtual Life* (London: Routledge, 1999), 90.

36. Carter, telephone interview with the author, 23 December 2002.

37. Slavoj Zizek, "How the Non-Duped Err," *Qui Parle: Literature, Philosophy, Visual Arts, History* 4, no. 1 (1990): 1–20.

38. Zizek, "How the Non-Duped Err," 4.

39. Zizek, "How the Non-Duped Err," 3.

40. Jacques Lacan, "Seminar on 'The Purloined Letter,'" in *The Purloined Poe*, ed. John P. Muller and William J. Richardson, trans. Jeffrey Mehlman (Baltimore: Johns Hopkins University Press, 1956), 37.

41. *American Candidate,* at www.fxnetwork.com/candidate (accessed 12 January 2003).

42. Ulrich Beck, *Risk Society: Towards a New Modernity* (London: Sage, 1992), 56.

43. Kevin Robins and Frank Webster, "The Revolution of the Fixed Wheel: Information, Technology and Social Taylorism," in *Television in Transition*, ed. Phillip Drummond and Richard Paterson (London: British Film Institute, 1985), 36–63.

Chapter Two

The Promise of the Digital Revolution

According to the makers of a digital appliance called TiVo, Gil Scott-Heron got it wrong. Television *will* be in the forefront of the revolution against the homogenous forms of mass-produced culture and advertising for which it has so often been blamed, or so its promoters say. It will undermine the cultural hegemony of its own executives and return control to the viewers.

This was the message of the summer of 2000's opening marketing salvo for TiVo, which featured a commercial in which two hefty blue-collar types hurled a network executive through his plate glass window. The message: Interactive digital technology will wrest control of your television from the captains of the culture industry and return it where it belongs—snug in the hand wielding the remote control. Lining up alongside TiVo's marketers, interestingly, were the pundits, including Anthony Lewis of the *New York Times*, who greeted TiVo as "the beginning of the end of another socialistic force in American life: the mass market."[1] Against the background of the new technology, Lewis wrote, "The entire history of commercial television suddenly appears to have been a Stalinist plot erected, as it has been, on force from above rather than choice from below."[2] This is quite an achievement for a technology that allows viewers to decide what they're going to watch and when by digitally recording and storing TV shows and keeping track of viewer preferences. As Lewis's own article suggests, the real revolution heralded by TiVo is not the transfer of control to viewers but a quantum leap in the ability of programmers and marketers to monitor consumers. Digital recorders like TiVo and Replay,

accumulate, in atomic detail, a record of who watched what and when they watched it. Put the box in all 102 million American homes, and you get a pointillist portrait of the entire American television audience. . . . Already, TiVo and Replay know what each of their users does every second, though both companies make a point of saying that they don't actually dig into the data to find out who did what, that they only use it in the aggregate. Whatever. They know.[3]

The promise of shared control reveals itself, once again, as an invitation to productive self-disclosure. The parallel with reality TV is not exact, but it is certainly clear: Just as marketers off-load the work of consumer monitoring onto viewers who perform it in exchange for the promise of convenience and shared control, so producers, hungry for content, turn to selected members of the audience, inviting them to perform the work of self-disclosure in exchange for—in many cases—less than the minimum wage.

It should be clear by now that this is not a book about reality TV per se, but about how to think about reality TV within the context of the ostensible challenge to the mass media posed by the advent of new media. Broadly speaking, it is an attempt to highlight the characteristics of an emergent and ostensibly post-Fordist, postmass, and postmodern society by viewing them through the lens of one of its cultural artifacts. This means analyzing examples taken from popular programming in order to consider how the promise of the real is deployed and to what end. The goal is to suggest a framework for thinking about the political economy of online commerce, the lure of voyeurism, and the fate of ideology critique in a savvy postmodern era ostensibly characterized by flexibility, customization, and decentralization.

The rhetoric of the digital revolution assumes a fundamental discontinuity between the old media and the new. This assumption is predicated on the dramatically new technological capabilities of the Internet, which presumably herald a rupture with more traditional forms of one-way, top-down media production. However, placing these apparently disparate media technologies within their respective socioeconomic contexts helps smooth over the image of rupture. The goal of this chapter, then, is to provide the historical context for a consideration of the revolutionary promise of new media (enlisted by reality TV) and some of the decidedly nonrevolutionary uses to which media new and old are being put. What such an analysis requires is not so much a theory of the media but rather what Raymond Williams calls a theory of culture: "the study of relationships between elements in a whole way of life."[4] The media—as the term itself indicates—serve as a convenient locus for a consideration of these (mediated) relationships. The following sections outline the related elements of the way of life that corresponds to the emergence of mass society and examines the role of the media in enacting and reinforcing these relations. The goal is to provide the background against which to consider the constellation of media developments associated with the advent of mass-customized society and its ostensibly revolutionary challenge to industrial mass society. In keeping with the goal of tracing interrelations between elements in a whole way of life, I will juxtapose significant characteristics of the development of mass media with related developments in other spheres of social practice, including manufacturing, popular culture, and the emerging interactive aesthetic that underwrites the "democratizing" promise of reality TV.

The central focus will be on the opposition between aspects of preindustrialized "traditional" society and those of modern, mass society that the advent of customized capitalism promises to overcome. The word *traditional* is placed in quotation marks because some of its more romantic characteristics can be attributed to the retroactive gaze of modernity. Traditional society is portrayed from the perspective of modernity as the locus of nonalienated handicraft production and of a rich and participatory community life—all of which are undermined by the advent of modernity and, eventually, mass society. This portrayal locates the perspective of modernity as the view from the realm of, as Theodor Adorno puts it, "the hardened and alienated."[5] One of the dominant themes of modernity is consequently that of loss—the loss of unalienated labor, of community, of tradition, and of an existence steeped in the deep meaning of shared ritual. It is the cumulative effect of these losses that Max Weber described as the "disenchantment"[6] of the world. This recurrent theme of loss has served not just as modernity's self-critique but also as an incitement to modernization itself: if we just move ahead fast enough, perhaps we can catch up to what has been left behind.

This incitement is recapitulated by the promise of the digital revolution: that we may finally be reaching the point at which dramatic technological advances make it possible to recapture the era of community, of participation, of fulfilling work and individualized goods that characterized the image of traditional society figured in modernity's backward gaze. Similarly, one of the recurring themes of reality TV formats that document the ongoing rhythm of the daily lives of their cast members is that of a return to premodern or traditional community. This is not merely a matter of coincidence: one of the distinctive characteristics of modernity is the *loss* of the forms of mutual monitoring associated with traditional community and the emergence of the distinctive anonymity of urban life. The demise of traditional society is associated with the replacement of a more generalized form of mutual surveillance by segmented and hierarchical structures of monitoring. Increasing scrutiny in the workplace is accompanied by increasing anonymity outside it. Interestingly, the promise to surpass the hierarchy of mass society (and its "top-down" model of monitoring) is accompanied by the resuscitation of forms of lateral surveillance and mutual monitoring associated with life in traditional, premodern communities. Consider, for example, the increasing role of cell phones as a means not just of communication but of mutual monitoring:

> Imagine being able to learn without dialing a single digit whether another person's phone is in use, or in the case of a cellphone, whether it is even turned on. Now imagine being able to do the same thing with any wired or wireless device of the future—whether it is in the car, in an airplane or at the gym. Not only could you learn whether a person is available for a chat, but you could also deduce what that person might be doing at that exact moment, all without exchanging a word. That is the idea behind a programming concept called presence awareness, which is based on the realization that appliances on a network can automatically be detected by other devices.[7]

Similarly, online databases like Google are becoming resources for lateral monitoring that can be used, for example, to research a new acquaintance, an academic colleague, or an upcoming date.[8] Reality TV makes the equation explicit: lateral monitoring (viewers watching selected members of the audience) hearkens back to premodern forms of community. *Survivor*, for example, explicitly invokes the themes of a return to preindustrial, premodern culture, as did the PBS reality series *1900 House*, which transported a family back in time, requiring the cast members to live as they would have at the turn of the last century. Similarly, *Big Brother* touts its "back-to-basics" environment and the need of contestants to return—ironically—to an unmediated environment: no mass media, no phones, and no newspapers—only face-to-face interaction.

In short, what emerges in the promise of new media is a tension very similar to that noted by Walter Benjamin in his excavation of the prehistory of consumer capitalism in the nineteenth century: the way in which the promise of the future resonates with the unfulfilled desires of a mythical past—what he referred to as an "ur-past." This resonance serves as one of the means whereby the "new" distinguishes itself from the immediate past: "The utopian images that accompany the emergence of the new always concurrently reach back to the ur-past."[9] The deployment of the unfulfilled potential of the ur-past may have politically progressive potential, insofar as it offers an alternative to the given state of affairs, but, as Benjamin's own analysis suggests, it can also serve as an alibi for the self-proliferation and extension of the logic of the present.

Far from viewing the heralded promise of a (digitally enhanced) reclamation of what was lost with the advent of modernity as an effective critique of industrial capitalism, we should understand it—at least within the context of e-commerce—as the continuation of a marketing strategy that hearkens back to the very origins of mass society: the promise to recapture what was lost by moving forward. It is thus to the origins of this society that we must turn in order to situate any understanding of the claims of the digital revolution, with the caveat that the following discussion of the emergence of mass society is meant to be suggestive, not exhaustive, and that the elements are chosen for their relevance to the promise forwarded by the propagandists of the digital revolution. This approach is inspired by Adorno's contention, summarized by Susan Buck-Morss, that history takes on meaning "only in relation to the present, and then only as a critical concept which demystifies the present."[10] Demystifying the promise of new information and communication technologies means considering their emerging uses not in isolation but in relation to each other and to their historical context.

The central features of the backdrop against which the promise of the digital revolution is deployed are the forms of rationalization and abstraction that come to characterize the "way of life" associated with mass society in the industrialized world. The models of top-down, centralized media production to which reality TV offers an ostensible challenge serve as integral components of the industrialized mass society to which the digital revolution opposes itself. Indeed, the central role of the Internet in the promise of the digital revolution relies on the implicit assertion that the mass media are deeply implicated in the formation of mass society: They provide not only the advertising that supports consumer society but also mechanisms for the rationalization of public opinion and the portrayal of politics as a public spectacle for mass consumption. If the printing press provided one of the earliest models of mechanized mass production, the commercialization of the mass media modeled the centralized and abstracted forms of production associated with mass society. In much the same way, the advent of interactive media both embodies and facilitates the emergence of flexible capitalism and mass customization. If, in other words, the "old" media were an integral component of the culture and economics of mass society, the question confronting us at the dawn of the so-called digital revolution is how the advent of new information technologies and their deployment shape the forms of commerce, art, and communication in the emerging society of mass customization.

The first challenge, then, is to define that period during which the characteristics of consumerist mass society came into their own: the first half of the twentieth century, which encompassed the dramatic productivity increases of industrial society, strategies for the rationalization of both mass production and mass consumption, and the rise of advertising-supported mass media with a nationwide reach. It is this era, of course, that eventually spawns the formulaic programming that reality TV ostensibly contests and the one-way, centralized mass media that the Internet promises to supercede. Early on, the emergence of advertising as a means of both subsidizing the mass media and rationalizing "an impersonal marketplace of vast scale" coincided with the efficiency gains brought about by the Fordist and Taylorist rationalization of production.[11] As scholar Darin Barney puts it, "While the Industrial Revolution enabled the production of vast quantities of an increasing variety of goods, the question remained as to how their consumption could be incited on an equivalent scale."[12] Transformations in the way people worked and the way they consumed constituted a dramatic reconfiguration of social life. Advertising historian Bill Leiss argues, for example, that traditional social patterns were eroded and replaced by the creation of "consumption communities":[13] "The functions of older cultural traditions in shaping consumption patterns and the sense of satisfaction for individuals have been taken over by media-based messages through which are circulated a great assortment of cues and images about the relationship between persons and goods."[14]

Antonio Gramsci argues that new forms of mass production required not only a new kind of consumer but the creation of a new kind of worker, and thus "a new form of society."[15] Henry Ford was very aware of the fact that the development of industrialized mass production required more than dramatic changes in technology and the workplace, but in the entire way of life of workers and consumers: "In 1916, Ford sent an army of social workers into the homes of his 'privileged' (and largely immigrant) workers to ensure that the 'new man' of mass production had the right kind of moral probity, family life, and capacity for prudent (i.e. non-alcoholic) and 'rational' consumption to live up to corporate needs and expectations."[16]

In other words, shifting forms of manufacturing are associated with a variety of social transformations. This chapter explores some of the features of this "new form of society" by considering the relationship between the emergence of the scientific management of mass production, the rise of the mass media, and the emergence of early twentieth-century modernism. The theme common to each of these developments is that of the rationalization of the production process and the associated increase in the division between mental and material labor that comes to characterize the way of life associated with mass society. In each of the realms discussed—manufacturing, the media, and art—the focus will be on the way in which the dictates of industrial rationalization structure social relations in ways that come to symbolize the shortcomings of modernity. In promising to surpass these shortcoming and thereby to complete the process of mass society's own self-overcoming, the digital revolution necessarily offers an explicit critique of this society and its contradictions. Thus, the emergence of so-called flexible capitalism interestingly co-opts the critique of industrial capitalism in order to propagate itself. Furthermore, just as the industrial revolution required changes in the elements of an entire way of life, the same might be said of the so-called digital revolution. The current and ongoing creation of a mass-customized society is predicated not just on the continual retraining of both workers and consumers in the use of interactive technologies, but upon their willing entrance into what this book calls the "digital enclosure" wherein they participate in the work of being watched. Because it enacts the productive role of this form of work, reality TV serves as a cultural formation that can be used to think through these changes, to interrogate and critique them.

FROM ENCLOSURE TO DIGITAL DEDIFFERENTIATION

Have you ever sent a fax . . . from the beach? You will.

—AT&T advertisement

[I]n Finland, some sauna-goers will soon be . . . participating in sauna-based videoconferences.

—Computer Dealer News, 22 February 2002

Perhaps the characteristic promise of new media—the one that has come to dominate the popular press and celebratory cyberfuturism—is that of a heightened flexibility enabled by interactive media. The revolutionary promise of the digital future, on this account, is to free us from the rigid spatial and temporal boundaries associated with the rationalization of modern society: the demarcation of the work day and of spaces of leisure, domesticity, consumption, and production. The dedifferentiated future is one in which we will be able to work or shop online during our morning commute—or, if we're tired of commuting, to work from the privacy of home or the local Starbuck's. The promise is one of flexibility and convenience for workers and consumers alike. This promise doubles as a strategy not only for increasing worker productivity, but for promoting the "de-institutionalization" of work.[17] The potential of telecommuting, at least for many low-end jobs, is to help employers offload the costs of office space and equipment, and perhaps eventually of the benefits associated with full-time positions onto a flexible, telecommuting workforce, for whom job security has become a distant, perhaps nostalgic memory.

But if interactivity and flexibility are being deployed as a strategy for the continued rationalization of consumption and production, how are we to explain the apparent appeal of the promise that we'll be able to continue to work *even while* we're at the beach or coffee shop? At least part of the appeal is related to the seeming challenge offered by mediated interactivity to the rigid patterns of consumption and production associated with mass society. The purported benefit of "flexibility" is that of individuation: the ability of workers to customize their working conditions according to their personal preferences and to overcome the cookie-cutter conformity of mass society. As Robins and Webster put it, "Domestic information networks facilitate the restructuring of patterns of time use on a more flexible and individual basis; they provide the technological means to break the times of working, consumption and recreation into 'pellets' of any duration, which can then be arranged in complex, individualized configurations and shifted to any part of the day or night."[18]

Flexibility, of course, is the watchword of post-Fordist production and marketing techniques, which rely on increasing specification, customization, and division of labor. At the same time, however, the promise of flexibility hearkens back to the customized forms of production and consumption associated with pre-modern life, and thus caters to pre-mass-society nostalgia. The constellation of mass society provides the background against which to consider not just the dedifferentiation of work and leisure associated with interactive forms of consumption but also the dedifferentiation of work and daily life enacted by reality TV itself, which transforms the rhythms of daily life into a value-generating activity by virtue of the fact that they can be monitored.

FROM THE ENCLOSURE MOVEMENT TO THE DIGITAL ENCLOSURE

The Emergence and Rationalization of the Industrial Work Space

The rationalization of production (and eventually of consumption and leisure) associated with industrial capitalism is based on the efficiency of centralized control associated with the characteristic *divisions* of mass society: between engineering and execution, producer and consumer, creator and spectator. The emergence of mass society can thus be situated within the broad historical context of the consolidation of capitalist social relations based on two complementary developments: "the accumulation of capital on the one hand, and on the other the creation of 'free' wage labour."[19] Historically, the emergence of these processes takes different forms in different locations, but of particular interest for the current discussion is Marx's description of the role played in England by the enclosure movement:

> The spoilation of the Church's property, the fraudulent alienation of the state domains, the theft of the common lands, the usurpation of feudal and clan property and its transformation into modern private property . . . all these things were just so many idyllic methods of primitive accumulation. They conquered the field for capitalist agriculture, incorporated the soil into capital, and created for the urban industries the necessary supplies of free and rightless proletarians.[20]

The private appropriation of property in modernity is a complementary process to that of the creation of a propertyless labor class forced into the position of selling its labor power. In this sense, the enclosure movement neatly sets into motion the processes of capitalist modernity. It lays the foundations for workplace surveillance even as it undermines precapitalist social relations.[21] The shift from feudal agrarian relations corresponds to a shift in the mode of economic exploitation and, crucially, the emergent economic rule of surveillance. Instead of the appropriation of surplus product by feudal lords associated with precapitalist forms of agrarian production, capitalism depends on the appropriation of surplus value. The former process relied heavily on the threat of force, whereas the latter relies on the insertion of exploitation into the wage-labor contract: an insertion that serves to mask the power relations built into the "free" decision to sell one's labor for a specified wage. As sociologist Anthony Giddens puts it, "The expropriation of workers from control of their means of production, creating a mass of saleable labour-power, involves the intrusion of class relations into the production process itself."[22] The spatiotemporal divisions inaugurated by the enclosure movement—the separation between spaces of work, domesticity, and leisure (at least for paid laborers)—laid the foundations for the boundaries that came to characterize the division of labor and leisure as well as the deployment of surveillance in the workplace. These divisions eventually underwrote the rationalization not just of the workplace but of the mass-produced forms of news and entertainment that came to characterize the second half of the twentieth century in the United States and Europe.

Associated with these dramatic transformations, according to the critics of modernity, was the loss of traditional culture bearings: the emergence of a sense of anomie associated with the loss of a stable and cyclical cultural life. Industrialization eventually required workers to enter not just into a labor contract but also into a distinct physical space operated and controlled by its owners, separated out from sites of domesticity and leisure. At the same time, the separation of the worker from the routines of agrarian life combined with the emergence of urban capitalism undermined traditional social relations, contributing to the dissolution of what Giddens, following Laing, calls "ontological security": "In the capitalist urban milieu . . . the routinisation of day-to-day activities is stripped away from tradition. In the 'everyday life' of capitalist urbanism large tracts of activity are denuded of moral meaning; they become matters of habit or of 'dull economic compulsion.'"[23]

The rise of industrial capitalism meant the disruption of the pace, space, and culture of traditional society. This disruption created the opening for the eventual rationalization of culture via the advertising and marketing industry: the replacement of traditional social cues with those of consumption and market status. It also triggered resistance on the part of workers "steeped in peasant rhythms" to "the new discipline of market relations . . . regular hours and days of work, punctuality, subordination to the machine, wage income as the sole means of subsistence."[24] The emergence of the scientific management of labor takes place within the context of the struggle over control of the labor process and the administration of this "new discipline of market relations." The resolution of the struggle in favor of a system of top-down, centralized control has become the implicit target of the critique mobilized by the publicists of the digital revolution — and implicitly by those who champion the democratic character of flexibility, interactivity, and customization.

As capitalism developed from a "putting out" (piece work) system to an industrial system, workers were aggregated within the space of the factory — a process that led to the spatial and temporal differentiation of work, domesticity, and leisure. Giddens suggests that this differentiation can be understood as the first step in the scientific management of labor: "The main phenomenon, in fact, that promotes the separation of home and work-place is the recognition of employers that labour discipline is more satisfactorily sustained if workers are under one roof."[25]

The emergence of a separate space for work (the factory workshop) during the advent of capitalist modernity simultaneously allows for the increasing rationalization of production *within* the work space through the division of labor and the introduction of machinery that transforms handicraft production into simple, repetitive motion. Indeed, it is the internal rationalization of the work space that, in conjunction with the development of mechanized forms of production, lays the groundwork for the dramatic productivity increases of the industrial revolution and the further development of Fordist techniques of production.[26] Such productivity enhancements were predicated on the realization that the machine can serve as a means of ensuring greater control not just over raw materials but also over the worker. Thus, the development of automated technology in the workplace served the specific goal of routinizing and simplifying the worker's contribution so as to lower labor costs and discipline the workforce.[27]

The division of labor also resulted in a series of spatial divisions internal to the factory itself, the most significant of which was the segregation of manual from mental labor. It is this division that comes to underwrite the characteristic split between management and labor, as well as the centralization of control that came to typify both industrial and mass media production. Labor historian Harry Braverman describes the progressive implementation of this separation associated with the technique of scientific management, a process whereby management monopolizes the knowledge required for a particular manufacturing process in order to "control each step of the labor process and its mode of execution."[28]

The hallmark of scientific management is the segregation of conception from execution described by Braverman.[29] This fundamental division comes to characterize mass society as a whole, especially insofar as the monopolization of creative control in the hands of the few parallels the increasing monopolization of control over the means of production—not just of consumer goods but also of cultural products such as news and entertainment. Indeed, it is the thrill of undermining this centralized control that is deployed by the promoters of reality TV who hype the producers' ostensible "loss" of control over an unscripted and unrehearsed cast as an authentic challenge to the centralized and hierarchical production processes associated with mass society and mass culture.

Within the factory, the division between conception and execution—"mental" and "manual" labor—serves as a physical manifestation of workplace social relations. Once these relations become congealed in spatial form, the resulting boundaries help naturalize them. Braverman recounts, for example, Frederick Taylor's observation that even if a worker did have the knowledge to participate in the design process, the spatial requirements of scientific production would render such participation impossible:

> The practical use of scientific data also calls for a room in which to keep the books, records, etc., and a desk for the planner to work at. Thus all of the planning which under the old system was done by the workman, as a result of his personal experience, must of necessity under the new system be done by the management in accordance with the laws of science; because even if the workman was well suited to the development and use of scientific data, it would be physically impossible for him to work at his machine and at a desk at the same time.[30]

This spatial segregation creates the need for a detailed system of record keeping based on the monitoring not only of production rates and efficiency levels but of the minute details of workplace activity. Precisely because those responsible for engineering are not directly involved in the manufacturing process, they need a detailed record of the physical activity of the worker that takes the form of Frank Gilbreth's famous time and motion studies.

It is worth highlighting the fact that this redoubling of the worker associated with scientific management—the creation of a data record that comes to stand for the worker and that can be used as a form of manipulation by proxy—is not a new development but one associated with the rise of industrial capitalism. Much has been made of the redoubling of the subject in the data banks of the information revolution. Deleuze coined the term "dividual" to refer to the no longer discrete (in)dividual, who finds him- or herself multiplied in myriad databanks. Similarly, Mark Poster describes the data image of the subject as a "second self," and Phil Agre calls it a "digital shadow."[31] All three associate this redoubling with the information era—a claim that only makes sense if one locates the origin of this era not in the digital revolution, but in the industrial revolution, as Robins and Webster do.[32] The digital double, in other words, traces its roots to the use of data about workers to rationalize the production process. The pioneers of scientific management abstracted the worker's activities from their immediate context and reconstructed them in the "planning department," where they served as a second self that could be manipulated according to the dictates of efficiency enhancement— and then imposed back on the worker.

The development of the prodigious productive power that made possible the era of mass production depended on what Braverman describes as the rationalization of production: the consolidation of techniques not only for monitoring workers but for centralizing control over the manufacturing process.[33] In the place of handicraft work, which depended on a specialized skill set, scientific management instituted routinized, repetitive labor that depended on surveillance of workers assigned to perform homogenized tasks. The role of the worker was to participate without controlling. If Taylorism consolidated the division of mental from material labor, thereby decreasing control of the worker and increasing that of the manager, Fordism further shifted the balance by subordinating the pace of the worker to that of the assembly line. Under Fordist strategies of rationalization, supervision becomes *automated*; the need to monitor workers devolves onto the machine itself.

This dissolution of traditional forms of production, and the consequent disempowering of the laborer, is one of the central themes of the critique of modernity that has, intriguingly, become a commonplace in the celebratory reception of new media. Although this assessment has long been associated with a left/critical perspective (as well as certain strands of antimodern conservative elitism), it has since been co-opted by the promoters of the revolutionary potential of new media. According to this critique, the creative potential of labor (as fulfilling) is neutralized when it is reduced to the commodity form of labor power and the worker's connection is no longer to the manufacturing process as a whole but to a predetermined set of fragmented and abstracted gestures. Work becomes a denatured practice that echoes the empty, self-proliferating logic of production for its own sake.

The promise offered by the digital revolution is to renature work and empower workers by overcoming the constitutive divisions of the modern workplace. As futurists Steve Pruitt and Tom Barrett put it in their discussion of the work space of the future, "Cyberspace will free an individual from space and time constraints."[34] The result, according to their description, will be a more creative, engaging, and individuated workplace, one in which knowledge workers (the authors have little to say about menial labor, perhaps on the assumption that it will become automated) will have opportunities for lifelong learning and benefit from "tremendous job mobility."[35] The appeal is to a combination of premodern dedifferentiation and postmodern flexibility as two combined lines of flight from the constraints of modernity. If workers feel constrained by boring repetitive labor, they will, in the digital future, have to upgrade their skills constantly. If they feel hemmed in by what the *New York Times* calls the last remaining pockets of "corporate socialism"—"jobs for life, employee and customer loyalty, all for one and one for all,"—the workforce of the future will be caught in a cycle of perpetual competition and the constant search for the next new job: "Electronically nomadic, cyberspace workers will live wherever the electronic cyberspace infrastructure reaches [assuming they can afford it]. . . . Separated from the stress caused by crowded and polluted urban areas and able to instantly turn to their real environments for recreation and exercise, cyberspace workers will lead highly productive and healthy lives."[36] That is, of course, if they aren't weighed down by the stress of having to continually retrain and compete with workers around the world for jobs with no security.

Indeed, the world described by Pruitt and Barrett sounds more like an employer's dream than a worker's paradise, providing firms with the ability to free themselves from burdensome obligations and costly benefits, to offload the costs of overhead and retraining onto telecommuters, and to force workers to compete with each other globally, thus driving wages down to the level of the cheapest workers in the least expensive markets. To streamline their own costs and compete globally, workers may well have to relocate to the least expensive locations, which are not likely to be the healthiest and most recreation friendly. The nomadic, monadic, worker is a futuristic ideal of the capitalist imaginary: the elementary particle of a perfectly friction-free workforce.

The virtual work space envisioned by corporate futurists doesn't just allow employees to work wherever they might be located, but also permits a level of worker supervision that makes Taylor and Gilbreth look like amateurs. Thanks to the miracle of interactivity, not just every motion of workers can be remotely monitored but also their conversations and interactions, where they go online, and every detail of their work. To the extent that non-business-related interactions have migrated onto the Internet, they become monitorable and targets for elimination in the name of efficiency, as is the case of the virtual water cooler activity that has been renamed "cyberslacking." In an echo of Gilbreth's preoccupation with the cumulative loss generated by even a fraction of second squandered per hour, companies promoting their surveillance software have already documented the economic losses, reportedly in the billions, resulting from employees surfing the net on company time.[37] In the "corporate virtual work space" of the future, it seems unlikely that employees will have the spare time for cyberslacking, but even if they do, it can be taken into account by the employers who pay them on a per-project basis, presumably compensating them only for the time that they actually worked—strictly according to the digital record.

The economic potential of digital dedifferentiation isn't based solely on allowing employees to continue working outside of the work space proper, but also to render non-work-related activities economically productive to the extent that they can be monitored. Thus, the border between work and leisure is eroded from both directions. As in the case of the workplace, the promise on offer to consumers is increasing flexibility, convenience, and control. The reality is that of the increased rationalization of consumption. To the extent that it enacts this dedifferentiation, reality TV serves as a compact metaphor for the productivity of the online economy: self-disclosure of even the most mundane variety is increasingly economically valuable in a mass-customized economy. The reason for this increasing productivity is twofold: First, it reanimates the logic of consumer capitalism described by Tiziana Terranova wherein consumers are compensated for their loss of control over the production process by the compensatory promise of control and fulfillment via consumption; second, it facilitates the forms of customization and niche marketing associated with the emerging online economy.[38] Within the "digital enclosure," the border between the rationalization of production and that of consumption disintegrates.

The Digital Enclosure

What the factory floor was to the mode of production in industrialized mass society, the "digital enclosure" is to the mode of consumption emerging in the mass customized, online economy. Legal scholar James Boyle uses the term to describe the process whereby information or other forms of content once available in the public domain come to be enclosed by digital "fences" erected by technological innovations and legal controls such as encryption and the Digital Millennium Copyright Act (which bans the unauthorized decryption of copyrighted material).[39] In this usage, the term *digital enclosure* refers to ways in which the online commons is being privatized.

I propose a somewhat broader reading of the notion of digital enclosure—one that refers back to the land enclosure movement that made possible the segregation of the space of work from those of leisure and domesticity (a separation that facilitated the productive deployment of surveillance). *Digital* enclosure can correspondingly be understood as the process whereby activities and transactions formerly carried out beyond the monitoring capacity of the Internet are enfolded into its virtual space. In the United States, examples might include the attempt by online booksellers to replace brick-and-mortar stores or the development of digital forms of television delivery. The process is still very much in its early stages, but it is being heavily underwritten by investments in start-up dot-com enterprises and by the enthusiastic and breathless predictions of the mass media. It is hard to avoid the barrage of stories that describe the revolutionary potential of online music delivery, online book publishing, and online shopping—all of which enable the increasingly comprehensive monitoring of consumer behavior.

From an economic perspective, the process of digital enclosure relates to the earlier enclosure movement insofar as it promises to compel entry into a particular social relation—one of surveillance—by preempting alternative spaces. Writing for the *American Prospect,* Toby Lester notes that entrance into what I call the digital enclosure is often voluntary (at least for the moment), but he describes the way in which consumers are compelled to go online for an increasing array of transactions by "the tyranny of convenience."[40] The current trend suggests that, increasingly, alternatives to this tyranny will be foreclosed. If, in other words, the latest work of a popular author or musical group is available *only* online, consumers are compelled to enter a virtual space within which certain, very detailed forms of monitoring can take place.

The spatial strategy of digital enclosure can thus be seen to parallel that of the land enclosure movement: Both compel entry into a specific space within which surveillance can take place. Moreover, both enact an internal segregation of that space (with the emergence of the engineering department and the digital database) to allow for proprietary access to information that can be accumulated, stored, and manipulated to enhance efficiency. However, the difference between these forms of enclosure also needs to be highlighted. First, and perhaps most important, is the fact that the process of digital enclosure does not (yet) take place through the direct (or even the indirect) threat of physical violence. Moreover, the process of digital enclosure encompasses not the sphere of labor proper but precisely those areas that were previously exempted from direct forms of surveillance characteristic of the workplace: the spheres of domesticity, recreation, and consumption.

Entry into the digital enclosure promises to *undo* one of the constituent spatial divisions of capitalist modernity: that between labor and leisure. The dismantling of this division operates as a form of dedifferentiation whereby spaces of leisure and domesticity are rendered economically productive. Dedifferentiation tends to work only in one direction; it does not make work more like "free time" but, rather, tends to commodify free time by transforming it into time that can be monitored, recorded, repackaged, and sold. If the land enclosure movement helped separate spaces of labor from those of leisure and domesticity so that labor time could be more efficiently exploited, the digital enclosure reaches out to embrace what was left over: free time. The anticipated productivity of the digital enclosure is thus predicated on a self-reinforcing spiral of surveillance and self-disclosure. Downloading a book or programming a digital television set generates information that can be commodified, repackaged, and eventually incorporated into customized products whose consumption generates ever more specific demographic information. Viewed in this way, the power of surveillance within the digital enclosure can be understood in Foucaualdian terms, as an incitement to productivity. Entry into this enclosure allows for the rationalization of the labor of consumption—an activity that had hitherto been relatively expensive to monitor as comprehensively as factory labor.

Monitoring the digital enclosure is relatively inexpensive because of the interactive capability of the Internet, which allows consumers to participate in the production process and thereby to perform valuable work for producers. The goal of marketers is to induce consumers to enter this enclosure and thereby to establish an ongoing relationship of surveillance via interactivity. The incentive to enter into the digital enclosure remains historically distinct from the incentive to enter into the monitored space of the factory workshop. In the latter case, the incentive was quite direct: deprived of access to the means of agricultural production— open farmland—those who had no capital resources had little choice but to sell their labor power under the conditions offered, which came to include submission to comprehensive workplace surveillance. In the case of the digital enclosure, which is still in its early stages, a variety of strategies to induce entrance are at work. In some cases, submission to surveillance becomes a condition for obtaining a service that is only available online. Thus, for example, Internet service providers (ISPs) routinely track information about users (although there are some ISPs that guarantee privacy in exchange for a fee). Often users are offered the promise of a bonus in exchange for the information they provide, as in the case of free e-mail services that monitor the browsing habits of users stored in the form of electronic "cookies"—information about websites the client has visited. Typically, these services do not allow access to users who have turned off their cookies, thereby rendering the record of their browsing habits inaccessible. Taken to its limit, the logic of digital enclosure works toward the goal of foreclosing offline consumption options: if consumers want or need a particular product, they would have no choice but to enter into a relationship characterized by electronic monitoring. Far from serving as a form of empowerment, monitored interactivity has the potential to become a comprehensive system for monitoring both workers and consumers.

The strategy of portraying surveillance-based monitoring as a means of countering the very forms of control it serves to reinforce inaugurates a self-stimulating cycle. When the *New York Times* tells its readers that the advent of interactive digital television is "the beginning of the end of another socialistic force in American life: the mass market,"[41] it contributes to the deployment of what might be called, with apologies to Foucault, "the mass society repressive hypothesis." The latter underwrites the ostensibly subversive potential of interactivity even as it replicates and intensifies the relations it ostensibly undermines. The most familiar version of this hypothesis suggests that mass production worked to stifle the forms of individuation and self-expression that will be unleashed in the upcoming digital revolution, that the incitement to divulge our consumption-related behavior (and what else is there, from a marketing perspective?) paradoxically represents a subversion of the totalitarian, homogenizing forces of the mass market. As in the case of the deployment of the repressive hypothesis, the promised subversion turns out to be an incitement to multiply the very forms of self-disclosure that serve the disciplinary regime they purportedly subvert. The role of the media in this self-stimulating cycle is taken up in the following section.

FROM MASS TO INTERACTIVE MEDIA

Information Rationalization

> Instead of reading what other people think is news and what other people justify as worthy of the space it takes, being digital will change the economic model of news selection . . . In fact, under these conditions, you might be willing to pay the *Boston Globe* a lot more for ten pages than for a hundred pages. . . . You would consume every bit. . . . Call it *The Daily Me*.
>
> —Nicholas Negroponte in *Being Digital*[42]

The digital critique of the mass media is directly related to its critique of mass production: the products of the news and culture industries are homogenous, and control over information concentrated in the hands of the few. Readers and viewers don't have enough say in determining the forms of news, entertainment, and culture they consume. In response, writers like Nicholas Negroponte and Bill Gates predict that the Internet will challenge the top-down model of information delivery associated with the rise of mass media.[43] Their claim is that the erosion of the boundary between production and consumption works to the advantage of the viewers/readers whose preferences will shape the news and entertainment they consume. To understand the appeal of this promise, once again, requires a brief consideration of the logic of mass society, this time translated into the realm of media practice.

The rise of advertising as the "linchpin" of consumer society was dependent on the development and rationalization of commercial media during the nineteenth century.[44] Specifically, the commodification of news in the late nineteenth century analyzed by media historian Gerald Baldasty incorporates elements of the rationalization of production outlined above and anticipates the increasing social importance of advertising in the following century.[45] According to Baldasty, as the news came to be viewed as a commodity, its producers adopted the technique of mass production in the form of "patent insides": ready-made newspaper templates complete with "general news, innocuous editorials, feature articles, and advertisements" that left space open for the insertion of local content.[46] Compounding this homogenization of content, the division of labor within the newsroom (the "factory" of news production) was consolidated with the emergence and institutionalization of the beat system. Finally, the recognition that the real product produced by mass circulation newspapers was an audience to be sold to advertisers led to techniques for manufacturing this audience in the most efficient way possible. This meant consolidating markets, fostering broad appeal, and, consequently, backing away from partisan associations that might alienate some fraction of the readership. The commodification of news, in short, played a role in its packaging as mass market entertainment: "The search for 'vivid, bright, and pyrotechnic stories' led to coverage of disasters, murder, suicide, love triangles, elopements, gossip, and any truly odd story."[47] The emergence of a professionally produced, commercial, mass circulation newspaper stands in the same relation to the eighteenth-century press as the emergence of mass production to handicraft production. It becomes another symptom of the transition from traditional participatory forms of production to modern, rationalized ones.

The critique of the mass media, like that of mass society, mobilizes a sense of loss that is exploited by the promoters of the promise of interactivity. The transition from revolutionary but preindustrial forms of public information to mass-produced media is associated with the rise of the forms of centralized manipulation and passive consumption attributed to the culture industry. James Carey, for example, portrays the preindustrial American colonial press as a participatory, interactive, community-centered medium:

> Pubs were presided over by publicans who were often publishers as well. Publicans picked up information from travelers who often recorded what they had seen and heard on their journeys in log books stationed at the end of the bar, and from conversations in the pub. . . . In other words, the content of the press was by and large the spoken word, the things being said by public men in public places.[48]

This account draws heavily on Jürgen Habermas's discussion of the emergence of modern publicity in European public houses and coffee houses. His invocation of the *Tatler* newspaper, for example, emphasizes its role in promoting the continuation of public conversation by other means: "The periodical articles were not only made the object of discussion by the public of the coffee houses but were viewed as integral parts of this discussion. . . . The dialogue form too, employed by many of the articles, attested to their proximity to the spoken word."[49]

Carey and Habermas both offer their discussion of the participatory ("skilled") public as the starting point for a narrative of decline. This narrative, which traces the so-called refeudalization of the public sphere—the transformation of publicity from a form of participatory debate into a strategy for manipulation (as epitomized by public relations)—parallels the narrative of the deskilling of the labor force outlined by Braverman.[50] In both cases, control is centralized and the participation of the many—be they workers or members of the public—is routinized. Indeed, Habermas's description of the decline of publicity as active participation bears a strong resemblance to Braverman's description of the de-skilling and disempowering of the workforce: "A public of citizens that had disintegrated as a public was reduced by publicist means to such a position that it could be claimed for the legitimation of political compromises without participating in effective decisions or being in the least capable of such participation."[51] Carey similarly considers the rationalization of public opinion as a strategy for what the founder of public relations, Edward Bernays, described as the process of "engineering consent":[52] "The press no longer facilitated or animated a public conversation. . . . It informed a passive and privatized group of citizens who participated in politics through the press. What conversation remained was orchestrated by the press in the name of a superior knowledge and superior instruments of inquiry into just what was going on."[53] The process of refeudalization (Habermas's term) might, in this sense, be understood as that whereby the skills that empowered the public (rational-critical debate, participatory deliberation, etc.) are professionalized and relegated to the members of a small elite in an attempt to gain and centralize power over the public.

The professionalization and commercialization of the news industry gave rise to the distinction between the roles of reader and writer (one that remained blurred in the public houses and coffee houses), shattering the (handicraft) image of journalism as conversation continued by other means. It also effectively eclipsed activist forms of journalism, including the working-class and suffragist press in the late nineteenth and early twentieth centuries. Jon Bekken's history of the working-class press at the turn of the century and Linda Steiner's discussion of suffrage periodicals both offer examples of the kind of participatory news production that echo Carey's nostalgia for the colonial press.[54] The readers of these periodicals were often their writers, and the motive was not profit but political discussion and the consolidation of a community of interests. Both Bekken and Steiner highlight the difficulties faced by periodicals that attempted to buck the contemporaneous trend of politically neutral, advertising-supported news commodities. Steiner, for example, notes that the suffrage periodicals "generally failed" because of a lack of commercial support, and Bekken attributes the extinction of the working-class press during the Great Depression to "the collapse of the community institutions that supported and often published these papers . . . the postwar Red Scares, and . . . tightened restrictions on immigration."[55]

A certain nostalgia for the lost "golden era" of participatory media production thus comes to characterize the rhetoric of the digital revolution. In this sense, the celebrants of new media have incorporated strands of the arguments of media critics like Habermas and Carey, suggesting that the new media can resuscitate what was best about the old. If the problem of the mass media is that they are top-down, mass produced, and homogenous, if they relegate viewers and readers to the role of passive spectators, the promise of digital dedifferentiation is to erode the barriers that kept them from participating. Interactivity is positioned as the resuscitation of participation: the elimination of the differentiation between reader and writer, viewer and producer. In practice, however, we are forced to ask whether this promise lives up to its potential. To what extent does the type of participation envisioned by futurists like Negroponte and Gates amount to meaningful control? It's one thing to be able to customize one's choices and quite another to expand the range within which customization can occur. A newspaper that allows its readers to read only about the issues that interest them does not necessarily provide a broader or different range of topics, views, and news than a mass-produced one. Nor does it promote the ability to "talk back" in any more meaningful way than by providing a customized set of preferences. What such a paper does do, however, is help acclimatize readers to a world in which submission to detailed monitoring is the flip side of customization. Just as new technologies allow the workplace to expand so as to include the home, the airport, and even Starbuck's (which is currently in the process of equipping its cafés with high-speed Internet access), so, too, does the digital enclosure expand to encompass activities hitherto largely beyond the scope of comprehensive surveillance. Newspapers will *need* to know our content preferences and reading habits in order to whittle down their mass-produced content (and ads) to fit our idiosyncratic interests. The interactive infrastructure and the habituation of consumers to the digital enclosure it creates become crucial preconditions for mass customization.

Interactive Media

The promise of new media to challenge the one-way, top-down structure of the mass media is highlighted by technologies such as TiVo that equate viewers with programming directors able to customize their viewing preferences. This form of customization is, according to Bill Gates, just the beginning. He anticipates a world in which not just the timing and choice of programs will be customized, but in which the content itself can be adapted to viewer preferences—allowing them, for example, to choose the type of ending they want, the setting of the movie, even the actors.[56] Gates understands that customization points in the direction not only of allowing the consumer to personalize entertainment (or news) but also of making the consumer the star: "You might watch *Gone with the Wind* with your own face and voice replacing Vivien Leigh's (or Clark Gable's). Or, see yourself walking down a runway wearing the latest Paris fashions adjusted to fit your body or the one you wish you had."[57]

The promise of customization and the promise of reality TV overlap insofar as they offer to make the viewer the star, via interactive technology. At the same time, it's hard not to read in this promise the solipsism of what Adorno calls identity thinking: the attempt to eliminate difference that results in the subsumption of the external world to what is already known. The same might be said of Negroponte's description of the *Daily Me*: the perfection of niche marketing reinforces its own version of homogeneity. Gates, in attempting to imagine the most appealing scenario for digital customization, comes up with the promise that everywhere viewers look, they may find only themselves: as the stars of the shows they watch and the characters in the advertisements, the creators of the artworks they view, and of the products they consume. The *i* that designates "interactivity" overlaps with the *I* of identity thinking.

On the level of public relations and advertising—the selling of a lifestyle, as it were—the news and entertainment media continually underscore and reinforce the claims of convenience and control associated with the "digital revolution." The discourse is carried over relatively intact from the marketing and business literature to the mainstream media (with occasional exceptions). But such ideological support is just one aspect of the role played by communication technologies in the would-be emergent paradigm of mass customization. New media technologies are a central component of mass customization in several ways: they make possible the convergence that dedifferentiates the spheres of consumption, production, and leisure; they facilitate the interactivity that simultaneously redifferentiates products and services; and, finally, they enable the surveillance that commodifies the labor of production.

It is important to add that since the culture of mass customization is still in its formative stages, the role of the mass-customized media remains largely an anticipated one. Futurists ranging from Bill Gates to Alvin and Heidi Toffler are currently spinning out scenarios that media giants and dot-com start-ups are hoping to exploit for profit.[58] Thus, any attempt to trace the outline of the interactive, customized economy must necessarily focus on preliminary efforts toward fulfilling the forecasts of the futurists, whose predictions help create a blueprint for capital. The example of TiVo described earlier offers a glimpse of the direction in which the mass media are headed: that of increasingly customized forms of delivery. Mass customization, in this context, refers to the customer's ability to choose when and where he or she will watch a particular program. Gates's conception of interactivity pushes a bit further: toward the notion that viewers will eventually be able to customize the programming itself. The goal will be, as in the case of hypertext, to allow the viewer to shape the content of the show—to become, in some sense, a coproducer. The following chapters claim that this goal is anticipated by the way in which particular reality TV formats (CBS's *Big Brother* in particular) incorporate viewer participation into the program's content.

The media in the "after-mass" of interactive technology offer one more blow to the 1950s model of broadcasting in which the major networks monopolized a mass audience. This "mass" model was already destabilized in the 1970s with the advent of cable TV and the VCR. The move toward proliferating channels and time shifting will be pushed even further by devices like TiVo and Internet-based television, which allow viewers to watch their chosen programs at their leisure—and in some cases to bleep through commercials with a fast-forward capability that leaps ahead in thirty-second intervals (no more overshooting the end of the commercials and then rewinding). These new versions of television threaten to render obsolete the mass advertising paradigm: not only can advertising no longer be pegged to the demographics of time (who's watching when), but bleeping through commercials becomes easier than ever.[59] That might sound like a relief, but such forms of media consumption set the stage for a shift toward the paradigm of mass-customized advertising. If, as telecommunications companies envision, the Internet is eventually to become the platform for the delivery of all forms of home entertainment, every customized set of viewing preferences will be recorded by service providers. Broadcasters will thus be able to monitor viewing patterns with accuracy far beyond that of the relatively crude system of the Nielsen ratings.

What, then, is to become of the paradigm of mass advertising? The short answer is that it becomes integrated into entertainment programming and simultaneously becomes customized—at least according to the vision outlined by the cyberfuturists. Lewis suggests that one potential response to the new television technology will be a shift toward product placement as the dominant advertising model.[60] Bill Gates describes how such a paradigm might work even more effectively via an interactive medium like the Internet. He envisions a world in which movies and television programs could serve not only as vehicles for product placement but also as online catalogs: "If you're watching a video of *Top Gun* and think that Tom Cruise's aviator sunglasses look really cool, you'll be able to pause the movie and learn more about the glasses or even buy them on the spot— if the film has been tagged with commercial information."[61] The world Gates imagines is one in which actors double as catalog models and in which every item that appears in a movie—from the protagonists' wardrobes to the resorts they visit—can serve as a hot-link to promote consumption. This was the advertising model anticipated in the 1998 movie *The Truman Show*—which offered a prescient take on the accelerating trend toward surveillance-based reality TV. Rather than breaking into the content to air an advertisement, *The Truman Show* dedifferentiated advertising from narrative by working the advertisements into the show itself: all of the products in the protagonist's house, in the yard, and at work doubled as advertisements. The result is the extension of the process of dedifferentiation to the boundary between advertising and content—a boundary that has long been contested in the U.S. commercial media. The reality TV trend has been at the forefront of this dedifferentiation process, as evidenced by the integration of sponsors into the content of successful shows like *Survivor* and *American Idol*. As *Survivor* producer Mark Burnett put it, the show "is as much a marketing vehicle as it is a television show. My shows create an interest, and people will look at them, but the endgame here is selling products in stores—a car, deodorant, running shoes. It's the future of television."[62]

The complete convergence of entertainment and consumption must be understood as one of the central goals of online commerce, and this understanding allows the logic of current practices of the culture industry to fall into place. We have been hearing more and more about product placement in recent years, and it has become increasingly clear that promotional campaigns for movies, as in the extreme case of the first *Star Wars* prequel, serve as much to market spin-off products as to sell the movie itself. Without the interactive capability of the Internet, product placement functions merely as an unzappable form of advertising. Delivered over the Internet, however, it transforms the "passive" viewing experience into an "active" shopping experience and helps to further dedifferentiate the pursuits of leisure, consumption, and production. This process of dedifferentiation—which is a leitmotif in the literature on mass customization—is presented as a counterparadigm to the forms of differentiation associated with the era of mass production and consumption. It promises to push the process of commodification to its logical extreme while simultaneously claiming to challenge the stultifying division of labor characteristic of mass production.

The advertising example helps demonstrate how interactivity and surveillance form one version of what business consultant Joseph Pine describes as the feedback loop of mass customization.[63] Interactivity allows formerly "passive" and anonymous viewers to make their viewing and consumption decisions known to marketers in advance. The labor that goes into these decisions—formerly decommodified and thus unproductive from the point of view of capital—can then be used to generate customized and individualized marketing strategies. Habituating consumers to this kind of surveillance-based customization means overcoming the historical association of surveillance with totalitarian forms of oppression and exploitation. It requires, in short, the repositioning of surveillance as a form of consumer convenience and a means of "adding value" to a media product. Thus, in addition to spreading the word of the impending "revolution" and of the myriad technological achievements that will enable it, the mass media are also starting to serve as a kind of experimental training ground for interactive uses of new communication technologies.

Consider, for example, the ratings success of the first "interactive" version of the television show *Dateline*. Aired in July 1999, the program urged viewers to log onto the Internet in order to cast "guilty" or "innocent" votes in response to the television coverage of a murder trial. The show—which integrated television and the Internet—took top ratings for the week.[64] Viewed as an isolated instance of a successful marketing gimmick, the ratings success of a *Dateline* episode in the middle of the rerun season is not particularly striking, but viewed within the context of the discourse of mass customization, it takes on a certain resonance. The success of such a show may well attest to the effectiveness of the oft-repeated message that interactivity is somehow empowering and hence desirable. It also helps define interactivity according to the parameters outlined by the system of mass customization: participation at the point of consumption that adds value while leaving untouched the relation of power between those who own the means of production and those who consume its products.

Television shows like the interactive *Dateline* do more than celebrate the "active" audience; they help train viewers to use television in new ways that fit neatly within the paradigm of mass customization. If one of the hurdles faced by mass customizers is that of convincing an occasionally wary populace that surveillance is to be embraced, programs like interactive *Dateline* suggest to viewers that they gain more control when they "participate" in the show they are watching rather than passively absorbing it. To drive home the point, *Dateline* host Jane Pauley introduced the show by hyping its interactive aspect: "And now, our special interactive *Dateline,* where you weigh the facts and decide."[65] Presumably viewers also weigh facts and decide even when they aren't registering their votes online, but those decisions only gain significance (and the recognition of Jane Pauley) when they are aggregated by *Dateline* and displayed on the television screen. The notion that surveillance somehow makes preferences effective and real is a useful one for the purveyors of mass customization, who depend on the ready participation of consumers in the commodification of their desires.

INTERACTIVE CULTURE AND THE RETURN OF THE REAL

> Interactivity . . . will destroy the elite divide between those who can create and those who can't.
>
> —Peter Gabriel, *Time*, 1995

In his criticism of a reductionist view of culture, Adorno argues, "A dialectical theory which is uninterested in culture as a mere epiphenomenon, aids pseudo-culture to run rampant and collaborates in the production of evil."[66] Interestingly, the result of such a perspective is to take even popular cultural seriously—not as a form of escape from social reality but as an integral component of its reproduction. This is perhaps why Adorno was doubly fascinated with culture: with exploring the critical potential of some cultural forms and the ideological character of others. The argument so far has suggested the ways in which cultural processes both typified and enabled emerging economic paradigms. The mass media not only adopted the model of factory production but helped sell its goods and promote the values of consumer culture. Similarly, the deployment of interactive media both enacts and enables mass customization. If mass society was associated with a way of life based on concentrated surveillance in the workplace and the segmentation of the working day, flexible capitalism is associated with the generalization of surveillance and the dedifferentiation of the boundaries between production and consumption.

Just as a shared logic of rationalization via the abstraction of conception from execution can be traced in the seemingly disparate elements of mass society, the notion of interactivity can be used to explore the relationships between the elements of the way of life envisioned by the proponents of the emerging digital economy. The ostensible opposition between the two social formations comes to rest on the promise of interactivity to overcome abstraction, a promise embodied by the impetus to "get real"—to counter the contrived forms of top-down manipulation characteristic of mass-produced culture. The connection to the real is perhaps the central contribution to the equation of democracy with the new "interactivity" observable in the current pop cultural obsession with reality-based programming, from webcams, to amateur porn, to reality TV, and even car chases.[67] In 1999, at the dawn of the resurgence of reality TV, residents of Los Angeles—the city famous for its car-chase films—could subscribe to a pager system that would alert them when *real* car chases were being aired on TV news stations. The appeal, once again, was access to unproduced reality—a chance to sidestep the contrivances of the culture industry, an industry that had come to be characterized by the same set of abstractions as the factory: the production by a select few of formulaic entertainment for the consumption of the many.

The ambiguity in the term *popular culture* itself points to the shift from participatory cultural forms associated with pre–mass society to the products of the culture industry. Media scholars Alan O'Connor and John Downing offer an anachronistic definition of popular culture: that which is produced by the people. Crucial to this definition is its participatory aspect.[68] The reference is to the "folk" cultures in which the distinction between producer and consumer remains blurred by the role of the participant. However, this definition is certainly not the currently dominant one. The term *pop culture* is more likely to invoke images of Britney Spears and The Backstreet Boys than the Irish jigs and Balinese shadow puppets discussed by O'Connor and Downing. Indeed, the definition of popular culture that comes to characterize mass society seems to incorporate two of the definitions proposed by Williams: "work deliberately setting out to win favour with the people" and works that are "well-liked by many people."[69] Thus, the semantic shift that takes place within the adjective *popular*—from "created by the people" to "created for the people"—parallels the shift in the term *publicity* from public accountability to public relations.

As culture is commodified and its production rationalized, responsibility for production is monopolized. The participation of the public is reduced to that of consumer/spectator. The hope offered by the advent of the network society is that the converse might be true: that the return of public participation via interactivity might revitalize not only politics and production but also culture—that the interactive aesthetic is a more democratic one than either of those provided by mass society: high culture and the culture industry. Reality TV partakes of the appeal of the interactive aesthetic by taking it literally in order to challenge the abstracted relations of cultural production and reception with the promise of the return of the real. Abstraction is associated with separation and differentiation as well as with the split between concept, execution, and consumption. Undoing abstraction—and reality is offered as an antidote to abstraction—means overcoming the constitutive divisions of modernity, which is the promise of reintegration. The irony is that flexibility and mass customization simultaneously promise to pursue the logic of segmentation, stratification, and customization to its logical extreme. Nevertheless, the implicit appeal is to the role that participation will play in leveling the hierarchies and overcoming the divisions. Perhaps one of the most fascinating elements of this appeal is the way in which it mobilizes mediation to counter the effects of the mass media in the cultural realm: interactivity allows access to a reality that one-way, centralized media could stage only as spectacle.

The Interactive Aesthetic

One of the areas in which a critical assessment of the promise of interactivity has been most conspicuously absent is in the popular and theoretical reception of new media in the cultural realm—particularly in the realm of art. It is perhaps because this realm has been so thoroughly abstracted from the practical realm in modernity that the idealistic promise of interactivity as democratization can be given free play in it, liberated from some of the more obvious contradictions that confound such a promise in the political and economic realms. At the same time, precisely because of this abstracted character, the role of interactivity in the arts reinforces many of the metaphors for the promise of interactivity enlisted by the celebrants of new media to sell interactivity in the economic and political spheres.

Reality TV, to the extent that it, too, draws on these metaphors of participation and democratization, partakes in the promise of the digital aesthetic to counter the hierarchies of modernism. If the aesthetic of high modernism was associated with the abstract relations that parallel those of mass society itself, interactive digital culture is portrayed as a means of surpassing the separation between the celebrity artist and the anonymous mass audience. The notion of the (inter-)"active" viewer, reader, and listener is central to many digital works and has been used to underwrite the claim that computer art radically "democratizes" the aesthetic experience.

In his discussion of digital culture, Richard Lanham argues, for example, that the interactive character of the digital aesthetic counters the "oppressive" nature of the canon: "The traditional idea of an artistic canon brings with it, by the very 'immortality' it strives for, both a passive beholder and a passive reality waiting out there to be perceived."[70] Digital art, by contrast, promotes viewing as an active, transformative process, according to Lanham: "All of this yields a body of work active not passive, a canon not frozen in perfection, but volatile with contending human motive. Is this not the aesthetic of the personal computer?"[71] Similarly, Douglas Robertson argues that interactive, hypertext composition frees the reader from the dictates of the author: "It allows the ordering of the text to follow the reader's cares and interests rather than the author's."[72] Negroponte writes that the computer ushers in an age of widespread and democratized creativity accompanied by "a new era of opportunity and respect for creative avocations—lifelong making, doing, and expressing."[73] No longer will creative practice be limited to the fortunate few, for computers turn the "tools to work with" into the tools of creativity: "there will be a more common palette for . . . self-expression and group work."[74] This new aesthetic, according to such authors, overflows the boundaries

of cyberspace; it is the aesthetic of the Internet itself and consequently of contemporary life.[75]

It is hard not to discern in Lanham's attack on the canon a critique of the abstracted, autonomous modernism that critics fault for distancing itself from the
day-to-day reality of contemporary viewers. Interactive artworks challenge this
autonomy by ostensibly undermining the relations of production that made it possible. The crucial connection to be drawn between the realm of high culture and
the advent of mass society is the way in which the turn away from realism (toward
abstraction) coincides with the separation of the mental from the manual labor of
artistic production. The artist Lazlo Moholy-Nagy, one of the original members of
the Bauhaus school, highlighted this division of labor when "To demonstrate that
other possibilities existed in art-making apart from hand skills . . . , [he] ordered
the fabrication of a work of art by telephone."[76] Duchamp's "ready-mades"
demonstrate a similar point insofar as they "reduce the aesthetic consideration to
the choice of the mind, not to the ability or cleverness of the hand."[77] It is significant, then, that the objects Duchamp chose as ready-mades were not items taken
from nature but rather mass-produced industrial objects. These products—turned
into artworks by the mental "labor" of the artist—were simultaneously the creation
of an industrialized manufacturing process reliant on the rationalization of production and the separation of mental and manual labor. Duchamp's gesture is a
shocking one precisely because it reintroduces into the realm of mental labor a
product of industrial (deskilled) manual labor—thereby highlighting the gulf between the two at the same time as it points out the commonality between the realm
of aesthetic production and that of mass production.

Thus, the high culture that asserts its autonomy in the face of an increasingly
commodified society characterized by the rationalization of popular culture retains a certain similarity to mass production insofar as it relies on the abstraction
of the mental from the material. The opposition between high and mass culture
tends to background this shared logic, which can perhaps be discerned in the gulf
between artist and spectator that parallels and starts to merge with the gulf between celebrity and fan (Picasso and Hemingway both come to epitomize the
overlapping character of the celebrity/artist). In a similar vein, Harvey attributes
the growing distance between cultural producer and consumer at least in part to
the demands of a commodified art market in which celebrity cachet helps produce
marketable works: "The result was often a highly individualistic, aristocratic, dis-
dainful . . . , and even arrogant perspective on the part of cultural producers."[78]

The interactive aesthetic promises to counter this elitism, thanks to the logic of
digital dedifferentiation. No longer is the site of artistic production removed from
that of its reception, no longer is the artwork walled in and fenced off, and no
longer do these walls reinforce the division between the creative (active) artist
and the "passive" viewer. In her book on hypertext fiction, Janet Murray describes in more accurate terms the reconfigured role of the "active" viewer, stop-
ping short of Lanham's "the author is dead, long live the reader (as author)" rhet-

oric. For Murray, hypertext enables the interactive aspect of the digital aesthetic described by Lanham, but that doesn't mean the viewer becomes the author. Rather, she argues that the viewer should be described as an "interactor":

> The interactor, whether as navigator, protagonist, explorer, or builder, makes use of this repertoire of possible steps and rhythms to improvise a particular dance among the many, many possible dances the author has enabled. We could perhaps say that the interactor is the author of a particular performance within an electronic story system.[79]

The result is that the nature of authorship changes:

> Authorship in electronic media is procedural. Procedural authorship means writing the rules by which the texts appear as well as writing the texts themselves. It means writing the rules for the interactor's involvement. . . . It means establishing the properties of the objects and potential objects in the virtual world and the formulas for how they will relate to one another.[80]

The text is no longer fixed, but the rules whereby it operates are. The *process* and the terms of the relationship become the author-supplied content. In many ways, this transformation serves as an apt description of the post-Fordist "postmodern" digital economy: people will design and shape their own products, but in so doing they will reinforce the procedural logic that shapes their interaction. What is important for the replication of the digital economy in this account is not the nature of any particular product but rather the reproduction of a given set of rules. It is the givenness of these rules that keeps the "mass" in "mass customization." This model allows one work to result in a variety of possible performances, just as reality TV formats offer the combination of repetition and originality. Indeed, reality TV offers a commodified example of procedural authorship: the producers craft the set of rules whereby cast members (and sometimes audiences) shape the show. Each season of *Survivor* or *The Real World* follows the same set of conventions but relies for new content on the contributions of selected members of the audience.

The promise of interactive works, then, is predicated on the contention that viewers are not "merely" passive—that they are, in some sense, cocreators. Such has long been the contention of so-called reception theories of the media, which argue that although viewers don't shape the production of media texts, they play an active role in interpreting those texts—and thereby partake in the production of their significance.[81] It is also echoed in Foucault-inflected approaches that view the notion of authorship as a discursive strategy to control the subversive potential of the text. As Foucault puts it in "What Is an Author?": "The author is therefore the ideological figure by which one marks the manner in which we fear the proliferation of meaning."[82] Both of these critiques of "authority" are directed against the modernist conception of the artist as the embodiment of the rarefied (abstracted) creator separated from the site of reception and consumption. Both, in other words, are motivated by a critique directed against the abstract relations of mass society, insofar as each discerns domination in these relations. If "authority" is oppressive, then interactivity is, by contrast, portrayed as subversive of rationalized social relations. If abstraction is elitist, realism is democratic.

The ostensible challenge to modernism offered by interactivity is the dissolution of the hierarchical relationship between artistic creator and viewer/reader. The more celebratory strands of reception theory enact this dissolution as if by magic, implicitly asserting that such a relationship never *really* existed: the viewer was a creator all along. However, these approaches rely on the very split they promise to overcome: reception can be equated with production insofar as it is abstracted from the production process and relegated to an autonomous realm of its own. This realm belies its autonomy to the extent that it promises to offer political purchase on the very processes from which it has been abstracted. The claim that autonomous "meaning making" can challenge relations of domination in the political and economic spheres highlights the incoherence of such an approach, as Turner suggests: "The obvious limitation to the progressive effect of this multitude of textual possibilities is that the textual system may well be more porous than the social system; making over the meaning of a television program may be much easier than climbing out of a ghetto."[83] At the same time, the desire of reception theorists to counter the notion that reception is "merely" passive implies a certain recognition of the rationalization of the relations of production that minimizes worker and consumer control over the production process. It offers a symbolic challenge to (and compensation for) these relations by arguing that if the privileged position of control lies on the side of the mental labor, reception also implies control on the part of the viewer, since it is yet another form of mental labor. Taken to its extreme, the argument suggests that it doesn't much matter what is actually produced, that the real labor of production takes place in making meaning out of whatever raw material is provided. If consumers are excluded from control over the production process, they are promised compensation in the form of their control over consumption, which is, in turn, termed symbolic production.

This promise highlights the *real* perception of a lack of control. Amid the various debates over Marx's conception of alienation, it should be noted that marketing and advertising strategies continue, implicitly, to base themselves on it. How else is one to interpret the repeated compensatory promise of control over one's own practice (of consumption) as a form of authentic self-expression and fulfillment? It is hard not to discern in the logic of marketing an implicit reliance on the vicious cycle that Marx's theory attempts to explain. Advertising would not be half so effective if it delivered on its promise: if the products it sold effectively addressed the desire for control and fulfillment. Rather, they offer as the realization of this promise the embodiment of the lack to which advertising caters: the alienated product of alienated labor—the commodity.

The promise of the more celebratory strands of reception theory lines up neatly with this strategy, arguing, *with* the advertising industry—whether they admit it or not—that the site of consumption can double as a site of meaningful creative activity. This promise is patently false insofar as it works to background the congealed social relations and institutional practices that it helps to reproduce. The lure of interactivity, however, is a more complex one, insofar as it allows access to the site of production and to the production process itself. Interactivity thereby offers to push a step further than reception theory in order to resolve the latter's contradictions. If the subversive potential of reception is based on an untenable asymmetry—the assertion that production doesn't determine reception, but reception can challenge domination at the site of production—interactivity offers to eliminate the asymmetry. The promise of interactivity is to "real"-ize the assertion that reception is actually a form of production, offering ways in which viewers can take an active role in contributing to the finished product.

Virtual Realism

In the realm of digital aesthetics, the promise of digital interactivity also overlaps with that of an ostensibly empowering form of realism: the ability to create forms of virtual reality limited only by the power of the human imagination. In his study of digital art, Stephen Holtzman describes the appeal of the "real" as one of the defining aspects of digital aesthetics: "The Holy Grail of computer graphics is to create 'photo-realistic' images—computer-generated images indistinguishable from photographic images of the real world. In virtual worlds, the aim is to create an experience that seems completely real."[84] Tellingly, David Zeltzer of the MIT Media Lab invokes the same metaphor: "True virtual reality may not be attainable with any technology we can create. . . . Nevertheless, virtual reality serves as the Holy Grail of the research."[85] The invocation of the Grail myth holds a certain resonance for the current analysis insofar as it refers, in its pre-Christian form, to the cure for an ailing king, suffering from his wounds and presiding over a country turning into a wasteland. Translated into the register of the critique of mass society, the return of the real (albeit in virtual form) promises a cure for a culture suffering from the self-inflicted wounds of its own abstracted social relations.

It is perhaps one more trace of the implicit link between the return of the real and the promise of interactivity that virtual reality invokes the same self-contradictory logic as mass customization. Indeed, it is possible to read the latter through the former. The term *mass customization* is meant to represent not a temporal regression to an era before that of mass production but a surpassing of the opposition between handicraft and mass production—one that incorporates the benefits of both. In this sense, the promise of customization or individuation might be considered a virtual one: customization will take place to the extent that it conforms to the set of rules defined by producers. Without this conformity, the prefix *mass* would lose its meaning, or, to put it in more concrete terms, the mass manufacturing of customized products would be impossible. Virtual reality anticipates the types of virtual individuation and customization associated with digital interactivity: they offer only a virtual form of individuation—a simulacrum of individuality.

Perhaps one more area of overlap between these two terms can be discerned in the way they participate in the form of idealism that Adorno critiques as constitutive subjectivity. The "Holy Grail" of mass customization is the goal of creating a reality completely determined by its human creators and yet indistinguishable from uncreated nature. The fantasy, then, is one of absolute autonomy from nature, the dissolution of its stubborn objectivity and its replacement with a creation of the technologically enhanced subject—a subject invoked by Freud's description of "a kind of prosthetic God" who, "when he puts on all his auxiliary organs . . . is truly magnificent."[86] The enhanced subject becomes the unfettered master of cyberspace. As Holtzman puts it in his rhapsodic paean to the promise of virtual reality, "I imagine the possibilities of a world free of physical constraints and made from the infinitely malleable material of the virtual."[87] This fantasy coincides with that of pure autonomy from nature, which philosopher Simon Jarvis describes as an insistence that the subject should be "self-constituting and self-sufficient," freed from material determinations.[88]

Whereas Jarvis argues that the version of critical materialism outlined by Adorno acknowledges that freedom *requires* a "heteronomous element," the goal of virtual reality is, by contrast, to abolish heteronomy outright. Virtual reality seeks to transform the mediated into the immediately real—which is the definition of the naturalization of second-nature. This gesture is paralleled by the argument of reception theorists outlined above, insofar as their goal is, once again, the dissolution of the artifact and the consequent immediacy of the *interpretation*—which becomes the "real" product, no longer mediated in any meaningful (determinative) sense by the artifact itself. Again, we confront the antipathy to otherness that seems to characterize the solipsism of the digital world envisioned by futurists like Negroponte and Gates: a world in which we can roam the globe, shop, work, even make love, without every leaving the privacy of our homes. This solipsism is neatly summed up by the experiment of a man who renamed himself DotComGuy in order to prove that he could live in his house for a year getting everything he needed over the Internet (his experiment is discussed in greater detail in chapter 3).

But what of the promise of interactivity, which, as I have noted, doesn't dissolve the artifact per se, but goes reception theory one better by offering access to the productive process that reception theory backgrounds? In so doing, it fails to account for the fact that, viewed from a slightly different perspective than that offered by the publicists of the new economy, interactivity functions as labor. One might as well say, in other words, that even mass production is "interactive" insofar as it couldn't take place without the contributions of the members of the workforce who participate in the production process. Similarly, television and fine arts are all interactive, insofar as they require the (albeit) "passive" participation of an audience. The promise that interactivity (the labor of being watched) represents a more authentic, hence fulfilling, form of participation seems to be predicated on the fact that it takes place outside of the traditional work space and the social relations that characterize it. It takes place, in short, in the spheres to which the fulfillment foregone through the sale of labor power has been deferred: those of leisure and domesticity. If panoptic forms of surveillance came to be associated with labor within the modern office or factory, synoptic monitoring became, at the same time, associated with celebrity and the attainment of a position removed from that of the mass. Reality TV represents an intermediate and at times indeterminate form of monitoring: both a form of work and a celebrity holiday, both participation and submission. In this respect, it provides a neat segue into the era of interactive media, in which the TV we watch will watch us back, ostensibly for our own good.

The search for cheap programming is certainly one of the reasons for the proliferation of the reality format, but it is also worth considering how such a format fits into the logic of mass customization. To what extent does the equation of ubiquitous surveillance with entertainment help defuse the perceived threat posed by a computer network that promises to one day monitor every consumption decision we make? How might the suggestion that surveillance serves as an effective confirmation and validation of the "reality" of a situation (as in the case of MTV's *The Real World*) help encourage consumers to regard their self-commodification as a form of "self-expression"? These are some of the questions that will be addressed in the following chapters.

The notion that the labor of consumption is somehow fulfilling *in itself* fits neatly with a paradigmatic aspect of mass customization: convergence. The convergence of different forms of media (print, radio, TV) anticipated by the Internet parallels the convergence of functions (advertising, entertainment, production), as well as the dedifferentiation of spheres of labor, leisure, and consumption envisioned by the proponents of mass customization. The interactive *Dateline* program provides one example: The attempt to combine one-way television programming with the interactivity (and surveillance) offered by the Internet serves as a kind of transitional stage—TV with interactive training wheels—for mass customization. It takes a known medium and attempts to integrate it with some of the key characteristics of an emergent medium. This convergence is paralleled by other communication technologies that further the process of dedifferentiation. Home computers, personal digital assistants (PDAs), beepers, and cell phones all help bridge the divisions between home, work, and recreation—divisions that gained their clarity within the highly differentiated system of mass production. In Bill Gates's world, all of these various functions would be absorbed into the Internet. At the limit, the Internet represents the ultimate form of dedifferentiation: Within the digital enclosure, our lives become reducible to the universal medium of digital exchange: the bit.

The crucial question is, Who benefits from dedifferentation process? The business literature argues for a win/win scenario in which the consumer gains added convenience, and the producer remains "at the controls" of an economy cranking up the production cycle to a more frenetic pace. Above and beyond the promise of added convenience lies the ostensibly "revolutionary" challenge to the shortcomings of mass society. The recognition of these shortcomings highlights the collision between the rationalization of mass society and liberal conceptions of freedom and individualism. The provision of consumer goods for a mass market relied upon techniques of mass production that homogenized both products and the labor associated with their manufacture.[89] Furthermore, it helped concentrate economic power (and political power) in the hands of an increasingly rarefied economic elite. The productivity gains associated with the rationalization of production did contribute to elevated material standards of living, and in this sense they helped justify the promise of mass society. At the same time, they contributed to the creation of the "mass" of consumers, laborers, and readers/viewers, on one hand, and the centralization of control in the hands of what sociologist C. Wright Mills calls the "power elite," on the other.[90] The contradiction, as Slavoj Zizek, among others, notes, was eminently productive, since improved access to material goods could be repeatedly offered as a means of compensating for the "massification" of the public.[91] Thus, the alienation of the masses was not just a lament of the critics of mass society; it was also an advertising strategy for products that offered to overcome it (and thus helped reproduce it).

Mass customization promises to make good on this promise by allowing both increased access to a wider range of material goods, and the ostensible democratization of the production process. The thrust of this promise is that, in radical discontinuity with the logic of mass society, customization will deliver on the equation of democratic freedom with the freedom of the market. However, the version of digital interactivity being deployed in online commerce and new commercial media represents the continued deferral of this promise. Or, to put it another way, it represents not the overcoming of the contradiction between the "free" market and democratic freedom but its continued exploitation. The underlying continuity between mass society and mass customization, then, cannot be traced through any one sphere of social practice, but rather in the logic that links the contemporaneous development of the promise of new media in both cultural and material production and consumption.

The argument that the digital enclosure represents an extension of the logic of mass society suggests that what we are likely to see in coming years is not the dismantling of monopoly capital but the increased concentration of control over the means of production. As Darin Barney notes, digital information and communication technologies allow for the centralized control of ever more extended corporate organizations, allowing companies to operate more effectively on a global scale.[92] The flurry of merger activity (of unprecedented scope) over the past several years seems to favor this scenario rather than the promise of decentralization. For example, the Federal Trade Commission noted that in fiscal year 2000, "more than 4,900 [merger] filings were made, a record number. This continues a 10-year trend, in which the number of filings has more than tripled since 1991. Some of the largest mergers in history were proposed this past year. The value of reported merger transactions now exceeds $2 trillion each year—an 11-fold increase in the past decade."[93] This merger activity is not all related to the telecommunication industry (although the sector has certainly seen its fair share of record-breaking mergers in the past several years), but it certainly refutes the claim that technological developments are working to decentralize control over productive resources. On the contrary, the incunabulum of the digital era has been characterized by the acceleration of the concentration of wealth and economic control in the United States and abroad.

If the *mass* media served not only to advertise the benefits of mass consumption but also as examples of the logic of mass production in every aspect, then the question remains as to how the *interactive* media will function within the era of mass customization. Reality TV may not brainwash viewers into equating surveillance with self-expression, but it reinforces the way in which this equation has come to characterize the logic of the mass-customized economy. The goal of the following chapters is to discern the social realities that are enacted in the artifice of the latest programming trend: to determine just what is real about reality TV.

NOTES

1. Michael Lewis, "Boom Box," *New York Times Magazine*, 13 August 2000, 36.

2. Lewis, "Boom Box," 37.

3. Lewis, "Boom Box," 42.

4. Raymond Williams, *The Long Revolution* (New York: Columbia University Press, 1961), 46.

5. It is this self-positioning of modernity that the term *postmodern* suppresses. The simplistic version of postmodernism pilloried by Terry Eagleton in *The Illusions of Postmodernism* (Oxford: Blackwell, 1996) imagines that a perspective from which modernity appears as characterized by oppressively false claims to totality must locate itself somehow beyond modernity (hence the addition of the misleading prefix). The current argument suggests, on the contrary, that this perspective has always been incorporated into modernity itself in the form of a self-stimulating nostalgia for what has been lost. This loss is registered in the postmodern "discovery" of the falsity of modernist totality. This charge represents not a rupture with Enlightenment reason but its logical extension. Consequently, the argument that the digital revolution is not revolutionary at all parallels the argument that postmodernism doesn't represent a definitive break with modernism. In this sense, the current account is sympathetic with J. M. Bernstein's contention that postmodern theory is more accurately described as "philosophical modernism" (Jay M. Bernstein, "The Causality of Fate: Modernity and Modernism in Habermas," *Praxis International* 8, no. 4 [January 1989]: 407–25).

6. Max Weber, "Science as a Vocation," in *From Max Weber: Essays in Sociology*, ed. H. H. Gerth and C. Wright Mills (New York: Oxford University Press, 1946).

7. Lisa Guernsey, "You Can Surf but You Can't Hide," *New York Times*, 7 February 2002, G1.

8. For a detailed examination of mutual "Googling," see Neil Swidey, "Nation of Voyeurs," *Boston Globe Magazine*, 2 February 2003, 10–34.

9. As quoted in Susan Buck-Morss, *The Dialectics of Seeing: Walter Benjamin and the Arcades Project* (Cambridge, Mass.: MIT Press, 1995).

10. Susan Buck-Morss, *The Origin of Negative Dialectics* (New York: Free Press, 1977), 168.

11. Roland Marchand, *Advertising the American Dream: Making Way for Modernity, 1920–1940* (Berkeley: University of California Press, 1985), 9.

12. Darin Barney, *Prometheus Wired: The Hope for Democracy in the Age of Network Technology* (Chicago: University of Chicago Press, 2000), 12.

13. William Leiss et al., eds., *Social Communication in Advertising* (Toronto: Metheun, 1990), 59.

14. Leiss et al., eds., *Social Communication in Advertising*, 62.

15. Antonio Gramsci, *An Antonio Gramsci Reader: Selected Writings, 1916–1935*, ed. David Forgacs (New York: Schocken, 1988), 291.

16. David Harvey, *The Condition of Postmodernity* (Cambridge: Blackwell, 1990), 126.

17. Barney, *Prometheus Wired*.

18. Kevin Robins and Frank Webster, *Times of the Technoculture: From the Information Society to the Virtual Life* (London: Routledge, 2000), 117.

19. Anthony Giddens, *A Contemporary Critique of Historical Materialism* (Berkeley: University of California Press, 1981), 117.

20. Karl Marx, *Capital: Volume 1. A Critical Analysis of Capitalist Production* (New York: International Publishers, 1992), 895.

21. Anthony Giddens, *A Contemporary Critique of Historical Materialism* (Berkeley: University of California Press, 1981). Giddens defines surveillance in two ways, both of which are implied by the use of the term in this book: first, "the accumulation of 'information'—symbolic materials that can be stored by an agency or collectivity. Second, the supervision of the activities of subordinates by their superiors within any collectivity" (169). The hierarchy implicit in the use of these terms highlights the asymmetry of surveillance: corporations get to know much more about workers and consumers than vice versa. Also implicit is the issue of control: who is able to extract profit from the exercise of surveillance. The business literature argues that consumers gain additional "satisfaction" from a customized product, in part based on the belief that they have, in some way, participated in the production process. This satisfaction, however, is an artifact of the way in which consumers have been systematically excluded from control over the production process—it is symbolic compensation for this exclusion, which, notwithstanding the propagandistic promise of mass customization, remains in place.

22. Giddens, *A Contemporary Critique of Historical Materialism*, 9.

23. Giddens, *A Contemporary Critique of Historical Materialism*, 11.

24. Giddens, *A Contemporary Critique of Historical Materialism*, 54. Giddens argues that the apparent relative prosperity of workers in industrialized societies is coupled with an increase in the sheer amount of time and effort extracted by workplace discipline. The

amount of time devoted to work in such societies is, he writes, often greater than that required for survival in agrarian or hunter-gatherer communities (22).

25. Giddens, *A Contemporary Critique of Historical Materialism*, 10.

26. Harry Braverman, *Labor and Monopoly Capital* (New York: Monthly Review Press, 1974).

27. David F. Noble, *Force of Production: A Social History of Industrial Automation* (New York: Knopf, 1984).

28. Harry Braverman, *Labor and Monopoly Capital* (New York: Monthly Review Press, 1974), 119.

29. Braverman, *Labor and Monopoly Capital*.

30. Braverman, *Labor and Monopoly Capital*, 115.

31. Deleuze, Gilles, "Postscript on the Societies of Control," from *OCTOBER* 59 (Winter 1992): 3–7; Mark Poster, *The Mode of Information* (Chicago: University of Chicago Press, 1990); Phil Agre, "Wish List," *The Network Observer* (May 1996), at dlis.gseis.ucla.edu/people/pagre/tno/may-1996.html (accessed 20 January 2003).

32. Kevin Robins and Frank Webster, *Times of the Technoculture: From the Information Society to the Virtual Life* (London: Routledge, 2000).

33. Braverman, *Labor and Monopoly Capital*.

34. Steve Pruitt and Tom Barrett, "Corporate Virtual Workspace," in *Cyberspace: First Steps*, ed. Michael Benedikt (Cambridge, Mass.: MIT Press, 1991), 401.

35. Pruitt and Barrett, "Corporate Virtual Workspace," 402.

36. Michael Lewis, "Boom Box," *New York Times Magazine*, 13 August 2000, 54–107; Pruitt and Barrett, "Corporate Virtual Workspace," 403.

37. Keith Naughton, "CyberSlacking," *Newsweek*, 29 November 1999, 62.

38. Tiziana Terranova, "Free Labor: Producing Culture for the Digital Economy," *Social Text* 63, no. 18 (2000): 2, 42.

39. James Boyle, "Foucault in Cyberspace: Surveillance, Sovereignty and Hard-Wired Censors," 1997, at www.wcl.american.edu/pub/faculty/boyle/foucault/htm#iv (accessed 10 February 2003).

40. Toby Lester, "The Reinvention of Privacy," *Atlantic Monthly* (27–29 March 2001), 28.

41. Lewis, "Boom Box," *New York Times Magazine*, 36.

42. Nicholas Negroponte, *Being Digital* (New York: Knopf, 1995).

43. Negroponte, *Being Digital*; Bill Gates, *The Road Ahead* (New York: Penguin, 1996).

44. Leiss et al., eds., *Social Communication in Advertising*, 59.

45. Gerald Baldasty, "The Rise of News as a Commodity: Business Imperatives and the Press in the Nineteenth Century," in *Ruthless Criticism*, ed. William S. Solomon and Robert McChesney (Minneapolis: University of Minnesota Press, 1993), 98–121.

46. Baldasty, "The Rise of News as a Commodity," 102.

47. Baldasty, "The Rise of News as a Commodity," 107.

48. James Carey, "The Press, Public Opinion, and Public Discourse," in *Public Opinion and the Communication of Consent*, ed. Theodor L. Glasser and C. T. Salmon (New York: Guilford, 1995), 179–80.

49. Jürgen Habermas, *The Structural Transformation of the Public Sphere* (Cambridge, Mass.: MIT Press, 1991), 42. As this description might suggest, John Durham Peters goes on to locate a certain logocentrism in Habermas's "distrust of representation." He argues

that Habermas fails to come to terms with the inherently mediated nature of face-to-face interaction, a failure that does much to explain the latter's mistrust of mediated representation. Peters suggests that coming to terms with the mediated nature of all communication might provide the basis for resuscitating the potential of the mass media in promoting democratic discourse (John D. Peters, "Distrust of Representation: Habermas on the Public Sphere," *Media, Culture and Society* 15 [1993]: 541–71). Interestingly, it is this Habermasian distrust of representation and mediation that characterizes the paradoxical utopian promise of the Internet: that the development of new media can help eliminate mediation altogether. Thus, the goal of the Internet—as espoused by such efforts as MIT's "Oxygen" project—is to make the interface perfectly transparent. This goal of transparency, as will be discussed in later chapters, corresponds to the false reconciliation described by Adorno, wherein the constitutive divisions of modernity are declared to be overcome via technology.

50. Jürgen Habermas, "The Public Sphere: An Encyclopedia Article," in *New German Critique* 1, no. 3 (1974): 49–55; Braverman, *Labor and Monopoly Capital*.

51. Habermas, *The Structural Transformation of the Public Sphere*, 221.

52. Edward Bernays, "The Engineering of Consent," in *The Annals of the American Academy of Political and Social Science* (March 1947): 114–15.

53. James Carey, "The Press, Public Opinion, and Public Discourse," in *Public Opinion and the Communication of Consent*, ed. Theodor L. Glasser and C. T. Salmon (New York: Guilford, 1995), 179–80.

54. Jon Bekken, "The Working-Class Press at the Turn of the Century," in *Ruthless Criticism*, ed. William S. Solomon and Robert McChesney (Minneapolis: University of Minnesota Press, 1993), 151–75; Linda Steiner, "Nineteenth-Century Suffrage Periodicals: Conceptions of Womanhood and the Press," in *Ruthless Criticism*, 66–97.

55. Solomon and McChesney, eds., *Ruthless Criticism*, 93; Bekken, "The Working-Class Press at the Turn of the Century," 168.

56. Bill Gates, *The Road Ahead* (New York: Penguin, 1996).

57. Gates, *The Road Ahead*, 101.

58. Alvin Toffler and Heidi Toffler, *Creating a New Civilization: The Politics of the Third Wave* (Atlanta: Tower, 1995).

59. Peter H. Lewis "Making Television Searchable," *New York Times*, 22 April 1999, G1.

60. Lewis, "Boom Box," 36.

61. Bill Gates, *The Road Ahead*, 188.

62. Mike Sager, "What I've Learned: Mark Burnett," *Esquire* 136 (July 2001), at www.esquire.com/features/learned/010701_mwi_burnett.html (accessed 14 December 2002).

63. Joseph B. Pine, *Mass Customization: The New Frontier in Business Competition* (Cambridge, Mass.: Harvard University Press, 1993).

64. Louis Irwin, "Interactive Dateline Is #1," *Studio Briefing*, at studio@usa.net, 14 July 1999.

65. "Death in the O.R.," *Dateline*, 13 July 1999, NBC Television, transcript at www.lexis.com (accessed 28 August 1999).

66. Theodor Adorno, "Cultural Criticism and Society," in *The Adorno Reader*, ed. B. O'Connor (Oxford: Blackwell, 2000), 205.

67. An article on the popularity of web-enabled amateur porn notes that the genre has become so successful that it has spawned an ersatz version of "shamateurs"—professionals who portray themselves as amateurs (Nick Galvin, "The Porn Star Next Door," *Sydney Morning Herald*, 10 January 2003, 27).

68. Alan O'Connor and John Downing, "Culture and Communication," in *Questioning the Media: A Critical Introduction*, ed. John Downing, Ali Mohammadi, and Annabelle Sreberny-Mohammadi (London: Sage, 1995).

69. As quoted in John Storey, *An Introduction to Cultural Theory and Popular Culture* (Athens: University of Georgia Press, 1993), 6.

70. Richard A. Lanham, *The Electronic Word: Democracy, Technology, and the Arts* (Chicago: University of Chicago Press, 1993), 38.

71. Lanham, *The Electronic Word*, 51.

72. Douglas S. Robertson, *The New Renaissance: Computers and the Next Level of Civilization* (Oxford: Oxford University Press, 1998), 156.

73. Negroponte, *Being Digital*, 221.

74. Negroponte, *Being Digital*, 221.

75. Lanham, *The Electronic Word*.

76. As quoted in Margot Lovejoy, *Postmodern Currents: Art and Artists in the Age of Electronic Media* (Upper Saddle River, N.J.: Prentice Hall, 1989), 55.

77. As quoted in Lovejoy, *Postmodern Currents*, 58.

78. David Harvey, *The Condition of Postmodernity* (Cambridge: Blackwell, 1990), 22.

79. Janet H. Murray, *Hamlet on the Holodeck: The Future of Narrative in Cyberspace* (New York: Free Press, 1997), 153.

80. Murray, *Hamlet on the Holodeck*, 152–53.

81. See, for example, the discussion of reception theory in David Morley, *Television, Audiences and Cultural Studies* (London: Routledge, 1992), and Graeme Turner, *British Cultural Studies: An Introduction* (Boston: Unwin Hyman, 1990).

82. In Paul Rabinow, ed., *The Foucault Reader* (New York: Pantheon, 1984), 119.

83. Turner, *British Cultural Studies*, 122.

84. Steven Holtzman, *Digital Mosaics: the Aesthetics of Cyberspace* (New York: Simon & Schuster, 1997), 43.

85. As quoted in Michael Heim, *The Metaphysics of Virtual Reality* (New York: Oxford University Press, 1993), 123. The program for a recent exhibition of digital art at the Whitney Museum in New York City opened with the claim that "while photography revolutionized the arts by superceding painting's claim to represent the 'real,' digital technology has become the ultimate tool for capturing the nuances of the 'unreal.'" A few lines later, however, the program noted, "Perhaps the effect most commonly associated with digital technology and the arts is 'virtual reality.' While its most extreme form—complete alternative realities replete with all five senses—remains the stuff of fantasy, digital media have made possible the creation of simulated environments of remarkable veracity" ("The Works," BitStreams [official website], at www.whitney.org/bitstreams/ [accessed 24 July 2001]). The ultimate fantasy of the new medium, then, is the return of the real.

86. Sigmund Freud, *Civilization and Its Discontents* (New York: Norton, 1961), 38–39.

87. Holtzman, *Digital Mosaics*, 41.

88. Simon Jarvis, *Adorno: A Critical Introduction* (New York: Routledge, 1998), 191.

89. Pine, *Mass Customization*.

90. C. Wright Mills, *The Power Elite* (New York: Oxford University Press, 1957).

91. Slavoj Zizek, *The Fragile Absolute, or, Why Is the Christian Legacy Worth Fighting For?* (London: Verso, 2000).

92. Barney, *Prometheus Wired*.

93. Federal Trade Commission, "FTC Wraps Up Record Year in Anti-trust Enforcement with New Mix of Litigation and Guidance," at www.ftc.gov/opa/2000/10/antitrustfy2000.htm (accessed 30 January 2001).The *New York Post* reported in 1999 that the nation's two top investment banks, Goldman Sachs and Morgan Stanley Dean Witter, were engaged in a race to see which would be the first to consult on a record-breaking $1 trillion worth of deals (mergers and acquisitions) in one year. The top deals included telecoms, such as Vodafone's bid for Mannesmann and the Qwest/USWest merger (Sandra Angulo, "Race for $1 Trillion," *New York Post*, 18 November 1999, Business, 1).

Chapter Three

Rediscovering Reality

The return of the real is a recurring motif not just in the conventional mass media, but also in the development of digital media.[1] On the one hand, we are deluged with proliferating reality formats, from those that rely on found video, like *When Animals Attack* and *Busted on the Job*, to slick productions like *Survivor*, and, recently, to gross-out shows like *Jackass* and *Fear Factor*. On the other hand, we are increasingly exposed to innovative uses of digital media that allow us to make our own "reality shows." Webcam pioneer Jennifer Ringley gained an international reputation when, as a college student in 1996, she turned an inexpensive digital camera on herself and started a website called "Jennicam." At its height, Jennicam, which featured occasional masturbatory displays (eventually phased out) in addition to the details of Jennifer's daily life, reportedly attracted some five million hits a day—ratings that approach those generated by cable television programs.[2] Ringley seemed to single-handedly demonstrate the "revolutionary" potential of the Internet. After all, she was but a young woman with paltry resources and no background in media production, and she managed to produce a popular show on a shoestring budget without the benefit of a production crew. Single-handedly, she seemed to herald the success of an alternative media model—one that had haunted the imagination of media critics for decades: an ordinary person seizing control of the means of media production. Furthermore, she attracted her millions of fans in two ways—first, by taking on the active role of producer rather than the passive one of viewer, and by similarly encouraging her audience to talk back via online chats; second, by providing them with a steady diet of "reality" in place of the predigested news and entertainment programming that are the staple formats of the mass media. Moreover, Ringley was able to support herself—at least for a time— on the revenues from subscription fees paid by fans to receive more frequently updated images from the cameras in Ringley's room.

Drawing on the power of reality to counter mass-produced, commodified programming, Ringley seemed to embody the promise that the Internet would place the means of media production in the hands of the people. With its emphasis on a form of alternative media production explicitly opposed to the "cheesy" conventions of commodified entertainment and the attempt to create an online community for Jennifer, her friends, and fans, her project seemed perhaps in some distant way to anticipate the utopian yearning of Douglas Kellner's claim that new media would enable "ordinary citizens and activists themselves to become political actors and communicators, to reproduce and disseminate information, and to participate in debates and struggles, thus helping to realize Gramsci's dictum that anyone could be a public intellectual."[3]

Ringley was hailed in the popular press not as a revolutionary but as an attention-getting curiosity (who laid the groundwork for DotComGuy's attempt to enlist the webcam as an advertising gimmick), and she became a darling of the mass media, which seemed singularly unthreatened by her one-woman appropriation of the means of media production. The mainstream media coverage garnered international attention for Ringley's project and helped inspire a spate of imitators. The *New York Times* estimated that some quarter million people around the world have taken to "exposing their lives part time" and noted that a million webcams were sold in 1999 alone.[4] The founder of Earthcam.Com, which features many of these sites, estimated there would be some thirty-six million webcams online by 2005, documenting everything from the intimate lives of individuals to landscapes and urban vistas.[5]

Ringley has since spawned numerous imitators, some of whom have gone commercial, sparking an Internet-based voyeurism industry that will be discussed in greater depth later in the chapter. In keeping with the promise of homemade media production pioneered by Jennicam, computer makers like Apple anticipate that digital video will be one of the "killer apps" of the next generation of computers, which are being equipped with editing programs to allow "everyone" not just to be the star of their own show but the director, producer, and production crew as well. Similarly, the new generation of cell phones includes models equipped with the ability to capture and send digital images and video. Taken to the limit, futurist Howard Rheingold imagines a future in which everyone is equipped with wearable, portable video devices that allow them to take over the role of recording and documenting the world from the official sources:

> What if people beamed WearComp video to the Web, offering continuous views of breaking events that hitherto have been available only from Newscorp, AOL-Time-Warner, and Disney? Would it be possible to turn the table on the surveillance society and counter the media monopolies? What would be the effect on public opinion if thousands of WearComp-equipped citizens webcast all they saw and heard?[6]

Access to the means of media production promises to empower the people.

The first step, seemingly, is to hand over airtime to the real people. In this respect, the parallel development of reality programming on TV and online occasionally converges, as in the case of the *Big Brother* series, which represented an early and, by some measures, successful attempt to merge television with the Internet. *Big Brother*, thanks to the online feed, was both a TV show and a webcam site, with four live camera feeds available at all hours online. Unlike Jennifer Ringley, these people *never* left the house, so there was always something to watch, even if it was only people sleeping. This convergence of TV and Internet is, by all accounts, the direction in which the industry is headed, and it surfaces in developments ranging from the AOL/Time Warner partnership to Bill Gates's recent introduction of so-called Ultimate Television, which combines VCR functionality with delivery of web-based content.[7] As if to prepare us for inevitable convergence, television is already working hard to incorporate the Internet into conventional programming, providing websites for popular formats. Moreover, anthropologists employed by telecommunication corporations are being enlisted to study the ways in which convergence can foster more active viewing practices — even to the point of promoting a more active viewing posture.[8] Perhaps the next step will be an attempt to redesign the physical space within which viewing takes place, including the construction of furniture that promotes interactivity (an "interactive" La-Z-Boy with a keyboard and mouse pad built into the padded arms, perhaps). Sheer inertia may render the couch-potato style of viewing resistant to change, but the prospect of an increasingly "active" form of viewing may not be as farfetched as it seems in an era in which electronic multitasking is becoming the norm. A generation that talks on the phone while driving, instant-messages while working, and surfs the Web in class may find it perfectly normal to shop online while watching TV. Indeed, the advent of the bottom of the screen "crawl" on cable news channels seems to cater to the multitasking habit by providing viewers with something to read *while* they watch TV. The very restiveness of younger generations in front of the TV — they can't *just* watch, it seems — bodes well for the coming era of interactive TV.

Interestingly, this hybrid attitude of viewing/participating characterized several of the people with whom I chatted online during visits to the *Big Brother* website. These were viewers who logged on to the Internet to chat about the television series while they either watched the show on television or online. As if those two activities weren't enough in themselves, some of the people with whom I spoke engaged in both while at work — alternating between job tasks, watching the live Internet feeds from the *Big Brother* house, and sending intermittent messages to one of the online chat rooms devoted to the program. Because the video and audio portions of the show were available over the Internet, all three activities could take place on the same computer monitor. Consequently, the online video feeds came to serve, in some cases, as the visual equivalent of background music, providing kinetic "wallpaper" for the desktops of people keeping track of the action in the *Big Brother* house while they were working. The broadcast version of the show attempted to capitalize on this activity by incorporating the participation of viewers into the weekly hour-long recap show — a fact that encouraged fans to post their own contributions to the website with the hope that their messages might be read on the air. The computer thus served a dual role for viewers: it allowed them to monitor the *Big Brother* house, but it also allowed AOL to monitor online interest in the show by recording visits to the webpage and incorporating comments posted online into the broadcast version. Thus, the *Big Brother* format offers multiple opportunities to explore the integrated elements of spatial enclosure, interactivity, and the work of being watched.

The following chapters bring these strands of the argument to bear on a consideration of several different reality formats. The focus will be on genres that rely on comprehensive surveillance of the daily lives and unscripted interactions of people who agree to participate in making their private lives public. Shows like *The Real World* and *Temptation Island* fit into these categories, as do more recent game-show formats like *The Bachelor* and *Joe Millionaire*, which film not just the dramatic moments in the courtship process but the daily lives of those who agree to live on location during the course of the filming—their "behind-the-scenes" discussions while cooking, hanging out, and preparing themselves for their dates. Such shows are of central interest because they rely on willing submission to comprehensive forms of commercial (as opposed to state) surveillance. The need to narrow the focus to a particular subset is also a result of the fact that, despite the fact that we all seem to have a notion of what we mean when we use the term *reality TV*, there isn't any one definition that would both capture all the existing genres and exclude other forms of programming such as the nightly news or daytime game shows. One of the definitional problems is created by the fact that much of the academic literature on reality TV has been devoted to a consideration of law enforcement genres like *Cops* and *America's Most Wanted*, which has led to the assertion that reality programming is based on "civic action" (such as solving crimes) or on the presentation of "dangerous events, unusual situations, or actual police cases."[9] Such definitions are clearly inadequate to the proliferating genres that have nothing to do with crime, police action, or dramatic events. Indeed, even seemingly ready-made associations about reality TV—that it is based, for example, on the lives of "real" people, as opposed to professional actors—are routinely violated (as evidenced by the appearance of well-known actors on celebrity reality shows). The general term *unscripted entertainment* embraces reality TV but also professional sports, political debates (more or less, on both counts), dog shows, and so on. In short, our reasons for thinking about the reality TV phenomenon will necessarily shape what we mean by reality TV, and rather than attempting to make all of the various formats fit one general definition, I will focus on the subset of unscripted entertainment reliant on willing submission to comprehensive monitoring of the rhythm and events of daily life.

My goal is not so much to provide an exhaustive analysis of the reality TV genre in general—a futile undertaking—as to use elements of the reality trend as a means of thinking about the deployment of the promise of mediated interactivity in the emerging information economy. Guiding this approach is Theodor

Adorno's assessment of the promise of the "real": "the mind is indeed not capable of producing or grasping the totality of the real, but it may be possible to penetrate the detail, to explode in miniature the mass of merely existing reality."[10] The details I have in mind are examples of reality programming, recognized not just as superficial cultural phenomena, but as invoking and feeding on deeper social tensions and developments. To set the stage, the following section includes a brief introduction to the genre of reality television and to the shows that will be discussed in subsequent chapters.

REALITY AS A GENRE: THE STORY OF *AN AMERICAN FAMILY*

> Hey, you're always saying, "Bring me real life. Bring me street life." And, like, "One man's mundane and desperate existence is another man's Technicolor."
>
> —Tick, in the original treatment of James Cameron's *Strange Days*

Reality-based entertainment is as old as human society itself and runs the gamut from "people watching" to the Roman circus. Considered within the narrower context of the mass media, reality-based films that record the rhythms of daily life were, as documentary filmmakers Ilisa Barbash and Lucien Taylor argue, one of the first manifestations of the moving picture medium. The inventors of film-based motion pictures, Louis and Auguste Lumière, "churned out film after film about apparently inconsequential moments of daily life: workers leaving their factories; a train arriving at the station . . . and lumberjacks going about their work."[11] This early slice-of-life cinema anticipated the mundane character of shows like *Big Brother* and *The Real World*, which often focus on the details of daily life: cast members sweeping the yard, washing the dishes, and sitting around the table with nothing much to say. Similarly, although a webcam site like Jennicam has its occasional moments of drama and titillation, the vast majority of the content is devoted to the routine details of daily existence. The most common image on Jennicam is either Ringley's empty chair in front of the computer or her bespectacled face, blue in the glow of the computer screen, staring slightly off camera as she works on the computer.

With the development of documentary film, recording the rhythm of daily life became not just a historical genre, but, as Barbash and Taylor note, an anthropological one—a way of presenting the lives of other people, often in far off lands. In this sense, the medium served as a means of overcoming spatial and temporal boundaries, re-creating either historically or geographically distant lives. The advent of the reality genre takes place when documentary techniques are used not to document the daily life of geographically and culturally remote peoples but to study the lives of proximal, contemporary figures as representatives of typical—hence real—people. The fictional sitcom and family drama anticipated this genre by relying upon scenarios based on the daily, domestic routines of fictional families like the Cleavers and the Ricardos. It provided a glimpse behind the facade of suburbia into the domestic lives of American families. Insofar as such shows focused on private rather than public life, they helped draw back the curtains on the internal dynamics of family life and provided a "behind-the-scenes" look at gender and family relationships, albeit fictional and often idealized.

The turn to real families took place in 1973 with the release of the PBS series *An American Family*, which documented the daily life of the Loud family and famously chronicled the parents' divorce and the eldest son's decision to come out of the closet.[12] Promotions for the original series, which compressed seven months worth of filming (three hundred hours of raw footage) into twelve weekly one-hour installments, presciently billed the Louds as "TV's First Real Family."[13] The show triggered many of the responses that have characterized the media coverage of the current spate of "reality" shows: laments over the decline of the private sphere and the role played by television in promoting an inordinate fascination with celebrity, as well as musings on the educational—indeed anthropological—character of the show (with frequent quotes from Margaret Mead, who described the advent of this form of reality TV as very possibly "as important for our time as were the invention of drama and the novel for earlier generations").[14] The show also triggered a debate that has long characterized the practice and reception of documentary film: How does the artifice of filmmaking impact the "reality" of what it seeks to portray? The response of *An American Family*'s producer Craig Gilbert anticipated those of later reality producers: "If reactions were modified because of the camera, those reactions were still valid."[15] In other words, the conditions might have been artificial, but the responses were real. What might be meant by this definition of "validity" will become a central concern of the upcoming consideration of the audience response to the artifice of reality TV.

It is perhaps not insignificant that *An American Family*, as the first manifestation of a "reality" TV format that provided comprehensive documentation of the rhythm of proximal daily life, occurred during the period characterized by both theorists and business consultants as the transition to post-Fordist, or flexible capitalism.[16] Reality TV emerged during a period in which the destabilization of mass society was accompanied by a reformulation of the boundaries that helped maintain its social and cultural hierarchy. If indications of the breakdown of the postwar Fordist model of industrial production became evident in the early 1970s, the era of flexible capitalism that emerged in its wake coincided with challenges to the cultural order of 1950s-era America. Media theorist Josh Meyrowitz, for example, interprets the "question-authority" mentality of the 1960s generation as a result, at least in part, of the role that television played in eroding the boundaries that enclosed the private lives of the powerful and famous—bringing them down to the level of "real" people: "Most people who step forward into the television limelight and attempt to gain national visibility become too visible, too exposed, and are thereby demystified. The more we see them, the more ordinary they appear."[17] The hit reality show *The Osbournes*, based on the daily life of heavy metal rocker Ozzy Osbourne and his endearingly eccentric family, provides a contemporary example of the demystification facilitated by the intimacy of the medium. Once feared and reviled as another "satanic" element in popular music—the Marilyn Manson of his day—Ozzy Osbourne has become the bumbling, harmless hero of a family show, the addled Ward Cleaver of the dawn of the millennium. Meyrowitz claims that a similar demystifying intimacy helped undermine the cultural authority (if not the economic and political power) of elite groups and individuals: "We have the perspective of stagehands who are aware of the constructed nature of the drama. . . . Rather than being fooled, we are willingly entertained, charmed, courted, seduced. Ironically, all the recent discussions of how we are being manipulated may only point out how relatively visible and exposed the machinations now are."[18]

As Andy Warhol's famous observation about fame suggests, the erosion of the boundaries that separate celebrities from the mass doesn't just allow for the details of celebrities' private lives to flood the airwaves, but creates the potential for an inversion of the celebrity equation: willingness to expose one's private life could, as the Louds discovered, lead to celebrity. If the limelight that revealed the most personal and intimate details of celebrities' lives demystified them, if it brought them "down" to the level of ordinary people, the corollary was that ordinary people could, through mass mediated self-disclosure, attain a degree of celebrity. Interestingly this ostensible democratization coincided with and may have played some role in enabling increasing economic disparity. The breakdown of the postwar settlement associated with the decline of Fordism was accompanied by increasing economic stratification. As economist Paul Krugman noted in a *New York Times* article about the return of the "Gilded Age":

> [The United States] became a middle-class society only after the concentration of income at the top dropped sharply during the New Deal, and especially during World War II. . . . Income then stayed fairly equally distributed until the 1970s. . . . Since the 1970s, however, income gaps have been rapidly widening. . . . After 30 years in which the income shares of the top 10 percent of taxpayers, the top 1 percent and so on were far below their levels in the 1920's, all are very nearly back where they were.[19]

We are faced, then, with an interesting conjunction: the historical moment marked by the role of television in the ostensibly democratic demystification of authority (the era of Watergate and Warhol) and the advent of the first reality show based on the daily lives of real people, corresponds to the *return* of an era of increasing economic inequality. This moment brings together several strands of the argument: Mass customization emerges as an effective marketing strategy in an era of increasing economic stratification even as it promises increased democratization.[20] The deployment of the offer of shared control becomes more ideologically important at a time when real control over economic resources is becoming increasingly concentrated. At the same time, increasing stratification requires more comprehensive forms of marketplace monitoring in order to rationalize the production and marketing processes for an ever wider range of goods for a more segmented market. The offer of participation both compensates (symbolically) for growing inequality and serves as an inducement to submit to the forms of interactive monitoring relied on by producers to reduce uncertainty in an increasingly diversified market.

Highlighting this conjunction is the turn-of-the-millenium resurgence in the "democratic" genre of reality TV alongside public awareness of the return of the robber-baron capitalist/industrialist. Krugman notes, for example, that the average CEO compensation jumped from thirty-nine times the pay of an average worker in the earlier 1970s to more than a thousand times the pay of an average worker thirty years later.[21] *The Economist* called the explosion in CEO compensation during the same time period "the largest peacetime transfer of wealth in history."[22] The promise of the dot-com boom and the long bull market of the 1990s seemed to incarnate the American Dream: anyone could cash in, but, as the fallout of the dot-com crash indicated, only a select few reaped the benefits.[23] Against this background, it is not hard to discern the appeal of reality TV insofar as it keeps alive the promise that "anyone" can make it in an era when the concentration of wealth and ownership in the hands of an increasingly rarefied group of elites is becoming increasingly obvious.

In a similar vein, the same time period that marked the decline of Fordism and the start of a three-decade trend of increasing economic inequality coincided with the return of the lottery and its resurgent popularity. Like reality TV, the lottery represents a fast-food version of the American dream and thereby serves as compensation for the centralization and concentration of wealth and power. After being banned in the late nineteenth century, and then reinstated in one state (New Hampshire) in 1964, the popularity of lotteries boomed in the 1970s and continued to grow in the 1990s, along with the size of the payoffs and the lengths of the odds against winning.[24] Annual lottery sales increased from about $1 billion in the late 1970s to some $35 billion in the late 1990s, based in no small part on the games' appeal to those living in the least wealthy neighborhoods.[25] Reality TV is, in many of its incarnations, a lottery of celebrity; it invites viewers to submit tapes and apply to be on the shows with the promise that they might find themselves transformed instantaneously into TV stars. Reality TV deploys the promise of greater equality based not just on the offer that anyone might become famous but on the symbolic portrayal of celebrities who are "just like us"—if you overlook their fantastic wealth.

This presumed leveling effect was borne out by the case of the early reality show *An American Family*. In a mutual cycle of adulation, Andy Warhol was a public fan of the show, and the Louds' eldest son was, in turn, a fan of Warhol, to whom he had written as a teenager.[26] In 1973, however—when talk shows still depended on celebrities and before reality TV had become a phenomenon in itself—the idea that inviting cameras into the home could transform "real" people into celebrities was still a relative novelty. As Lance Loud put it in an interview during an anniversary screening of the series,

> I remember one of the reasons my family went along with it was that we didn't even *get* PBS in Santa Barbara. We thought it was going to be right up there with a trout fishing TV series. No one imagined it was going to be anything major. . . . And literally overnight, we went from being, like, normal nerds to much-criticized and nationally vilified nerds.[27]

Documentary was one of the staple formats of PBS in its early years, and the turn to an exploration of the private life of a contemporary family was—like the current crop of reality formats—facilitated by the development of increasingly compact and versatile filmmaking equipment. Barbash and Taylor argue that, with the development of portable, synchronized sound-recording equipment in the 1960s, new possibilities for less intrusive forms of documentary production emerged: "Because the new equipment was so portable, new arenas of human experience were opened up to scrutiny—in particular, people's private and domestic lives."[28] The available technology, then, combined with the culture of television celebrity as well as the experimental approach of PBS filmmakers to produce the first reality TV series. Additionally, the show's producer, Craig Gilbert, brought his background in anthropological film (as the producer of *Margaret Mead's New Guinea Journal*) to the project, which he described as a means of finding out "how the enormous technological, social, and cultural changes of the past half-century have affected the daily life of an American family."[29] The program was thus presented as a social experiment that might provide useful information about life in the United States. This reflexive anthropological approach—turning the camera around so as to study representative members of contemporary society in their natural habitat—remains a pervasive motif in the way producers, fans, and cast members describe reality shows like MTV's *The Real World* and CBS's *Big Brother*. Jennifer Ringley of Jennicam fame compared her webcam site to the Nature channel, describing the occasional images of her sex life that go out over the Web as being no different from the nature shows that document the mating habits of animals around the world.[30]

Turning away from content to a consideration of form, perhaps the hallmark of the reality format is its incorporation of a variety of genres: fiction, soap opera, and documentary. Indeed, future permutations of the genre recycle fictional fare by transposing it into the realm of the real, as in the case of the proposed remakes of successful 1960s shows like *Green Acres* and *The Beverly Hillbillies*. Such infusions of the real promise to rejuvenate exhausted formats by overcoming the abstracted relations of the industrial production of culture.

The ostensible challenge to the rigid hierarchies of mass production promised by the "return of the real" aligns itself with the formal challenge to the authenticity of the visual image itself. In the digital era, not only is it easier to capture and record reality; it is also easier to manipulate the images that are captured.

Thus, Arild Fetveit has suggested that the push for the real is a compensatory reaction to the increasing loss of faith in the evidentiary (or indexical) character of
photography: "[T]he proliferation of reality TV could be understood as an euphoric effort to reclaim what seems to be lost after digitization. And what seems
lost is not only a belief in the evidential powers of photography, but as much a
sense of being in contact with the world by way of indexicality."[31] Fetveit's formulation captures the ambiguity of the promise of digital flexibility, for the promise to reinstate indexicality—to capture evidence of the real—is facilitated by developments in the very digital technology that undermines trust in representation.
The emergence of total surveillance as a means of capturing reality and the vir-
tualization of reality go hand in hand. In the case of a show like *Big Brother*, the
technology works in the direction of restoring access to the real, thanks to the
round-the-clock surveillance enabled by the video feeds.

The opposition that Fetveit delineates between the indexical, evidentiary quality of photography, on the one hand, and its "symbolic, illustrative" quality, on
the other, recapitulates the terms of the critique of abstraction: that the artifice of
filmmaking ostensibly deprives its images of substance and credibility. This critique needs to be located within the context of the social relations associated with
the culture industry. Mistrust of artifice—of what Fetveit describes as the symbolic character of photography—associates it with the formulaic mass production
of cultural products for passive consumption. This wariness toward the symbolic,
which will be explored in greater detail in chapter 8, can be traced back to the political exchanges that characterized the early days of cinema, according to Fetveit,
who cites Soviet theorist Viktor Schklovsky. In 1926 Schklovsky claimed that pioneering filmmaker Dziga Vertov's work was compromised by its contrived character: "The man who departs on broad skis into the snow-covered distance is no
longer a man but a symbol of the departing past. The object has lost its substance
and become transparent."[32] The thinning of experience—the loss of substance—
connotes the loss associated with modernity and eventually comes to stand for the
loss associated with homogenized, mass-produced culture. In formal terms, then,
the revitalization of the visual medium promised by reality TV requires the rehabilitation of indexicality and, with it, the dense substantiality of the real. This is
the promise of shows that offer to revitalize fictional formats by injecting them
with elements of the real.

The bridging of the formats of fiction and reality can be traced to *An American
Family*. From a formal point of view, Ruoff argues that the series was a hybrid
documentary film—a transitional form that incorporated elements of anthropological documentary and popular television.[33] In a sense very similar to that of a
reality show like *Big Brother*, the PBS series might be considered an experimental transitional form that blended elements from an older medium with those of
the new. Ruoff argues that the show's hybrid approach works to break down the
"fixed distinctions between reality and spectacle, public and private, narrative
and nonfiction, film and television."[34] This dismantling of binary oppositions par-

allels that described by Harvey in his assessment of the cultural transformation from modernity to postmodernity, which he associates with the emergence of post-Fordist capitalism.[35] The effect is achieved in technical terms by the blurring of formal techniques of observational documentary (which lacks the direct address of expository films) into the episodic and repetitive structure of a soap opera. Indeed, *An American Family* was repeatedly described, in ways that anticipate the explicit goal of shows ranging from *Big Brother* to *Temptation Island*, as a "real-life" soap opera, or, as *Time* magazine put, it the "Ultimate Soap Opera."[36] In keeping with the theme of dedifferentiation, reality TV erodes the boundaries between a variety of standard formats as well as the formal conventions that helped distinguish between them.

THE RETURN OF REALITY TV

An American Family did not immediately inspire a spate of imitations, despite the fact that it helped boost PBS ratings.[37] The reality TV trend was yet to develop into a full-fledged media phenomenon. Other reality formats, including shows like *Cops* and *America's Funniest Home Videos* emerged in the late 1980s and early 1990s as the multiplication of channels on cable TV led producers to look for less expensive forms of programming. However, the documentary format based on the comprehensive monitoring of the rhythm of its subjects' daily lives lay largely dormant until it was revitalized in 1990 by documentary filmmaker Jon Murray and his production partner Mary-Ellis Bunim. According to Murray, *An American Family* served as a direct inspiration for MTV's *The Real World* and its later spin-offs, including *Road Rules*.[38] His stated goal was to remake *An American Family* for the MTV generation.

Both of the programs that resulted preserve the observational format of *An American Family*. This format, as Barbash and Taylor suggest, is well suited to the promise of replicating reality "as it happened." Rather than adopting an "expository" or "reflexive" approach, shows like *Road Rules* and *The Real World* eschew third-person voice-overs and avoid showing any trace of the filmmakers. Drawing on Barbash and Taylor's terminology, the MTV shows might be considered a hybrid format that combines observational techniques with the *cinema verité* strategy of deploying the camera "as a deliberate provocation."[39] The observational segments are intercut with scenes shot in a confessional room where cast members speak directly to the camera and share their thoughts and reactions to the day's events. The half-hour segments are tightly edited and the narrative flow is bolstered with occasional captions describing the location or the event being filmed and with superimposed background music. However, by far the largest portion of the half-hour segment is built from scenes and dialogue shot and edited in observational fashion. In this sense, the format promotes what Barbash and Taylor describe as an "interactive" viewing experience, since documentaries shot in the observational style, "let the spectators put the pieces together for themselves: they proceed by implication rather than demonstration, and so demand a more active viewing experience."[40] This formulation neatly summarizes the interactive potential of reality TV, which might be one reason why the promise of reality TV is turning out to play so well in an era whose buzzword is "interactivity."

The attempt to update the format of *An American Family* for the MTV generation garnered a moderate degree of success, with ratings for *The Real World* continuing to grow over the course of the last decade. However, the real commercial breakthrough for the format was a result of its cross-pollination with another successful (partially) unscripted format—that of the game show. The marriage was perhaps a natural one, considering the phenomenal success of *Who Wants to Be a Millionaire* first in the United Kingdom and then in the United States (and many other countries). Indeed, this phenomenally successful quiz-show format draws on a central tenet of the reality format: that the game is open to ordinary people, not just prodigies. The mass appeal is perhaps expressed by the fact that *Who Wants to Be a Millionaire* was so popular it actually transformed the typical pattern of telephone traffic in the United States. By early 2000, the telephone company noted that the standard lull in telephone activity in the evening (postwork) hours was interrupted by a jagged peak at 10 P.M. (Eastern time), representing the thousands of phone calls made to the *Who Wants to Be a Millionaire* hotline at the end of the show.[41] The show had tapped into the appeal of the real: fans hoped that they could be more than just passive viewers, that they might have a chance to participate in the show. Unlike more highbrow formats, *Who Wants to Be a Millionaire* plays up this appeal, starting off the show with simple questions that can be answered by the average ten-year-old. The contestants are portrayed not as knowledgeable nerds possessed of exceptional intellectual capacity, but as "real" people, and they are thus encouraged to relate details of their home and work lives and to reveal their thought processes to the audience, thinking out loud as the host patiently awaits an answer.

Given the success of this type of game show, which weaves in the personal aspects of the contestants with the appeal of a lottery-sized jackpot, it is perhaps not surprising that the next step was its cross-breeding with a reality format. Indeed, one of Europe's most successful reality shows, *Big Brother* was the brainchild of a production company known primarily for its game-show lineup. The format's Dutch originator, John de Mol, said that the inspiration for the show was neither *An American Family* nor *The Real World* but rather Biosphere 2, which had been in the news when the producers were trying to come up with a new game show.[42] *Big Brother* was the result of a two-hour brainstorming session and was pitched by Endemol (which also served as supervising producer for *Who Wants to Be a Millionaire* for much of Europe) as "part social experiment, part real-life soap, and part competition."[43] The combination was a smash hit in the Netherlands, drawing more than 53 percent of the nation's viewing audience for its finale, and has since gone on to ratings success in Germany, Great Britain, and Italy.[44] The combination of the documentary approach with the cash reward of a show like *Who Wants to Be a Millionaire* promised to be such an effective draw that CBS reportedly paid more than $20 million for the rights to the format and premiered the show during the summer of 2000.[45]

The new format also drew on the energy of what Neal Gabler has described as the increasing tendency to package news events as entertainment spectacles.[46] The famous image of O.J.'s white Ford Bronco leading the California police on a low-speed chase must be counted among those cultural events, along with *An American Family* and *Who Wants to Be a Millionaire*, that shaped the emergence of the current reality TV boom. After the long run of blockbuster news spectacles that characterized the 1990s, from the Persian Gulf War and the O.J. trial, to the JonBenet Ramsey murder investigation, the Oklahoma City bombing, and the Clinton intern scandal, it is perhaps not surprising that viewers have grown accustomed to a taste of the real in their prime-time diet. Moreover, there can be little doubt that, as Gabler suggests, we are invited to experience reality as split subjects who recognize both the authenticity of its visceral impact and the way in which this authenticity can be enlisted as a form of entertainment. The Bill Clinton/Monica Lewinsky scandal is instructive in this regard insofar as it highlighted the split that characterized the reception of news *as* entertainment. In retrospect, it is clear that viewers (unlike many politicians and pundits) recognized the scandal primarily as a form of entertainment: they wanted to watch, but as titillation rather than a political event. The seemingly paradoxical result was high ratings for both the scandalous news coverage and for the president. In other words, rather than taking the scandal seriously as a political fiasco and indignantly supporting Clinton's impeachment, viewers enjoyed the entertainment value of the spectacle while recognizing its absurdity as a political event. Indeed, the political fallout worked to Clinton's advantage and resulted in the downfall of Newt Gingrich and a net loss for Republicans in the midterm elections (not to mention the surprising spectacle of notorious pornographer Larry Flynt helping dethrone Gingrinch's successor).

The phenomenal success of reality as a form of entertainment has led to the familiar cycle whereby news outlets come to rely on the next blow-out story—the next Lewinsky affair or Ramsey murder. Increasingly, rather than relying on their news departments to sniff out the next big story in the lineup, networks have turned to the entertainment sector to manufacture a steady diet of reality as spectacle. The migration of reality toward entertainment is complemented by its converse. On the one hand, we see the increasing commodification of reality as entertainment, as when producers tally the ratings for the Gulf War or for Monica Lewinsky's televised testimony. Prior to the 2003 Iraq war, cable news stations reportedly calculated the potential ratings impact: "CNN is hoping to reclaim its past glory by becoming the leading source of information about the war on TV, and, its executives hope, the highest-rated one on cable."[47] On the other hand, we see the increasing packaging of entertainment as reality: the *Survivor* contestants interviewed on morning news shows and featured on the covers of weekly news-magazines like *Time* and *Newsweek*. As if to highlight the eroding boundary be-tween news and entertainment, the producers of the first U.S. season of *Big Brother* turned to network news announcer Julie Chen, who reprised her role in subsequent seasons.

REALITY ONLINE

The consolidation of reality as a form of entertainment—and the complementary development of entertainment based on reality—coincides with the emergence of webcam sites discussed earlier in the chapter. Rather than emphasizing the sen-sationalized aspect of reality, webcams, from their inception, focused on the mun-dane character of daily life—an element that had been neglected by the increas-ing sensationalization of both news and entertainment. In this respect, personal webcams anticipate the role of surveillance in the online economy. As opposed to police surveillance, commercial surveillance is not predicated on catching the ex-ceptional moments or even the "subversive" scenes of our lives but rather the mundane moments that characterize the routine rhythms of consumption. As if to highlight this point, the website generally acknowledged as the first public online webcam featured a close-up of the coffee machine in a computer lab called "The Trojan Room" at Cambridge University. As the site's cocreator, Quentin Stafford-Fraser, tells it, the coffeepot was shared by several researchers, some of whom had to travel several flights of stairs to make their way to the coffeepot—a trip that "often proved fruitless if the all-night hackers of the Trojan Room had got there first."[48] So the programmers decided to create a system that would allow anyone with access to their local network to see for themselves whether there was enough coffee to make it worth the trip. In 1993, the coffee cam migrated to the Internet and went public as the first live, twenty-four-hour webcam show. "Since then, hundreds of thousands of people have looked at the coffeepot, making it un-doubtedly the most famous in the world." *Wired* magazine reported in 2001 that the coffeecam site received more than 2.4 million visitors since it first went public.[49]

Since the "coffeecam" first went online, the development of cheap, easy to use digital cameras has triggered the proliferation of webcam sites that rival the mun-dane quality of their predecessor: Webcams that allow visitors to watch the corn grow in an Iowa cornfield, monitor the exploits of a hamster in his cage, and fol-low the lifecycle of an ant colony. A webcam on Loch Ness even allows visitors to keep an electronic eye out for the mythical monster "Nessie." In the era of comprehensive surveillance, even the mythical is rendered transparent. These web-cam sites represent the flip side of sensationalistic reality entertainment: a sheer fascination with the ability to peer into the mundane existence of strangers (from the privacy of one's home or office). It is the very banality of what is being watched that underwrites its reality: the coffee machine is not a contrivance to entice viewers and sell advertising. In all of its triviality, sitting there, slowly filling up, it is palpably, drearily "real." Certainly there is a voyeuristic element—one that has been exploited by commercial pornography sites that ostensibly allow subscribers access to hidden cameras placed in changing rooms, bathrooms, and bedrooms. But even in the case of the hamster cage or the camera in someone's house trained on the attic floorboards to capture the mouse that may or may not live there, the cameras appeal to a drive for transparency: the desire to see, thanks to technology, what would otherwise remain hidden from view. The goal of transparency aligns itself with the challenge to the abstracted relations of mass society that leave so much hidden from sight, including the sites of media, political, and industrial production.

It is thus not surprising that webcams seemed to allow reality programming entrepreneurs to make an end-run around the mainstream media. During the peak of the dot-com boom, even the lowly webcam seemed to offer the possibility of a winning ticket in the start-up lottery. Thus it was that during the halcyon days of the high-tech economy—at the dawn of the new millennium—an entrepreneurial-minded former employee of the AirTouch corporation decided to change his name to DotComGuy and live his life online. For the former Mitch Maddox (a.k.a. DotComGuy), the decision was more than a lifestyle decision; it was also a business decision. By living his life in front of twenty-five cameras installed in his house and yard, DotComGuy hoped to demonstrate the benefits of e-commerce, ordering everything he needed online so that he wouldn't have to leave his home for a year. As an online advertisement for e-commerce—an entrepreneurial Truman Burbank—DotComGuy hoped to turn his website into a for-profit corporation that would generate enough money to support his handlers and to earn him a $98,000 paycheck for his year-long stint in the DotCompound.

DotComGuy, was, in short, attempting to demonstrate how the Internet made it possible for an ordinary guy with access to some relatively inexpensive hardware to put on his own show and support himself from the proceeds. His case is instructive precisely because it explores the intersection of interactivity, e-commerce, and reality programming—hence its role as an introduction and explication of several of the themes that will be developed in the following chapters on reality television.

DotComGuy's attempt to steer his webcam in an entrepreneurial direction started swimmingly. Piggybacking on the kind of media blitz that he could count on in the wake of Jennicam and the contemporaneous dot-com boom, his online "show" drew sponsors and captured the attention of viewers, who generated more than a million hits a day for the website during its first few months of operation.[50] However, by the end of the year, the euphoria over the online economy had been replaced by a healthy dose of skepticism, and as the Nasdaq headed south, so did DotComGuy's revenues. On New Year's Day 2001, DotComGuy left the compound behind and forfeited his $98,000 payday, keeping as payment only those products that the company had purchased or received for promotional purposes over the course of the year.[51] He also gained a wife—an online fan who became his girlfriend while he was in the DotCompound and his fiancée on the day of his departure. More important, from a media studies perspective, DotComGuy stumbled across one of the truths of the emerging online economy: the fact that being watched is an increasingly important form of labor in the online economy.

THE TOTAL INSTITUTION: FROM COMPULSION TO VOLUNTARY SUBMISSION

The thread that unites Jennicam with DotComGuy—and with reality programming in general—is that the creators of both sites recognized the potential of the work of being watched. Jennifer Ringley avoided commercializing her site, but DotComGuy took the opposite approach, realizing that if the reality trend was taking off, he might be able to just live for a living—to earn his keep by agreeing to live a fully monitored life. For DotComGuy, the DotCompound was what Erving Goffman describes as a "total institution"; there was, according to the site's premise, no alternative space to that of surveillance—and production.[52] Even when he was asleep, DotComGuy was still working, thanks to the fact that his digitized image was surrounded by the banner advertising of his sponsors. In this respect, the DotCompound anticipated the productive ideal of the digital enclosure: a space within which the rhythm of daily life could be comprehensively and exhaustively monitored.

The total institution is a site of compulsory, comprehensive supervision: a jail or asylum. The similarity between the DotCompound and a jail cell was not lost on Maddox, whose website included an "About DotComGuy" section that started with the question "Why am I doing this . . . Why volunteer for lockdown? I get that question a lot."[53] Of course, the very fact that he could evoke the image with irony suggested a crucial difference between his high-tech home and a high-tech prison: He was there by choice, for his own benefit. At any time, he was free to give up his life of perpetual surveillance and disappear into relative anonymity. Indeed, he had promised himself a hefty fee for undergoing the rigors of "lockdown," delivered in increasing installments, so as to provide the incentive to remain in the house for a full year. According to the schedule of payments outlined on his website, he was to receive half of his anticipated income as the final monthly installment. If he left the house before finishing out the month, he would be giving up at least half of his salary.

The DotCompound thus represents an interesting hybrid: the marriage of the comprehensive surveillance associated with a "total" institution, in which surveillance is pervasive, with the "freely" agreed-on character of wage labor. This hybrid space of surveillance resembles that of a work space insofar as privacy is exchanged for a salary in a freely entered-into arrangement (in this case, between DotComGuy and his production company). Unlike a work space, however, there is no alternative space of free, unsupervised time. DotComGuy's time is never free—in the sense of nonproductive. To the extent that his life is the show, he is working all the time. In this respect, he anticipates the logic of the digital enclosure taken to its extreme. He embodies an early version of what Bill Gates describes as a fully "documented life" enabled by the portable digital technology:

> Your wallet PC will be able to keep audio, time, location, and eventually even video records of everything that happens to you. It will be able to record every word you say and every word said to you, as well as your body temperature, your blood pressure, the barometric pressure, and a variety of other data about you and your surroundings. . . . It will be able to track your interactions with the network—all of the commands you issue, the messages you send, the people you call or who call you.[54]

To the extent that the "wallet PC" Gates describes is interactive—that is, "within" the digital enclosure—or that similar data can be gathered by computers with which we will interact throughout the course of the day, all of this information is potentially available to others. The notion of wearable computers might have seemed a bit outlandish a few years ago, but the proliferation of networked mobile phones and personal digital assistants has started to transform the computing landscape in the direction indicated by Gates. As the *Ecomomist* recently observed in a cover article on the future of computing, "The switch to mobile devices is thus a logical long-term step."[55] Finding ways of making mobile computing not just technically possible but physically comfortable has led to the development of clothing and accessories designed to accommodate portable devices and even pioneering efforts in the creation of so-called smart fabrics that incorporate electronic circuits and "affective jewelry" that incorporates inexpensive biosensors of the type envisioned by Bill Gates.[56] Perhaps sometime in the not-so-distant future advertisers will be able to measure our physiological responses to ads in addition to our click-through rate. The obverse of wearable computing is the emerging attempt to create interactive environments: spaces that monitor the people in them and interact with their portable devices. MIT's Project Oxygen, for example, is dedicated to developing embedded interactive devices that would be as pervasive and ubiquitous as air—hence the name of the project. The creation of invisible, always-on interactive computing anticipates an era in which the spaces we move within not only respond to us but also generate a detailed record of our movements, our actions, perhaps even our vital functions.

The result is the anticipated emergence of the ultimate data double: the mother lode of data mining. DotComGuy's online experiments anticipate such a life: one of full self-disclosure. However, the failure of his project doesn't necessarily reflect on the economic viability of the documented life, for he was attempting to profit from it as a form of celebrity synopticism: the many watching the few. The real economic value of the documented life relies on the tried-and-true panoptic model: the few (marketers, advertisers, and data miners) monitoring the many. The beneficiaries will be those with ready access to centralized data collection and storage—those, in other words, who control the means and mode of surveillance—not those being watched. The enticement offered to those who are watched, at least for now, is that of the convenience of an interactive world that adjusts to the user's needs and preferences while naturalizing the monitoring process as a pervasive and eventually invisible feature of the digital economy. The themes of this strategic appeal can be discerned in the tagline for MIT's Project Oxygen that asserts, in utopian fashion, that pervasive computing is "Bringing abundant computation and communication, as pervasive and free as air, naturally into people's lives."[57] We already provide all kinds of information about ourselves to strangers: how we look, the way we dress, and so on. Wearable computing promises a quantum leap in the information that might be made publicly available and raises the question of how much control we will have over that information.

The fact that a selected few members of the audience are finding synoptic success by joining the ranks of celebrity (whether via webcam or prime-time reality TV) should not overshadow the reality of an emerging economy in which the vast majority of noncelebrities are being recruited to participate in the labor of being watched by subjecting the details of their daily lives to increasingly pervasive and comprehensive forms of high-tech monitoring. This reality is perhaps borne out by the fact that the economically successful webcam sites are not the homemade "entrepreneurial" ones like Jennicam, or even the explicitly commercial DotComGuy, but rather sites like VoyeurDorm, which employ "real" people willing to submit themselves to comprehensive surveillance as a form of wage labor. These sites make explicit the role of submission to surveillance in the online economy: Because it generates commodities that can be bought and sold, it can be considered a form of work. Such sites also import the mainstream media model of synoptic surveillance: They rely on the rationalization of the work of being watched rather than on the democratization of access to the means of media production. The VoyeurDorm women don't reap the reported multimillion-dollar profits from the site; rather, as one newspaper account put it, they are wage slaves who "receive free tuition, free rent and a modest salary. They work in shifts that include scheduled parties and lingerie shows. No drugs are allowed. They can show as little or as much skin as they like."[58] Their work is the work of being watched.

WHY CALL IT WORK?

It is obvious that in the case of a site like VoyeurDorm or in the *Big Brother* house being watched is a form of work. After all, those who agree to turn their private lives into a mediated spectacle are being paid for it. The parallel between this kind of labor and that of the monitored consumer, however, requires a more detailed explanation. The purpose of pointing out the parallel is to suggest that the interpretation of the act of being watched as a form of work, or value-generating labor, offers a much-needed alternative to the terms of the contemporary critique of online surveillance, which tends to pit convenience against personal privacy. The drawback of the privacy argument so frequently mobilized by the critics of ever more pervasive forms of commercial surveillance is, as social theorists including David Lyon and Oscar Gandy have suggested, that the attempt to secure privacy rights has a disturbing tendency to work as much in the interest of the corporations doing the monitoring as in that of the individuals being monitored.[59] The development of demographic databases relies heavily on the protection accorded private property, since these databases are only profitable to the extent that the information they contain is proprietary. As sociologist David Lyon puts it, "Privacy grows from the same modern soil as surveillance, which is another reason for doubting its efficacy as a tool of counter-surveillance."[60]

As an alternative to the popular portrayal of the proliferation of corporate surveillance as exacerbating the invasion of privacy, this chapter suggests an approach influenced by the concerns of political economy. Conceived of as a form of work, the activity of being watched can be described in terms of differential access to the means of surveillance and to the benefits that accrue to the exploitation of this labor. The operative question is not whether a particular conception of privacy has been violated but rather, What are the relations that underwrite entry into a relationship of surveillance, and who profits from the work of being watched? This approach draws its inspiration from Kevin Robins and Frank Webster's assessment of the information revolution as "a matter of differential (and unequal) access to, and control over, information resources."[61]

The productive aspect of the labor of being watched, despite frequent allusions to Foucault, all too often gets short shrift in the critical literature on surveillance. Anthony Giddens, for example, in his discussion of surveillance in *A Contemporary Critique of Historical Materialism*—which refers directly to the work of Foucault—emphasizes the oppressive top-down power of the surveillance state: "'Classical social theory' did not recognise the potentiality of what has become in our day a fundamental threat to human liberties, totalitarian control maintained through a society-wide system of surveillance, linked to the 'policing' of day-to-day life."[62] Similarly, Clive Norris and Gary Armstrong, who have written on the deployment of closed-circuit television, emphasize the homogenizing and pacifying effects of surveillance, invoking Foucault's argument that surveillance serves as a means of "controlling and disciplining the institutionalized populations."[63] Lyon also emphasizes the policing and categorizing aspects of surveillance, especially within the context of the shift toward preventative surveillance as a form of categorical suspicion.[64] Finally, Gandy stresses the role of panopticism in sorting consumers into "classes and categories" thereby consolidating "power gains of bureaucracies, both private and public, at the expense of individuals and the nonorganized sectors of society."[65]

All of these authors make the link between surveillance and capitalism, but a strong trace remains of what Foucault describes as the insistence in the West on "seeing the power it exercises as juridical and negative rather than technical and positive."[66] This tendency is also reflected in the public debate over online privacy, which centers on the "invasion" of privacy and the oppressive surveillance capacity of the state. In short, the emphasis is on the ways in which disciplinary surveillance creates "docile bodies" and not on the more suggestive aspect of Foucault's analysis: the spiraling cycle of productivity incited by disciplinary regimes. As he puts it in *Discipline and Punish*, "Let us say that discipline is the unitary technique by which the body is reduced as a 'political' force at the least cost and maximized as a useful force."[67] Docility is certainly one of the goals of discipline, but the real power of surveillance is a relentlessly productive and stimulating one: "The Panopticon . . . has a role of amplification; although it arranges power, although it is intended to make it more economic and effective, it does so not for power itself . . . its aim is to strengthen the social forces—to increase production, to develop the economy . . . to increase and multiply."[68] This power—and not the sterile juridical "repressive" gaze of Big Brother—is what attracts the interest and the capital of the online economy.

Surveillance via interactivity serves as an incitement to productivity by dedifferentiating spaces of consumption and production and thereby allowing for the deployment of the monitoring gaze as a means of rationalizing both processes simultaneously. In this sense, it brings the rationalization process full circle: The division that initially facilitated surveillance by bringing workers into a monitored work space is superceded by the extension and generalization of the monitoring process itself. Anthony Giddens notes that this original differentiation was the characteristic strategy of capitalist modernity, which relied on the enclosure movement to force workers into a monitored wage–labor arrangement and thereby, eventually, to enter into a monitored work space.[69] The characteristic spatial division of modernity—that which precipitated out a space devoted exclusively to monitored labor—gave rise to the discrete character of activities that had previously been intermingled: consumption, production, and leisure. As media scholar Nick Couldry notes, this segregation carries over into the sphere of media practice, helping to reinforce the symbolic power of media institutions.[70] Limited access to the site of media production helps underwrite the division between those who shape the news and those who consume it. This division works to naturalize the way stories are framed and presented, in large part because the editing and writing processes remain inaccessible to the general public. Centralizing and concentrating the planning process in a particular location reinforces the deskilling of the nonparticipatory audience.

The promise of the digital revolution is to overcome this hierarchical arrangement between both planning and execution and consumption and production. The webcam movement reinforces this promise by ostensibly challenging the spatial segregation of unmonitored domestic space and monitored work space.

The space of production is no longer inaccessible to audience members formerly relegated to the role of passive consumption. In a webcam-enabled world, a domestic site like a dorm room or household can become a site of production in its own right; the clear division between sites of domesticity, leisure, and labor is eroded. Reality shows like *Big Brother* and *The Real World*, which, like webcam sites, are predicated on comprehensive surveillance, highlight this process of dedifferentiation by taking as their production site a "real" home in which the cast members are living their lives. As in the case of DotComGuy, these cast members are working *while* going about their domestic lives, cooking, cleaning the bathrooms, relaxing in the living room, and so on. This spatial dedifferentiation is a recurring motif of the online economy, in which, we are told, we will be able to work from home, to shop without leaving the privacy of our home office, and so on. At the same time, from a marketing perspective, we will be able to generate value while going about the routines of our daily lives, sending signals about our consumption habits with every TV show we watch, every carton of milk we buy, every website that catches our attention. It's not just that we'll be able to work from home, in other words, but that domestic activities that didn't used to generate value can be captured, recorded, and commodified, thanks to the extended reach of the monitoring gaze facilitated by the digital enclosure. As work becomes more integrated into our domestic lives, domesticity becomes increasingly productive.

Interestingly, this dedifferentiation process enlists the appeal of the real, insofar as it harkens back to a time before the "artificial," abstract divisions instituted by the rise of mass society. Prior to these divisions, of course, the activities of work, domesticity, and leisure often took place within the same space—or closely overlapping spaces. The home, for many, was a site of production: a place for making the homemade products whose manufacture migrates outside of the household with the rise of consumer society. Similarly, work spaces, for practical reasons, were not far removed from domestic space. A generalized exclusive, monitored work space hadn't yet crystallized. Thus, the appeal of dedifferentiation is bolstered by the romanticization of a premass existence, allowing the promoters of the online economy to enlist the promise of a return to all that was wholesome and rewarding about premass society. DotComGuy views his compound precisely in these terms—as a space that, thanks to modern innovation, harkens back to the integration of work space and home: "It's all cyclical. . . . In the past when you worked, when you were a farmer or you were a blacksmith, it was attached to your house. You're also seeing the same thing with Internet and e-commerce."[71] Adopting the celebratory rhetoric of the business world futurists, DotComGuy, a former human resources officer, argues that this "return" to a more integrated way of life restores a lost balance between work, leisure, and domesticity, allowing workers to perform more efficiently: "I think you can get a lot of work done at home. . . . You talk about creating balance in people's lives—the Internet has the potential in some aspects to help add to that balance between the workplace and home and helping people better balance all the challenges in their lives, especially with today's hectic work environment."[72]

The notion of a restoration of "proper" balance, however, has a tendency to mask the fact that the balance tends to shift in the direction of more time spent in value-generating activity, hence the increasingly hectic and competitive work environment referenced by DotComGuy. The ways in which the home, the café, even the beach and the airport all come to serve as alternative work sites thanks to networked devices (cell phones, laptop computers, and other wireless Internet devices) warrant a book-length study of their own, but I want to touch briefly on their reflection in the image of the DotCompound as a place where one can work without leaving the privacy of one's home. The corollary of this dedifferentiation of work and leisure is that workers no longer have to stay within the boundaries of the work space in order to be subject to the forms of monitoring associated with work. With respect to work proper, the business world has been quick to recognize the potential advantages of the digital enclosure, as Rifkin points out:

> Companies such as AT&T have begun to introduce the idea of the "virtual office." Employees are provided with a mobile office, complete with laptop, fax, and cellular phone, and literally sent home. . . . Telecommuting not only increases employee productivity, but also reduces the amount of office space necessary to conduct business. Dun & Bradstreet Software cut its real estate costs by 30 percent by implementing telecommuting plans.[73]

Corporate futurists Steve Pruitt and Tom Barrett take the model of the virtual office even further, exuberantly describing a future in which workers will be able to commute around the world without leaving home, thanks to the power of virtual reality. Suggestively, the virtual work space they envision takes the form of a wearable computer, a virtual reality suit that, when donned, gives the user the illusion of being in a virtual office and allows access to stored files and network connections.[74] This virtual work space allows for greater flexibility at the same time as it eliminates the need to commute—or even to shower and dress—thereby minimizing downtime. The spatial dedifferentiation that allows the work space to reach out and subsume spaces previously external to it is accompanied by an anticipated dedifferentiation of activities—the so-called multitasking associated with media convergence. Perhaps the image of the office worker logged on to "DotComGuy" (or shopping on eBay) while writing computer code anticipates a converged world, in which the spatial and temporal distinctions between the labor of work and consumption blur into one another. From the perspective of capital, what Pruitt and Barrett call the "personal virtual workspace" has two advantages: It promises to facilitate detailed and comprehensive employee monitoring, and it offers to make labor markets increasingly competitive and flexible. Within such a virtual work space, every action taken by the worker could be recorded. Indeed, the suit anticipates the potential benefits to employers of a fully documented life: the creation of a detailed, high-resolution digital double for the purposes of either record keeping or rationalization of the work process. Such a suit might also be technologically tailored to protect the worker's privacy, but this would likely make the worker less competitive in a labor market that can draw on workers from around the world.

The "unprecedented freedom" that Pruitt and Barrett anticipate for the future workforce turns out to be, in significant ways, a negative form of freedom for the worker—freedom from benefits and job security. This translates into a somewhat more positive form of freedom for employers—freedom from the burden of a long-term commitment to workers and their welfare: "If the individual takes full advantage of cyberspace and becomes an independent economic unit, he will need to become more self-reliant. Health care and financial cushions [by which the authors mean retirement and unemployment benefits] may become the responsibility of the individual."[75] In an increasingly fluid and flexible labor market, continual job shifting and retraining would become the norm and, likely, the responsibility of workers. The advantages of efficiency accrue heavily on the side of the corporation to the detriment of the worker, as Darin Barney suggests: "teleworking often entails a 'shift in the capital costs from the employer to the workers . . . [whereby] workers are expected to absorb the costs of doing business.' Overhead costs, including equipment and supplies . . . , utilities . . . , training . . . , and maintenance are, in many cases, borne by the teleworkers themselves."[76]

At the same time, the virtual work space promises to do away with one of the major sources of market "friction" on the production side: the relative geographic fixity of the workforce. Admittedly, Pruitt and Barrett treat only a particular class of worker—the trained engineer with the ability to earn enough money to afford the hardware and software to participate in such a market. Nevertheless, the benefits of a fluid labor force to corporations may prove to be significant enough to warrant the creation of portable corporate workstations that can be shifted to regions that boast the lowest wage for menial labor (e.g., data entry or data mining). Physical labor rooted to a geographic location (mining, construction, etc.) seems to have only a small role to play in the imagination of the prophets of the information society, at least for the moment.

It is worth noting a gaping inconsistency in much of the mass customization literature. It tends to overlook the fact that mass production and the stultifying forms of labor it fosters promise to remain alive and well in the digital economy. Indeed, even one of the most respected mouthpieces of the business world, the *Wall Street Journal*, has acknowledged the debilitating forms of mass production that accompany the booming computer industry: "While American industry reaps the benefits of a new, high-technology era, it has consigned a large class of workers to a Dickensian time warp, laboring not just for meager wages but also under dehumanized and often dangerous conditions."[77] As theorist Tiziana Terranova puts it, the realization that "[w]orking in the digital media industry is not as much fun as it is made out to be" is creating a "necessary backlash against the glamourisation of digital labour, which highlights its continuities with the modern sweatshop and points to the increasing degradation of knowledge work."[78] Her descriptions invoke not only the free labor provided by America Online "volunteers" who worked long hours as unpaid chat hosts but the sweatshop-like call centers described by Darin Barney. These call centers provide an example of the ability of networks to take advantage of the new "flexibility" of the workforce. Such work can be performed remotely thanks to the lowered cost of long-distance telephony that allows employers to seek out the cheapest labor markets, using workers in India or Ireland to service callers in the United States.

As cultural geographer David Harvey suggests, in an era of flexible accumulation, many modes of production—patriarchal, feudal, and Fordist—can coexist. For the purposes of the current argument, the central emphasis will be on the claims made for the mode of production dubbed "mass customization."[79] But this emphasis must be qualified with the recognition of the fact that mass customization—despite the assumptions of its celebrants—coexists with many of the forms of production that it purportedly supercedes. It exists, in short, as one layer of production, limited to the more prosperous consumers in more prosperous nations, on top of many others. It offers solutions to a set of concerns that are specific to a distinct class and a particular level of market development. It seems evident, for example, that mass customization emerges as a paradigm only in markets in which consumers have both the leisure time and the disposable income to assist in the production of customized products and to pay for the privilege of doing so.

DotComGuy represents the promise of the privileged form of dedifferentiation: that the worker might be able to benefit from the convenience associated with the high-tech merger of home and work space. When asked how he views his home, DotComGuy replied that it serves as domestic space, office, production studio, and even concert hall (since he invited live bands to promote themselves by performing concerts in the DotCompound) on a regular basis. At the same time, as an advertisement for the future of online consumption, DotComGuy anticipates the productivity of the work of being watched. Within the enclosure, every consumption decision represents a double value: that realized in exchange and that which can be generated by the information about the exchange. Political economist Vincent Mosco, following Eileen Meehan, terms this second value—that which goes into the formation of the consumer's data double—a "cybernetic commodity"—an artifact of monitoring and surveillance practices: "These practices are part of the commodification process because the information they produce is used in the production of commodities, like newspapers or television situation comedies, and are cybernetic because the outcome of the production process is the production of a new commodity."[80] Such a formulation neatly restores the original meaning of "cybernetic"—feedback control—to cyberspace, in which the generation of cybernetic commodities becomes increasingly easy and inexpensive. The value of this information necessarily increases in proportion to its comprehensiveness, hence the goal of those whom Robins and Webster term "consumption engineers": to create a "global 'network market place' in which ever more activities come 'online.'"[81] The enterprise is by no means new, as Robins and Webster's analysis of Sloanism (the management of consumption associated with the marketing industry) suggests, but it is greatly enhanced by the deployment of sophisticated information and communication technologies to render "the Scientific Management of consumer life more efficient and automatic"— and, of course, cost-effective.[82]

THE NEW WORLD OF WORK

Being watched is a vital component of the traditional modern workplace insofar as the rationalization of factory and office work of all kinds is based on the ability to monitor workers. However, the rationalization of activity outside the workplace—and of consumption in particular—has remained somewhat limited by the inability to subject it to equally comprehensive forms of monitoring. The digital enclosure promises to change all that by allowing for the comprehensive monitoring of consumption-related activities (which, from a marketing standpoint, include virtually all activities insofar as they contribute to the creation of a demographic profile).

The DotCompound anticipates this aspect of the digital enclosure insofar as the work performed by DotComGuy is neither database entry nor computer programming but simply that of being watched. If everything had gone according to plan, DotComGuy would have received his $98,000 payday simply for drawing audiences to his site. That it didn't work out for DotComGuy doesn't mean that the work of being watched will not be an integral component of the online economy. The Internet anticipates a world in which the mass media model is inverted: Many people are watched by the few, who compile, sort, and aggregate information about consumers in order to design ways of rationalizing the consumption process. In short, it envisions a world in which interactive media allow for the organization of leisure/consumption activity precisely along the lines previously limited to work. The rationalization of the online economy is not limited to the realm of production since the dedifferentiation process is based on the crucial recognition that consumption can double as a form of value-generating labor— not just because it generates sales revenue but because it generates commodifiable information.

DotComGuy enacts the appropriate attitude of the wired consumer: a thoroughly contemporary, almost "hip," lack of squeamishness toward surveillance. As the following chapter notes, this is the attitude of the reality TV celebrity as well as of the webcam celebrity. Webcam pioneer Jennifer Ringley, for example, dismisses the fetishization of privacy as a form of self-deception:

> I honestly think the concept of privacy is a mental fabrication. It's a convenient way to imagine we're hiding the things we like least about ourselves, and therefore

negates us from responsibility for them. . . . Realistically . . . we should be able to defend our actions to ourselves, to know why we do what we do and to come to peace with it, or to change what we cannot accept.[83]

Perpetual surveillance is to be welcomed as a means of confronting and challenging one's own beliefs and actions rather than feared as a form of social control. Indeed, Ringley sees herself as an advertisement for the personal benefits of self-disclosure: "I think most of what people go into private to hide—their bodies, their silly habits, their insecurities—is only doing more harm than good by being hidden. . . . I'm not doing Jennicam to show the world my details necessarily, but hopefully to show generally that owning up to these things isn't a bad thing, it's great!"[84] Voluntary submission to comprehensive surveillance becomes a therapeutic experience, a theme taken up in more detail in chapter 6.

The equation of self-disclosure with convenience and even substantial personal gain is underwritten by the example of for-profit personal webcam sites, which short-circuit the middleman by marketing directly to the public. Such sites enact the commodification and rationalization of self-disclosure. The potential of a website to serve as a portable work space was recognized early on by Ringley, when Jennicam had high ratings (upward of several million hits a day) and was the subject of extensive media coverage.[85] At the time, Ringley said she was approached by a soft drink company with an offer of $10,000 a month to leave bottles of its product around her house. She turned down the offer to protect the authenticity of the site, because, "it would . . . make the site about as real as the *Real World* or any of the other cheesy productions mainstream society produces. Once I start fabricating the content, especially for the sake of money, it's not worth even doing anymore."[86]

Despite the apparent commercial appeal of Ringley's site, the promise of entrepreneurial economic empowerment via webcam is by no means a secure one, as DotComGuy demonstrated. Those who can support themselves via webcam remain few and far between—and overworked. When Jennifer Ringley was able to support herself from her webcam site (before she took the job that now keeps her away from the cameras for most of the day), she said the work was all-consuming and, at times, exhausting: "It feels like I'm working all the time : / . . . Moving back towards a traditional job and spending less time on the site will help that hopefully. I'd like to feel a little less guilty when I actually *do* leave the house :)."[87] Because she spent her life online for a living, any attempt to have a life beyond the camera (which meant beyond her house) undermined her livelihood. Despite her fascination with the webcam and its socially constructive possibilities, getting a job meant escape from the work of being watched.

One economically successful variant of the webcam phenomenon is the adult-oriented sites—many of which are run by companies that hire models to perform online. As both Ringley and Voog discovered, sex improves online ratings and generates revenue. Voog saw the number of visitors to her site increase after net-casting a sexual encounter with her boyfriend, and Ringley's masturbatory shows helped boost ratings early on.[88] The relation between reality TV and pornography is, I suggest in the following chapters, not an incidental one. Voyeurism is an undeniable aspect of the appeal of reality TV and lends this appeal a distinct erotic charge. Indeed, the question of sex embeds itself in any format based on the perpetual monitoring of the private lives of a group of people (especially when they're cooped up together in a house or on a tropical island). At the same time, pornography carries with it the promise of the real: that the act of copulation is neither imitated, as in fictional movies, nor stylized, as in erotica, but presented in all its raw, mundane, reality.[89]

The invocation of the real is, in keeping with the current discussion of reality TV, coupled with that of interactivity. Suggestively, one of the more successful adult-oriented sites, TheWetlands.com, which was started by a self-described soccer mom and an unemployed funeral home worker, relies on the interactive capability of the Internet to invite real-time feedback from subscribers. Drawing on the promise of showing all there is to show of *real* people, instead of "air-brushed Malibu Barbie dolls," the site's founders claim to have built their personal website into a lucrative business that receives some four hundred thousand visits per day (as of this writing, the online tally for the month boasted more than four million hits).[90] The site not only invites paying members to "participate" online by directing the couple's lovemaking, it also promises that selected viewers will be invited to participate more directly: "This is the site where many of the featured wives have actually had sex with our lucky members. Maybe YOU will join our next 'members gangbang.'"[91] The site, in short, enlists the promise of *Who Wants to Be a Millionaire* into the register of online porn. Based on the financial success of the subscriber-supported site, the couple has recruited other "real" couples to join their site, which, according to MSNBC documentary, made $6 million in 1999.[92]

In keeping with the constellation of reality programming, the Wetlands site also mobilizes the equation of the return of the real with the resuscitation of community to differentiate their site from other online sex sites. What makes them unique, according to the site's promotional material, is not just that they feature regular, everyday folk but also, and not incidentally, that their site "is an actual community of sexually free-spirited adults."[93] Once again, the appeal of the real is lined up alongside that of the resuscitation of community, as well as of the critique of the abstraction of artifice—whether it be in the form of television sitcoms or glossy, air-brushed porn.

The equation of the real with the unedited coincides with a rejection of the all-too-predictable illusions produced by the culture industry. Reality programming, both online and on TV, caters to the recognition that "all images are concocted" by no longer backgrounding the site of production. Such formats bring viewers straight to the production site—where the promise of reality in its untampered form is, paradoxically, resurrected.[94] The form of demystification proffered by reality TV is echoed by sites like Jennicam and DotComGuy, where we can see the protagonist/producers in all their uncut glory. We can find them, in some cases, wandering around in their underwear, watching TV, staring glassy-eyed at the computer. We can read in their online journals about the tribulations of daily life: getting new software to work, going to the Department of Motor Vehicles, dealing with parents, paying the bills, and so on. Even the Wetlands relies on behind-the-scenes images: a photo of the "set" where the action takes place in the suburban home of its protagonists.

The promise of democratization is underwritten not just by the fact that webcam celebrities are "real" people like the rest of us, but by the ability of viewers to communicate and interact with the stars. Interactivity offers access to, and perhaps some modicum of control over, the site of production. One relatively popular nonadult site, DriveMeInsane.com, allows viewers to control a variety of appliances in the owner's home: lamps, Christmas tree lights, and even a radio-controlled toy car. Visitors who enable the site's audio feed can hear their own e-mail messages read back to them by a voice synthesizer.[95] Once again, the promise of interactivity turns out to be the ability to find one's own reflection in the surrounding world, enacting the digital solipsism envisioned by Bill Gates: a world in which the movies one watches and the ads all feature the same leading character: that of the viewer. This is the substance of Ana Voog's assessment of the appeal of her own site as a Rorschach test for visitors: "Whatever I'm doing, it has nothing to do with me—it has to do with what they're thinking I am, and that is what they are."[96]

CONVERGING MEDIA

Voog's interpretation of the appeal of her site translates well into the register of reality TV and goes partway toward explaining its popularity: the ability to identify with the real members of the cast. Indeed, much of the online discussion in the reality TV fan sites discussed in upcoming chapters centered on speculation regarding what viewers would do if *they* were in the *Big Brother* house or the *Survivor* island. Against the background of the burgeoning promise of interactivity as democratization, formats like *Big Brother*, *Survivor*, and *Temptation Island* emerge, then, as a pastiche of other demonstrated successes—the inbred offspring of a game show, a documentary, tabloid TV, and the latest media technology. They represent the industrialization and mass marketing of the promise of interactivity, and in so doing, they stand in the same relation to the personal webcam site as the factory is to the home business. DotComGuy was right: One can work by being watched all the time, but it doesn't pay quite as well as he had hoped, at least not for the majority of employees. The producers and the networks are the ones who realize the bulk of the profits. The promise of democratization takes the form of the lottery: Selected viewers have a chance to win fame and perhaps a shot at fortune. As a concession to their claim to realism, these shows tend to incorporate an element of reflexivity. Unlike *The Real World* and *An American Family*, formats like *Big Brother*, *Survivor*, and *Temptation Island* all thematize their production process to some extent. In the case of *Big Brother*, for example, both the series premiere and its finale featured a "behind-the-scenes" look at the *Big Brother* house and production studio. The transitions to and from advertisements also featured the *Big Brother* logo coupled with an image of the production studio's control panel. Throughout the show, the remote control cameras in the corners and the microphone dangling from the ceiling were featured topics of conversation and signified the omniscient presence of the producers and the audience. Similarly, *Temptation Island* included occasional shots of the production crew, including an extended meeting of two of the contestants with the show's producer. *Survivor* generally stuck closer to the observational style, although it did incorporate an emcee, and a postfinale reunion show that provided a backstage glimpse of the "reality behind the reality show." MTV's *The Real World* has spawned a spin-off industry of behind-the-scenes shows and "tell-all" books. As for webcam sites, the production process is an ongoing theme of sites like Jennicam and Anacam, which not only provide specifications of the equipment being used but frequently discuss various aspects of webcam life in the daily journals and diaries that accompany the online images.

The addition of the reflexive element highlights the extra step that these shows have taken toward the promise of reality: the introduction of the production process itself as an element of the content. The argument up to this point suggests that this reflexivity is directly related to the interactive promise of the reality format insofar as both underwrite the challenge to the "abstraction" of mass production described in the previous chapter. If viewers are to be included by proxy in the production process, the corollary is that they are not completely excluded from the space of production; they get to share a glimpse behind the wizard's curtain. The space of production and planning is made accessible rather than invisible in degrees varying from show to show. At one extreme are those variants of reality programming that allow real people to create their own shows: the webcam sites. At the other are the highly produced spectacles like *Survivor* that allow the audience to participate by proxy, since the "stars" are real people selected from the audience.

Spanning the extremes is the promise that interactivity will tear down the barriers associated with mass society: between audience and spectacle, consumer and producer, passive viewing and active participation. Many reality TV fans, for example, also create fan sites devoted to particular shows or cast members. However, the result has not been a transfer of power and control from the power elites of Hollywood to the masses but rather a shift in the burden of labor from paid actors and writers to the viewers from whose ranks the cast is drawn and whose free labor on fan sites helps add value and interest to often lackluster performances. As the *New York Times* notes, the success of the post-*Survivor* generation of reality shows including *American Idol*, *Joe Millionaire*, and *The Bachelor* threatens (or promises) to transform the economics of the television industry: "Writers are petrified," according to an unnamed executive, "This could change the whole economics of this town. Studios have to be scared to death."[97]

In keeping with the transition to more "flexible" forms of production, reality TV itself offers an alternative model to the industrial, high-fixed-cost model of production associated with TV since the 1950s. Rather than relying on expensive formats sold to networks at a loss that can be recouped in syndication, reality TV heralds an era of quick-hit formats that make money during their first run but have little to no value as reruns.[98] The goal is no longer to dominate a time slot for years on end with the same format and cast, but to undermine the boundaries of the traditional television season: "Instead of the time-honored formula of introducing shows en masse in September and ending them in May, broadcast networks want to stagger the shows' debuts and banish repeats from the schedule almost entirely."[99] This dedifferentiation of the standard seasons—including the period of summertime "hiatus" during which cable shows try to draw viewers away from the networks—coincides with the dedifferentiation between content and advertising. Working the advertising into the content of the show further erodes the industrial model of television production that emerged in the wake of the talk show scandals of the 1950s. However, as in the case of flexible manufacturing, viewer participation doesn't necessarily correspond to viewer empowerment. Rather, it helps producers lower costs and rationalize both production and marketing. Cast members may not have stormed the inner sanctum of the culture industry, but they're working away at providing it with cheap and popular programming.

NOTES

1. The return of the real also has its analogue in popular music: Producer T-Bone Burnett recently attributed the phenomenal success of the American folk music soundtrack for the movie *O Brother, Where Art Thou* (which went platinum and topped the country music charts) to the audience's desire for less heavily produced and more humanly "real" music, complete with all of the imperfections of nonsynthesized music ("T-Bone Burnett Discusses His 'American Roots' Music," NPR, 28 July 2001, Scott Simon interview).

2. Emma Brockes, "Welcome to Me TV," *The Guardian* (London), 10 December 1999, Features, 2.

3. Douglas Kellner, "Globalisation from Below? Toward a Radical Democratic Technopolitics," *Angelaki* 4, no. 3 (1999): 109.

4. Marshall Sella, "The Electronic Fishbowl," *New York Times*, 21 May 2000, 54.

5. *MSNBC Reports:* "Look at Me! The Webcam Explosion," MSNBC, 29 August 2000.

6. Howard Rheingold, *Smart Mobs: The Next Social Revolution* (Cambridge, Mass.: Perseus, 2002), 168.

7. Gary Dretzka, "He Got Game: Bill Gates Promotes Versatile Xbox," *Chicago Tribune*, 18 January 2001, N4.

8. Ken Anderson, "Technology and Convergence of the Digerati," white paper, MediaOne Labs, 1999.

9. These definitions are summarized in Jon Dovey, *Freakshow* (London: Pluto: 2000), 79–80.

10. Theodor Adorno, "The Actuality of Philosophy," in *The Adorno Reader*, ed. B. O'Connor (Oxford: Blackwell, 2000), 38.

11. Ilisa Barbash and Lucien Taylor, *Cross-Cultural Filmmaking* (Berkeley: University of California Press, 1997), 15.

12. More broadly defined forms of reality programming certainly predate *An American Family*, including shows like *Candid Camera*, which debuted in 1948 and *Queen for a Day* (1956). These shows, however, belong to the "exceptional moments" brand of reality programming, whose descendents include programs like *Funniest Home Videos*, *When Animals Attack*, and, of course, the current incarnation of *Candid Camera*.

13. Shana Alexander, "The Silence of the Louds," *Newsweek*, 22 January 1973, 28.

14. Abigail McCarthy, "An American Family & The Family of Man," *Atlantic Monthly* (July 1973), 72.

15. McCarthy, "An American Family & The Family of Man," 75.

16. David Harvey, *The Condition of Postmodernity* (Cambridge: Blackwell, 1990); Joseph Pine, *Mass Customization: The New Frontier in Business Competition* (Cambridge, Mass.: Harvard University Press, 1993).

17. Joshua Meyrowitz, "Mediating Communication: What Happens?" in *Questioning the Media: A Critical Introduction*, ed. John Downing et al. (London: Sage, 1995), 48.

18. Meyrowitz, "Mediating Communication," 49–50.

19. Paul Krugman, "For Richer—How the Permissive Capitalism of the Boom Destroyed American Equality," *New York Times*, 20 October 2002.

20. See Pine, *Mass Customization*.

21. Pine, *Mass Customization*.

22. "Share and Share Unalike," *The Economist*, 7 August 1999, 37.

23. Mark Gimein, "The Greedy Bunch: You Bought, They Sold," *Fortune*, 11 August 2000.

24. Dan Morain, "Lotteries on a Roll," *Los Angeles Times*, 1 February 1987, 1.

25. Morain, "Lotteries on a Roll," and Brett Pulley, "Waiting for Riches," *New York Times*, 22 May 1999, A1.

26. Kevin Delaney, "'An American Family' Visits the Andy Warhol Museum" (1996), at members.aol.com/kdel691586/love/amfamily.html (accessed 12 December 2000).

27. Delaney, "'An American Family' Visits the Andy Warhol Museum."

28. Barbash and Taylor, *Cross Cultural Filmmaking*, 28.

29. Stephanie Harrington, "An American Family Lives Its Life on TV," *New York Times*, 7 January 1973, Sec. II, 19.

30. Jennifer Ringley, e-mail correspondence with author, 17 September 2000.

31. Arild Fetveit, "Reality TV in the Digital Era," *Media, Culture, & Society* 21 (1999), 798.

32. Fetveit, "Reality TV in the Digital Era," 791.

33. Jeffrey Ruoff, "'A Bastard Union of Several Forms': Style and Narrative in *An American Family*," in *Documenting the Documentary*, ed. Barry Grant and Jeannette Sloniowski (Detroit, Mich.: Wayne State University Press, 1998).

34. Ruoff, "'A Bastard Union of Several Forms,'" 288–89. It's probably worth pointing out that Ruoff's description doesn't take into account the fact that anthropological

documentary had dispensed with some of these boundaries for years, extensively documenting the private lives of particular groups—primarily those comprised of nonwhite, nonwestern peoples living in "undeveloped" societies. The pioneering aspect of *An American Family*, then, lies not so much in its documentation of the rhythm of day-to-day life but in its documentation of affluent white Americans (living in Santa Barbara, California), not just for anthropological purposes but for the entertainment of their contemporaries.

35. Harvey, *The Condition of Postmodernity*.

36. "The Ultimate Soap Opera," *Time*, 22 January 1973, 36.

37. Delaney, "An American Family."

38. Jon Murray, telephone interview with the author, 20 October 1999.

39. Barbash and Taylor, *Cross-Cultural Filmmaking*, 30.

40. Barbash and Taylor, *Cross-Cultural Filmmaking*, 28.

41. Seth Schiesel, "New AT&T System Displays a 'Millionaire' Bonus," *New York Times*, 14 February 2000, C4.

42. Peter Larsen, "Spanish Were Watching as *Big Brother* Stole the Show," *Financial Times* (London), 18 March 2000, 10.

43. Larsen, "Spanish Were Watching."

44. Marshall Sella, "The Electronic Fishbowl," *New York Times*, 21 May 2000, 50–104.

45. Drew Jubera, "Oh, 'Brother': Ratings Fall as Boredom Rules," *Atlanta Journal and Constitution*, 11 July 2000, 4C.

46. Neal Gabler, *Life: The Movie: How Entertainment Conquered Reality* (New York: Knopf, 1998).

47. Jim Rutenberg, "Reality Shows Set Off Fight over Awards," *New York Times*, 12 February 2001, C1.

48. "The Trojan Room Coffee Machine," at www.cl.cam.ac.uk/coffee/coffee.html (accessed 12 December 2002).

49. "Farewell Seminal Coffee Can" (7 March 2001), at www.wired.com/news/culture/0,1284,42254,00.html (accessed 14 December 2002).

50. Mitch Maddox, telephone interview with the author, 16 September 2000.

51. Libby Copeland, "For DotComGuy, the End of the Online Line," *Washington Post*, 3 January 2001, C2.

52. Erving Goffman, *Asylums: Essays on the Social Situation of Mental Patients and Other Inmates* (New York: Doubleday, 1961).

53. "About DotComGuy," at www.dotcomguy.com (accessed 14 September 2000).

54. Bill Gates, *The Road Ahead* (New York: Penguin, 1996), 303–4.

55. "Computing's New Shape," *The Economist* (23–29 November 2002): 11.

56. Melissa Witkowski, "Wearable Computing," unpublished manuscript.

57. "Project Overview," MIT Project Oxygen, at oxygen.lcs.mit.edu/Overview.html (accessed 15 June 2002).

58. Huettel, "Voyeur Dorm Is Test of Cyber Law," 1B.

59. David Lyon, *The Electronic Eye: The Rise of Surveillance Society* (Minneapolis: University of Minnesota Press, 1994); Oscar Gandy, *The Panoptic Sort: A Political Economy of Personal Information* (Boulder, Colo.: Westview, 1993).

60. Lyon, *The Electronic Eye*, 21.

61. Kevin Robins and Frank Webster, *Times of the Technoculture: From the Information Society to the Virtual Life* (London: Routledge, 2000), 91.

62. Anthony Giddens, *A Contemporary Critique of Historical Materialism* (Berkeley: University of California Press, 1981), 175.

63. Clive Norris and Gary Armstrong, *The Maximum Surveillance Society: The Rise of CCTV* (Oxford: Berg, 1999), 18.

64. Lyon, *The Electronic Eye*.

65. Gandy, *The Panoptic Sort*, 52.

66. Michel Foucault, *Discipline and Punish: The Birth of the Prison*, trans. Alan Sheridan (New York: Pantheon, 1977), 121.

67. Foucault, *Discipline and Punish*, 221.

68. Foucault, *Discipline and Punish*, 208.

69. Giddens, *A Contemporary Critique of Historical Materialism*.

70. Nick Couldry, *The Place of Media Power* (London: Routledge, 2000).

71. Mitch Maddox, telephone interview with the author, 16 September 2000.

72. Mitch Maddox, telephone interview with the author, 16 September 2000.

73. Jeremy Rifkin, *The End of Work: The Decline of the Global Labor Force and the Dawn of the Post-Market Era* (New York: Tarcher, 1996), 150.

74. Steve Pruitt and Tom Barrett, "Corporate Virtual Workspace," in *Cyberspace: First Steps*, ed. Michael Benedikt (Cambridge, Mass.: MIT Press, 1991), 403.

75. Pruitt and Barrett, "Corporate Virtual Workspace," 406.

76. As quoted in Darin Barney, *Prometheus Wired: The Hope for Democracy in the Age of Network Technology* (Chicago: University of Chicago Press, 2000), 146.

77. As quoted in Jim Davis and Michael Stack, "The Digital Advantage," in *Cutting Edge: Technology, Information, Capitalism and Social Revolution*, ed. Jim Davis, Thomas Hirschl, and Michel Stack (London: Verso, 1997), 121–44, 134.

78. Tiziana Terranova, "Free Labor: Producing Culture for the Digital Economy," *Social Text* 63, no. 18 (2000): 1, 2.

79. David Harvey, *The Condition of Postmodernity* (Cambridge: Blackwell, 1990).

80. Vincent Mosco, *The Political Economy of Communication* (London: Sage, 1996), 151.

81. Robins and Webster, *Times of the Technoculture*, 101.

82. Robins and Webster, *Times of the Technoculture*.

83. Jennifer Ringley, e-mail to the author, 12 December 2000.

84. Jennifer Ringley, e-mail to the author, 12 December 2000.

85. Kathryn Balint, "All the Web's a Stage; Would-be Stars May Find Their 15 Minutes of Fame by Posting Their Talents on the Internet," *San Diego Union-Tribune*, 13 June 2000, E-1.

86. Jennifer Ringley, e-mail to the author, 12 December 2000.

87. Jennifer Ringley, e-mail to the author, 12 December 2000.

88. Mike Clothier, "More Folks Watching Web Cameras and Waiting," *Chicago Tribune*, 7 October 1999, 7; Jennifer Ringley, e-mail to the author, 12 December 2000.

89. It is significant, with respect to the deployment of the promise of access to the real, that one of the recurring, deeply disturbing mythologies of the hard-core porn industry is that of the "snuff" video: a movie in which the sexual object (usually the woman) is not only penetrated and tortured but killed. A permanent change in the world—the destruction of a human life—marks the fatal reality of the act. It is perhaps not surprising that certain of the more pornographic subsets of the current mainstream reality genre move in the same direction: from depictions of car chases to disasters in which people survived, to those in

which they didn't. Or, by the same token, from people living together on an island, to people warring with each other using paintball guns on an island, to people engaging in dangerous and death-defying stunts (as in the case of MTV's *Senseless Acts of Video*).

90. "The Story of the Wetlands," at www.wetlands.net/Site01/index.html (accessed 12 November 2002).

91. "The Story of the Wetlands" (accessed 2 January 2003).

92. *MSNBC Reports:* "Look at Me!"

93. "The Story of the Wetlands" (accessed 12 December 2000).

94. The promise of an immediate reality offered by such formats takes on the character of an infinitely receding horizon. Consider, for example, MTV's *The Real World*, which has built a subsidiary industry on the marketing of "behind-the-scenes" books and shows. We are still waiting for a behind-the-scenes look at the making of the behind-the-scenes show.

95. Pamela O'Connell, "Online Diary," *New York Times*, 10 October 2002, G3.

96. Jon Bream, "Art around the Clock," *Minneapolis Star Tribune*, 22 September 1998, 1E.

97. Bill Carter, "Reality TV Alters the Way TV Does Business," *New York Times*, 25 January 2003, A1.

98. Carter, "Reality TV Alters the Way TV Does Business."

99. Carter, "Reality TV Alters the Way TV Does Business."

Chapter Four

The Kinder, Gentler Gaze
of Big Brother

Big Brother may have been portrayed as hostile and forbidding during the Cold War era, but he is currently receiving a glossy Hollywood makeover as a poster boy for the benefits of high-tech surveillance. His rehabilitation is a crucial component of the developing online economy, which is increasingly reliant on the economic value of information gathered through sophisticated interactive communication technologies. However, before he can be openly embraced by the captains of industry, he has to win public acceptance as a nonthreatening—even entertaining and benevolent—pop-culture icon.

A recurring theme of this and the following chapters is the way in which reality TV helps to reposition the portrayal of surveillance and highlight its advantages not to the watchers but to the watched. The approach will be one of triangulation that relies not just on a consideration of particular TV shows but on the reception of these shows by viewers and the media. I rely, therefore, on a variety of sources to piece together the portrait of the new Big Brother: media reports; personal interviews with reality TV cast members, fans, and producers; and audience surveys. In assembling empirical evidence—interviews, surveys, and texts—the goal has been to provide the "analytically isolated elements" that might be arranged in conjunction with one another to provide a fruitful way of rethinking the revolutionary promise of the Internet. The approach is one influenced by Theodor Adorno's version of Walter Benjamin's constellational approach, which draws on the combination of empirical evidence and theory to help illuminate the "logic of the matter." This logic cannot be read directly from the opinions evinced in surveys, interviews, and observations of chat rooms and bulletin boards. Nor can it be reduced to the intentions (stated or interpreted) of the producers and creators of cultural artifacts or to the driving economic imperatives shaping the development of the online economy. Rather, this logic lies in the juxtaposition of these elements within the present social context—a context that necessarily incorporates the materialized contradictions of contemporary capitalist society. The goal is not to prove that reality TV is conceived, produced, and received as an advertisement for the benefits of self-disclosure in an increasingly interactive media environment. Instead, it is to provide one possible interpretation of an emerging pattern in the reception and portrayal of contemporary forms of commercial surveillance and to demonstrate the fruitfulness of this interpretation as a means of thinking about shifting cultural and economic patterns in the information age.

The moment that, for me, defined the co-optation and commercial domestication of Big Brother occurred just before the 2000 "summer of reality TV" in the United States, during an interview with one of the cast members of the 1997 *Road Rules* season, Holly. *Road Rules* is a spin-off of MTV's *The Real World*, which features seven twenty-somethings living together in a house for several months while their daily lives are videotaped for broadcast in edited-down half-hour installments. On *Road Rules*, cast members live in a Winnebago caravan and are tasked with completing several challenges as they drive from one town to another (often in a foreign country). The group's adventures, failures, conflicts, and love lives are duly videotaped and edited into half-hour segments for broadcast.

According to Holly, every season the cast comes up with a nickname for the members of the camera crew who document their waking hours. Her cast nicknamed its crew "Big Brother," which, in practical terms, meant, as Holly put it, "if we needed something we'd be like into the radio, 'uh Big Brother, we're just wondering if we're going to leave in the next hour or if we're going to be here for three' . . . and then someone would walk up and say 'just to let you know we're going to leave in 45 minutes.'"[1] The nickname may have come from recollections left over from a junior high school English class, but the historical reality of Big Brother had apparently changed for this savvy, post–Cold War generation. The totalitarian specter was gone, replaced by the increasingly routine, annoying but necessary intrusions of commerce in the form of the entertainment industry. A decade after the fall of the iron curtain, in an era when commercial surveillance has become an increasingly important structural component of flexible capitalism, Big Brother is reconstituted not as a symbol for all that is wrong with surveillance but as a popular global game show format, poking fun at the idea that there's anything scary about perpetual monitoring. Indeed, the figure of Big Brother seems to have undergone the televisual demystification of authority figures described by Meyrowitz: from authoritarian monster to harmless figure of ridicule.[2]

For Holly and her companions, the Big Brother nickname was a bit of flip irony—perhaps one more indication that they're neither fooled nor particularly troubled by the commodification of their private lives for mass consumption. This lack of concern or, to put it a bit more strongly, the fascination with self-exposure and celebrity has, in the wake of the recent explosion of reality formats, recently become the object of media speculation and criticism. The shows are seen as testimony to an inordinate fascination with voyeurism on the one hand and fame on the other—pathologies of a society in which the public sphere has been eclipsed by the private. This chapter takes the argument in a slightly different direction, one that bemoans neither celebrity obsession nor the erosion of personal privacy (although it certainly lauds neither). Drawing on interviews with cast members of MTV's *Road Rules* and press coverage of both *Road Rules* and *The Real World*, I consider how such programs help define a particular form of subjectivity consonant with an emerging online economy: one that equates submission to surveillance with self-expression and self-knowledge. This equation is crucial to the rationalization of consumer labor anticipated by the architects of an online economy that relies on surveillance not only as a means for customizing consumer demand but for adding value to products and creating new ones. By democratizing celebrity, such programs help reinforce the notion that a surveillance-based society can overcome the hierarchies of mass society. Since this research was conducted, the burgeoning success of reality TV in the United States has offered many further examples of the arguments outlined in the chapter, some of which I take up in the following chapters.

RATIONALIZING THE WORK OF WATCHING

Before exploring the version of surveillance portrayed on *The Real World* and *Road Rules*, it is worth taking a closer look at the notion of the work of being watched introduced in earlier chapters. If "watching" commercial messages is a form of work, as scholars Sut Jhally and Bill Livant (drawing on the work of Dallas Smythe) have argued, then the work of being watched helps to rationalize this labor.[3] Indeed, the productivity of surveillance, for the purposes of this discussion, can be understood as being parasitic upon other forms of labor. As the classic description of Frederick Taylor's success in boosting the productivity of the day laborer "Schmidt" suggests, surveillance is indispensable in generating the efficiency gains associated with scientific management. Taylor notes that before selecting Schmidt, he observed the entire workforce for four days, allowing the managers to select four workers upon whom to concentrate their efforts: "A careful study was then made of each of these men. We looked up their history as far back as practicable and thorough inquiries were made as to the character, habits, and the ambition of each of them."[4] Moreover, Schmidt's training consisted of being supervised by a manager who observed his every action, timing him with a stopwatch, and dictating Schmidt's actions down to the most specific detail. The result of all this monitoring and managing—the rationalization of Schmidt's labor—was that his daily productivity almost quadrupled. The activity of being watched wasn't productive on its own, but coupled with another form of labor (in Schmidt's case, hauling pig iron), it helped multiply the latter's productivity.

Sut Jhally and Bill Livant's description of watching as work suggests a similar consideration of the role that surveillance plays in the productivity of viewing.

Their analysis is straightforward: Audiences perform work by viewing advertising in exchange for "payment" in the form of programming content. The viewing of advertising is productive because it helps "speed up the selling of commodities, their circulation from production to consumption. . . . Through advertising, the rapid consumption of commodities cuts down on circulation and storage costs for industrial capital."[5] Furthermore, they argue that there exists a point beyond which it is no longer efficient to attempt to require audiences to work more (a limit, e.g., in the number of commercials audiences are willing to watch during a one-hour program). The problem for those who would exploit the labor of viewing/consumption is to find a way around this limit. Jhally and Livant propose two possible paths: merging content with advertising and developing techniques to make viewers "watch harder."

The DotComGuy website, thanks to its dedifferentiation of the show's content (DotComGuy's daily existence) from its advertising (for all the products and services Maddox relies on in order to survive without leaving his house), exploits the potential of the first path. To watch the DotComGuy website is to watch a perpetual commercial: the advertising content *is* the entertainment content. Reality shows like *Survivor* and *American Idol* that integrate products into the content of the show (e.g., by having contestants "race" each other in cars provided by the sponsor) are at the forefront of the dedifferentiation between content and advertising. A proposed reality show called *The Runner*, developed by celebrities Matt Damon and Ben Affleck's production company LivePlanet, is perhaps the most ambitious attempt so far to exploit the advantages of blending advertising and content. The show would feature one contestant who has to evade capture in the continental United States for thirty days while accomplishing fifteen set tasks during the same period. Members of the viewing public (both online and on television) would be invited to attempt to capture the contestant and thereby win the $1 million prize. If no one succeeds, the runner takes home the money. The format of the show represents the further extension of several aspects of the reality TV trend and its promise of participation. The audience participates in the show—providing from among its ranks not only the runner but a cast of thousands (at least) attempting to capture him or her. Moreover, by virtue of their participation, audience members become contestants on the show, gaining a chance to take home the grand prize. Perhaps the most ingenious aspect of the format, however, is its use of corporate tie-ins to merge content and advertising. The "tasks" to be completed by the runner would all involve the show's corporate sponsors, meaning that audiences would have to do the work of researching sponsors as they track the runner. Thus, for example, the runner might be assigned, as one account puts it, to visit "a McDonald's in New Mexico during a set 48-hour period. . . . The Runner will carry a hidden camera (and hidden cameras will follow him) as he, for instance, moves from a Caesar's Palace buffet in Las Vegas to a Miller brewery tour in Milwaukee to a rock concert in Atlanta."[6] In each case, the television show would serve as a form of promotion for the sponsors of each event, and all of the events would have commercial tie-ins.[7]

The boundary-blurring effect can be read as one more instance of the process of dedifferentiation that takes place within the digital enclosure. If the rationalization of consumption relies upon the fact that sites of consumption and labor are no longer distinct, a show like *The Runner* demonstrates how the distinction between viewing as leisure/entertainment (the "content") and watching as work (the advertising) erodes. The interactive component of the digital enclosure thus further dedifferentiates the constitutive divisions of mass society. Taken to its limit, this dedifferentiation tends toward the convergence of entertainment, advertising, and consumption envisioned by Bill Gates; every detail in every program is not just an ad but a clickable link that facilitates instant, friction-free consumption. This integration of activities becomes one of the anticipated results of convergence within the digital enclosure.

THE MASS-CUSTOMIZED MEDIA

A second strategy for making audiences work harder is to rationalize their labor by breaking the advertising market down so as to ensure that each viewer works as efficiently as possible. The parallel to the scientific management of production is straightforward: the task of watching is broken down according to the specific characteristics of the viewer. The rationalization strategy is based on "the specification and fractionation of the audience," which leads to "a form of 'concentrated viewing' in which there is (from the point of view of advertisers) little wasted watching."[8] In other words, as in the case of Schmidt, what is needed is detailed information about the audience labor force—both its background and its behavior. The commodification of this information has already been institutionalized as the secondary market in ratings, whose growth accompanied that of the electronic mass media. The labor of being watched goes hand-in-hand with the work process: viewers are monitored so that advertisers can be ensured that the work of watching is getting done. As Jhally and Livant suggest, however, advertisers also need more specific information: demographic profiles of the audience for particular shows that allow them to ensure the work of watching isn't being wasted, that advertising messages are being sent to those most likely to participate in the consumption of the goods being advertised.[9]

Within the context of the mass media, the labor of being watched faced certain limitations, both structural and cultural. Watching may be a form of work, but it doesn't take place within a centralized space that would allow broadcasters to stand over viewers with a stopwatch, as in the case of the disciplining of the factory labor force. Moreover, the bourgeois tradition of privacy, combined with the more recent rhetoric of the Cold War and a certain libertarian strain in the U.S. psyche have contributed to a mistrust of centralized forms of surveillance. We accept a level of supervision in the workplace that we so far haven't been willing to tolerate in the privacy of our homes. The notion that the workplace divides our time into that which is subject to work discipline (and hence to surveillance) and that which is "free" is, as Giddens suggests, characteristic of the mode of wage labor in modernity: "Two opposed modes of time-consciousness, 'working time' and 'one's own' or 'free time,' become basic divisions within the phenomenal experience of the day."[10] Surveillance, within this schema, is associated with time that is not free but that is, rather, subjected to the asymmetrical power relations of the workplace, underwritten by the workers' subordination to the owners of the space and resources of production.

The productive potential of the labor of being watched is further limited by the structure of the mass media model, which can only develop the logic of market fractionation up to a point. It is desirable to isolate an affluent demographic but to continue to subdivide it beyond a certain point would be counterproductive. For example, pushing the logic of niche marketing to its extreme, it would be absurd to produce a prime-time television program for a market of one, regardless of that individual's disposable income. Moreover, because the kind of surveillance that takes place in the realm of consumption extends into the individual's private space and free time, detailed monitoring has tended to be relatively costly and has relied to a large extent on the consent of the monitored. Thus, the television industry has contented itself with the relatively rough sampling results offered by the Nielsen ratings, rather than attempting more detailed and comprehensive approaches to managing the work of watching. The advent of interactive, networked forms of content delivery, however, promises to overcome the limitations to consumer surveillance and thereby to develop the potential of the work of being watched to its fullest.

If the advent of cable television allowed for market segmentation only up to a point, the development of digital delivery allows for its extension all the way down to the level of the individual viewer. Bill Gates, for example, argues that advertising appeals can be custom-tailored to fit individuals thanks to the malleability of digital content:

> The net will be able to make much finer distinctions among consumers and to deliver each consumer a different stream of advertising. . . . The Ford Motor Company might want affluent people to be shown a Lincoln Continental ad, young people to see a Ford Escort ad, rural residents to watch an ad for full-size pickup trucks, and everybody else to see a Taurus ad. Or a company might advertise the same product for everyone but vary the actors in the ad by gender or race or age.[11]

The same logic could be extended to products other than media programming. Computers will, for example, allow "[i]ncreasing numbers of products—from shoes to chairs, from newspapers and magazines to music albums" to be "created on the spot to match the exact specifications of a particular person."[12] Half a decade after Gates, *Wired* magazine, in its April 2001 "Megatrends" issue, named "personal fabrication on demand" as one of the top emerging trends of the new millennium.

A mass medium like television requires the additional apparatus of a separate industry—that of the ratings system—to monitor viewers. By contrast, interactive media offer the potential to integrate the labor of watching with that of *being* watched. This is the crucial aspect of new media from the perspective of the on-line economy. Consumers can be monitored while they are surfing the Internet, they can be monitored while they are reading, listening, or shopping. Interactive media offer the ability to generate cybernetic commodities with a minimum of ef-fort and expense. They are a veritable goldmine of demographic information. Moreover, they are a necessary gold mine from the perspective of a customized economy which needs consumers to turn themselves into DotComPeople in order to keep the productive machinery supplied with detailed information about every aspect of their daily lives.

Like DotComGuy, corporate futurists portray the mass customized economy's reliance on surveillance in benign terms. Gates, for example, envisions a world in which software "agents" (computerized database programs) "will try to get you to fill out a questionnaire about your tastes. . . . The information you furnish will go into a profile of your tastes, which will guide the agent. As you use the system for reading news or shopping, the agent will be able to update your profile."[13] We are already starting to see this process at work on websites and browsers that gather and store information about the online behavior of computer users. In many cases, this form of online monitoring is rather more surreptitious than Gates suggests, as the users of the RealPlayer music utility found when they learned that detailed information about their listening habits was being automatically relayed from their computers to RealPlayer's parent company.[14] The use of computers' cookies by online marketers like DoubleClick to keep track of browsing habits and customize advertising is certainly less transparent to consumers than the sce-nario envisioned by Gates.

The parallel between the rationalization of consumption via the work of being watched and the rationalization of production carries over into the realm of pric-ing. In a mass-customized market, prices are no longer standardized, as demon-strated by the emergence of companies like PriceLine.com, which allow con-sumers to bid on goods and services formerly offered at a standardized price. Amazon.com's recent experiments in "variable pricing" anticipate this process of disaggregation, by attempting to charge customers different prices for the same product, based on demographic information gleaned from purchaser cookies.[15] This approach translates the logic of workplace rationalization into the realm of consumption. If the division of labor reflects Babbage's observation that labor can be compensated more cheaply if it is broken into its constituent parts,[16] a sim-ilar rationale applies to consumption. Breaking the market into its constituent parts allows the maximum price to be charged to each consumer. These two forms of rationalization mirror each across the (increasingly blurred) divide that sepa-rates production from consumption within the digital enclosure.

Flexible, customized production doesn't operate solely on the basis of direct interaction with consumers. Rather, it creates secondary markets for demographic information that has been collected, sorted, and packaged by middlemen. Thus, consumer labor is a source of profit both directly as a means of adding value to a particular customized product, and indirectly when information generated by consumers is aggregated and sold as a commodity in its own right. Companies such as Axciom, DoubleClick, and EquiFax (not to mention ZapMe!—a company that once offered to donate computers to schools in exchange for being able to monitor the surfing habits of schoolchildren) profit from the sale of such commodities. According to the *Nation*, EquiFax alone makes $2 billion a year by trafficking in so-called personal information.[17]

The argument so far can be summarized as follows: The speculative value of the online economy is dependent, at least in part, on the anticipated economic benefits of customized forms of marketing and production that rely upon increasingly pervasive and comprehensive forms of consumer surveillance. If the success of e-commerce is similarly predicated on the development of a "new person" who has the right kind of attitude toward the benefits of online surveillance, then it is worth considering some of the cultural formations that exemplify the values and behaviors associated with the new economy. The goal of the remainder of the chapter is to explore how a program like *Road Rules* exemplifies the "right kind of attitude" for the online economy. The new economy relies on the assumption that individuality can be recovered from mass society through the process of individuation via customization—that consumers can express their uniqueness by participating in forms of customized production. Crucially, this participation comes about largely through the surveillance process—hence, the equation of pervasive monitoring with creativity and self-expression that is one of the hallmarks of the current generation of reality programming.

SURVEYING THE REAL

If, as the producers of *The Real World* and *Road Rules* admit, the scenarios they portray are, in many respects, contrived, what, then, constitutes the claim to "reality" put forth by such shows? The answer appears to be twofold. First, the characters are not professional actors, and, second, the show's action is unscripted. However, these two criteria do little to separate out the genre of *The Real World* from a broad spectrum of programming, ranging from game shows and talk shows, to programs like *Cops* (based on videotapes of real car chases and arrests, set mostly in southern California), and *Funniest Home Videos*. A further qualification needs to be added to shows like *The Real World* to distinguish them as a genre unto itself: the fact that they are based not on the documentation of exceptional moments but on the surveillance of the rhythm of day-to-day life. This rhythm may take place in a contrived context, but the distinguishing element of *The Real World* and *Road Rules* is that the surveillance of the characters is, for the period they are on the show, comprehensive. The only time cast members were not taped was when they were sleeping, showering, or going to the toilet.[18] In the end, the show airs only a tiny fraction of the total footage it gathers—typically distilling twenty-two half-hour episodes from more than two thousand hours of videotape.[19] Nonetheless, the premise of the show is that the cast members live in a panopticon—not everything they are doing is taped and watched, but they have to live with the knowledge that their words and actions could, at any time, be recorded for broadcast.

My goal is not to question the definition of "reality" implicit in *The Real World* or to hold it up against some yardstick of what reality *really* is, but rather to explore the way in which this definition functions to reinforce the logic of a surveillance-based interactive economy outlined earlier. Cultural forms like *The Real World* ought not to be considered in isolation from the socioeconomic contexts within which they emerge and gain a certain degree of acceptance. Placing such forms within a broader social context helps illuminate their significance and perhaps to defamiliarize them in a theoretically productive manner.

Consider, for example, the first component of the reality format outlined above: the fact that cast members are drawn from the viewing public, and not from the specialized ranks of professional actors. This fact has its practical appeal to producers, insofar as it helps make reality programming cheaper than conventional dramas and sitcoms. Furthermore, it adds to the fantasy appeal of such shows by democratizing it. As Murray puts it, "I think the audience that watches the show thinks that they have an opportunity to be on it."[20] The appeal apparently works—and as in the case of the lottery, there is anecdotal evidence to suggest that the fantasy can come true. Dan Detzler, a former cast member of *Road Rules*, said that being a fan of the show was what inspired him to apply: "There's a bunch of kids in the front of the camera . . . and you're sitting on the couch, thinking, 'That could be me.'"[21] In this sense, reality TV replicates the promise of interactive commerce: that viewers/consumers will have a greater ability to participate actively in the production process.

Part of the claim to "reality" of a show like *The Real World*," then, relies on the explicit assertion that the control of specialists over the program has given way to that of the "real" people it documents—nonspecialists, just like members of the audience. As coproducer Mary-Ellis Bunim suggested in a newspaper interview, the role of producer and audience has, in a sense, been reversed: the producers sit back and watch while selected members of the public put on the show: "All we have to do is stand back and let it happen. . . . We're flies on the wall."[22] Bunim's coproducer, Jon Murray, is a bit more candid about the control the producers have in the editing process, but he still stresses the element of cast control: "We don't have a lot of control during the production process, what we have is the control to make choices during the editing."[23] This model parallels that of interactive commerce outlined earlier: viewers/producers provide the content that adds value to the program/product that is then repackaged and sold back to them. Of course, not all audience members have a chance to participate in providing content. But their ability to contribute is further expanded by the producers' use of video footage sent by cast rejects to liven up behind-the-scenes shows about the casting process for

The Real World. Indeed, several of the would-be cast members I interviewed for this chapter pointed out that even if they didn't make it onto the show, they might at least make the highlight tape of the auditions featured in the behind-the-scene background episodes. The production staff has plenty of material to choose from, considering the fact that each year some fourteen thousand would-be cast members send in videotapes demonstrating their prime-time potential, and thousands more line up at locations across the nation for open casting calls.[24]

The myth offered up by programs like *The Real World* is that audience members gain meaningful control over the content of television programming when that programming becomes "real." Content becomes liberated from the inbred coterie of scriptwriters and directors, to be replaced by the spontaneous rhythms of real conflict and real romance—the twin foci of every season of *Road Rules* and *The Real World*. The reality of the programs becomes dependent on perpetual surveillance, which is presented as the antidote to artificial interactions—to "acting." As coproducer Bunim puts it, "You can't sustain a character that isn't true to yourself, day and night, for thirteen weeks. It's just not possible. It would drive you mad."[25] Perpetual surveillance, on this account, doesn't compel conformity; rather, it reveals authentic individuality.

The contribution of cast members to the show is decidedly not their acting ability—indeed, when one cast member began to play to the camera on *The Real World*, other cast members derisively started to call her "the actress."[26] The cast members' contribution is their ability to "be real"—to reveal their authentic reactions and to just be themselves. This emphasis on authenticity epitomizes the goal of *The Real World* format, according to its developers. As producer Murray, a former documentary filmmaker, puts it, "We're very strict about not influencing the action. If you only bring cameras in when something exciting is happening, then you affect the cast. We don't want them to know what we think is important and not important. We don't want to turn these people into actors."[27]

The result of this ostensible striving for authenticity is not only the purported "loss of control" of the producers, but the portrayal of the program as a kind of social experiment, whose outcomes always remain uncertain. As Murray puts it, "We try to cast really interesting people who, when they come together, something interesting is going to happen. . . . It's like a chemical experiment—you wait to see what kind of compounds are going to be created, and then apply all of the principles of drama to it."[28] In keeping with this experimental mentality, the producers are not above tweaking the cast members' environment in order to generate interesting results. Sarah, a cast member of the 1997 *Road Rules* season, said that if the action seemed to be slackening on the Winnebago, the producers would cut back on the cast members' cash allowance: "They purposely put us in a situation where we didn't have any money or any food to watch us argue about it."[29] In recalling the ways in which the producers attempted to create tension and conflict, Josh, also a member of the 1997 season of *Road Rules*, echoed Murray's description of the show: "I knew going into it it's kind of a human experiment, kind of to see how people react under certain situations. . . . I knew that going in and it doesn't really bother me."[30]

This knowing attitude characterizes several of the cast members interviewed for this chapter. Despite Bunim-Murray's assertion that *Road Rules* represents a willful relinquishing of producer control, cast members knew that the way they were portrayed and the way they lived, down to details of money, food, and shelter, were out of their control. Their contract stipulated that they permit the comprehensive documentation of the rhythm of their day-to-day lives in return for wages that they said amounted to less than minimum wage for the number of hours they spent on location and the gift of a VW Beetle at the end of the season. As in the case of online services like AllAdvantage.com, cast members were directly compensated for access to the rhythm of their daily lives. In this respect, reality TV shows serve as the perfect metaphor for the online economy: they directly exploit the work of being watched as a source of cheap labor. Furthermore they demonstrate just how gratifying being watched all the time can be. Pervasive surveillance is presented as one of the hip attributes of the contemporary world— a way not just to express oneself but an entrée into the world of wealth and celebrity. In this respect, the reality trend aligns itself with the efforts of the proponents of the new economy to destigmatize surveillance and reposition it as a form of convenience. We are not "working" for the marketers when we submit to pervasive monitoring on this account; rather, they are facilitating their slavish devotion to our every whim and fancy, in an ongoing attempt to serve us better.

SURVEILLANCE CHIC

Nevertheless, the attempt to encourage entry into the digital enclosure is complicated by the prevailing public mistrust of centralized forms of surveillance and by the conventional distinction between monitored labor time and "free" time. Exploiting the labor of being watched means subjecting free time to forms of surveillance traditionally associated with the workplace, centralized control, and top-down power. Public awareness of the attempt to extend the reach of surveillance by the Internet is reflected in surveys like the 1999 *Wall Street Journal*–NBC poll, which revealed that "privacy is the issue that concerns Americans most about the twenty-first century, ahead of overpopulation, racial tensions, and global warming."[31] Lawmakers have recognized the importance to the digital economy of assuaging these concerns. For example, in describing the benefits of proposed Federal privacy legislation, Senator Ernest Hollings of South Carolina emphasized its economic significance: "For many, privacy concerns represent the only remaining obstacle impeding consumers' full embrace of the Internet's ample commercial opportunities."[32] The problem with such legislation is that it threatens to dry up the flow of surveillance-generated information that is the lifeblood of the economy it seeks to promote.

The more promising approach, from a corporate perspective, has been to attempt to reposition surveillance as a form of consumer control. The popular reception of the Internet as a means of democratizing the one-way, top-down mass media model certainly works in favor of this attempt. The more we view this enclosure as a site for the potential revitalization of community and democracy, the more inviting it appears. Which is not to dismiss this potential outright, but rather to note how neatly it lines up with the promise forwarded by those who would use the potential of interactivity to rationalize the labor of being watched.

Indeed, in the case of advertising, customization and interactivity are offered as technological solutions to the problem that advertising itself created. Consumers are being blackmailed with the question "Wouldn't you rather be targeted by ads for products you're actually interested in than barraged by advertising for products that are completely irrelevant to your needs and wants?" Corporations hoping to avoid the stigma of Big Brother are further assisted by the legal culture in the United States, which has designated them as part of the "private" sector. If Big Brother famously represented the threat of totalitarian government intrusion, corporations can distance themselves by making an appeal to the fact that they're interested in providing goods and services, not in securing totalitarian domination. Furthermore, they can argue that the information they gather remains, in the legal sense, private. Otherwise, of course, they could not exploit its economic value.

The negative aspect of a campaign to champion the advantages of surveillance might be understood as the attempt to stigmatize any unreasonable fear of self-disclosure as a tacit admission that there is something to hide. Seen from this perspective, a program like *Road Rules* goes a long way toward promoting a subjective attitude of self-disclosure as a form of being honest to oneself and others. The version of reality that is valorized in such a program is one that can be achieved only through full disclosure. Significantly, the attitude that equates honesty with openness to surveillance is a common attribute of the *Road Rules* cast. Here's how cast member Josh put it: "I think I got chosen [to be on the show] because I kind of just wear my life on my sleeve—you know what I mean? I really don't have anything to hide from anybody, I don't have any skeletons, and I'm a real honest kind. They don't want somebody to get on the show that's going to be hiding what they're feeling or what they're thinking or whatnot."[33] Gladys, who was kicked off the show after a conflict with another cast member escalated to physical violence, echoed Josh's sentiments: "I'm very open with everything, whatever I've done in my life . . . and I've gotten over it. . . . I told them, 'Listen, I smoke weed all the time. I don't do any other drugs. I smoke weed. I drink. That's about it.'"[34] The producers make no secret of what they are looking for in the show and, consequently, what is valorized by the show. According to coproducer Bunim, "We try to cast people who have a natural openness."[35]

Interestingly, this message seems to have come through loud and clear to the thousands of teens and twenty-somethings who regularly turn up for Bunim-Murray's open casting calls. At the 17 November 2001 open casting call in New York City, I interviewed more than seventy-five aspiring reality TV cast members, almost all of whom said that their main strategy for getting on to the show was to be "open" and "honest," and just "be themselves." This was apparently the lesson that they had learned from watching the show—that what was valorized in the cast members was their honesty. All of the would-be cast members unsurprisingly expressed minimal reservations about being watched all the time, with many claiming that they had very little privacy in their lives, and that they would eventually become accustomed to being on camera all the time. According to the show's cast members, they weren't far off the mark. Holly of *Road Rules* fame noted that even though there were times when she felt more shy than other cast members, part of the experience of being on the program meant becoming not only accustomed to constant surveillance but almost reliant on it: "You honestly get used to it; it's just part of your everyday life. . . . I went through withdrawal for the two weeks after I got home. . . . I looked forward to that for so long, having my own time and my own space, and then when I got there, it was so lonely."[36]

Holly's personal experience echoes the eventual acceptance of *The Real World* format itself, the appeal of which, according to its producers, was not immediately evident. That meant in the beginning that cast members were not always so easy to come by as they are now, said producer Bunim: "Can you imagine approaching people on the subway and saying, 'How would you like to live in front of cameras eighteen hours a day, seven days a week?' People thought we were nuts."[37] In past years, of course there has been no shortage of applicants, and the producers no longer have to scour the streets and Laundromats for willing victims as they did for the first season—all they have to do is put out a casting call. It is worth considering this process of surveillance acclimatization within an even broader context: If Holly can grow reliant on—almost addicted to—being constantly under surveillance, if programs like *The Real World* can win popularity as accepted and legitimate formats wherein self-disclosure via surveillance is valorized as authentically "real," can the population as a whole be rendered dependent on perpetual monitoring? Perhaps the secret to making surveillance more acceptable is not to lessen its extent but, on the contrary, to universalize it—or, to borrow a metaphor from the folks at MIT's Media Lab, to make it as invisible and ubiquitous as oxygen (with the help of ever more sophisticated and unobtrusive monitoring technology).

In his survey of attitudes toward surveillance, Oscar Gandy notes that greater television exposure is associated with greater acceptance of the statement that: "The more businesses know about me, the better they can meet my individual needs."[38] Furthermore, increased exposure to television also correlates with greater acceptance of the view that, "The only people who are concerned about privacy are people with something to hide."[39] As in any survey research of this nature, the question of causality remains open. However, for the purposes of this paper, it is perhaps not insignificant to note that the attitude toward reality valorized by *The Real World* and *Road Rules* corresponds neatly to what Gandy defines as the corporate "hegemonic" attitude toward the panoptic sort: the delegitimation of privacy concerns and the presentation of corporate surveillance as beneficial to the consumer.

The positive benefits of the type of "reality" made available through surveillance television are twofold. First, as noted earlier, control over reality is ostensibly ceded by proxy to the audience. The audience reclaims a modicum of participation in the production process via its representatives: the chosen few selected to join the cast. This participation parallels the participation of consumers in an interactive economy in which consumer labor is figured as the resuscitation of creative labor—of the possibility that, to paraphrase Marx, the product of the worker's activity can also be the *object* of that activity.[40] The promise of interactivity within the sphere of e-commerce is that labor and life activity are reunited—that the labor of customized consumption can offer the fulfillment of creative life activity.

This promise is recapitulated by the promise of the real in reality TV: that surveillance provides a certain guarantee of authenticity, and that this authenticity becomes a process of self-expression, self-realization, and self-validation. Holly, for example, describes the television episodes in which she appears as a kind of journal that allows her to share her experience with her friends and family, as well as the general viewing public: "I'd gone and had this experience, but I could never describe the things I saw, the things I did, and the feelings I felt to everyone. And then you think, oh, wait, they're going to see it on TV. . . . And that's the whole point about validation. It [being on *Road Rules*] validates what you did and why you were there."[41]

One of the common themes that emerged from the interviews with cast members (and from their quotes in news accounts) was that being on the show served as a learning experience—a means of getting in touch with themselves and others. Josh, for example, described the show as a means of testing his self-knowledge—knowledge cultivated during a winter retreat in a cabin in the Colorado mountains before joining the *Road Rules* cast: "What I got out of the show is that all of the characteristics that I figured out about myself were put to the test throughout the show during certain situations. . . . And everything that I had come to the conclusion on while living in Colorado was held true by the tests that were presented to me. . . . So I came away from the show being even more confident in who I am."[42] Rebecca, who was on the 1997 *Real World* cast in Atlanta, similarly described being on the show as an exercise in self-discovery: "I'm so much more open-minded than I ever have been. . . . Seeing that first show, it's amazing how much you have changed."[43]

This appeal to the therapeutic potential of surveillance recurred in the first U.S. season of *Big Brother*, which made personal growth one of its weekly themes, thanks to its reliance on celebrity doctor Drew Pinsky (of *Loveline* fame) as the show's "health and relationship expert." Every week, during the live, hour-long show, Pinsky would describe how the cast members were being transformed by their *Big Brother* experience. Typical of Pinsky's approach was his assessment of the way in which Jordan, a twenty-seven-year-old exotic dancer from Minneapolis, reacted to the fact that she had been nominated for banishment by her housemates: "She told us a couple of nights ago [during a conversation with her housemates] she's come to learn and change, and God bless her, she has. . . . She's willing to be more honest . . . to look at her feelings more honestly and fess up to them."[44] Pinsky's comments tended to equate the willingness to be "open" on camera (to submit oneself to comprehensive monitoring) with "being real," and, consequently, with personal growth. Thus, he praised those houseguests who, over time, "opened up" in front of the camera—not just for getting into the spirit of the show, but for demonstrating signs of personal growth. If, as Lears[45] argues, the promise of personal growth and authentic experience served as an advertising strategy that capitalized on a waning sense of reality that accompanied the abstraction of mass society, Pinsky's comments advertise the benefits of surveillance by celebrating the ostensibly therapeutic benefits of the access to "reality" it provides.

Furthermore, Pinsky argues that the show's benefits extended to its viewers: "We are all the ones doing the watching . . . and we do that because we want to learn something about ourselves, and we want to learn something about other people."[46] This observation invites the show's audience to look at the cast not only as experimental subjects, but as people with whom to identify. For viewers, learning about the houseguests (who serve as a representative sample of the "real" population) means learning about themselves. As cast member Jamie put it in a post-season interview, "The cool thing about 'Big Brother,' [is that] the 10 people in the house came from all walks of life and everyone . . . the fans can probably identify with someone on the show and maybe they can learn."[47] The general value of self-disclosure as a form of personal growth was highlighted not just by the producers and the show's host, who asked every houseguest how they had been changed by their *Big Brother* experience, but by the houseguests themselves. As Cassandra put it during a heart-to-heart chat with Brittany, who was worried about how she was getting along with the other houseguests, "Everyone here is on a journey to learn about themselves."[48] Moreover, to hear the houseguests tell it, whether they won the cash prize or not, the journey was a successful one. Even Will, the first guest to be kicked off (after two weeks), claimed not only that he learned about himself, but that the show had served as a public forum to test the courage of his convictions: "All life experiences have some influence on you, so this was one that allowed me to get a feel for the . . . community and how they view my opinions."[49] Crucial to the account of their time in the *Big Brother* house was the role of the monitoring gaze in forcing the houseguests to take responsibility for their actions. Cassandra, for example, likened the presence of the cameras to a maternal gaze: "I was always aware of the camera presence, but I always was concerned about if I were on the outside . . . and if my mother could see me, would she be upset with what I'm doing. So the camera for me was like my mom's eye."[50]

Josh, a former model, described having an audience as a way of making himself aware of the consequences of his own behavior. By the end of the show's run, he told the host, Julie Chen, "Living in here has made me a better person in the sense that I can treat people the way I've always wanted to treat them. . . . I think I can walk out of here and be a better person in society and help people out better."[51] This assessment of the benefits of being watched explains his remark to Brittany, several weeks earlier, after being confronted by her and two of the other women in the house for being a flirt: "Everyone should have an audience"— presumably to help them learn about themselves and to keep them honest.[52] Rather than being described as an invasion of privacy or as an oppressive form of manipulation, the process of being watched all the time was positioned, in these accounts, as a challenge (e.g., like an Outward Bound adventure) that forced cast members to learn about themselves and to develop as individuals. This sentiment was pervasive throughout the course of the show and in the postseason interviews in which cast members participated. For example, Jamie, a veteran of beauty pageants who was quite accustomed to the limelight and who was also the houseguest who spent the most time talking about the value of the *Big Brother* "experience," described her time on the show as follows: "For the first time, I'm learning how to be in a group, and I'm feeling more comfortable. This is like challenging all your traits and standards, but it's challenging them in the public eye. You can't not be you."[53] Cassandra also repeatedly described her experience with twenty-four-hour surveillance as a personal challenge: "I was looking for something that was a challenge for me and I certainly found it. I grew a lot from this. . . . I learned a lot about myself."[54]

Eddie, the grand prize winner, fittingly noted that he not only learned from his time on the show but developed a respect for the technological innovations that made his brush with celebrity possible: "I learned a newfound love and respect for my family and learned a new appreciation for modern technology."[55] Indeed, the technology that made it possible for Eddie to be watched twenty-four hours a day around the world helped him earn $500,000 without leaving the (highly public) privacy of his home. What better endorsement for the advantage and convenience of pervasive surveillance? Not only does the monitoring process allow one to learn about oneself—to express one's unique individuality—not only does it serve as a forum for self-expression—a way to "get one's message out to the world," but it also provides tangible economic benefits.

In short, willing subjection to surveillance on the *Big Brother* show comes to serve as a demonstration of the strength of one's self image—of one's comfort level with oneself. Being "real" was a proof of honesty, and the persistent gaze of the camera provided one way of guaranteeing that "reality." Furthermore, in a teeming society wherein one's actions often go unnoticed by others, the implication is that the reality of those actions can be validated if they are recorded and broadcast—they become more real to oneself to the extent that they become real for others. Surveillance is a kind of institutionally ratified individuation: it provides the guarantee of the authenticity of one's uniqueness. Coproducer Jon Murray believes that people who want to be on the show are seeking this kind of validation: "I think there is a feeling that this is a very complex global world, that people want to count, they want to feel like they're having some kind of impact. . . . You know when you're at a college campus and you're waiting in those long lines to register for classes, and when as a freshman you're sitting in a lecture hall with 400 other kids, it's very easy to feel like you're sort of the smallest cog in the wheel, and I think this idea of being able to be on one of these shows and have your opinion heard by your peers in a large way is very exciting."[56]

CONCLUSION

The paradox of a surveillance-based economy is that it pretends to individuals that they count—that they are worthy of individual attention—even though all it really wants to do is count them—to plug their vital statistics into a marketing algorithm. Even Winston Smith must have had the illusion that, as subdued and circumspect as he was, he counted as enough of a threat to warrant the mobilization of Big Brother's extensive resources against his petty subversions. Smith, of course, was not, in himself, a threat, merely one more ruse for the proliferation of power. Similarly, a television show like *The Real World* although it implicitly promises the democratization of creative control and productive power, serves also as a form of acclimatization to an emerging economic regime predicated on increasingly unequal access to and control over information. It also validates the pervasive surveillance of the rhythm of day-to-day life as a contemporary commonplace—a form of convenience and entertainment. The celebrity status attained by participants on the show highlights the promise that authentication via surveillance has its tangible rewards. Big Brother's gaze no longer symbolizes the threat of mass homogeneity but the promise of a paradoxical mass individuation.

This is a promise that needs to be handled very carefully. On the one hand, it invokes a familiar critique of a society in which authentic individuality has been subordinated to the dictates of mass production and the mass media. It further offers a critique of the passive spectatorship associated with the refeudalization of the public sphere. But at the same time, the promise remains complicit with an emerging paradigm of mass customization that rehabilitates individuation only to commodify it. As labor power before it, personal information can be extracted from consumers only to be sold back to them in a congealed commodity form. This ambivalence in the promise of mass customization recapitulates an oft-noted ambivalence in the political potential of new information technologies in general.

However, the foregoing discussion of mass customization suggests that our notion of ambivalence itself must be modified. The binary distinction between a passive, refeudalized public sphere and active (or interactive) revitalized politics is outdated. Too often, the critique of the mass media is accompanied by an uncritical celebration of the inherently progressive virtues of participation. This celebration manifests itself in the equation of participation with democratization. The

Gemeinschaft nostalgia that characterizes much of the writing on media and democracy is particularly prevalent in Habermas-inspired discussions of a pre–mass
media public sphere. Typical of such approaches is James Carey's description of
the deterioration of public life that accompanied the rise of a mass commercial
press which, "no longer facilitated or animated a public conversation. . . . It informed a passive and privatized group of citizens who participated in politics
through the press."[57] The notion of public participation is central to Habermas's
own account of the refeudalization of the public sphere: "a public of citizens that
had disintegrated as a public was reduced by publicist means to such a position
that it could be claimed for the legitimation of political compromises without participating in effective decisions or being in the least capable of such participation."[58] This instrumental use of publicist means represents the co-optation of the
language of publicity, as Peters observes: "In writings by theorists such as Jeremy
Bentham . . . and John Stuart Mill . . . 'publicity' meant openness of discussion and
commerce as well as popular access to government. Today publicity only suggests
public relations."[59] Peters goes on to argue that this semantic transformation parallels Habermas's description of the transformation from "critical participation" to
"consumerist manipulation."[60] The linkage that is called into question in the era of
new media interactivity is implicit in the term *critical participation*—that participation promotes democratization. It is important to understand the appropriation
of the critique of the mass media elaborated above by the deployment of the promise of participation in the interactive economy. In some sense, this critique helps
lay the foundations for the marketing of the interactive economy, which provides
a market solution to the depredations of mass society. Are the mass media too uni-
vocal? The Internet allows audiences to answer back. Are homogenized mass-
produced goods foisted on the consumer? Mass customization will allow consumers to design products and services to fit their individual needs. Does mass
production deskill the workforce? In the digital era, workers will have to *constantly* retrain themselves and upgrade their skills in order to compete in the increasingly fluid labor market. Does mass society promote passive consumption?
The interactive economy will revitalize active participation.

   Television shows like *The Real World* suggest that new media offer a third possibility between the passive evisceration of publicity as spectacle and the revitalization of democracy through the reclamation of publicity as public debate. This
third possibility is a hybrid combination: the democratization of publicity *as* public relations. In a world in which the public sphere has been debilitated to the extent that publicity is reconfigured as spectacle, this third alternative ought not to
come as a surprising one. The democratizing promise offered by the Internet in the
era of e-commerce is not that everyone will be able to participate in a revitalized
public sphere but that everyone will be able to participate in politics as celebrity.
No longer will it just be the president whose private life is subjected to micro-
scopic examination and "public" debate. Now it will be the private life of the person on the street—of anyone who trains the webcam on him- or herself—or any-

one who makes the final casting call for *The Real World*. If politics has been reduced to public relations, its democratization results not in a repoliticized public sphere but in equal access to celebrity as self-promotion (public relations). Providing access to the means of publicity makes it possible for everyone to actively participate in self-commodification. This is the pessimistic conclusion drawn by Baudrillard in his discussion of reality TV (a discussion that anticipated both *Big Brother* and the webcam trend): "We are exposed to the instantaneous retransmission of all our facts and gestures on whatever channel. We would have experienced this before as police control. Today it is just like an advertising promotion."[61] Webcasters, like reality TV cast members, aren't rehabilitating the political character of publicity but are, paradoxically, democratizing publicity as celebrity. As Ana Voog, who notes on her FAQ page that she hates politics, puts it, "I guess it was my goal for a while, and it still is my goal, to become an icon."[62] This is the language not of Gramsci but of Hollywood Boulevard. Victoria, one of the inhabitants of the Tampa, Florida–based webcam site VoyeurDorm, describes her webcam work as a way to get a foot in the door of the entertainment industry: "This is just an everyday movie. . . . I'm in a movie every single day of my life, and that's how I look at it. . . . Like I'm an actress every single day."[63] Consider, also, the gushing enthusiasm of a seventeen-year-old girl who drove several hours to get a chance to be one of the audience members interviewed live on camera by the host of MTV's *TRL* show: "It's like, 8 zillion people watch this show, and I get to advertise myself."[64] Indeed, many of the young people who stood in line for hours in New York City to audition for *The Real World* in the fall of 2001 told me the same thing: their agenda was a combination of self-discovery and self-promotion, and, at times, self-discovery through self-promotion. Another way to describe this combination is as willing self-promotion, or what Reginald Whitaker has described as voluntary submission to the "participatory panopticon."[65] If politics has been reduced to consumerism, self-expression has been reduced to marketing oneself, a reduction that falls only one step short of the friction-free fantasy that, through submission to surveillance, consumers will perform the work necessary not just to market themselves but to market *to* themselves.

The lesson of reality TV for media critics is that a two-way, participatory medium is by no means an inherently progressive one. And this is not just because of imbalances in the flow of information, but also because of the economic value of consumer participation. The more willing consumers are to send information about themselves "upstream," the better for those companies in a position to exploit such information. Thus, approaches to new media that celebrate the progressive aspect of interactivity run the danger of co-optation by marketing strategies that appeal to the democratic potential of the Internet. Programs like *The Real World* reinforce that marketing strategy by equating self-disclosure with freedom and authenticity. *The Real World* is a place, in other words, where people can individuate themselves—can differentiate themselves from the mass—by willing submission to pervasive surveillance. This real world, of course, is precisely the world imagined by the architects of mass customization. Reality becomes mass customized just as the online economy starts to become a reality.

NOTES

1. Holly, personal interview with the author, 12 November 1999.

2. Joshua Meyrowitz, "Mediating Communication: What Happens?" in *Questioning the Media: A critical Introduction*, ed. John Downing, Ali Mohammadi, and Annabelle Sreberny-Mohammadi (London: Sage, 1995).

3. Sut Jhally and Bill Livant "Watching as Working: The Valorization of Audience Consciousness," *Journal of Communication* 36, no, 3 (1986); Dallas Smythe, *Dependency Road: Communications, Capitalism, Consciousness, and Canada* (Toronto: Ablex, 1981). Without getting into the specifics of what might count as labor in a materialist analysis, it seems sufficient for the current argument to note that marketers and advertisers are willing to pay to ensure that the activity of watching ads takes place. Indeed, as noted earlier, they are even willing to pay audiences directly. There is some question as to what precisely they are paying for, although I would argue that is one more input into the creation of the final commodity, whose attributes include not just its physical qualities but the reputation of these qualities (and the extent to which the desired reputation is known to consumers). This is why, for example, brand names themselves are assigned values in the business world, even though they are not material objects. When it comes to the work of being watched, there is little doubt, once again, that whatever the debates going on in the world of orthodox materialism, the business world understands this as work that generates demographic commodities to be bought and sold. This recognition is perhaps inimical to a hypostasized distinction between consumption and production proper, but not to the somewhat more nuanced reading of the critique of political economy outlined by David Harvey (in *Limits to Capital* [Oxford: Blackwell, 1982]). Following Marx, Harvey argues not just that production and consumption exist in "a mediating relationship to each other," but that "production and consumption relate to each other so that 'each of them creates the other in completing itself, and creates itself as the other'" (80). Furthermore, "consumption 'as need' is itself an intrinsic moment of production when set within the context of a process of social reproduction. . . . [V]alue must be understood in terms of the underlying unity of production and consumption" (81). The rationalization of consumption and that of production complement and complete one another. Entry into the digital enclosure allows for the former process to catch up with the latter.

4. Taylor, as quoted in Harry Braverman, *Labor and Monopoly Capital* (New York: Monthly Review Press, 1974), 104.

5. Sut Jhally and Bill Livant, "Watching as Working: The Valorization of Audience Consciousness," *Journal of Communication* 36, no. 3 (1986): 125.

6. Andy Serwer "What Do These Guys Know about the Internet?" *Fortune*, 9 October 2000, 112.

7. As of this writing, *The Runner*, which had been purchased by ABC, was shelved in the wake of the 11 September terrorist attacks, presumably because the idea of a nationwide manhunt seemed somewhat less entertaining—and perhaps a bit too close to what was taking place in reality—in the ensuing months.

8. Jhally and Livant, "Watching as Working," 125.

9. Jhally and Livant, "Watching as Working."

10. Anthony Giddens, *A Contemporary Critique of Historical Materialism* (Berkeley: University of California Press, 1981), 137.

11. Bill Gates, *The Road Ahead* (New York: Penguin, 1996), 194–95.

12. Gates, *The Road Ahead*, 188.

13. Gates, *The Road Ahead*, 191.

14. Doug Bedell, "FTC to Survey E-commerce Sites on How They Use Customers' Data," *Dallas Morning News*, 2 March 2000, 1F.

15. Wendy Grossman, "Shock of the New for Amazon Customers," *Daily Telegraph* (London), 26 October 2000, 70.

16. Specifically, Babbage writes that "the master manufacturer, by dividing the work to be executed into different processes, each requiring different degrees of skill or force, can purchase exactly that precise quantity of both which is necessary for each process; whereas if the whole work were executed by one workman, that person must possess sufficient skill to perform the most difficult, and sufficient strength to execute the most laborious, of the operations into which the art is divided" (as quoted in Braverman, *Labor and Monopoly Capital*, 79–80). It is perhaps not a coincidence that Babbage, credited with the invention of the first computer, anticipated the forms of rationalization to which his device would eventually contribute.

17. Simon Garfinkel, *Database Nation: The Death of Privacy in the 21st Century* (Cambridge: O'Reilly, 2000), 11.

18. Holly, personal interview with the author, 12 November 1999.

19. Drew Jubera, "Entering the Real World," *Atlanta Journal and Constitution*, 12 June 2000, 1C.

20. Jon Murray, telephone interview with the author, 20 October 1999.

21. Neal Justin, "Reality Bits: The Most Compelling New TV Soaps Are All about the Ordinary Days of Our Lives. Ready for Your Closeup?" *Minneapolis Star Tribune*, 22 June 1998, 1E.

22. Paul Farhi, "The Spin on "Real World," Cast Members Say the MTV Show Adds Its Own Spice to a Duller Daily Life," *Washington Post*, 4 November 1999, C1.

23. Murray, telephone interview with the author, 20 October 1999.

24. Richard Heft, "Cues from the Real World," *Glasgow Herald*, 17 October 1998, 14.

25. Farhi, "The Spin on 'Real World,'" C1.

26. Farhi, "The Spin on 'Real World.'"

27. Sharkey, "Living in 'The Real World': Entering Its Sixth Season, MTV's Video-verite Series Has Established Its Own Brand of Show," *Mediaweek*, 1997 July 21, 17.

28. Marc Weingarten, "MTV Moves the "Real" Fishbowl to Honolulu," *Los Angeles Times*, 14 June 1999, F2.

29. Sarah, telephone interview with the author, 4 December 1999.

30. Josh, telephone interview with the author, 4 December 1999.

31. Toby Lester, "The Reinvention of Privacy," *Atlantic Monthly* (March 2001): 27. These results, of course, predate the growing acceptance of government surveillance associated with war against terrorism.

32. Stephan Labaton, "U.S. Is Said to Seek New Law to Bolster Privacy on Internet," *New York Times*, 20 May 2000, A1.

33. Josh, telephone interview with the author, 4 December 1999.

34. Gladys, telephone interview with the author, 5 December 1999.

35. Marc Weingarten, "MTV Moves the 'Real' Fishbowl to Honolulu," *Los Angeles Times*, 14 June 1999, F2.

36. Holly, personal interview with the author, 12 November 1999.

37. Peter Brownfield, "Reality-Based TV Raises Questions about Privacy," *Buffalo News*, 28 June 1998, 2.

38. Oscar Gandy, *The Panoptic Sort: A Political Economy of Personal Information* (Boulder, Colo.: Westview, 1993), 165.

39. Gandy, *The Panoptic Sort*, 165.

40. David McLellan, *Karl Marx: Selected Writings* (Oxford: Oxford University Press, 1977), 250.

41. Holly, personal interview with the author, 12 November 1999.

42. Josh, telephone interview with the author, 4 December 1999.

43. Tim Klass, "'Real' Spotlight Sometimes Glowed, Glared," *San Diego Union-Tribune*, 17 June 1998, E-1.

44. *Big Brother*, WKNC, Denver, 20 July 2000.

45. T. J. Jackson Lears, "From Salvation to Self-Realization," in *The Culture of Consumption*, ed. Richard Fox and T. J. Jackson Lears (New York: Pantheon, 1983).

46. *Big Brother*, WKNC, Denver, 29 September 2000.

47. Available at www.hand-quilted-fabric-arts.com/bb (accessed 14 January 2003).

48. *Big Brother*, WKNC, Denver, 23 August 2000.

49. *Big Brother*, WKNC, Denver, 29 September 2000.

50. *Big Brother*, WKNC, Denver, 13 September 2000.

51. *Big Brother*, WKNC, Denver, 29 September 2000.

52. *Big Brother*, WKNC, Denver, 16 August 2000.

53. *Big Brother*, WKNC, Denver, 23 August 2000.

54. *Big Brother*, WKNC, Denver, 13 September 2000.

55. Eddie, telephone interview with the author, 16 January 2001.

56. Jon Murray, telephone interview with the author, 20 October 1999.

57. James Carey, "The Press, Public Opinion, and Public Discourse," in *Public Opinion and the Communication of Consent*, ed. Theodor L. Glasser and C. T. Salmon (New York: Guilford, 1995), 379.

58. Jürgen Habermas, *The Philosophical Discourse of Modernity* (Cambridge, Mass.: MIT Press, 1996), 221.

59. John Durham Peters, "Distrust of Representation: Habermas on the Public Sphere," *Media, Culture and Society* 15 (1993): 543.

60. Peters, "Distrust of Representation," 543.

61. Jean Baudrillard, "The Virtual Illusion: Or the Automatic Writing of the World," *Theory, Culture & Society*, 12 (1995): 97.

62. *MSNBC Reports*, "Look at Me! The Webcam Explosion," MSNBC, 29 August 2000.

63. *MSNBC Reports*, "Look at Me!"

64. George Myers, "As Seen on TV in Video Age, Everyone Wants to Get into the Act," *Columbus Dispatch*, 2000 March 5, 1A.

65. Reginald Whitaker, *The End of Privacy: How Total Surveillance Is Becoming a Reality* (New York: New Press, 1999).

Chapter Five

Access to the Real

The reality TV show that most rigorously adhered to the promise of portraying unedited access to the mundane daily routine of its cast members was the first season of the U.S. version of *Big Brother*. The previous chapters have largely skirted the question of the promise of the real, focusing instead on the emerging economic function of surveillance and the rehabilitation of its pop culture portrayal. This chapter and the following one will attempt to explore in more detail the status of the contrived reality characteristic of the genre and the ways in which viewers respond to and interpret the promise of access to surveillance-based reality.

The U.S. version of *Big Brother* was not, it should be noted, a particularly interesting show. It attracted a fair amount of viewer attention early on, not least because it piggy-backed on the success of *Survivor*, with which it briefly overlapped. However, it soon became clear that *Big Brother* was, in some sense, much more "real": the content was built around ten people living in a bland, prefabricated home, with no media access, no books, and not much to do all day. The net result was a rather boring show about a desperately bored group of people that played a little bit like a jailhouse drama, minus the drama; a portrayal of what it would be liked to be locked up all day, just trying to figure out how to pass the time until parole. This blunt and boring "realism" of *Big Brother*, combined with the fact that, at least during the first season, anyone with Internet access could watch the live feeds from several cameras in the house, enabled the show to approach the "ideal type" of its particular subgenre: that of the comprehensive documentation of the mundane rhythms of daily life. It is the realism of the show, and the way this was interpreted by both fans and cast members, that serves as a starting point for the discussion of the deployment of the promise of reality.

THE RETURN OF *BIG BROTHER*

The premise of the U.S. version of *Big Brother*, as outlined in its webpage, was that ten contestants, representing "a cross-section of personalities, ethnicities, geographies, and sexual orientations," would live together in a house constructed by the producers on a lot in Studio City, California.[1] To win the show's cash prizes, contestants agreed not to leave the house and its small, attached garden until they were voted out by members of the audience. Each week, the "houseguests"—as the show's producers called them—were allowed to nominate two of their housemates to be banished. The two or more houseguests who received the highest number of nominations were then selected for potential banishment. Throughout the following week, viewers were urged to phone in their vote for who should be expelled—at a cost of $0.99 cents per call. A week after the nominations were announced, one houseguest was selected to leave based on the results of the audience vote. The banishment process continued until there were only three houseguests left, and the audience decided who would win the first-, second-, and third-place prizes of $500,000, $100,000, and $50,000.

Within the *Big Brother* house, contact with the outside world was limited; there were no phones, televisions, radios, or computers in the house, which the webpage described as a "back-to-basics" environment.[2] Houseguests were told they would have to "grow their own vegetables, bake their own bread, and tend a flock of chickens. Even the hot water [was] rationed."[3] With the emphasis on gardening, on tending the chickens, and so on, the *Big Brother* house hearkened back to the era of handicraft-based community. Indeed, the paradoxical absence of the mass media (in a show created by and for these media) was described as a return not only to face-to-face community but as an incitation to participatory forms of entertainment. The houseguests, as the show's host, Julie Chen, observed in the premier episode, had to find ways of entertaining themselves rather than relying on the products of the entertainment industry. Interestingly, their ability to do so would determine the fate of yet another product of the culture industry. The *Big Brother* house thus became a mass media experiment in watching people deprived of the mass media. The house was not completely back-to-basics, of course; it was wired with remote-controlled cameras and microphones. Behind the one-way mirrors that lined every room (including the bathroom) were studios that housed the videographers who worked around the clock supplementing the footage from automated cameras in the corners of the house and in its yard. There were no spaces where houseguests could escape the watchful electronic gaze of the video cameras. Even when they turned off the lights, the cast members' nocturnal activities were monitored by "night-vision" cameras, and the live microphones captured their snoring and rustling. There was only one place where the houseguests could escape each other: a closet-sized room, painted entirely red, where they could speak directly to (and be interrogated by) the producers, who referred to themselves collectively as "Big Brother." The nominations for banishment were conducted in the Red Room, as were occasional interrogations with houseguests who seemed to be engaged in conflicts or potential amorous relationships with their roommates (in other words, when budding plot lines needed to be developed).

The houseguests were not, moreover, left entirely to their own devices. In order to introduce tension and a modicum of drama into the house, the producers assigned them daily and weekly challenges, ranging from requiring them to answer trivia questions about each other to completing a jigsaw puzzle and learning how to juggle. The challenges resulted in prizes and penalties, the most significant of which was the loss of grocery money to buy necessities that weren't provided by the garden and the chickens. As the show dragged on, and it became apparent that viewers weren't going to flock to the television in record numbers to watch a group of bored, restless inmates complete a jigsaw puzzle, the producers attempted to come up with ways of inciting drama in the house by allowing the cast some minimal contact with the outside world, including phone calls to loved ones, a meeting with a Hollywood casting director, and even a trip to the Emmy Awards for one houseguest. The producers even offered on one occasion to pay $50,000 to any houseguest who would volunteer to leave so they could replace him or her with a more dynamic character (the offer was refused). The stated goal of the challenges, of the limitations on hot water and groceries, and of various other instigations contrived by the producers, was to create an atmosphere that would force the houseguests into negotiating stressful situations and potential conflicts. The intent was ostensibly anthropological and socially therapeutic, according to the show's producers: "*Big Brother* will capture emotions, inspire discussions on human behavior and confront long-held opinions on privacy."[4] The behavior of humans in their natural habitat was to be placed on display for the purpose of public contemplation, even edification. In keeping with this line of reasoning, the official website of the show's second-place winner, Josh, described the show as "an experiment in human behavior and strategic planning."[5]

Unlike other reality shows of its kind, including both *The Real World* and *Survivor*, *Big Brother* aired five days a week, concurrently with the time the contestants were in the house. This left little time for editing, which was reflected in the half-hour and hour-long segments that aired nightly. *Survivor*, *The Real World*, and even *An American Family* were all shot in advance and then edited into weekly hour or half-hour segments. In the case of *Big Brother*, moreover, the online feeds were aired largely unedited, but they were subject to a twelve-second delay, and were continually monitored by AOL representatives to ensure that nothing offensive to the sensibilities of family viewers would go out over the Internet.[6]

As the weeks passed, and it became clear that *Big Brother* was, in some ways, a bigger hit online than on television, the producers began to incorporate material taken from the website into the show. Thus, the site offered a disclaimer similar to that for the houseguests, allowing *Big Brother* the right to broadcast postings to the site. The website became a monitored space not dissimilar to that of the *Big Brother* house, providing television content in the form of the interactions of the "real people" who visited the site. Moreover, the site hosted polls and contests that allowed viewers to name their favorite houseguests, to write haiku and short stories about the house, and thereby to express their reactions to the show "creatively" and interactively. The distinguishing element of *Big Brother* was that the surveillance of the houseguests was, for the period they were on the show, comprehensive. The premise of the show was that the cast members lived in a panopticon—not everything they were doing was necessarily taped and watched, but they had to live with the knowledge that at any moment, their words and actions could be taped for broadcast and might be going out live over the Internet.

GETTING REAL

Two formal developments that distinguish *Big Brother* from other programs in the genre are of central importance to a consideration of its relationship to the digital enclosure. The first was the adoption of a reflexive style that incorporated the production process itself. The second was the integration of the Internet in a manner that promised access to the site of production. These developments clearly complemented each other; both ostensibly shattered the fourth wall and invited the viewers behind the scenes. In this sense, the *Big Brother* series took the promise of the real a step further than shows like MTV's *The Real World* and *An American Family*, both of which maintained the conventions of observational documentary by keeping the producers, videographers, and cameras out of the frame. If previous reality shows staked a claim to reality by promising to show the unscripted interactions of real people, *Big Brother* went one step further by revealing the process whereby these interactions were documented. The cameras became characters in the show itself—serving in some cases as the focus of the shot, especially when it became clear that cast members were reacting to or discussing the fact that they were being filmed.

Several early episodes featured a clip in which Jordan, a twenty-seven-year-old exotic dancer from Minneapolis, experimented with a remote control camera, changing directions as she walked down a corridor in order to watch the camera follow her every move. The sound track for the shot was provided by the whine of the servomechanism that moved the camera and by Jordan's assessment of the situation: "Oh, that's creepy." One of the other oft-repeated clips featured the eventual winner, Eddie, talking directly to the camera as he chewed on a slice of pizza, asking the technician behind the scenes if he wanted a bite. When the remote-controlled camera started to turn away from him, Eddie moved to block it, saying, "Look at me when I'm talking to you."[7] This form of direct reference and direct address to the camera is conspicuously absent from shows like *Survivor* and *The Real World*. Perhaps one other detail highlights this difference between *The Real World* and the first season of *Big Brother*: when cast members in the *Big Brother* house entered the Red Room for their confessional moments with producers, one framing shot included the lens of the camera to which they were speaking, and the audio track included the voice of the producer. In *The Real World* confessional, by contrast, the framing shot is a straight headshot, with no camera in sight, and viewers never hear the voice or see a trace of the invisible producer. Rather, they are positioned as the invisible viewer, directly spying on the cast members.

Supplementing the *Big Brother* claim to realism was the deployment of the Internet by the program's producers. On one level, this deployment simply furthered the promise of access to the real. It pushed the definition of reality TV beyond that of previous reality formats by providing twenty-four-hour live video and audio feeds from the *Big Brother* compound for the entire run of the show. Not only was the *Big Brother* version of reality unscripted, undirected, and unacted, it was also, at least online, unedited; a promise that none of the other reality shows could make. This additional step in the deployment of the promise of reality created an interesting tension in the response of viewers. On the one hand, many of them said the twenty-four-hour feeds helped them to really get to know the houseguests, and thereby brought them one step closer to the reality of the *Big Brother* house. This access to reality seemed to underwrite the frequent claim by fans that they liked the show precisely because it was less contrived than other prime-time programs. On the other hand, the access to the twenty-four-hour feeds allowed viewers to play the Internet off against the television show, arguing that their direct access to the *Big Brother* house allowed them to see just how manipulative the television show was. In this respect, the promise of "behind-the-scenes" access catered to a certain sense of savviness: it offered to demonstrate to viewers the contrivance behind the show's claim to realism.

The appeal of the real, in this context, becomes the promise of access to the reality of manipulation, which the jaded viewers already knew to be the reality of entertainment programming (and, arguably, all commercial programming). The interesting result was the demonstration of the way in which this promise could be effectively commodified, as the *Big Brother* series, among others, demonstrates. This fact has some interesting implications for those strains of critical media theory that work to expose and denaturalize the way in which media events are framed, for it suggests that denaturalization doesn't necessarily contest the media's social power to frame the issues. Rather, the process of denaturalization is more ambiguous than some of its celebrants suggest. On the one hand, the denaturalization of production, at least from the perspective of ideology critique, seems to rely on a socially progressive promise. This promise is rehearsed by those strands of media theory and activism exemplified by media watchdog groups like FAIR (Fairness and Accuracy in Reporting) and writers including Ben Bagdikian, David Barsamian, Edward Herman, and Noam Chomsky, who work to demonstrate the ways in which the media frame stories according to the interests of dominant sectors of society.[8] Demystification is also the goal of those forms of cultural studies and critical sociology that demonstrate how media artifacts participate in the reproduction of capitalist social relations. The implicit hope is that the denaturalization of the production process—the foregrounding of the constructed nature of media truths—will help challenge what media scholar Nick Couldry calls its "symbolic power."[9] He describes this power in terms of "an asymmetry in people's ability to constitute social reality itself. As James Carey has argued, 'reality is a scarce resource'; 'the fundamental form of power is the power to define, allocate and display this resource.'"[10]

Highlighting the way in which such power is monopolized and exercised, on this account, may help to delegitimize it. On the other hand, as Couldry notes, there is plenty of evidence—not least in the realm of reality TV—to suggest that the process of denaturalization can be absorbed, and indeed exploited by the media industry, a theme that will be taken up in more depth in later chapters. Couldry specifically invokes the example of reality TV in his discussion: On the one hand, such programming has the potential to demystify the production process by blurring the boundary that separates the privileged site of production from "real" people. On the other, he notes that "it could be argued that such programmes, by affirming television as the site for watching such 'reality' footage . . . , simply extend the ambit of the media's 'naming' authority; they legitimate television as a ritual form of public surveillance."[11] At the same time, they perform the double gesture of providing limited forms of access without ceding control. The result is a form of demystification that is not at all empowering: the manipulative character of prime-time programming is conceded and simultaneously portrayed as a given and unchangeable feature of the medium. The result is an odd kind of ideology critique that I explore in more depth in chapter 8: the power of media elites is both exposed and naturalized.

Participatory Reality

The *Big Brother* format pushes the promise of access to reality further not just by highlighting the production process and providing access to unedited footage, but also through its incorporation of audience participation. It offers to include viewers not just by proxy, but directly, based on their participation in web-based forums and contests. If, as producer Jon Murray suggests, shows like MTV's *The Real World*, are predicated in part on the promise that the viewers can participate vicariously through their identification with the "real" people who make up the cast, *Big Brother* certainly invokes the same promise. At the same time, the format does more than offer the promise of indirect or vicarious participation. Via the Internet, it makes the promise direct: you, the viewer, can participate right now. Just go to Big-Brother2000.com and post your comments, register your opinion in the polls, and enter your haiku in a contest that might lead to your work being read on the air.

The Internet component of the show bolsters access to the real behind the fiction by inviting viewers into a space of comprehensive surveillance: one from which they can gain the fullest view of the houseguests and one that functions at the same time as a form of comprehensive surveillance of the viewers themselves, whose preferences and responses are exhaustively tapped and mined. In this respect, the promise of reality functions as an incentive to enter into the digital enclosure — and to, in turn, offer oneself up as an element of that reality, as a *participant* in it. Interactivity as participation is offered as a means of undoing the abstraction of mass society: of pulling back the wizard's curtain.

During the airing of the first season of *Big Brother*, I spent at least four hours a week (often more) in the live chat rooms, conversing with fans and gathering transcripts of online discussion about the show. I also collected posts from the bulletin board on the official *Big Brother* website. The resulting transcripts totaled well over a thousand pages of comments, chat, praise, and rants. During the first season of *Survivor* in 2000, I also sent letters to the editor to newspapers across the country asking for reality TV viewers to send their thoughts about the appeal of reality TV to me, either electronically or by mail. The result was more than 150 letters and e-mails — about 80 of which I followed up on with further questions.

While the newspaper responses were certainly not a representative sample, they provided some interesting insights into the thoughts of viewers who felt strongly enough about the genre to make the effort to write. The online samples were perhaps a more accurate reflection of the group described by Rebecca Gardyn as avid viewers — 70 percent of whom reportedly go online to discuss the reality shows they watch.[12] What emerged over the course of combing through the transcripts, letters, and e-mails, while monitoring the media coverage and the shows themselves, were several themes in the audience response that I explore in some depth in this and the following chapters. My goal has been not just to extract recurring motifs in the audience response but to try to connect these with the theories of e-commerce, surveillance, and the appeal of reality TV outlined in previous chapters. The hope is that by juxtaposing a critical analysis of the shows with the responses of fans and interviews with producers and cast members, some fruitful patterns for thinking about the social significance of the genre might emerge.

THE REAL THING: PRIME-TIME POSITIVISM

In both the interviews I conducted online and the surveys I received from viewers across the country, one of the most common explanations for the popularity of reality TV was that it offered an alternative to the predictability of fictional programming. As one respondent put it, "It's a change from the same old thing. One never knows how a situation will turn out."[13] Similarly, another viewer observed, "this type of voyeur style TV show is a natural progression resulting from a lack of creativity in television programming in general."[14] The apparent distaste for prime-time programming was manifested in the repeated assertion that "truth is stranger than fiction" and therefore, perhaps more entertaining. It is not hard to discern in these responses the strains of a critique of the abstracted, nonpartici-patory character of mass culture. It is just a short step from these sentiments to those invoked by the critics of mass society: fiction has become mass produced, standardized, and stultifying. The way to break through this abstract artifice is to get real: to draw on the actions and interactions of authentic people rather than the cardboard cutouts that have worn so thin as to be unable to withstand scrutiny.

Even more common in the interview and survey responses than the assertion that reality TV is less contrived than fiction is the contention that it is *more* than mere entertainment, insofar as it leads to knowledge of human nature. Thus, for one fan, *Big Brother* isn't just "'reality TV'; it's 'anthropology TV.'"[15] Appar-ently, the fact that the show was often painfully slow moving and dull as com-pared with the standard prime-time fare merely highlighted the reality of its sci-entific rigor, at least for some viewers who took the "it's not supposed to be entertaining, it's an educational experience" approach. This is the stance adopted by one anonymous post to the *Big Brother* website: "I think most people miss the truly remarkable aspect of Big Brother. It isn't merely entertainment for your ple-beian sensibilities. It's a sociological, psychological, and anthropological experi-ment."[16] In other words, studying human nature requires the painstaking patience of an anthropologist in the field. However, since this particular form of anthro-pology was being conducted in the heart of the American dream—a studio lot in Los Angeles—the viewers weren't learning about distant populations but about themselves. One fan whom I interviewed in AOL's *Big Brother* chat room said that he and his wife view the show as an opportunity to predict the future of American society by generalizing from the viewer reactions (as recorded in the voting process) to the houseguests. The fact that viewers seemed to vote off the most controversial and conflict-oriented cast members thus boded well for a less-ening of tensions in society (so much for the predictive power of reality TV).

From the empirical standpoint, the contrived nature of the house takes on the aspect of a laboratory setting, and in its very artificiality serves to guarantee the authenticity of the sociological interactions being monitored. Thus, whereas some viewers point out the artificial premise of the show, others liken it to the con-trolled conditions necessary for a "scientific" study of human interaction. Cutting the houseguests off from the external world, controlling every aspect of their lives down to how much food they have and what tasks they must perform sets up a situation in which the producers are lab assistants and the viewers are interested students of human nature. Thus, as a post to the website put it, "The aspect of con-finement, and the fostering of genuine (somewhat) relationships in an artificial situation is key" to the anthropological character of the show.[17] Other posts liken the house to a lab and the cameras to microscopes that allow for the observation of the minute details of human interaction.

Picking up on the metaphor of the microscope, it is the comprehensive and per-vasive character of the round-the-clock surveillance that stands as the guarantee of authentic reality. Thus, the gaze of the viewer comes to stand as the litmus test of whether characters are being "real" or not. The most common definition of "real" in this context is the willingness of a houseguest to "be" him- or herself rather than attempting to play a role in order to manipulate either the audience or the other houseguests. The repeated form of praise in the chat rooms, where the most common activity was to debate who should win and who the fans' favorite characters were, was that a cast member was being "real." Interestingly, the show's eventual winner, Eddie from Long Island, was easily the character most often praised in this fashion. Viewers complained that he was often rude to other houseguests, didn't contribute as much to the chores, and spent much of his time sleeping, but his redeeming feature was that he was, at least, "real." In the words of one chat room participant: "Eddie should win, he is the only one in the house that is willing to be honest enough to play the game, the way it should be played, he has no fear nor concern about what the others in the house think of him, he is always true to himself and his own beliefs. . . . Eddie is 'The Real Thing.'"[18]

The standard of authenticity was, for the viewers, provided by their own omniscience. The ability to see how each houseguest interacted not only with various roommates, but with the producers in the Red Room, allowed viewers to argue that they could discern who was being "phony." The ultimate crime of a houseguest was, from the point of view of authenticity, to be caught being two-faced: presenting one façade to the houseguests and another to the producers (or the audience); or, to be caught betraying roommates behind their backs. A close second was to abstain from "getting real," by clearly withholding one's thoughts and feelings in order to control one's public image. These standards helped create an interesting tension in viewer interpretations of the show, which veered between describing the goal as an experiment in who could be the most "real" and as a competition in which houseguests had to "play the game" in order to win the grand prize. Debates often erupted in the chat rooms over whether the houseguests should be strategic—hence manipulative and "phony"—or whether they should just "be themselves" and let the cards fall where they may. The defenders of the benefits of authenticity collapsed this tension by arguing that the best way to win—hence, the most effective strategy—was not to be strategic: to be "real."

KEEPING IT REAL

The way the audience voted over the course of the season rewarded the strategy of being as "real" as possible. Those characters perceived to be duplicitous because of the way they manipulated their housemates were the first to be voted off. Perhaps even more significantly, the popularity of characters shifted as soon as they were perceived to be trying to manipulate either the audience or their roommates. The most obvious example was that of George, a forty-three-year-old roofer from Illinois, who was early on hailed as the representative of the "common man"— someone who never would have made it on TV if not for the emergence of the "reality" trend. Consequently, during the first weeks of the show, George was frequently hailed as one of the most "real" characters on the show, but his reputation changed drastically after several events transformed him into a potential phony, from the perspective of both viewers and fellow cast members. He began to confound viewers after his first nomination for banishment when he started appearing in the house's confessional room (the Red Room) in a variety of disguises, pleading with the American public not to oust him. His mocking imitation of an Arab convenience store owner quickly earned George the online reputation of being either bigoted or, at best, insensitive. Even more damaging, however, was his parody of a previously banished houseguest (Karen, a forty-four-year-old housewife, also from Illinois) that earned George the reputation of a back-stabber. His reputation further eroded when the rest of the cast learned that George's wife and a radio station in his home town had banded together to offer his supporters free telephone calls to ensure he wasn't banished from the house. Although the network, the producers, and the radio station all insisted that the free calls had not made a difference in the election results (both George and another houseguest, Brittany were nominated, and Brittany was banished), this apparent attempt to fix the vote was construed by viewers as unfair manipulation. The fact that George's wife made a cryptic reference to the fact that his "plan" was "working perfectly" during a brief phone call he had been allowed in the Red Room made George the target of an evolving conspiracy theory in the chat rooms. From being viewed as a friendly, disingenuous family man, he became the subject of protracted speculation: had he and his wife planned his victory from the start, and what secret strategy were they using to ensure his win? A rumor quickly spread in the chat rooms that George was sending secret signals to his wife over the Internet cameras, using the masks that houseguests had made of themselves and hung on the wall to indicate whom his wife and her cohorts should banish next.

This controversy was fueled inside the house, when Brittany, shortly after being banished, was allowed to talk to one of the remaining houseguests and told him about the radio station organizing free telephone calls to banish George's opponents. At the same time, members of an online chat room pooled their resources to hire an airplane to fly cryptic messages over the *Big Brother* compound, urging the houseguests not to trust George. The result was that George started to be portrayed in the chat rooms as someone whose bumbling harmlessness concealed a cunning and nefarious strategy. In the house, the cast was clearly discomfited by news of George's wife's "get out the vote" campaign, and he was nominated and banished shortly after the rumors of his strategy spread.[19]

In the end, the audience voting pattern reflected the impulses of the chat room participants: the imperative to "keep it real" by banding against those houseguests perceived as phony or manipulative. Whereas the decline of George's reputation and his subsequent banishment offer perhaps the most dramatic example of this imperative, the fate of Jamie, a twenty-seven-year-old beauty queen from Washington state, is also suggestive. Jamie was, from the very beginning, criticized by online viewers for being too image-conscious. Viewers made fun of her for always being perfectly made up for the camera and frequently accused her of not being up-front and honest with her housemates about her thoughts and feelings. A frequent sentiment in the chat rooms and on the bulletin boards was that since Jamie was "just plain not willing to talk," she should be banished from the house and replaced by an alternate.[20] By not being up-front about her thoughts and feelings, viewers argued, Jamie was not playing according to the spirit of the game. As an online post to the *Big Brother* webpage put it, "I just think Jamie is less deserving of the final prizes because she obviously has a problem being herself and being open and honest about her feelings."[21]

These sentiments reflected discussions within the house triggered by housemates who challenged Jamie for trying to control the way she was being portrayed. Her closest friend in the house, Curtis, a twenty-nine-year-old lawyer from New York City, repeatedly accused Jamie of avoiding particular discussion topics out of concern that these might become "storylines" in the television show. Curtis, who was one of the final three houseguests and ended up taking home the $50,000 prize, repeatedly expressed his philosophy that the only way to cope with the conditions of the house was to stop worrying about the cameras and just "be himself." In response to Jamie's refusal to talk about certain topics—and to evade "Big Brother" by leaving her microphone off on one occasion—Curtis told her, "this is reality television, everything we do becomes a storyline. You do have a lot of control over the so-called storyline just by being whoever you are or want to be . . . this thing is about our lives and our reality. . . . It's about whether you're going to bottle it up inside so it's never said aloud."[22] Curtis, in short, echoed the criticism that had been directed against Jamie in the chat rooms and argued that the best strategy was not to strategize—to "be real." Of course, the corollary of this observation, one that echoed the marketing efforts of the *Big Brother* genre, was that reality had itself become a strategy.

The real turning point in Jamie's popularity occurred when she made a decision that many viewers regarded as confirming her instrumental approach to the show. Early on in the season, Jamie admitted to her housemates that she was an aspiring actress, a confession that earned her the nickname "Hollywood" and prompted the show's producers to offer her a show-biz "reward" for winning one of the daily challenges (a trivia contest about the cast): a brief interview with a prominent Hollywood casting director. The twist was that she had to decide between the interview and a brief reunion with her mother in the Red Room. Her decision to leave her mother waiting (a bit tearfully) in the wings and to meet instead with the casting director resulted in a flurry of criticism in the chat rooms. The substance of the accusations against her was that the decision demonstrated her true colors: she was in the *Big Brother* house in order to jump-start her acting career—a fact that compromised her ability to "be real." Jamie became, in other words, just as phony as the actors whose *absence* was part of the guarantee of reality made during the show's premier episode ("no professional actors, no scripts, no second takes"). The typical response in the chat rooms to Jamie's choice was exemplified by a visitor to the website, who observed that: "She never chose to speak with her mom when she was there. instead she was greedy enough to opt to speak to the agent. she had a choice. how do you think the mom feels? . . . The true face shows."[23]

The recurring sentiment was that Jamie had dropped the mask (that she was on the show "for the experience") to show her true face—which revealed that she was attempting to contrive her portrayal on the show. As another post put it, "Jamie hides behind a mask, she's in it for herself. All her talk about "being close like family" is lies. If the way she treated her mother is anything like the "Family" in the house, then everyone is in big trouble!"[24] Jamie's decision also earned her the opprobrium of L.A. *Times* columnist Brian Lowry, who described the scenario as follows: "Jamie, one of the 'Big Brother' inmates, was presented the opportunity Thursday to meet with her mother—who was flown in for the occasion—or a Hollywood casting director. If you think she chose Mom, you haven't been paying attention to just how pathetic the yearning for celebrity has become."[25] The irony of this criticism is manifold: Not only is Lowry's entertainment column reliant on the very celebrity it disparages, but his accusation replicates the paradoxical attitude toward reality expressed in the chat rooms. Once Jamie decides to sacrifice her privacy in order to become a "reality" celebrity, she should behave as if she isn't at all interested in celebrity. In so doing, she would presumably distinguish herself from the rest of the professional actors in Los Angeles. Jamie did have her defenders, who argued that if she were their daughter, they would have wanted her to take advantage of the opportunity—after all, celebrity is one of the benefits of "reality TV." However, the tide had turned, and Jamie was voted off the show the following week.

From the perspective of the promise of the real, it is interesting to note the way in which the "interactive" aspect of the show—the incorporation of viewers into the banishment process—was enlisted by viewers to, in a sense, pursue the promise of the real by voting off the characters who seemed the most strategic or manipulative. The paradoxical result of this approach, which was repeatedly noted in the media coverage, was that the audience worked to make the show less interesting by voting off cast members who sparked controversy or created tension. This tendency of the audience to shape the show in a way that made it boring (and then to stop watching, as evidenced by the gradual decline in ratings for the show) was taken by critics to highlight an inconsistency in the viewing public. On the one hand, viewers were apparently interested in shows that featured drama, conflict, and contrivance; but on the other hand, they weren't willing to take responsibility for fueling that conflict—at least insofar as it was real and had real consequences for the show's cast members. The obvious comparison to be made was between *Big Brother* and *Survivor*, whose striking ratings success was attributed in large part to the fact that the most devious and manipulative contestants made it to the final episodes, thereby escalating the strategic nature of the competition and heightening its drama. The crucial difference between the shows, in this re-spect, was that *Survivor*, whose winner, Richard Hatch, was portrayed as a devi-ous antihero, didn't rely on the viewing audience to decide who would be elimi-nated from the competition. As the *New York Times* put it, "the [*Survivor*] audience, which loved to hate Richard, never had a chance to vote him off the is-land."[26]

One explanation for the fact that viewers chose to make the show so boring they wouldn't watch is that, as the *New York Times* put it, they tend to vote "more with their hearts than their tastes."[27] However, the argument of this book suggests an alternative explanation: viewers were attempting to make good on the prom-ise of reality by eliminating the show's "actors." If reality TV is supposed to be about "real" people, then the people who contribute to reducing it to a contrived entertainment spectacle must be banished. The result is that the promise of real-ity works to background the contrived nature of the show itself: So as not to ap-pear phony (an appearance that could get them banished from the house), the houseguests are compelled to contrive an obliviousness to the reality of their sit-uation: that they are being monitored in order to create marketable entertainment, to compete for a cash prize, and to parlay their self-exposure into a career in "the Industry."

The cast members themselves frequently referred to the role that the viewing audience played in keeping them "real" during the course of the competition. Thus, when Jamie was concerned that Karen, a housewife from Illinois, was talk-ing about other houseguests behind their backs, she observed, "You'd think the cameras would keep you more honest."[28] Indeed, cast members repeatedly in-voked the cameras when questions about the honesty of their roommates were raised. The general contention was that the all-seeing audience would take care of those who were duplicitous, phony, or otherwise manipulative. As Curtis put it, "Eventually you're just going to be yourself . . . or if you are different, I can't imagine the public would let you stay here."[29] Indeed, this impression seemed to be verified for the cast by the fact that all of the houseguests who were accused in the airplane banners of being untrustworthy were eventually banished from the house, including both Jamie and George. It was also not lost on them that the two most obvious manipulators in the house were the first to be kicked out of the house.

During the show's finale, Brittany, a twenty-six-year-old pharmaceutical repre-sentative from Minnesota, who was banished several weeks before the end of the series, observed that the viewers had picked out the three winners based on their authenticity. She made it clear that this authenticity was verified not so much by her own impressions in the house as by the testimony of the omniscient viewers:

You get out [of the *Big Brother* house] and you have your friends and family—people who you trust and love—saying things. You talk to camera people who have been there behind the scenes twenty-four hours a day and you get all this information, and the three people that I heard the least about that didn't match with what I thought in my head were those three, so I know for sure everything I thought of those three was the same thing all my friends and family and the camera people and CBS thought.[30]

In the end, the banishment process worked to secure the implicit equation of surveillance with authenticity. The monitoring process itself was portrayed not as a form of manipulation but as the *antidote* to manipulation.

The promise of *Big Brother*, then, is twofold: First, it allows access to reality via electronic surveillance. The viewers are put in the position of authenticating reality in the *Big Brother* house thanks to the extensive surveillance network to which they have access. The online discussions suggested that viewers took this task seriously, devoting much of their time to establishing who was being phony and who real. Second, the interactive component of the show ostensibly provided viewers control over reality—specifically, the control to keep things real by banishing the "actors." Once again, the promise of interactivity was deployed as a means of participating in a challenge to the manipulations of the culture industry.

The promises of interactivity and surveillance paralleled and reinforced each other. On the one hand, surveillance allowed viewers access to reality—it was the necessary precondition for their participation in the show. On the other hand, in expressing their preferences via the voting process (for which they had to pay), the viewers subjected themselves to another form of monitoring—one that allowed them to participate in shaping the content of the show. The fact that this particular form of participation was not as successful as producers had hoped highlighted the contradiction in the show's premise: that it was supposed to provide commodified entertainment even as it promised to counter the manipulative tendencies of the entertainment industry.

A RIFT IN THE REAL

A central tension in the audience response resulted from the thematization of this contradiction. On the one hand were those viewers who criticized houseguests for being manipulative (hence phony): for trying to win by playing their companions against each other or by playing to the audience. These were the viewers who seemingly adopted the definition of reality put forth by the producers; that "reality" means people are not acting. Indeed, the mistrust toward acting (as a form of contrivance/manipulation) goes hand-in-hand with the rejection of fiction outlined earlier. The goal is to purify interaction by cleansing it of artifice. Being real meant the denial of the palpable artifice of the show: the cameras, the contrived challenges, the laboratory-like isolation, and, above all, the fact that the cast members were embarked on an encounter with celebrity. Authenticity, oddly enough, meant behaving as if nothing out of the ordinary were taking place.

This model of authenticity has some interesting implications for the acceptance of the digital enclosure. It suggests that comprehensive surveillance doesn't oppress its subjects or make them behave unnaturally; rather, it keeps them honest. Furthermore, it suggests that the best way to deal with comprehensive surveillance is to just "be oneself." This is the moral to be read from Brittany's analysis of the show: the winners were the ones who adjusted to surveillance by remaining themselves and not altering their behavior for the cameras. In a context wherein surveillance has become part of everyday reality, being real means treating surveillance as nothing out of the ordinary. This approach, in short, enacts a form of habituation to the routine and comprehensive surveillance of the rhythm of day-to-day life.

However, not all the viewers took the promise that the cameras provided access to reality in such a straightforward fashion. The defenders of George, of Jamie, and of some of the cast members who were banished early on in the show for trying to stir up tensions in the compound frequently pointed out that the show was, after all, a game, and that it was therefore not unreasonable to expect the contestants to devise strategies for taking home the grand prize. Being "real" was perhaps one strategy—but it needed to be recognized as just that. The reality of the show was, according to this interpretation, that it was just a game wherein authenticity functioned as a ruse to win cash. This recognition opened the field up in pragmatic fashion to whichever strategy might prove most effective. Thus, when the rumor surfaced that George and his wife had a secret plan to capture the top prize, his defenders argued that it would be foolish not to be strategic: "It's a game. Win win win. You can't take home $500,000 by sitting on your thumbs. Have to have a plan. What's wrong with that."[31] Or, as another pragmatic realist put it in a post to the online bulletin board: "It's a game and yes people are going to have to stab people in the back."[32] This brand of realism lined up with an unsentimental view of the program as, after all, a form of entertainment that drew its dramatic tension from the competition between the houseguests.

These fans echoed the frustration of the producers not just with the audience for voting off the most controversial and disruptive characters, but with the houseguests for trying so hard to get along with each other rather than competing. As one post put it, "they need to get over the love in the house and play the game."[33] This sentiment was echoed in repeated defenses of the first two characters to be kicked out. Jordan (a twenty-seven-year-old exotic dancer from Minneapolis) and Will (a twenty-eight-year-old youth counselor from Philadelphia), who, while they may not have been the most likable characters, kept the show interesting, according to numerous posts to the chat rooms and bulletin boards. As one former fan put it, "I started watching and BB was interesting and exciting, now that all the quote 'TROUBLEMAKERS' are gone, the show is BIG AND BORING . . . GET ALTERNATES or STOP THEM FROM RUINING THE SHOW."[34] Viewers who criticized the show for not being entertaining enough tended to take a "realistic" approach to prime-time programming: they recognized themselves as viewers who needed to be entertained with drama, action, sex, and conflict. This assessment reflected a certain savvy cynicism, the consequences of which are explored in the following section.

REALISM AND THE "SAVVY" RESPONSE

One way to characterize viewers' praise for the manipulators who kept the show lively is as a further step toward the promise of the real: an assessment of what is "really going on" in the *Big Brother* show. Since it's all just a game orchestrated for the viewers' entertainment, the program can be evaluated according to its entertainment value. Indeed, part of the entertainment value for fans was apparently provided by the live access to the show that allowed them to discern just how contrived it was. The live feeds enhanced the promise of access to the real by offering viewers the unedited content from which the nightly broadcast segments were constructed. The result of this access was to foreground the production process itself, and thereby to allow online viewers to thematize the way in which the show was being manipulated and produced even while billing itself as "reality" TV. On Couldry's account, such access might have served as a form of demystification insofar as it allowed viewers to see how the editors framed the content of the nightly television show. However, *Big Brother* helped show how the promise of demystification could be co-opted as a marketing strategy. If part of the appeal of the show was precisely the way in which it allowed viewers to see through the promise of reality, this served, paradoxically, as one more savvy promise of access to reality: "You, the Internet viewers can see the 'real' truth of 'reality' TV: the way in which we edit the show in order to manipulate reality."

One of the ways in which viewers picked up on this promise was to discuss how the editing process allowed producers to manipulate the portrayal of particular houseguests. Very often participants in the online chats would argue, for example, that Eddie was being portrayed as nicer than he really was, or that Jamie's portrayal didn't do justice to how open she had been with her housemates. As one fan of the online feeds put it, "Watching the 24/7 streams are the ONLY way to have the BB experience. I don't think BB lends itself to 30-minute encapsulations. The editing that is done cannot help but be 'creative.'"[35] Often, online viewers noted that they were privy to details about the show that were edited out of the broadcast version. Particularly significant to such viewers were those moments when the producers provided scripted lines to the houseguests, as in the case of a mock "roast" of three houseguests who had been nominated for banishment:

> If you were watching this show without having access to the Internet you would not know that the roast, talk show, and many other scenes were scripted by show writers. The houseguests are deliberately being falsely portrayed. By the time America

& Canada see the houseguests they have been reduced to puppets. It is just a TV show and of course the point is to get high ratings, but it's somewhat insulting to TV-only viewers that CBS is practically writing the show and at the same time proclaiming it "reality."[36]

What this viewer—among many others—expressed was that the Internet feeds gave him access to the *real* reality of the television show: the fact that it was artificial. In this sense, paradoxically, the Internet, once again, allows access to the real: to the truth of its artifice.

The resulting version of realism accords with a certain postmodern savviness, which "recognizes" behind every promise of truth or authenticity the reality of an illusion. Sociologist Todd Gitlin locates this turn toward the savvy within the context of political news coverage, which, he argues, has responded to political manipulation of the media by developing a cynical metacoverage that describes the way in which such manipulation takes place—a move that at least keeps journalists from looking gullible. The result, however, is not to challenge the manipulative character of politics, but to privilege it and naturalize it—and what's more, to devote even more time to covering manipulation. This metacoverage is what Gitlin terms a "postmodern fascination with surfaces and the machinery that cranks them out, a fascination indistinguishable from surrender."[37]

He goes on to argue that this particular form of surrender—a preoccupation with manipulation that concedes the postmodern point that it's all just a power game—coincides with a fundamentally "depoliticized" society because it negates the promise of politics to be about anything other than manipulation.[38] Significantly, Gitlin's description of the way savviness functions in politics is directly applicable to the *Big Brother* fans' savvy debunking of the show's claim to reality:

> Savviness flatters spectators that they really do understand, that people like them are in charge, that even if they live outside the Beltway, they remain sovereign. Keeping up with the maneuvers of Washington insiders [or, in the case of *Big Brother*, with the strategies of Hollywood producers], defining the issues as they define them, savviness appeals to a spirit both managerial and voyeuristic.[39]

Gitlin's reference to the attitude of the voyeur is telling for the current discussion of reality TV: *Big Brother* exemplifies the equation of spectatorship with participation. After all, the viewers are, according to the show's premise, the ones who control the show's outcome by choosing whom to banish from the *Big Brother* house.

This promise of participation is taken even further by the Internet component of the show, which allowed the spectators' contributions to become part of the TV program's content. What is of particular interest for the current argument is the way in which, as Gitlin puts it, savviness flatters viewers and allows them to adopt the stance of insiders. This description is particularly apt for those viewers who, in their knowing assessment of the reality of *Big Brother* as a form of prime-time entertainment, become self-reflexive about their own role as viewers, seeing themselves, *through the lens of the producers*, as consumers who need to be entertained, who require drama and conflict, sex and violence, in order to participate in making a show popular. The disturbing result is that savviness allows viewers to adopt the same low estimate of themselves that they attribute to the producers. The way in which savviness allows them to identify with the producers also helps them to empathize with the need to manipulate the show for ratings. For example, with reference to the first houseguest to be booted, Will (who openly admitted that he tried to keep things interesting in the house by fueling tensions), many posts echoed the sentiment of the viewer who wrote, "Will provides conflict . . . what is a story without conflict? Not one heck of a lot."[40] An exchange in one of the chat rooms made a similar point:

> BBfan1: mega was there for a reason.
> BBfan2: what reason?
> BBfan3: stir the pot............
> BBfan4: ya LD.. its called RATINGS~~~
> BBfan5: They are all there for a reason
> BBfan1: ratings[41]

These "realistic" assessments of the show generally occurred in response to viewers who wanted manipulative house guests like Will banished so that the interaction in the house would be less disruptive and less "contrived." The gist of the savvy response was that these viewers weren't being realistic about the goal of television entertainment, and, implicitly, that they weren't being honest to themselves about what makes a show interesting. Thus, a frequent rejoinder to critics of Will was, as one of many posts put it, "He makes for good TV. Every show, fiction or not needs a villain. What else would you watch if it wasn't for Will?"[42] The frustration voiced by these "savvy" fans with respect to those who ended up prevailing (by voting off the most controversial characters) echoed that of the show's producers, who seemed stunned by the fact that viewers were eliminating precisely those characters who made the show interesting, and then complaining that it was dull.[43] The savvy viewers, then, are those who, knowingly or not, touch on the contradiction of the *Big Brother* premise: a successful entertainment commodity has a hard time making good on its promise to overcome the abstracted relations of the entertainment industry without undermining its commercial value. They consequently chastise those viewers who want to see reality realized, and argue in favor of the same old predictable formats to which these viewers had imagined reality TV might provide an alternative. The lesson to the "naïve" viewers was the need to be realistic about what entertains them. As one online post put it, with respect to the controversy over Will: "I say learn to love to hate William and his outspoken—maybe even obnoxious—ways because he needs to STAY. Ratings is what it is all about."[44]

The question remains as to what fascination reality TV might hold for these savvy viewers. The answer seems to be that since, to remain a popular TV series, it can't do without the staple, formulaic conventions that audiences have grown to expect, one thing it can do is to cater to savviness by showing how it relies on these conventions. It does so by providing access to the production process, and letting savvy viewers—especially those with access to the online feeds—see precisely how the producers construct "reality." The switch from the "naïve" viewer expecting unmediated reality to that of the savvy viewer looking to see how this promise is constructed is nicely summed up by one of the posts to the *Big Brother* bulletin board:

> I started watching this show as an experiment in human psychology/sociology. I thought it would be very compelling and it was in the first couple of weeks until I caught on to what the media was attempting to do to me. Now, it's an experiment in how the media can manipulate the American public—no less fascinating.[45]

Carrying their empathy for the producers even further, several contributors to the webpage offered suggestions for how to spice up the action in the house and boost ratings. Their identification with the priorities of the "manipulators" exemplifies Gitlin's contention that savviness allows viewers to "define the issues as insiders define them" and highlights, once again, the equation of watching and participating. In so doing, it works to naturalize the imperatives of the entertainment industry, leading savvy viewers to silence those who would impose an "ought" on TV (by asking it to deliver on its promise) with the admonition of what TV naturally and necessarily *is*. Thus, in response to those viewers who pointed to the contradiction of reality TV by noting that the promise to turn control over to the audience was merely a ratings gimmick, the savvy reply is, Get real—accept the industry for what it is. At least that way you won't be a dupe. For example, in response to charges that CBS was behaving immorally by attempting to manipulate people's emotions for ratings, one viewer argued, "TV CAN'T be morally wrong. That is the definition of television. If it's not graphically violent, sexual, or morally wrong, America won't watch it. Do you think a new 'Walton's' or 'Brady Bunch' would get the same ratings as 'Survivor' or 'Big Brother'?!!! I think not."[46] The naturalization of the commercial model places it beyond the reach of questions of morality: it retains the status of an ahistorical given—a brute fact of nature: as amoral as an earthquake.

Thus, as Gitlin notes, the logic of savviness works in a conservative direction, naturalizing the status quo in the very attempt to not be duped by it. Being a savvy realist means admitting how things really are—sacrificing a particular illusion of progress in order to avoid being seen as a dupe. Along the same lines, literary critic Terry Eagleton argues (in terms paralleling Gitlin's) that relativist, pragmatist postmodernism—in its savviest form—operates in a fundamentally conservative register: "Postmodern end-of-history thinking does not envisage a future for us much different from the present, a prospect it oddly views as a cause for celebration."[47] This argument picks up on Adorno's conception of ideology in the era of "late capitalism." Thus, Simon Jarvis notes that Adorno, in an article on Karl Mannheim's sociology of knowledge, observes "that the most prevalent form of philistinism today is not a crude faith in progress, but an undifferentiated cynicism appealing to an unalterable human baseness."[48]

This description neatly sums up the sentiments of those viewers who "realistically" assess the importance of entertainment value to the *Big Brother* series. Such an assessment of the conservative role of savvy cynicism points to yet another aspect of Adorno's attempt to take seriously the function of illusion. On the one hand, Adorno argues that the illusion of a reified "second nature" has real social consequences that cannot be dispelled merely by pointing out the "illusory" nature of their cause.[49] Taking illusion seriously, however, also means salvaging the moment internal to it that promises things could be otherwise. For example, the reality of the illusion of freedom might be assessed as its role in legitimating current forms of exploitation as the result of freely entered-into relations of exchange: workers shouldn't complain about working conditions because they agreed to them when they accepted the job, and they are "free" to leave. In a similar vein, the famous Anatole France quote about the law debunks the illusory promise of equality: "The Law, in its majestic equality, forbids the rich, as well as the poor, to sleep under the bridges, to beg in the streets, and to steal bread." The savvy move, then, would be to debunk the promise of freedom or equality: to show how they really serve merely as a ruse for exploitation—and therefore to discard such notions as one more bit of ideology. Society is about power and the claims of freedom and equality are nothing more than alibis. Such a move would be just as naturalizing and regressive as clinging to the illusion. As Jarvis puts it, "Under high capitalism, the characteristic form of ideology was a faith in illusory universals. But in late capitalism the most worrying prospect is that the very idea that our social experience could change will be lost altogether. In these circumstances the attempt to dispel all illusion may merely serve the idea that the real is the absolute."[50] This is what I take Zizek to mean when he argues that "the stepping out of (what we experience as ideology) is the very form of our enslavement to it," and, when, in tones similar to Gitlin's he refers to the ironic self-distancing way in which "'postmodern' cynical ideology functions."[51] Perhaps the appropriate response to the savvy subject, which will be taken up in greater depth in the chapter on *Temptation Island*, is Adorno's contention that cultural criticism "is ideology as long as it remains mere criticism of ideology."[52] The nonduped find themselves victims of their own savviness.

It is tempting, and perhaps useful, to read the savvy viewer through Zizek's elaboration of Lacan's description of the right-wing intellectual, who plays "the role of what he is in fact, namely, a 'knave.' In other words, he doesn't retreat from the consequences of what is called realism; that is, when required, he admits he's a crook."[53] This admission parallels that of the savvy viewers, who while perhaps bemoaning their own tastes, are at least willing to confess to having them. The savvy viewer self-consciously avoids the trap of the dupe, who adopts the position that the mass media cater to the "lowest common denominator" from which he or she is excluded, as the exception. The savvy move is to identify with the lowest common denominator, and thereby to avoid the ostensibly self-deluded, face-saving attempt to place the blame for popular tastes on an abstract and nebulous mass. The savvy viewer embraces the subject position interpellated by the crassest of mass appeal movies, and takes a certain pleasure in this identification, rather than bemoaning the low quality of mass culture. This is what is meant by "facing up to the consequences of realism": naturalizing the given.[54] The hip response is not to write off popular culture for its mass appeal, but to revel in the self-conscious knowledge of this appeal; sure, it's silly, and tasteless, and makes an unsubtle play to the baser audience instincts, but once we can acknowledge this fact, we can revel in it. If we know we're being manipulated after all—and like it—then we aren't really being manipulated, are we? This, of course, is the appeal of the promise to step outside of reality: the false freedom of the nonduped that is the theme of chapter 8.

Although the two interpretations of the promise of the real enacted by viewers seem at odds, they retain a significant affinity. The first interpretation—what might be termed the "positivist" reading—asserts the importance of liquidating subjective interference in order to get at the reality of the situation. The role of the producers, according to this reading, is to set up a social experiment and then not to tinker with it, so as to preserve the integrity of the results. Viewers who adopt this reading repeatedly criticize the producers for violating the integrity of their own premise by contaminating the Petri dish of the *Big Brother* enclosure and allowing contact with the outside world. The isolation of the compound—as highlighted in the show's opening credits with the dramatic promise of "no outside contact"—protects the objectivity of the experiment. In keeping with this premise, viewers repeatedly criticized the producers for introducing scripted elements into the show and thereby hindering direct access to the real. This positivist response is typified by the following post: "I personally like the show and I think I originally got hooked because the premise was real people in an unreal situation. How will they cope? Interact? etc. It started out that way, but now there is so much interference and restriction imposed by Big Brother, they aren't free to interact on their own anymore."[55]

The contrived premise of the show, on this reading, actually replicated the controlled conditions of the laboratory—the artifice necessary for the acquisition of scientific knowledge through experimentation. The imperative of any such experiment, once it has been set up, is that the observer must not interfere in ways likely to bias its outcome. By introducing contaminants, producers reduce the experiment to the formulaic, contrived approach it had promised to surpass. The paradox of this reading is that it naturalizes contrivance as the basis for the real. The "unreality" of the original premise serves as the unquestioned, given basis from which reality is to be derived. In this sense, the positivist approach and the

postmodern approach described by Gitlin overlap. Postmodern savviness identi-
fies the "truth" of this positivism by acknowledging the contrived basis of reality
without—and this is crucial to both Gitlin's and Eagleton's account—*challenging*
it (or acknowledging its historical contingency). In other words, if the positivist
approach of fans who see the social experiment as a means of studying real social interactions attempts to eliminate subjective influences, it simultaneously
naturalizes contrivance as a necessary tool. The postmodern approach achieves
much the same effect by asserting there is nothing but contrivance: both leave the
stark *givenness* of contrivance intact. This overlap might be one way to approach
Jameson's claim in *Late Marxism*, that

> . . . what Adorno called positivism is very precisely what we now call postmod-
> ernism, only at a more primitive stage. The shift in terminology is to be sure mo-
> mentous: a stuffy petty-bourgeois republican nineteenth-century philosophy of sci-
> ence emerging from the cocoon of its time capsule as the iridescent sheen of
> consumerist daily life in the Indian summer of the superstate and multinational cap-
> italism.[56]

In his discussion of the trajectory of the "demise" of the subject from positivism to postmodernism, Jameson neatly outlines the mistrust of artifice that I
have located in the attempt to counter abstraction with the promise of reality:

> Positivism becomes postmodernism when it has, like philosophy on the older para-
> digm, fulfilled and thereby abolished itself. Adorno insists on one side of its mission,
> thereby giving us one useful description: it wants to abolish the subjective, as that
> takes the form of thoughts, interpretations and opinions (perhaps it also wants to
> abolish the language that corresponds to these things: poetic, emotive, rhetorical).
> This is to say that it is a nominalism, and as such wants to reduce us to the empiri-
> cal present.[57]

Which is, perhaps, an apt description of the positivist promise of "reality" programming.

Whether we take the savvy route or the positivist one, we are left with the same
result: the reality of artifice. The following chapter picks up on a related question:
that of the relation between the promise of reality and the resuscitation of authentic experience. Or, put somewhat differently, it considers how the promise of
reality TV both exploits and defers the desire for authenticity.

NOTES

1. "About Big Brother," at Big Brother (official webpage), www.bigbrother2000.
com (accessed 10 September 2000).

2. "About Big Brother."

3. "About Big Brother."

4. "About Big Brother."

5. Josh Souza, "The Big Brother Show," 2001, at joshsouzaonline.com/bigbrother. html (accessed 6 January 2002).

6. Heather Perram, AOL producer, personal interview with the author, 17 February 2001.

7. *Big Brother*, WKNC, Denver, 29 September 2000.

8. Ben Bagdikian, *The Media Monopoly* (Boston: Beacon, 1997); David Barsamian, *Stenographers to Power: Media and Propaganda* (Monroe, Maine: Common Courage Press, 1992); Edward Herman and Noam Chomsky, *Manufacturing Consent: The Political Economy of the Mass Media* (New York: Pantheon, 1988).

9. Nick Couldry, *The Place of Media Power* (London: Routledge, 2000).

10. Couldry, *The Place of Media Power*, 7.

11. Couldry, *The Place of Media Power*, 187.

12. Rebecca Gardyn, "The Tribe Has Spoken: Reality TV Is Here to Stay," *American Demographics*, at www2.realitytvfans.com/newspub/story.cfm?id=3335 (accessed 5 September 2001).

13. Anonymous, e-mail to the author, 12 November 2000.

14. Anonymous, e-mail to the author, 18 November 2000.

15. Anonymous, e-mail to the author, 2 December 2000.

16. "The Boards," at BigBrother2000.com (accessed 3 August 2000).

17. "The Boards," at Big Brother 2000.com (accessed 3 September 2000).

18. "The Boards."

19. The dramatic transformation of George from the most "ordinary" and innocuous of the houseguests to the most devious and powerful among them was perhaps one of the most striking reversals that took place in the chat rooms over the course of the show. It resonates strongly with Zizek description in *The Ticklish Subject* of the deployment of the figure of Bill Gates as "evil-icon":

> He is no longer the corporate Big Brother running a rigid bureaucratic empire, dwelling on the inaccessible top floor, guarded by a host of secretaries and deputies. He is, rather, a kind of little brother: his very ordinariness functions as the indication of its opposite, of some monstrous dimension so uncanny that it can no longer be rendered public. . . . Gates, the Little Brother, the average ugly guy, thus coincides with and contains the figure of the Evil Genius who aims at total control of our lives. (Slavoj Zizek, *The Ticklish Subject* [London: Verso, 1999], 348)

Zizek's use of the Big Brother/Little Brother terminology is fortuitous, insofar as it echoes the houseguests' status with respect to the *Big Brother* that monitors their every action. However, the relevance of Zizek's analysis lies in his explication of the representation of uncanny evil in the guise of the innocuous Little Brother. Such a portrayal, he argues, functions as the obverse of reification: as, in other words, an illusory personalization of "objective social processes." He credits the first generation Frankfurt School theorists with the observation that "at the very moment when global market relations started to exert their full domination, making the individual producer's success or failure dependent on market cycles totally out of his control—the notion of a charismatic 'business genius' reasserted itself. . . . Does not the same hold true even more today, when the abstraction of market relations that run our lives is brought to an extreme?" (349). This analysis touches upon the question of the reality of material determination (irreducible to the intentions of social actors), and it can perhaps be adapted to offer one explanation for the portrayal of George in the *Big Brother* house. In its appeal to "reality," *Big Brother* offers to counter the "abstractions" of mass society and the mass media with a return to "back to basics" reality and "face-to-face" community. The appeal is a particularly ironic one, since it is made in the very context it ostensibly challenges. Drawing on Zizek, then, the intrusion of this abstraction into the very organization and operation of the show (which is after all, a product engineered for consumption) becomes personified in the uncanny cunning of George, who had appeared initially as the most "real" character in the house. But why isn't this manipulation personified for houseguests in the person of *Big Brother*—of the CBS producers? Cast members did frequently identify producers as the source of the manipulation to which they were subjected, however, they had agreed to this manipulation beforehand—it was part of the naturalized set-up of the show. Moreover, despite the show's reflexivity, the cast members don't come into direct contact with the producers except in the form of the disembodied voices that addressed them in the Red Room.

20. "The Boards," at BigBrother2000.com (accessed 25 August 2000).

21. "The Boards."

22. *Big Brother*, WKNC, Denver, 18 August 2000.

23. "The Boards," at BigBrother2000.com (accessed 21 August 2000).

24. "The Boards."

25. Brian Lowry, "Reality, in the Blinded Eye of the Beholders," *Los Angeles Times*, 29 August 2000, F1.

26. Bill Carter, "'Big Brother' Hopes to Engineer an Exit, Then Add a Face," *New York Times*, 4 September 2000, E1.

27. Carter, "'Big Brother' Hopes to Engineer an Exit."

28. *Big Brother*, WKNC, Denver, 5 August 2000.

29. *Big Brother*, WKNC, Denver, 5 August 2000.

30. *Big Brother*, WKNC, Denver, 29 September 2000.

31. "The Boards," at BigBrother2000.com (accessed 28 August 2000).

32. "The Boards."

33. "The Boards."

34. "The Boards," at BigBrother2000.com (accessed 18 August 2000).

35. "The Boards."

36. "The Boards."

37. Todd Gitlin, "Blips, Bites and Savvy Talk: Television's Impact on American Politics," in *State of the Art: Issues in Contemporary Mass Communication*, ed. David Shimkin, Harold Stolerman, Helene O'Connor (New York: St. Martin's, 1988), 215.

38. Gitlin, "Blips, Bites and Savvy Talk," 216.

39. Gitlin, "Blips, Bites and Savvy Talk," 217.

40. "The Boards," at BigBrother2000.com (accessed 28 July 2000).

41. "Chat," at BigBrother2000.com (accessed 2 August 2000). The screen names of chat room participants have been changed.

42. "Chat."

43. See, for example, Carter, "'Big Brother' Hopes to Engineer an Exit, Then Add a Face."

44. "The Boards," at BigBrother2000.com (accessed 25 July 2000).

45. "The Boards." In keeping with this assessment of the appeal of savviness, it is perhaps worth noting that a former contestant on the game show *Survivor* is suing the show's

producers for rigging the show to have her voted off early. The claim of "rigging" drew a flurry of media coverage and lead to more savvy speculation about just how "real" reality shows are. In reporting on the story, *USA Today* noted, "Of more than 5,500 Internet visitors to USATODAY.com, 65% believe 'Survivor' is rigged" (Cesar Soriano, "CBS Tribe Speak Out on Lawsuit 'Survivor' Not Rigged, They Say," *USA Today*, 8 February 2001, sec. 6D). Which just goes to show how savvy *USA Today*'s readers are. This kind of on-line voting, of course, is precisely the kind of two-way interaction with the media ("talking back," as it were) that corresponds to the promise of reality—and of reality TV. It offers the promise of "having one's voice heard" as a means of adding value to a commercial product.

46. "The Boards," at BigBrother2000.com (accessed 1 September 2000).

47. Terry Eagleton, *The Illusions of Postmodernism* (Oxford: Blackwell, 1996), 134.

48. Simon Jarvis, *Adorno: A Critical Introduction* (New York: Routledge, 1998), 66.

49. Theodor Adorno, "Subject and Object," in *The Adorno Reader*, ed. Brian O'Connor (Oxford: Blackwell, 2000), 137–52.

50. Simon Jarvis, *Adorno: A Critical Introduction* (New York: Routledge, 1998), 116.

51. Slavoj Zizek, *The Zizek Reader* (London: Blackwell, 1999), 60; Slavoj Zizek, *Looking Awry: An Introduction to Jacques Lacan through Popular Culture* (Cambridge, Mass.: MIT Press, 1997), 64.

52. Theodor Adorno, "Cultural Criticism and Society," in *The Adorno Reader*, ed. O'Connor, 203.

53. Zizek, *Looking Awry*, 45. The figure of the knave suggests that it is, perhaps, appropriate that George W. Bush seized the nation's helm during the era of "reality" television and will likely preside over its booming growth as a programming genre. For it was not hard to discern in the political rhetoric of his campaign the kind of savvy realism that seems such an integral part of the reception of "reality" TV—in which the scare quotes are integral to its savvy reception. One of Bush's main campaign strategies was to appeal to this savviness by admitting that he doesn't trust politicians any more than the voters do—and thus doesn't take the voters for dupes. By implication, Democrats, who still believed that politicians might work in the public interest, came off as dangerous dupes (or, more cynically, as taking the voters for dupes). Simply put, Bush's claim that he doesn't trust politicians fits neatly with Lacan's description of the knave as someone who, when required, "admits he's a crook." Which is why he cannot be called a hypocrite for the way in which he sealed his election victory. He warned us from the start, and for that he might be dubbed the first "reality TV" president.

54. Hence the popularity of the recent rash of movies that foreground the formulaic devices of the very movies they imitate: *Scary Movie, Austin Powers: International Man of Mystery*, and *Not Another Teen Movie*, for example.

55. "The Boards," at BigBrother2000.com (accessed 15 August 2000).

56. Fredric Jameson, *Late Marxism* (New York: Verso, 1990), 248.

57. Jameson, *Late Marxism*, 248–49.

Chapter Six

It's All about the Experience

Not everyone in a reality game show is able to win the grand prize—and for those who don't, there is no guarantee that they will be able to work their way into the fringes of the entertainment industry through advertising or cameo appearances. For example, for those in the *Big Brother* house who don't make it, the payment will be much less than the minimum wage: about $2 per hour for their time spent in the house. But there is, at least according to the houseguests, the possibility of having had an *experience* that was, as several of them put it over the course of the series, "priceless." The value of this experience, calculated within the context of the therapeutic ethos, represents an important part of the promise of reality and provides one more ostensible benefit of entry into the digital enclosure.

This promise recapitulates what cultural historian T. J. Jackson Lears describes as the relation between the rise of the therapeutic ethos and that of mass consumer capitalism in the early twentieth century.[1] In particular, he highlights the way in which advertising comes to enlist the sense of loss (of "traditional" society and its attendant values) associated with modernity to offer compensation in the form a revitalized richness of experience. In the era of ad campaigns that promise access to "The Real Thing," and to a reborn sense of excitement for those who "Do the Dew," it's clear that the therapeutic ethos retains its purchase. The equation that Lears discerns in advertising between the demise of traditional society and a need to counter a growing sense of "unreality" parallels the promise of the return of reality: to challenge the abstractions of mass society.

Specifically, Lears argues that the urbanization, industrialization, and secularization that accompanied the development of an "increasingly independent market economy" contributed to a waning sense of reality—one that resonates with sociologist Anthony Giddens's description of the disembedding effect of modernity: "For the educated bourgeoisie in the late nineteenth century, reality itself began to seem problematic, something to be sought rather than merely lived. A dread of unreality, a yearning to experience intense 'real life' in all its forms—these emotions were difficult to chart but nonetheless pervasive and important."[2] The result, Lears argues, was that this "feeling of unreality helped to generate longing for bodily vigor, emotional intensity, and a revitalized sense of self-hood."[3]

This description highlights the fundamental continuity between the promise of reality TV and the rationalization of consumption. As mass-produced products began to displace homemade ones, advertising portrayed the new products as a means of recapturing the lost authenticity of traditional society. The authenticity of homemade food and handicraft production was invoked as a tool for selling the very products by which they had been replaced. Lears argues that the invocation of a nostalgia for "the hard, resistant reality of things" coincided with a shift in advertising technique outlined by advertising historian Roland Marchand: the attempt to sell "the benefits instead of the product."[4] The therapeutic ethos promoted the ongoing search for "intense experience" as an antidote for what Boorstin described as "the thinner life of things" in industrial modernity: the homogenization and abstraction of centralized mass production.[5] The therapeutic appeal underwrote the attempt to sell the experiential benefits of products, rather than their more mundane attributes. Products were marketed on the strength of their ability to make up for the loss of the "ontological security" and authentic experience retroactively associated with traditional society. The result, Lears argues, was that advertising turned "away from the product and toward its alleged effects, away from sober information and toward the therapeutic promise of a richer, fuller life."[6]

The promise of reality TV recapitulates the promise of advertising developed during the advent of mass consumer society (and ever since). It does so in a manner that sells the attributes of the digital enclosure as a space within which experience is intensified. The therapeutic value of the *Big Brother* experience was one of the central themes of the show, as expressed both by the host and producers and by the houseguests themselves. To defuse competitive tensions and to come to terms with the fact that they might not win any prize money, the houseguests frequently reminded each other that they were in the house "for the experience."

THE REALITY OF EXPERIENCE

The experiential theme reached a climax in the house about halfway through the *Big Brother* season when producers attempted to bribe one houseguest into leaving the show so that they could introduce a new, livelier character to boost sagging ratings and counter the charge that the show was dull. During a live broadcast, the houseguests were presented with a suitcase containing $20,000. The money would go to anyone willing to pack up and leave the show that night, they were told. When it became clear no one was going to take the producers up on their offer, they brought in a second suitcase, containing an additional $30,000, upping the offer to the value of the show's third-place prize. Still, none of the contestants budged—not even the three who had been nominated for banishment that week. All of them claimed that the "experience" of the *Big Brother* house was worth more to them than the certainty of taking home the $50,000. Cassandra, the houseguest who was voted out that week, told the show's host on the night she was banished that she had no regrets about turning down the cash: "For me it was a question of integrity, I didn't want to be bought, I didn't want to sell my soul. If I took the $50,000, I'd be saying that's what the experience was worth, and it was priceless."[7]

The houseguests repeatedly echoed their appreciation for the value of their experience in the *Big Brother* house, when, for a short time prior to Cassandra's banishment, they agreed to walk out together rather than to continue to compete with each other. Once again, they justified the decision to themselves by arguing that just by virtue of sharing the *Big Brother* experience, they had already won. As Josh put it during the walkout deliberations: "You can always make more money in your lifetime, but you can't always have the experience."[8] Curtis agreed, echoing Cassandra's sentiments: "The time here is sort of priceless. . . . I'll leave with the memories."[9] Even Eddie, the show's eventual winner—who repeatedly asserted that if it weren't for the money, he had better things to do with his summer than spend it in "televised house arrest"—agreed (momentarily) to give up on the prospect of a cash prize, explaining his decision to producers in terms of the experience: "I walk in here without the *Big Brother* experience. I walk out of here with the experience. I come out of here a better person than when I walked in, I think."[10] Eddie described even the experience of being nominated for banishment as a learning process essential to the *Big Brother* experience. As he put it in a discussion with Jamie, who had, at the time, yet to be nominated for banishment, "You're being robbed of the experience, because you haven't had the experience of being nominated yet. I've gone through it twice and it's cool."[11]

Underlying this euphoric rhetoric of experience is the equation of surveillance with self-fulfillment: that being watched all the time serves to intensify one's experiences, and thereby to facilitate self-growth and self-knowledge. As in the case of *Road Rules*, the cast members repeatedly described their time on the show in terms of its educational and personal value. Indeed, every debriefing of a banished houseguest included a discussion of what that person had learned from his or her experience in the house.

The fascinating aspect of the repeated invocation of the intensity of the *Big Brother* experience is that what the houseguests were describing as priceless was the experience of comprehensive surveillance—one typically associated with oppression and control. In some sense, what they were doing was legitimating a particular form of discipline and exploitation as an enhancement of their individual experience. Put in less harsh terms, they freely entered into a relationship in which most of them would receive less than minimum wage for their participation in a show designed to earn the network millions of dollars. The incentive to enter into such an arrangement was based not just on the potential rewards (economic and otherwise) of celebrity, but also on the promise of the intensity of the proffered experience. In this sense, the appeal paralleled that of advertising in the therapeutic era outlined by Lears: the participants were being sold on the personal, therapeutic benefits of participation rather than on the actual attributes of that participation, which were somewhat less appealing, particularly for those who did not take home the prize money.

Paradoxically, what underwrote the promise that the surveillance experience was one of self-growth and betterment was the fact that it was presented in the guise of a contrived "social experiment." Presumably, the cast members would be outraged if they were subjected to such pervasive surveillance in their "real" lives. What made the experience worth having was the fact that it was not real, and what made it unreal, despite all the hype about "reality TV," was the fact that it was a television experiment—a pseudoeducational form of entertainment. In this sense, the houseguests' invocation of the significance of the "experience" of life in the *Big Brother* house offers an opportunity to interpret Theodor Adorno's claim that in the bourgeois era "the experiment became a surrogate for authentic experience."[12]

This assertion is certainly borne out by the way in which the houseguests legitimated their self-imposed incarceration as a pioneering experiment in television history—as part of something larger than the economic payoff for which they were competing. The most intense experience—in a world in which authentic experience has been eclipsed (in which, as Lears puts it, the experience of reality has "thinned")—is offered by the self-conscious thematization of the experiment as a means of gaining access to reality. The promise offered by the producers—and apparently accepted by the houseguests—was that the show was not just about economics. Of course, this promise was patently false within the context of the cutthroat competition for ratings that fueled the burgeoning reality trend. If the *Big Brother* series set out to provide a "groundbreaking" experience, as its publicity suggested, the measure of the success of this experience was precisely calculated in terms of rating and advertising revenues.

FROM EXPERIENCE TO THE EXPERIMENT

That the validity of experience can be calculated in dollars and cents is just one aspect of what Adorno means when he talks about the usurpation of experience by experiment. His deployment of the term experiment in this context alludes to his critique of positivism and identity thinking. This critique suggests that the positivist attempt to attain objectivity by subtracting the subjective moment of interpretation results in the hypostasis of the given.[13] Simply put, the attempt to gain direct access to the object backgrounds the role of the subject in constituting the given reality. This version of positivism offers an interesting approach to the claim to "reality" put forth on behalf of a show like Big Brother. There is a logic to the promise of reality TV that seems to resonate with the paradoxical, ironic, and often hyberbolic strategy of argumentation favored by Adorno: in an administered world, wherein the capacity for experience has been largely occluded, the most contrived and artificial of experiments poses as the most authentic of experiences. To push this observation one step further, there is an element of truth to this promise, insofar as it stages the reality of what experience has become in what Adorno described as an administered world—one in which experience is manufactured for consumption by the culture industry.[14]

Making sense out of this formulation requires a closer examination of Adorno's assessment of the fate of experience in late capitalism. Authentic experience for Adorno reaches beyond the general concept to encounter the specificity and particularity of the object.[15] When we really experience something—a sunset or a kiss—we don't experience it just in the abstract ("this experience falls into the general category of a kiss") but as a specific event that carries a surplus over and above that of its concept. This surplus necessarily highlights the inadequacy of the concept, the recognition of which gives rise to the "revolutionary moment of experience in which the criterion of truth is challenged."[16] Experience, in this sense, provides the motive force of thought insofar as it is able to reach beyond the hermetic and static mode of identity thinking, which always subsumes the particular to the general concept, and thereby finds in reality *only what is already given by the existing conceptual framework*. The role of experience is to highlight the inadequacy and contradiction of that framework, rather than to enlist the evidence of experience to shore the framework up thanks to the procrustean tailoring of the particular to fit the concept. The latter, while necessary for cognition is, for Adorno, always inadequate to its object, and it is this inadequacy which is suppressed by the instrumental mode of thought characteristic of both the dramatic technological advances and the economic depredations of capitalism. In crude terms, we might describe identity thinking as that form of instrumental reason that fails to account for its own role in shaping what it studies, thereby denying its own experience of the object. Simultaneously, for Adorno, it enacts the reduction of all use value to exchange value characteristic of capitalist society. Adorno's description of this suppression as a "withering of experience" resonates with the critique of modernity described by Lears in terms of the "thinning of experience."[17] In *Aesthetic Theory*, Adorno invokes this very image:

> The disproportion between the all-powerful reality and the powerless subject creates a situation where reality becomes unreal because the experience of reality is beyond the grasp of the subject. . . . The marrow of experience has been sucked out of the concrete. All experience, including experience that is removed from economic life, has been emaciated.[18]

Identity thinking is thus predicated on an evisceration of experience enacted by instrumental reason, which Adorno describes as a partial reason that attempts to pass itself off as the entirety of cognition. As philosopher J. M. Bernstein puts it:

> [F]rom the perspective of modernism, enlightened reason reveals itself as instrumental reason, means-ends rationality; because instrumental, then therefore as subjective;

because not the whole of reason, therefore as particular; and because it claims to represent the whole of reason, indeed it appears in practice as the whole of reason, then therefore, irrational.[19]

The part of reason that corresponds to authentic cognition of particularity is, according to Adorno, sundered from instrumental reason, and sequestered in the irrational realm of aesthetics in order to allow identity thinking to pursue its course unharassed. Hence, the significance of art and aesthetic theory in Adorno's critique of instrumental reason. His approach relies heavily on the notion that the realm of the aesthetic represents a cognitive experiential realm in which knowledge of particularity and nonidentity is not obtained through the subsumption of particulars to their appropriate concepts, but through a non-dominating form of cognition that Adorno (borrowing from and elaborating upon Benjamin's writings) terms "mimesis." Historian Martin Jay provides a useful gloss on Adorno's notion of mimesis:

> Mimesis . . . involves a more sympathetic, compassionate, and non-coercive relationship of affinity between nonidentical particulars. . . . Rather than producing a hierarchical subsumption under a subjectively generated category, it preserves the rough equality of the subject and object involved. More precisely, it assimilates the latter to the former in such a way that the unposited, unintended object implicitly predominates, thwarting the imperialist gesture of subjective control and constitution that is the hallmark of philosophical idealism.[20]

The reason for this detour through Adorno's aesthetic theory is to explore the nature of "experience"—so crucial to the *Big Brother* cast members' description of their time in the house—that corresponds to the social "experiment" upon which they are embarked. Adorno's formulation shows up both the falsity of this version of experience, insofar as it falls short of its own attempt to challenge the administered, rationalized relations of mass society, and its truth, insofar as it portrays the promise of authentic experience via social experiment for what it is: the real fate of experience in an administered world.

Such an argument depends on Adorno's own distinction between the forms of cognition associated with authentic experience and identity thinking. For Adorno, according to Brian O'Connor, authentic experience contains a mimetic element that allows subjective cognition to reach out beyond the historically given conceptual framework: "There is a non-identity between our concepts and the object, and consciousness of that non-identity produces a revision—a self-reflection—in our use of those concepts."[21] Identity thinking, by contrast, operates as a form of static, "unthinking inertia" precisely because it coincides with the suppression of the experience of non-identity—of the particularity of the object.[22] Dialectical thinking takes this particularity as its motive force. As Adorno puts it in *Negative Dialectics*, "The name of dialectic says no more than that objects do not go into concepts without leaving a remainder, that objects turn out to contradict the traditional norm of adequation."[23] It is precisely the point of Adorno's conception of experience that this remainder can nevertheless become an object of cognition. Furthermore, barring this possibility would render cognition itself impossible.

The regressive consequences of the evisceration of experience described by Adorno manifest themselves in the suppression of the recognition of contradiction that prompts a questioning of naturalized social relations. Moving beyond the positivist discovery of what is already given in the conceptual framework requires a consideration of the framework itself. Such, of course, is the agenda of so-called critical theory: a questioning of the presuppositions. Authentic experience opens up the possibility for this interrogation, whereas the waning of experience suppresses this possibility and reinforces the natural inevitability of the given. Thus, O'Connor argues that Adorno's account of the fate of experience provides him with "an invaluable model in that it allows him to explain what he takes to be the irrational acceptance by individuals in society of a social totality which is fundamentally antagonistic to them."[24]

If O'Connor is right, then Adorno's account potentially offers some insight into the portrayal of the surveillance-based commodification of the rhythm of daily life as "priceless" authentic experience in *Big Brother*. This portrayal certainly seems to conform to the model of the irrational acceptance by individuals of a totality that is fundamentally antagonistic to them. Thus, Adorno's analysis exhibits a certain affinity to Lears's account of the emergence of forms of advertising that deploy the promise of the revitalization of authentic experience. The increasing rationalization of daily life in accordance with the development of techniques of mass production and mass consumption, read in light of these two theorists, corresponds with the commodification of experience itself. Or, to put it slightly differently, even as rationalization comes to permeate and administer experience in industrial society, the advertising and culture industries respond with a compensatory commodified version of authentic experience. To adopt the technique of chiasmus so often deployed by Adorno, the historical experience of an administered world coincides with the administration of experience itself. In this sense, the artificial reality portrayed by *Big Brother*, in which interactions are constructed, manipulated, monitored, and commodified, corresponds to the historical reality of artifice in a society permeated by commodified forms of entertainment, experience, and interaction. Similarly, the perpetually monitored reality enacted by *Big Brother* corresponds to the social reality of increasingly comprehensive monitoring. It is this formulation that lends itself to Adorno's approach precisely because it highlights the way in which reality TV makes good on its claim (to portray reality). The assertion on the part of the houseguests that they are embarked on the recuperation of authentic experience is false insofar as it backgrounds the ways in which this experience is contrived and engineered, monitored, packaged, and sold. On the other hand, the assertion is true, insofar as it reflects the way in which the suppression of a constitutive artifice is the reality of experience in the world both within and beyond the confines of the *Big Brother* compound. The "real" world, insofar as it is orchestrated by the identity thinking that facilitates the naturalization rather than the critique of existing social relations, reflects the version of experience represented by the houseguests: little more than a reaction to stimuli provided by the producers.

The hermetic character of identity thinking that coincides with its inability to reach beyond the prison of the concept is enacted by the enclosure of the *Big Brother* compound. It is, it will be recalled, precisely this enclosure that guarantees the experimental authenticity of the reactions and interactions of the houseguests placed in the *Big Brother* laboratory. At the same time, the laboratory metaphor invokes the positivist attempt to bracket off those conditions that need to be called into question—the conditions that serve as the basis for authentic experience. This state of hermetic isolation replicates for Adorno the *subjective* correlate of the thing-in-itself: the self-enclosed, transcendental subject, for whom experience becomes a problematic category.

BIG BROTHER AND BOURGEOIS INTERIORITY

Adorno's early work on Kierkegaard provides a provocative metaphor for the hermetic subject of idealism—one that is useful for a consideration of the *Big Brother* house: that of bourgeois interiority. Adorno argues that the fitting image for the "shallow idealism" that encloses itself in the inward life of the spirit is "not the castle, with which Kierkegaard romantically compares inwardness," but "the imagery of the apartment interior."[25]

In elaborating on this imagery, Adorno refers to the descriptions in Kierkegaard's early writings of the "promenades in the parlor" engaged in by the character of the young Johannes Climacus (the name later adopted by Kierkegaard as a pseudonym). Prevented from leaving the apartment, Johannes is led by his father on walks through the hallways and rooms, which he imagines as, at times a garden, a beach, or a bustling street: "Thus the *flaneur* promenades in his room; the world only appears to him reflected by pure inwardness."[26] Interestingly, the intensity of the "experience" is heightened by its hermetic, isolated quality: "The father pointed out everything they saw; they greeted others passing by, cars noisily crossed their way, drowning out the father's voice; the cakes in the bakery window were more inviting than ever."[27]

The spatial enclosure of the *Big Brother* compound—or perhaps of the immobile telecommuter, surfing the world without leaving the office/bedroom, and even monitoring the *Big Brother* house online—might be construed as the twenty-first-century incarnation of self-enclosed bourgeois interiority. Insofar as this compound anticipates the space of the digital enclosure, the argument might be pushed further still: The version of interactivity associated with new media offers to realize the absurd technological extreme of bourgeois interiority. This extreme is represented by such ostensibly utopian versions of the future as inventor

Ray Kurzweil's description of a world in which humans are able to work, social-ize, and even have sex without leaving the privacy of their rooms—thanks to the advent of "virtual reality" technology.[28] Virtual reality serves as a literal-minded technological realization of the flexible reality of Climacus's apartment, which could transform itself instantaneously from a bustling city to a beach or a moun-tain trail.

Interestingly, from the perspective of the current discussion of reality TV, Adorno goes on to note that a standard piece of equipment in the nineteenth-century apart-ment is the window mirror, whose function was to "project the endless row of apart-ment buildings into the isolated bourgeois living room. . . . In their time . . . win-dow mirrors were commonly called 'spies.'"[29] It is suggestive that within this enclosure, the relationship to the external world—projected into the interior only in the form of "the semblance of things"—takes on the character of spying—of the voyeurism associated with the current proliferation of reality TV. If the promise of reality TV to its cast is that of the revitalization of authentic experience, the prom-ise to the audience is that of the ability to watch this revitalization from the safety of their homes: to substitute spying for experience.

If one of the "barriers to entry" discouraging participation in the digital enclo-sure is created by reservations about the invasion of privacy, reality TV repositions surveillance as a conduit for self-expression. The present discussion of *Big Brother* makes the case somewhat differently: the promise that the contrived, experimen-tal setting of the *Big Brother* enclosure somehow enhances authentic experience works to naturalize this contrivance and the exploitative character of the surveil-lance upon which it is based. Surveillance is not just naturalized; it is invoked as the guarantor of authentic experience. The *Big Brother* compound becomes the laboratory setting wherein the promise of direct access to reality is guaranteed by the abstraction of the experimental subjects from the real world. This abstraction works to naturalize the contrivance on which it is based by asserting the promise of unmediated access to reality via the subtraction of the subjective moment of in-terference (scripting, acting, directing). However, in so doing it highlights the way in which the contrivance (and surveillance) of life outside the compound is natu-ralized. Savvy fans pick up on the reality of this contrivance, a fact that adds yet another twist to the promise of reality: The process of naturalization need not al-ways be predicated on mystifying that which is naturalized—an observation that will be taken up in further detail in chapter 8.

Exposing contrivance for what it is can equally effectively work to naturalize it: "There's nothing but contrivance; that's just the way things are." Contrivance and nature collapse into one another. This collapse has some interesting conse-quences, insofar as it tends to neutralize the critical potential of the attempt to demonstrate the constructed nature of media content. The progressive potential of ideology critique is, to some extent, predicated on the assumption of a "naïve" public that takes the news stories they see and the values incorporated into their fictional entertainment at face value. Since viewers aren't aware of the way in which producers, directors, and network executives shape the information and values that are featured in mass media programming (incorporating their own values and imperatives in the process), the viewers are, on this account, more likely to interpret such programming as expressing natural and objective truths about the world. The hope forwarded by the critics is that allowing viewers to see the framing process in action might overcome their naïveté, creating a more critical and not so easily manipulated public.

However, the advent of the savvy viewer described by sociologist Todd Gitlin suggests a somewhat different story.[30] Viewers are by no means as naïve about the process of media production as some of the more optimistic strands of critical theory might suggest. Rather, reality TV—as well as certain forms of "savvy" advertising—relies heavily on the fact that viewers are self-consciously aware of the ways in which media power operates. For these savvy viewers, such programming foregrounds the contrived nature of celebrity per se by showing how network executives can transform people off the street into celebrities in just a few weeks. The invitation to viewers is not to seize control but rather to participate in the rationalization of their own viewing experience. Such is the version of democracy offered in the world of reality TV.

PARTICIPATION AS POWER SHARING

The final moments of the *Big Brother* season featured host Julie Chen summing up the role the audience had played in shaping the show. Facing directly into the cameras, she told viewers, "Your participation made this truly an interactive show. You changed the lives of ten people."[31] These concluding words picked up on a theme that the show's producers and writers had repeatedly emphasized over the course of the program's three-month run: that the audience was in control. In the opening show, Chen had implicitly likened the audience to the show's producers, noting that they would be able to see everything that took place in the house and then to decide the outcome.

The *Big Brother* series provides a nice example of the parallels between reality TV and the online economy because it was one of the first shows to bridge the gap between the two. AOL was CBS's online "partner," sponsoring the website and the chat rooms and contributing an Internet commentator, who appeared during the weekly live shows to provide observations about the activity on the *Big Brother* website and elsewhere online. In the case of *Big Brother*, the promise that the viewers—real people all—were sharing in the production of the show was bolstered by the program's format and, at least in part, by its use of the Internet as an auxiliary marketing tool.

Previous chapters have suggested that one of the characteristic aspects of the reality TV trend is the way in which it incorporates and reinforces the democratizing promise of new media, and that this promise works—at least in its corporate context—as a ruse for the rationalization of the labor of consumption. The *Big Brother* series demonstrates how the promise of reality does more than parallel that of interactivity. *Big Brother* offers some very practical examples of how the entertainment industry can avail itself of the capability of new media in order to incorporate the labor not just of representative viewers recruited as cast members but of all viewers. *Big Brother* was not a "mass-customized" program, because the television medium has not yet developed to the point of being able to provide such a product—which may also have something to do with the general consensus that *Big Brother* was a *failed* experiment in the integration of the new medium with the old. Nonetheless, this failure, insofar as it is a forward-looking one, is instructive for a consideration of the promise of interactivity: both as it was portrayed to viewers and consumers and as it was exploited by producers.

Big Brother pushed the promise of democratization further than most other reality formats to date. It is clear from just one viewing that *Big Brother* drew from a broader pool of potential cast members than shows like *Survivor* or *The Real World*. The inclusion of George, for example, seemed to violate many of the standards to which reality viewers had grown accustomed. A roofer from Rockford, Illinois, George had neither the typical show-biz face nor physique. The cast did include several younger, telegenic "houseguests," but George and Karen, a housewife from Illinois, seemed to prove that *Big Brother* was open to just about anyone. George picked up on this fact in an interview tape that was aired when he was introduced during the first episode of the show: "This doesn't happen to average working people. Answering an ad in a newspaper sending a tape off, and actually getting a call from Hollywood, California to come out and maybe try out for a TV show. Does that happen? No. But it did to me."[32] George, then, serves as an advertisement for the fact that, in the world of *Big Brother*, if it can happen to him, it can happen to anyone.

The representative element of audience participation has been the limit at which previous reality shows in the genre have stopped short. Viewers had little opportunity to participate directly in the show beyond the hope that they might be selected to be a cast member. *Big Brother* takes another two steps in the direction of participation. The first, as noted earlier, is in allowing voters to decide which of the nominees for banishment were asked to leave the house. The fact that they have to pay $0.99 for the privilege is reminiscent of the way in which purchasers of "mass-customized" products are charged extra for the luxury of incorporating their input into the production process. The second step is the integration of the Internet into the show, a move that both permits viewers enhanced access to the production process by allowing them to watch pre-edited scenes of life in the *Big Brother* house and by incorporating web postings and poll results into the content of the show.

This section explores how this promise of participation played out in practice through a consideration of two events in the *Big Brother* house. The first involves the control that cast members—considered, once again, as representative members of the audience—had over the show. The second involves the promise of participation deployed by the incorporation of the Internet. Both are meant to suggest how this promise was interpreted by those to whom it was presented, and how it functioned within the overall logic of the show. The first event, interestingly, involved the attempt of the cast members—representative members of the public—to follow through on the promise that they "controlled" the show by staging a coup against the manipulative power of the producers.

"THIS PLACE IS A TWO-WAY STREET"

One month into the *Big Brother* season, George, who had taken on the role of the "man of the people" in the house, had become troubled by several events. The first was the accusation made by former housemate Brittany that his wife was orchestrating a plot to ensure his win. Clearly concerned that this news (which turned out to be false) might make his roommates uncomfortable with him, George announced his attention to leave the house voluntarily. This decision seemed to be bolstered by his frustration over a series of airplane banner messages flown over the house accusing him of being untrustworthy. After mulling over his decision to leave voluntarily (even though he had not been nominated for banishment that week), he came to a dramatic conclusion that prompted him to gather his housemates together so he could share with them in prophetic tones his new plan for the house:

> You know what I figured out today? . . . That this place is a two-way street. It's right here and we never figured it out, but I figured it out, and it's so simple . . . it's so obvious. . . . There's more to this show than the stupid banishment and the stupid challenge and everything else. The show is meant to tell us and to tell the world that if we all stay together and if we all work together as one, we win.[33]

What this meant, according to George, was that all the houseguests should band together and walk out that week—making them all winners since they would all become the last remaining contestants in the house. During the ensuing conversation, it became unclear whether George believed that all those who walked out would split the prize money. What was clear was that he was arguing they would all be winners for deciding to stand together rather than to compete against each other for cash: "What they were trying to do was to break us all apart. They were trying to pit us all against us. . . . But last night it all kind of fell into place: they need us. . . . What happens if we leave? There ain't no show. We holded [*sic*] the cards in our hand all the time."[34]

In this respect, George's rebellion was aimed not only against the producers of the show but against its premise: the creation of dramatic tension by forcing people to live with each other in a close-knit, hermetic environment while competing with each other for a prize that only one person could win. The resolution of the contradiction envisioned by George was necessarily the destruction of the show itself. Interestingly, he argued that he had discovered the resolution that the producers had intended from the start: the lesson the show had been designed to teach both cast members and the audience was the importance of the cast *really* seizing control of the show and thereby ending it. Noting that the American cast of *Big Brother* had been the only one so far to succeed in one of the house's more time-consuming challenges (building a model of the *Big Brother* logo out of dominos so that they would all tumble in succession), George argued that perhaps they were also the only cast to discern the show's real import (the necessity of its own destruction): "This show is trying to prove a point to the world, it's not about who's the most popular guy, or woman. This show is made to prove a point that if people join together as one they'll win . . . but if one strays we lose. . . . If we *all* walk out as one, we're *all* winners."[35]

George's rebellion, then, relied on a literal interpretation of the promise of reality TV: that getting real means dismantling the relations of production and democratizing control of the production process. It is perhaps a telling reminder of the context within which this promise is deployed—the rationalized production relations of the culture industry—that the realization of the promise would mean the end of the show. Furthermore, it is indicative of the political undertones of the promise of interactivity that the housemates' initial response to George's plan focused on the revolutionary gesture of forswearing competition in favor of community. The housemates made the connection between giving up on their own hope for the prize money and depriving CBS of the revenues from a potentially successful show (at the time, they were unaware that the show had not lived up to its expectations). Eddie, for example, was quoted in the news coverage imagining how he would describe his decision to friends and family: "'What did you do this summer?' Trashed a CBS show."[36]

Furthermore, the houseguests repeatedly portrayed the possibility of walking out as a chance to "make history" in a revolutionary fashion. Josh noted, for example, that the decision to turn down $500,000 rather than having to "backstab" people to whom he had grown close would prove a moral point more valuable than the money itself. Curtis agreed: "Part of the reason for coming on the show was to be part of television and television history: you are creating a moment in television history."[37] Placed in perspective, the decision to band together rather than to compete, as George told Eddie, would earn the group its place in history: "When you're an old man, they're not going to remember you for the money. That money might be gone. They're going to remember you as Eddie: he got a chance to change things and how they really are."[38]

George and his housemates momentarily accepted the notion that they had gained control precisely because the show's content depended on their willing submission to comprehensive surveillance: this submission turned them into TV celebrities with the power to "make history" and to challenge the repressive relations that thwart community in the name of profit. Having been told that they were in control of the show, the houseguests took the promise literally, consumed with the heady notion that it was within their power to "trash" a CBS show in the name of solidarity. The proposed walkout was a significant moment in the show precisely because it raised the question of what happened when the cast attempted to take literally the promise of shared control.

One of the first things that took place was a relative flurry of media coverage. A Lexis/Nexis database search revealed that newspaper coverage of *Big Brother* increased more than 10 percent in the week of the proposed walkout. The week prior to the walkout had also been a big week for media coverage because one of the houseguests was temporarily released from the compound to attend the Emmys. Thus, it is perhaps a better comparison to note that newspaper coverage of the walkout week increased 50 percent over coverage the week before the Emmys (two weeks before the proposed walkout). Moreover, the ratings for the walkout week's live show were the highest since *Big Brother* had followed *Survivor* in the lineup, piggybacking on the viewership for the summer's runaway success.[39] The ratings went into a decline after the week of the proposed walkout and never recovered, dropping from a 12.5 share in the Nielsen ratings to a 9.5 share and then to a finale that drew only a 7.2 share (the finale aired on a Friday, typically a lower ratings night than the Wednesday and Thursday evening slots occupied by previous live shows).[40] As *Big Brother* producer Doug Ross noted, the proposed walkout introduced into the show some of the dramatic tension for which producers had been striving, sparking media interest (which served as free advertising) and perhaps contributing to a boost in the ratings (which rose from an 11 share to a 12.5 share).[41]

All of which might help explain the fact that, even though the house guests backed off of their plan the day after discussing it (after learning that no one would win any prize money if they walked, and after having had some time to think about relinquishing the *Big Brother* "experience"), the plan became the TV show's featured event of the week. Conceived on a Saturday and rejected on Sunday, the proposed walkout was featured on the following week's shows up until Thursday, when it was revealed that the only person leaving would be the houseguest banished that week. The promise of rebellion boiled down to a ratings-grabbing moment. This fact became readily apparent to Internet viewers, who were able to follow the rebellion's progression in real time, and knew that the plan was long dead even as the network continued to air promotional highlights. As one bulletin board post titled "Big Brother is finally happy with talk about leaving the house" put it, "Hey this is what BB wants. They have created excitement outside the house. They love it!!!!"[42] There was strong support in the chat rooms and on the bulletin board for the walkout, primarily reflecting anger on the part of the viewers toward the producers' transparent efforts to generate conflict and tension in the house (efforts that eventually deteriorated to the level of shorting the houseguests on their weekly supply of toilet paper and then telling them if they wanted more, they would have to spend their entire grocery allowance on toilet paper).

Producer Doug Ross's response to George's plan confirms the observations posted on the web: "We were only scared for about ten to fifteen minutes, then we realized whatever happens this is great: This is the controversy; this is the drama; this is the excitement that we always wanted."[43] Ross said that producers scrambled when they first heard of the plan, assembling to decide whether the show should end with the walkout or whether they would bring in a team of alternates and still award the grand prize (prorated according to the time actually spent in the house). Over the course of the weekend, he said the producers decided to scrap the show if the houseguests walked—a decision that apparently reflected the fact that the American version of *Big Brother* wasn't living up to their expectations.

In the end, the producers got what they wanted—more or less. They called those houseguests who seemed to have the most reservations about the walkout into the Red Room and explored their doubts. They also informed them that no one would get the prize money if everyone walked. The producers received some assistance from Eddie's mother, who paid an aerial advertising company to fly a message over the house urging him not to leave. Eddie decided, in the end, that he didn't want to be a "quitter": he had come to the compound to take home the money for his family and that he wanted to stick with that goal. Jamie, the would-be actress, admitted she didn't want prospective Hollywood employers to view her as someone who would leave a show in the middle of its run. Although she was cast, in this case, as a real person, she wanted to demonstrate her professionalism. Thus, the houseguests rather quickly shook off the euphoric moment of rebellion and came to the realization that the show's message was not the same as its promise—a realization underscored by producer Doug Ross: "George was 100 percent *in*correct in assuming that the real message of *Big Brother* was that they were all winners. . . . Indeed, that's not true."[44]

At the same time, however, it's not surprising that the cast members took seriously the promise that they were in control of the show—and that they could exercise this control to counter the "message" sent by the ratings-driven hunger for conflict, competition, and divisiveness. They were picking up directly on the implicit themes mobilized by the promise of reality: that real people could seize the reins, at least for a moment; that "being real" meant a lack of artifice and manipulation; and that a back-to-basics lifestyle meant a return to traditional forms of community that transcended the abstracted relations of contemporary society. Not all of the houseguests interpreted the promise of reality in this light, and Eddie, for example, repeatedly tried to get his housemates to acknowledge the fact that the main reason they were there was to compete for a big cash prize—that they *weren't* there for the "experience" but for the payoff (in this sense, Eddie represented the voice of "savvy" realism in the house—at times).

Other houseguests, including Jamie, George, and Josh, repeatedly suppressed the competitive aspect of their situation, extolling the virtues of learning how to get along with each other in their hermetic, microcosmic world. It is testimony to the power of the promise of "shared control" that George—not the most charis-matic of characters—was able to get everyone in the house, including Eddie, to at least temporarily agree to put the image of solidarity ahead of competition in an act of defiance toward the manipulations of the show's producers. Such ma-nipulation was what the promise of reality was ostensibly directed against, in the first place. That the promise is deployed by the very same hierarchy it ostensibly challenges is reminiscent of the promotion of the "revolutionary" promise of the Internet by some of the world's most powerful corporations.

The fact that the cast decided not to walk after all suggests that a realistic as-sessment took place once the initial excitement had worn off: that given the con-text within which they were operating, the historical agency they had imagined for themselves was little more than the illusory promise of an advertising cam-paign for a "revolutionary" new television product. That, when it came right down to it, Jamie was probably right (if a bit overoptimistic about the ratings po-tential), when, in reaction to George's revelation, she predicted that if they all walked off, "I see CBS bringing in six alternates, the ratings going through the roof, and the alternates receiving a tiny fraction of the prize money."[45] Despite this dose of realism, the house failed to erupt into the full-blown strategic scheming that characterized *Survivor* (much to the chagrin of its producers). In-deed, the cast retained its commitment to getting along with each other and en-joying the "experience" so much that during the final week, when asked who should win the grand prize, two of the remaining three houseguests, Josh and Eddie, each nominated the other. The fact that they won the top two prizes ($100,000 and $500,000, respectively) highlights, once again, the strategic po-tential of the promise of the real. If, in other words, the *Big Brother* show was marketed on the strength of this promise—of the potential of the show as a rev-olutionary "experience"—it's not surprising that the most effective strategy for the players was to be "real": to highlight the value of their authentic experience and to background the competitive, manipulative aspect of the show.

Having examined how the promise of shared control functioned in the *Big Brother* program as an advertising strategy, it is also worth considering the fact that producer Doug Ross attributes the show's relatively poor showing in the U.S. market at least in part to some of the real limitations the show placed on producer control. Echoing the refrain of reality TV producers from *An American Family* through *The Real World*, Ross argues that the format necessarily relies upon the content provided by its cast: "Even though there was a plan on what the show would be every day, we were subject to the whims of our contestants in the house."[46] But this wasn't as much of a limitation, he said, as were the time con-straints within which the producers had to operate. Because *Big Brother* was produced—like the evening news—on the basis of developments within the past twenty-four hours, the producers had to edit the show without knowing how it was going to turn out, and they had to do it quickly, generally in six to ten hours. In this respect, *Big Brother* represented a significant departure from previous *do Audience want Real Reality* (handwritten annotation)

programs in the genre—all of which were produced after the fact, allowing editors to shape the story based on an already known outcome. The format really did, in other words, sacrifice a degree of editorial control in order to convey the feel of "live" television (*Big Brother* aired five times a week during its first season, including one live episode each week to broadcast the banishments)—and Ross said the ratings took a hit because of this limitation. U.S. viewers, he said, are accustomed to tightly-edited entertainment programs with relatively high production values of the kind that cannot be achieved in the short time the "Big Brother" crew had to pull together a daily show. He added that unlike the European audience, which is habituated to evening soap operas with drawn-out plots that don't resolve themselves in one episode, American viewers are accustomed to prime-time fictional formats with largely self-contained narratives.[47]

Ross's argument suggests that the format really did impose restrictions on the artifice available to producers, one that forced them to rely heavily on the day-to-day actions of the cast for usable content. All of which made the ongoing efforts of the producers to instigate dramatic interactions over the course of the series appear more transparent—and, in some case, more desperate. The attempt to take a step closer to the promise of reality ended up highlighting the manipulative aspect of the show, and hence the paradoxical nature of its promise. By the same token, the cast members apparently took this promise as an authentic invitation to *not* cater to the public with the standard prime-time contrivances of conflict, sexual tension, and Byzantine plots. The audience—as the next section suggests—had to work hard to project such dramatic elements into the show, thereby taking some of the work of both cast and producers onto themselves. The way in which the *Big Brother* cast took up the promise of democratization reflects the assessment of the revolutionary promise of interactivity outlined in previous chapters. Reality TV relies on a surveillance-based participation that parallels the version of "interactivity" envisioned by the paradigm of mass customization. It was when the houseguests took this promise most literally—as a suggestion that they could take over the show and transform the message—that they were laboring most effectively for the producers, and generating *Big Brother*'s" highest post-*Survivor* ratings.

AUDIENCE LABOR

The promise of *Big Brother* as a reality TV experience was directed not just at cast members but also at viewers, who were guaranteed "a groundbreaking experience."[48] As active participants in the show, viewers would, or so the promotional material suggested, also be working on themselves—exploring their own reactions to the "reality" of the social interactions in the house and confronting "long-held opinions."[49] A significant part of that experience would take place for the viewers—as for the cast members—within an electronically monitored space: that of the official *Big Brother* website, and the Internet generally. One of the results of the show's reliance upon the Internet was the fact that, as producer Doug Ross put it, *Big Brother* was generally considered to be more of a success on the Internet than on television.[50] The success of the website was not unprecedented—the *Big Brother* sites had been popular and successful in both Germany and the Netherlands. In Germany, which has a population of some eighty-three million people, the official website generated more than ninety million hits during its first several weeks. In the Netherlands, with only fifteen million people, the official website received fifty-two million hits over the course of its three-month run. In the United States, the official website—hosted by America Online—became the top-rated new website for the month of July, with more than 4.2 million unique visits; midway through the series, the site was receiving bulletin board posts at the rate of one per second.[51] AOL estimates that over the course of its three-month run, the *Big Brother* website had a "unique home audience" of more than 9.4 million.[52]

The *Big Brother* website not only offered an invitation to "participate" in the *Big Brother* experience on a variety of levels, but also provided a source of instant demographic information and audience feedback to the producers of the television program. Producer Doug Ross said that one of the reasons the show was not as popular as it might have been was the failure to exploit the potential of this audience feedback—a failure that he attributes in large part to the reluctance of the Dutch production company Endemol to tinker with what had proven to be a highly successful format in Europe.

WE'RE ALL PART OF THE SHOW

It is perhaps useful to think of the *Big Brother* website in terms of the way in which it manipulates what communication scholar Nick Couldry describes as the "boundaries around the media sphere" that "reduce the chances of the media's authority ever being de-naturalised."[53] The standard image of the one-way, top-down industrial manufacture of media products locates these boundaries around the privileged site of media production: the private offices and editing bays where the final product is given shape. These spaces are, in some sense, the site of the "real" behind the façade of the reality portrayed by the media. They represent the place where reality is really manufactured—a privileged site of de-mystification, where the link between the values and priorities of media elites and the content of media programming is actualized.[54] The boundary between the sites of planning and decision making and that of viewing/consuming represents a spatial division of labor associated with the hierarchical and "abstracted" relations of mass society. Thus, it should come as no surprise that the critics of mass society keep trying to penetrate this boundary in order to expose what is *really* going on. However, from the standpoint of the rationalization of production, this boundary represents not the inner limit of a privileged domain, but the outer reach of comprehensive surveillance over the production process. The *Big Brother* website replicates the strategy of the digital enclosure by deploying the promise of access, participation via interaction, and, ostensibly, democratic accountability, as a means of extending the reach of comprehensive surveillance *qua* interactivity.

The direct promise of interaction (and of "democratic" accountability) is enacted by the claim that viewers shape the show through the voting process, which promises a form of offline participation. Such participation is not without its surveillance aspect: it provides producers with relevant demographic data about the geographic location of those viewers who care enough to vote. Significantly, it adds value to the show for producers, insofar as every call generates an extra dollar of revenue. In this respect, the promise of interactivity relies on the assumption that people are willing to pay to have a say in how the product they consume is shaped.

However, several further elements of the promise of participation are deployed by the website, which can be fruitfully compared to the *Big Brother* house itself, insofar as it served as a privately monitored space for social interaction removed from the context of the outside, or "real," world. One of the main attractions of the site was that it provided viewers not just with access to an unedited view of life in the *Big Brother* compound, but also a venue in which their voices could be heard. Furthermore, it drew heavily on the promise of virtual community—a promise that I have elsewhere identified in terms of the role that it plays in the ostensible challenge to mass society offered by online interactivity. In the chat rooms, the viewers find themselves in a position not unrelated to that of the houseguests: they are thrown into conversation with a group of strangers from disparate geographic locations in a space that is being monitored and that might provide them with a forum to have their opinions and thoughts aired on national television. As if to highlight this promise, the site's disclaimer warned visitors that their contributions could appear on television, and about three weeks into the show this happened when AOL spokeswoman Regina Lewis began reading selected posts on the air. The appeal of "having one's voice heard" on national TV—even though the posts were presented anonymously—was evidenced by Lewis's assertion that the number of letters to the website "increased tenfold" once she started reading them during the weekly live show.[55] Once viewers realized not only that their contributions were being monitored but that they might be aired, some of them started asking for their comments to be read on TV. In so doing, they were picking up on the promise of a two-way medium, one that would ostensibly allow them not just to watch, but to be heard. As one online plea put it, "PLEASE read my POST on the air tomorrow! I never have had anything on TV before, and it would be cool if I could get on for my opinions!"[56] This request carries the plaintive note of the desire for participation to which the promise of interactivity appeals, but it also smacks of the democratization of publicity as self-promotion. The author didn't indicate her age (although she wrote that she was from Peoria), but the plea is reminiscent of the teenager who drove several hours to the MTV studios in New York City to "advertise" herself. Thanks to the incorporation of the online posts into the weekly live show, the *Big Brother* chat rooms held out a similar promise to that of the *Big Brother* house: by entering into them and allowing one's reactions to be recorded, one could become part of the show.

The online viewers often made this comparison explicit, not just by imagining what they would do if they were in the house but by noting the similarity between the interactions in the chat rooms and those in the house. In several cases when members of a chat room used the "ignore" function to block the posts of other members who were being rude or obnoxious, they likened the exclusion to expulsion from the *Big Brother* house, as in "we banished 5 people from this chat room."[57] After the show's finale, when several of the online viewers had posted their farewells to both the houseguests and each other, one viewer summed up her reaction to the end of the show and the anticipated closure of the chat rooms in similar terms, highlighting the similarity between the departure of the houseguests from the *Big Brother* house and the emptying out of the chat rooms: "I think we've all been banished."[58] They had, indeed, been expelled from the space in which being monitored provided them with the chance to participate in the show they were watching.

The parallel between the chat rooms and the *Big Brother* house can perhaps be pushed a bit further with respect to the promise of the return to a participatory, pre–mass society community. The show's producers repeatedly described the *Big Brother* house as a "back-to-basics" setting in which the houseguests would have to occupy themselves without the benefit of mass-mediated forms of entertainment. As host Julie Chen put it during the show's premier episode, directly addressing the audience in a manner that is suggestive for the current argument: "Remember when your mother said to you when you were a kid, 'You've got to learn to entertain yourself'?. . . Well, our houseguests are going to take that to a whole new level."[59]

If getting "real" means surpassing the mass production of culture and returning to an era of craft-based, participatory culture, one implication is that viewers might have to participate in the process of entertaining themselves. In the *Big Brother* house, for example, the houseguests (bereft of TV, radio, computer, and newspapers) occupied themselves by writing their own songs, making up stories and skits, and creating artwork to decorate the house. Picking up on the parallel between the house and the chat rooms, one of the implications for the viewers was that they would also need to find ways to entertain themselves—rather than relying "passively" on the slow-moving, often breathtakingly boring show.

All of which is a particularly apt way of describing some of the effort that the viewers put into the website. During many of my visits to the chat rooms—in which I spent at least four hours per week for three months—I was impressed by the work that viewers were doing to *make* the show interesting to themselves. Frequently, the people in the chat rooms also had the live feeds from the *Big Brother* house on their computers while they were talking to one another—commenting on the action as it unfolded. However, the onscreen action was usually less than riveting, and it became readily apparent that what viewers were doing was trying to occupy themselves by coming up with conversational topics—with observations and provocations for their fellow chat room participants that would add some interest to what they were watching. The show served as the starting point for these viewers' attempts to entertain themselves. As a viewer put it one evening, by way of saying farewell to the AOL *Big Brother* chat room, "It's been real—and a lot more entertaining than live feeds."[60] "It's been real" is, of course, a standard colloquial sign-off that takes on added resonance within the context of the current discussion; it invokes, albeit unintentionally, the "authenticity" of the forms of truly popular culture in which the viewers are also participants. But the more salient point is that chat room contributions repeatedly echoed the sentiment that talking with other viewers was much more interesting than actually watching the show. The viewing experience became, in some sense, secondary to the discussion: a necessary prerequisite for participation in the online chats. This sentiment frequently crops up on reality TV websites, which have become a media phenomenon in their own right. Posters repeatedly say they watch the show so that they'll be able to participate in the online discussion. Part of the pleasure accorded to savvy viewers—one of the ways they are able to reconcile themselves to the entertainment programming whose limitations are obvious to them—is that of savagely critiquing the shows in online forums. Hence the success of websites like "Television without Pity" (www.televisionwithoutpity.com), which features sarcastic recaps of and repartee about popular television shows. The popularity of the sites hasn't escaped the notice of producers, who have, at times, responded to online critiques and have taken to assigning members of the production staff to monitoring the bulletin boards.[61]

Moreover, chatting wasn't the only effort that viewers put into *Big Brother*. By the end of the show's run, Regina Lewis of AOL noted that viewers had created more than fourteen thousand Internet home pages devoted to the show. Not all of them were complimentary, but they certainly represented a significant investment in time and energy by their designers, as well as a commitment to watching the show, whether to praise or mock it. The pages included everything from rants about the show to homemade animated movies featuring the houseguests. The online magazine *Salon* even included a section devoted to satirical summaries of the show. Contributors to one online site—which was largely critical of the show—ended up becoming part of it, since they pitched in to pay for several of the aerial messages that were flown over the house on a daily basis.[62] As Dr. Drew Pinsky noted, the plane messages became another "character" in the compound, inciting more tension in the house than any of the cast members, and serving as one of the dominant themes of the televised version of the show. In Los Angeles, other viewers were able to make their mark on the show through their fan activities, including an amateur painter who started selling his portraits of cast members online and a woman known only to the houseguests as "megaphone lady," who periodically tried to communicate with them over the compound walls before being chased away by security guards.

In a progression reminiscent of the movie *EdTV* wherein the protagonist—a San Francisco slacker chosen to be the subject of a twenty-four-hour reality show—found that his family and friends were slowly being sucked into his show, *Big Brother* repeatedly drew on friends, family, and assorted "person-on-the-street" interviews to widen the cast of "real" characters on the show. Once the live show started featuring visits to groups of fans, the fans started to organize in earnest. A town in Texas adopted George (despite the fact that he lived in Rockford, Illinois), and held a Texas-style "George Day" celebration, complete with high school marching bands and cheerleaders. A college in Vermont earned airtime on CBS with its offer of a scholarship to George's daughter, and an Illinois radio station got a plug for sponsoring free telephone calls to banish George's rivals in the house. CBS visited the homes of the cast's family members and local bars that had organized parties to support their hometown houseguests. The nature of the exchange was clear: those who were willing to do the work of promoting the show could become participants. Taken to the extreme, the content of the show was its own publicity—which is one way of conceptualizing the willingness of the houseguests to expose their private lives on television and online: their participation was their self-promotion. Shortly after the show ended, more than half of the houseguests had their own official websites, and Brittany, Eddie, Josh, and Jamie all acquired agents.[63]

It is also interesting to note that even though the houseguests repeatedly downplayed the role of the show's cash prize, the promise of celebrity remained a constant touchstone in their conversations. The decision to walk out, for example, although presented as an attempt to make a gesture that placed solidarity ahead of the machinations of the culture industry, also relied upon the publicity that the gesture would receive. The houseguests could imagine that their decision would "make television history" because they were confident that millions of people were watching them. The assumption that the media exposure could be translated into cash was one of the subtexts of George's plea to the houseguests to join him in his insurrection. Early on in his presentation, when he felt some of his housemates might be reluctant to give up the chance of winning the $500,000 prize, he told them, "If you're looking at the money part of it, I have a feeling there's going to be so much out there for us it's going to be unbelievable."[64]

The delusions of popularity cherished by the houseguests were a source of amusement to producer Doug Ross, who was particularly struck by the fact that when faced with a challenge that forced them to decide between true and false news headlines, the remaining houseguests guessed that most of the false headlines about former cast members cashing in on their celebrity were true (that, e.g., Karen from Illinois had landed a contract to host a cable television cooking show). As Ross put it, "All of them started developing a very grandiose sense of their own popularity, and they assumed that they had a much bigger impact than they were having."[65] Which is perhaps not surprising, considering that the implicit promise of the show is that win or not, just the exposure would provide empowering access to the realm from which "real" people are traditionally excluded.

Once they've gained access, interestingly, the temptation seems to be to adopt the role of manipulator rather than challenging it. In the case of *Big Brother* viewers, for example, once they were invited into the digital compound of the website, many of them adopted the role of advisor and collaborator, telling the CBS producers to make the show more interesting and thus boost ratings. Many of the posts to the *Big Brother* website took on the character of employee contributions to the office "suggestion" box: offering insight from the viewers' perspective that might help improve the show. Often these posts were among the longest and most thoughtful on the bulletin boards, clearly the results of time and effort on the part of the contributors. Also, these posts, unlike many others, often sparked discussion strands on the message boards, with one suggestion touching off several others, frequently addressed directly to the producers. One typical example posted to the *Big Brother* website offered to help out the producers:

> Want to raise your ratings CBS and AOL? You need MORE interactivity between the BB show and your viewers. Think about what has NOT been done yet on the Internet and do it with the BB website. . . . A few of my suggestions, and I'm not publicly revealing all that I've thought of ;) . . . . You need more interactive polls on your web site (Find out what your viewers really think. People LOVE to express their opinions.) . . . you need LIVE online chats with former banished house guests, you need LIVE online chats with members of the family of some of the house guests, you need more *ongoing* contests between your viewers.[66]

The post enacts its own assertion that "people love to express their opinions," implying a certain self-reflexive savviness. The claim replicates and internalizes the recognition enlisted by the online economy and reality TV that viewers can be more effectively manipulated (in order to increase ratings) via the promise of interactivity. Lurking in the background is a certain vulnerability to that promise: the distant hope that perhaps the show's producers might take the author up on the possibility of even better ideas to come—that a good post might earn the author a winning ticket for the lottery of reality TV fame.

One of the notable facts about the bulletin board is that it operated in the register of mass customization, allowing viewers to tell producers what they expected from their entertainment product. Another post, for example, tells the producers that they should "show the 10 big brother contestants family's reactions to their antics. I'd like to hear what Karen's husband and willy's girlfriend have to say."[67] One of the favorite responses of viewers was to put themselves in the producers' position in order to imagine how they would manipulate the cast members by coming up with ideas for challenges. For example, one viewer suggested that "one way to judge how well these people learn to live together would be to allow one hour of TV a day—they'd have to agree on what to watch. That would lead to some negotiating, bargaining, etc. Also, allow one hour of music—they'd have to agree on what kind of music to play."[68] Still others picked up on the mind games that producers occasionally played with the houseguests: "Tell the guests the show is bombing and if nothing happens soon, it will be removed" or "Reveal to the guests one secret about each other. Tell them in advance that it's coming. See them flip. . . . Hey, why not a personal challenge, if they fail, the secret is out."[69] Often the viewers demonstrated a slightly sadistic ingenuity that rivaled that of the producers: "Why not give them a treadmill and have it be their power supply? Want lights at night? Want the fridge to keep running? Well, better get a move on."[70]

Producer Doug Ross said that he and his counterparts at America Online were not unsympathetic to the pleas for "greater interactivity" and that they repeatedly tried to convince their Dutch counterparts to allow online viewers to choose a daily challenge for the houseguests from several alternatives contrived by the producers: "It was my opinion as well as that of most Americans working on the show, that we take information that we retrieved from the Web and use it to influence how we were programming the show."[71] He said the response from the show's Dutch production company, Endemol, was a reluctance to make changes in the format that relinquished any element of producer control: "The Dutch folks felt they didn't want to not be in control of selecting a challenge if that particular challenge was one that was needed at the moment."[72] Ross criticized this decision, arguing that such participation would provide one more way to provide "genuine and authentic interactivity between Web viewers and the TV show."[73] Indeed, the version of producer control that Ross seemed to be moving toward is very similar to that of Janet Murray's conception of procedural authorship wherein the author provides not a set script, but the rules for the viewer's involvement. Thus, Ross describes one of the show's weaknesses as a failure to fully exploit the interactive potential of Internet.[74]

He similarly noted that while the Internet represented an instantaneous source of feedback as to how audiences were reacting to particular developments in the house, producers did not systematically incorporate this feedback into the show. This fact perhaps represents the limits of the show's transitional format. Television, in its current form, cannot yet follow through on the promise of mass customization but relies instead on the traditional paradigm of mass marketing: averaging preferences in order to maximize consumer appeal. The crucial information from the point of view of the programmer is not so much the individualized preferences, but the fact that enough of these line up to create a mass audience. Ross said the *Big Brother* producers were conscious not so much of the specific content of the online posts, but of increases in the volume of posts in response to particular episodes.[75]

Thus, the show reflected the fact that the extent to which individual viewer contributions can be incorporated into current television programming is limited by the current state of the medium. *Big Brother* pushed that limit about as far as it could by incorporating viewers and their insights into the show. It also reported their responses to a variety of daily online polls featured on the website: ranging from who the most popular houseguest was to whether Jamie should have met with her mother instead of the casting director. The polling process, as scholars including Benjamin Ginsburg and Jürgen Habermas have noted, represents, within the context of mass society, the translation (and reduction) of democratic deliberation into the paradigm of market research (and its attendant strategy of public relations manipulation).[76] The ever finer and more frequent deployment of polling by marketers (and politicians) that coincides with emerging forms of flexible production falls short of the promise of mass customization. This colonization of democratization by the market model is reflected in the promise of *Big Brother*: that viewers shape the show according to their preferences, and thereby exercise control over the production process. The added benefit for producers is that they can introduce the poll results into the *Big Brother* house as one means of inciting tension and competition. The wealth of information about consumer preferences available through monitoring in the digital enclosure will not be fully exploitable until the technology and the format develop further in the direction of mass customization.

This section concludes with a brief comparison of the way fans reacted to the promise of shared control and the way the houseguests plotted to seize control and end the show. In the virtual space of the website, as in the show itself, there was a moment when viewers attempted to take the promise of shared control literally and stage a rebellion. The catalyzing moment came shortly after Brittany was banished following the voting campaign organized by George's wife and sponsored by an Illinois radio station that allowed his supporters to call in their votes for free. Although producers eventually revealed that the campaign did not alter the outcome, online viewers expressed outrage that the voting process had been "tampered with"—thereby undermining the implicit promise of democratic control. The outrage was in part a result of their evident surprise at the outcome. Brittany, who was kicked out instead of George, was generally considered to be one of the more popular houseguests, not least because of the results of an American Online poll in which web viewers selected her as their favorite cast member. The results of this poll not only were announced on the live television show but were revealed to the houseguests as well.

After the vote results were announced (during the same episode of the show that featured an interview with George's wife on the topic of her "get-out-the-vote" campaign), online viewers responded with an attempt to organize opposition to the allegedly tainted outcome. Some posts to the online bulletin board called for a boycott of the show, others for a boycott of the sponsors. It is interesting to see how readily this rhetoric of offended democratic sensibilities was translated into the realm of commodified entertainment. For example, one indignant viewer wrote:

> We spend our money to vote out these people. It's not reassuring to know that my one vote won't make a difference when a whole town bands together to vote for free. ... I hope the sponsors see how WE the people feel and start bailing out now or we shall begin boycotting them also. The People in America will not tolerate watching abuse.[77]

In a spurt of Internet "activism," another viewer composed an online petition and then posted the address of the petition on the official *Big Brother* website, asking viewers not only to sign, but to join her in a campaign to have George voted off the show. Finally, she called on the producers to "acknowledge that there has been a negative outcome from this television show," to apologize to Brittany and to consider bringing her back into the house.

The flurry of activity on the website was duly noted and announced on the show, not only during the live show, but as part of a daily challenge posed for the houseguests based on headlines "in the news." By the time of this challenge—two weeks after Brittany's expulsion—more than seventeen thousand Brittany fans had signed the petition, and the controversy over the "tainted" vote had generated hundreds of news articles. Jim Stone, the manager of WXRX Radio, which sponsored the free call-in campaign, noted in an on-line post to the *Big Brother* website that ratings had increased marginally after the incident.[78] The producers didn't apologize for the vote, but they did justify it repeatedly to reporters. In the end, Doug Ross said the attempted viewer rebellion had much the same effect as George's walkout plan: it momentarily injected drama and controversy into the show. Even better, it demonstrated that there were viewers who were deeply invested in the show's outcome. Radio manager Jim Stone implied viewers were taking the whole a thing a bit too seriously. "Do you realize this is just a TV show?" he asked in his online reply to Brittany's angry fans.[79] Producer Doug Ross, on the other hand, said he and his coproducers interpreted the response as an indication of just how seriously the viewers were taking the promise of reality: "We'd say, 'Isn't it phenomenal that people are really invested and they're hooked on it to the point that they can't get it out of their system.'"[80] As in the case of the cast rebellion, the moment when viewers took the promise of shared control most seriously coincided with the moment they were working most effectively to maximize the value of the show for its producers.

NOTES

    1. T. J. Jackson Lears, "From Salvation to Self-Realization," in *The Culture of Consumption*, ed. Richard W Fox. and T. J. Jackson Lears (New York: Pantheon, 1983).

2. Lears, "From Salvation to Self-Realization," 6.

3. Lears, "From Salvation to Self-Realization," 10.

4. Lears, "From Salvation to Self-Realization," 7; Roland Marchand, *Advertising the American Dream, Making Way for Modernity, 1920–1940* (Berkeley: University of California Press, 1985), 10.

5. As quoted in Lears, "From Salvation to Self-Realization," 7.

6. Lears, "From Salvation to Self-Realization," 18.

7. *Big Brother*, WKNC, Denver, 22 August 2000.

8. *Big Brother*, WKNC, Denver, 18 August 2000.

9. *Big Brother*, WKNC, Denver, 18 August 2000.

10. *Big Brother*, WKNC, Denver, 18 August 2000.

11. *Big Brother*, WKNC, Denver, 18 August 2000.

12. Susan Buck-Morss, *The Origin of Negative Dialectics* (New York: Free Press, 1977), 77.

13. Theodor Adorno, "Sociology and Empirical Research," in *The Adorno Reader*, ed. Brian O'Connor (Oxford: Blackwell, 2000), 174–92; Theodor Adorno, "Subject and Object," in *The Adorno Reader*, 137–52.

14. Gillian Rose, *The Melancholy Science: An Introduction to the Thought of Theodor W. Adorno* (London: Macmillan, 1978).

15. Brian O'Connor, "Introduction," in *The Adorno Reader*, ed. Brian O'Connor (Oxford: Blackwell, 2000).

16. O'Connor, "Introduction," 13.

17. Theodor Adorno, *Minima Moralia: Reflections from Damaged Life* (London: New Left Books, 1974).

18. As quoted in J. M. Bernstein, "Why Rescue Semblance? Metaphysical Experience and the Possibility of Ethics," in *The Semblance of Subjectivity*, ed. Lambert Zuidervaart (Cambridge, Mass.: MIT Press, 1997), 181.

19. Bernstein, "Why Rescue Semblance?" 233.

20. Martin Jay, "Mimesis and Mimetology," in *The Semblance of Subjectivity*, ed. Lambert Zuidervaart (Cambridge, Mass.: MIT Press, 1997).

21. O'Connor, "Introduction."

22. O'Connor, "Introduction."

23. As quoted in Simon Jarvis, *Adorno: A Critical Introduction*, 166.

24. O'Connor, "Introduction," 12.

25. Theodor Adorno, *Kierkegaard: Construction of the Aesthetic* (Minneapolis: University of Minnesota Press, 1989), 40–41.

26. Adorno, *Kierkegaard*, 41.

27. Adorno, *Kierkegaard*, 41. It should be pointed out that Adorno does not assimilate Kierkegaard to the category of shallow idealist, and that he is, as Gillian Rose points out, "most sympathetic . . . to Kierkegaard's refusal to posit identity between thought and reality and to his disposing of the 'autonomous ratio' as the foundation of knowledge" (Rose, *The Melancholy Science*, 63). Adorno argues—in a fashion typical to his immanent critique of those philosophies which he regards as significant expressions of the impasse of modernity—not that Kierkegaard is in idealist, but that his attempt to sidestep idealism remains antinomical and results in the absolutization of the individual. The result is the naturalization of how the individual has been construed, historically, under the reign of identity thinking.

28. Ray Kurzweil, *The Age of Spiritual Machines: When Computers Exceed Human Intelligence* (New York: Viking, 1999). The utopian and dystopian versions of "virtual reality" have a notable tendency to converge. Thus, Kurzweil's version of a future in which the "flesh" is no longer a necessary repository for our experiences—sensory or otherwise—bears a strong resemblance to the enslavement portrayed in the 1999 movie *The Matrix*, in which humans have been reduced to naked fetus-like creatures floating in amniotic fluid, experiencing the day-to-day reality of going to work, eating, making love, and so forth, "virtually" in the form of sensations programmed straight into the brain, bypassing the "reality" of the body's static physical existence.

29. Adorno, *Kierkegaard*, 42.

30. Todd Gitlin, "Blips, Bites and Savvy Talk: Television's Impact on American Politics," *Dissent* (Winter 1990): 18–26.

31. *Big Brother*, WKNC, Denver, 29 September 2000.

32. *Big Brother*, WKNC, Denver, 5 July 2000.

33. *Big Brother*, WKNC, Denver, 13 August 2000.

34. *Big Brother*, WKNC, Denver, 13 August 2000.

35. *Big Brother*, WKNC, Denver, 13 August 2000.

36. *Big Brother*, WKNC, Denver, 29 September 2000.

37. *Big Brother*, WKNC, Denver, 17 August 2000.

38. *Big Brother*, WKNC, Denver, 17 August 2000.

39. Rick Kissell, "Olympics Take Gold," *Variety*, 9 October 2000, 18.

40. Kissell, "Olympics Take Gold."

41. Doug Ross, telephone interview with the author, 18 January 2001.

42. "Boards," at www.BigBrother2000.com, 20 January 2001.

43. Doug Ross, telephone interview with the author, 18 January 2001.

44. Ross, telephone interview with the author, 18 January 2001.

45. *Big Brother*, WKNC, Denver, 13 September 2000.

46. Ross, telephone interview with the author, 18 January 2000.

47. Ross, telephone interview with the author, 18 January 2000.

48. "Chat," at BigBrother2000.com (accessed 2 December 2000).

49. "Chat."

50. Doug Ross, telephone interview with the author, 18 January 2001.

51. Laurie Flynn, "Compressed Data: Faltering TV Show Hits Stride on Web," *New York Times*, 18 September 2000, C4; *Big Brother*, WKNC, Denver, 13 September 2000.

52. Press release, AOL, 5 October 2000.

53. Nick Couldry, *The Place of Media Power* (London: Routledge, 2000), 178.

54. See, for example, Ben Bagdikian, *The Effete Conspiracy* (New York: Harper & Row, 1972), and Ralph Miliband, *The State in Capitalist Society* (New York: Basic Books, 1969).

55. *Big Brother*, WKNC, Denver, 26 July 2000.

56. "The Boards," at BigBrother2000.com (accessed 28 September 2000).

57. "Chat," at BigBrother2000.com (accessed 20 September 2000).

58. "Chat."

59. *Big Brother*, WKNC, Denver, 5 July 2000.

60. "Chat," at www.BigBrother2000.com (accessed 20 August 2000).

61. Marshall Sella, "The Remote Controllers," *New York Times*, 20 October 2002, 6, 68.

62. Steven Davey, "Brother Not Big," *Now*, 21–27 September 2000, at www. nowtoronto.com/issues/2000-09-21/next.html (accessed 2 January 2002).

63. Eddie McGee, telephone interview with the author, 16 January 2001.

64. *Big Brother*, WKNC, Denver, 13 September 2000.

65. Ross, telephone interview with the author, 18 January 2001.

66. "The Boards," at BigBrother2000.com (accessed 28 September 2000).

67. "The Boards."

68. "The Boards."

69. "The Boards."

70. "The Boards."

71. Ross, telephone interview with the author, 18 January 2001.

72. Ross, telephone interview with the author, 18 January 2001.

73. Ross, telephone interview with the author, 18 January 2001.

74. Janet Murray, *Hamlet on the Holodeck: The Future of Narrative in Cyberspace* (New York: Free Press, 1977).

75. Ross, telephone interview with the author, 18 January 2001.

76. Benjamin Ginsberg, *The Captive Public: How Mass Opinion Promotes State Power* (New York: Basic Books, 1986); Jürgen Habermas, *The Structural Transformation of the Public Sphere* (Cambridge, Mass.: MIT Press, 1991).

77. "The Boards," at BigBrother2000.com (accessed 2 September 2000).

78. "The Boards."

79. "The Boards."

80. Ross, telephone interview with the author, 18 January 2001.

Chapter Seven

Reality TV and Voyeurism

No discussion of the burgeoning reality TV trend can be complete without a consideration of its voyeuristic appeal. The power and control associated with the voyeuristic fetish is frequently evoked in popular descriptions of the appeal of reality TV, but it is rarely more than touched upon. Consequently, this chapter shifts from *Big Brother* to a discussion of a show that thematized the role of surveillance by incorporating it into the storyline.

Like *The Real World*, Fox's titillating, envelope-pushing show *Temptation Island* did not offer a cash prize. Instead, it based its appeal on the offer of a free trip to Belize, a stimulating "authentic" experience, and access to the truth about the cast member's "romantic relationships." In this regard, it picked up on the theme of self-knowledge and personal growth outlined in previous chapters. Moreover, in a self-reflexive gesture that has become the hallmark of television programming in the era of postmodern savviness, *Temptation Island* enacted the form of voyeurism to which it appealed. For viewers, the invitation was to receive intimate access to a relationship drama: Four couples would be split up and invited to date other people to see whether they would be willing to cheat on their significant other. The viewer was given the role of the keyhole-peeping private detective: following the cast members on their dates to see whether they would have sex with each other. At the same time, the element of voyeurism was incorporated into the show itself: cast members had to decide whether they wanted to see "highlights" of their significant others' dates.

The result was an interesting, if unintentional, exploration of the paradoxical form of impotent power associated with the position of the voyeur who participates by watching. It is this form of false control that links the position of the savvy voyeur with that of the interactive consumer envisioned by the promoters of the mass-customized online economy. In both cases, the form of control on offer turns out to be yet another form of submission. However, it is not quite enough to argue alongside Gitlin that savvy voyeurism is a form of surrender or, following

Zizek that "the gaze denotes at the same time power (it enables us to exert control over the situation, to occupy the position of the master) and impotence (as bearers of a gaze, we are reduced to the role of passive witness . . .)."[1] This chapter pushes the argument a step further, arguing that the role of the savvy voyeur doubles as a performance of the desire not to be "seen" as a dupe and, in this regard, as a form of submission to an imagined, omniscient gaze (which may not remain merely imaginary for long). Just as the offer of participation in the online economy via mediated interactivity reveals itself as a ruse of rationalization, so the burgeoning genre of voyeurism TV corresponds to the increasingly important economic role of an exhibitionistic form of self-disclosure. The threefold equation of participation (empowerment), access to reality, and total transparency (guaranteed by comprehensive monitoring) align themselves in the voyeuristic appeal of reality TV.

Temptation Island ended up disappointing the dire predictions of those who anticipated (with avid indignation) that it would devolve into a decadent exercise in infidelity and gratuitous sex. The show, which featured four couples invited to a tropical island to "test" their long-term relationships by dating attractive singles, was widely received as a new low in the already bottom-feeding genre of reality television. It was variously denounced by critics as a "morally bankrupt" network-sponsored attempt to induce promiscuity and infidelity, as "trash TV," and as a "perverse 'Fantasy Island'"—"[t]he latest appalling, offensive, amoral, how-low-can-we-go TV stunt."[2] A spokesman for the Parents Television Council (PTC) was widely quoted as saying that, "The producers of 'Temptation Island' should be ashamed of themselves for trying to force the destruction of four relationships for the entertainment purposes of those lowlifes who consent to watch this trash."[3] The PTC's executive director added, "If we're putting this kind of thing on TV as a form of entertainment, we might as well throw Christians to the lions. . . . It's disgusting and appalling. The idea that any company would sponsor this is unconscionable."[4] Even the show's blandly nonjudgmental host, Mark Wahlberg, conceded under questioning, "By no means will I defend it as noble entertainment. . . . It's adult over-the-top moralitywise. . . . But it doesn't reflect my morals."[5] The uproar apparently had some impact on the show's economic success, since several advertisers pulled their support, citing moral concerns. The chairman of one media buying service, for example, explained his decision to the press as follows: "I would never put our clients in a show like 'Temptation Island.' . . . The whole show is founded on a premise that is totally distasteful. The next step is the Roman Coliseum."[6]

This collective corporate/media indignation all centered on a series that, despite the hype, featured a minimum of profanity, no sex, and a finale in which all four couples declared their long-term loyalty to each other. Any purely content-based assessment of the program would have to concede that it was tamer than much of the prime-time fare that easily flies beneath the moral radar of advertisers and watchdog groups. What, then, explains the strong reaction to a show less revealing than a typical episode of *Baywatch*? Precisely the fact that it concerned not professional actors and models reading from a script but the "real" relationships of "real" people. The angry response to *Temptation Island* was ostensibly predicated on the notion that it's one thing to portray fictional sex and infidelity and quite another to manipulate the emotions of real people for the entertainment of viewers—just as it's one thing to portray Christians being fed to the lions and quite another to really send martyrs to their deaths. Of course, this parallel doesn't hold up: the *Temptation Island* couples all chose to participate in the show in exchange for a $3,000 stipend, a free trip to Belize, and ready entrée into the burgeoning world of "reality celebrity." Moreover, members of three out of the four couples went on record saying they decided to participate in the show as a means of giving their respective acting and modeling careers a boost.

If the claim to reality remains somewhat suspect—given the couples' admitted motivation for participating in the show—the assertion that *Temptation Island* undermines committed relationships and promotes promiscuity seems even more so. Perhaps the most realistic aspect of the series was its depiction of the economic potential of the exploitation of voyeurism (and exhibitionism) in an era characterized by the increasingly important economic role of electronic surveillance. Rather than attempting to plumb the depths of the reality of the couple's relationships, this chapter will explore the ways in which the logic of voyeurism enacted by *Temptation Island* traces the productivity of what Zizek (2000) describes as the "closed loop of perversion" typical of "late capitalist" market relations.[7] Drawing on the Lacanian description of the scopic drive, the goal is to demonstrate how the position of the voyeur (which recurs at several levels in *Temptation Island*) enacts not the desire to see and control so much as the drive to "make oneself seen."

The broader significance of this example resides in the fact that the role of making oneself seen, and hence of the scopic drive, is central to the emerging surveillance economy in which the transparency of the subject has an increasingly important role to play in the rationalization of production. Moreover, within a Lacanian framework it is crucial that what is at stake in the portrayal of voyeurism is the logic of the drive, which is, according to Zizek, properly perverse, insofar as "it finds satisfaction in . . . the very movement destined to 'repress' satisfaction."[8] Rather than retaining a fidelity to an ever-receding goal, in short, it finds its idiotic satisfaction in the closed cycle of repeatedly missing its goal, and thereby in the eclipse of the goal itself. In this respect, the connection between a psychoanalytic approach and social theory can be drawn: the logic of the drive describes the libidinal economy of the closed cycle of production/consumption *for their own sake*. The pervert, defined in these terms, embodies the subject position carved out by the market system for the mass-customized consumer: a shopper whose search for individuation through consumption always misses its mark.

PERVERSION, NOT SUBVERSION

The indignant reaction to *Temptation Island* as a threat to public morals implicitly assumes that perversion doubles as a form of subversion. What seems to trouble the critics, in other words, is the possibility that the portrayal of promiscuity as a form of entertainment will erode the moral fabric and that once viewers start taking pleasure in the emotional plight of "real" people, true moral decay will set in. This fear incorporates a certain willful disregard for the central role of ongoing "real" sex scandals in the mass media, obscuring the fact that the obverse of the ostensibly threatened public morality is an ongoing entertainment diet of human emotional trauma. The ideological moment, in other words, resides in the denial that the moral order championed by the indignant critics coincides with the immoral forms of entertainment that ostensibly threaten to undermine it.

To recast the argument in the terms suggested by Zizek, perversion (e.g., in the form of *Temptation Island*) cannot be equated with subversion (of the dominant moral order) *pace* those strains of performativity theory that suggest the hegemony of the dominant order can be challenged through transgressive forms of "acting out." In an era when the co-optation of transgression has become a prevalent mode of the dominant order's reproduction, this conclusion is by no means earth-shattering. Nonetheless, it provides an important qualification to those forms of reception theory as well as to those forms of cultural theory that champion the subversive character of "letting the freaks speak."[9]

Moreover, a psychoanalytic approach provides a useful set of terms for thinking through the ostensibly "transgressive" format of *Temptation Island*. Perversion, on this account, is to be viewed not as a (subversive) expression of the unconscious desire repressed by the dominant order, but rather as the expression of this order's *inherent* transgression: its "obscene, super-egotistical reverse." As Zizek puts it, "The deepest identification which 'holds a community together' is not so much identification with the Law that regulates its 'normal' everyday circuit as identification with the specific form of transgression of the Law, of its suspension."[10] In these terms, a program like *Temptation Island* ought to be viewed not as an attempt to "push the limits" of decency, but rather as paradigmatic of the moral order it ostensibly subverts. Apparent excesses of voyeurism such as the burgeoning reality genre, or perhaps the media spectacle surrounding Bill Clinton's sex life, can be viewed, on this account, as the flip side of forms of representative publicity that have come to count as politics. Given the central role of the exploitation of emotional trauma and sexual transgression to the entertainment industry, this argument seems rather more convincing than the indignant criticism repeatedly leveled against the show. *Temptation Island*, in short, is not a "new" low but the *old* one that we've been living with for quite some time. Thus, it is perhaps not surprising that the series earned Fox the highest ratings ever for its time slot, and also drew more of the coveted eighteen- to forty-nine-year-old demographic than any other Fox entertainment program of the season.[11]

Tellingly, the moral indignation over a series like *Temptation Island* has an important role to play as a form of publicity. The seemingly "transgressive" aspect of the format helped garner extensive publicity, providing Fox with far more free advertising than it received for its other reality series of the season: *Boot Camp*, which had a somewhat less provocative theme—"real" people enduring military style training subject to the discipline of "real" drill instructors. Indeed, the way in which these two shows complemented each other—one focusing on the rigors of discipline, the other on "forbidden" pleasures—enacts the description of transgression as the obscene underside/obverse of the moral law. As if to further emphasize this connection, Fox heavily promoted *Boot Camp* during *Temptation Island*, interspersing scenes of erotic tropical romps with images of boot camp discipline (e.g., people in fatigues doing push-ups while being yelled at by army officers). The decision to promote the one show during the other's run highlighted the implicit connection: what linked the format of transgression with that of discipline was the ostensible basis of *both* in "reality." The two shows were the twin poles of Fox's "reality"-based programming for the season. The Fox network itself, disparaged as a right-wing, Murdoch-spawned, sensationalistic media outlet might be viewed as the excessive obverse of the network system: not a subversive challenge to "quality" programming, but an expression of its constitutive underside: the obscene truth of self-righteously decent, objective, family-oriented programming designed to sell eyes to advertisers.

The success of *Temptation Island* and the role played by the indignant critics in helping to guarantee this success reinforce Zizek's assertion (following Freud and Lacan) that "perversion is always a socially constructive attitude"—not a socially subversive one.[12] The following sections will attempt to elaborate this socially "constructive" role within the context of the emerging surveillance-based economy associated with "flexible" capitalism.

PERVERSE SUBJECTS

Perhaps the most significant aspect of the version of psychoanalytic Marxism expounded by Zizek is the attempt to make a link between a Lacanian theory of the subject and the social relations of "late" capitalism—to describe, in short, the libidinal economy of contemporary capitalism. A central question addressed by this approach is that concerning the role of desire in the circuit of production and consumption for their own sake—a circuit that certainly deserves to be labeled perverse in the strict sense. Zizek describes this perversion in terms of the Lacanian logic of the "drive": "The most succinct definition of the reversal constitutive of drive is the moment when, in our engagement in a purposeful activity . . . the way towards this goal, the gestures we make to achieve it, start to function as a goal in itself, as its own aim, as something that brings its own satisfaction."[13]

The logic of capital—its substitution of means for ends—provides a paradigmatic example of the Lacanian logic of perversion insofar as it "finds satisfaction in . . . the very movement destined to 'repress' satisfaction."[14] Rather than attempting to break out of the self-proliferating cycle of a pursuit that always eclipses its goal (a cycle of exchange value that always eclipses use value), the subjective attitude of perversion is one that "gets off" on the repetition of this cycle: production for its own sake. This kind of productive cycle requires a similar self-fueling spiral in the realm of consumption: the ongoing attempt to fulfill needs while simultaneously endlessly deferring their fulfillment. Such attempts are staples of consumer society: the goal of gaining control over the environment by continuing to destroy it (e.g., buying sports utility vehicles because they are associated with the ability to conquer nature) or of expressing oneself through the purchase of products that always reduce the purchaser to the status of one more marketing statistic.

The discussion so far raises a central question regarding the periodization of capital. Why the stipulation that the perverse subject in question is that of "late" capitalism? The subjective attitude of capitalism in general, whether early, late, or somewhere in between, surely falls within the realm of the perverse. Thus, the designation of "late" points specifically to the ironic, self-distancing, reflexive attitude of ideology in the postmodern era. What seems characteristic of the contemporary "postmodern" attitude, in short, is the savvy stance outlined in previous chapters: a complacent "knowing" that takes pleasure in not having any illusions about society. This attitude of savviness is properly perverse insofar as it sacrifices the possibility of social struggle in order to claim the status of the "nonduped"—so as to recognize behind every social ideal the way in which it is deployed as a ruse of power (and thus deriving satisfaction from the knowledge of one's own impotence). The predominant perverse attitude of "late" capitalism is that which concedes the critical point—that, for example, power is increasingly lodged in the hands of a select few who control not just the economy, but politics and the mass media—without becoming the dupe of such critiques and imagining that things could be otherwise. Savvy subjects derive pleasure precisely from not being fooled by either the elite or the social critics: they know just how bad things are and just how futile it is to imagine they could be otherwise.

Gitlin invokes the example of political coverage to demonstrate this attitude, arguing that the trend of reflexive "metacoverage," which knowingly documents politicians' attempts to manipulate public opinion, serves to naturalize manipulation rather than contest it. This metacoverage is perverse in the sense outlined earlier insofar as it trumpets its own failure as its final satisfaction. It paradoxically devotes ever greater resources to coverage that demonstrates the futility of its own premise: that informing the public serves to empower it. It is precisely this perversity that media sociologist Todd Gitlin highlights when he notes that this surrender coincides with a fundamentally depoliticized society, precisely because it negates the promise of politics to be about anything other than manipulation. Significantly, Gitlin's description of savviness highlights its kinship with voyeurism: "One is already participating, in effect, by watching. 'I like to watch' is the premium attitude."[15]

Savviness is literally perverse insofar as it is expressed in the "premium attitude" of voyeurism and the fetishization of the scopic drive. It is equally perverse in the Lacanian sense: It gets off on the very cycle of failure that it highlights, exhibiting a certain scorn for the fuzzy hope of the duped: that things might be other than they are. Contesting the perverse logic of late capitalism, then, means avoiding the celebratory postmodern notion that perversion is subversive and, instead, highlighting its complicity. *Temptation Island* is perhaps a particularly telling example of this complicity insofar as its enactment of the default of voyeurism to the drive to "make oneself seen" exemplifies the socially *productive* role of surveillance (its socially constructive role, as opposed to its ostensibly subversive character).

PERVERSION 1: THE CAST

The driving tension of *Temptation Island*—its incitement to transgression within the narrative frame—is provided by what might be described as a sadomasochistic deployment of the gaze. Once the couples are separated from one another, they are allowed to see each other in person only during the process of picking their upcoming dates. This selection process takes place around a palm tree–lined swimming pool, with the couples divided into two groups according to gender. Members of each group select whom they want to "date" next from a lineup of bathing suit–clad members of the opposite sex. Thus, cast members do more than select a date; they also get to see whom their significant other selects. The tempters and temptresses make the most of this fact, taking the opportunity to rub it in by hugging or kissing their future dates in front of their dates' significant others.

One episode, for example, focused on the anger of a cast member named Billy after seeing a "tempter" embrace his girlfriend and carry her away from the swimming pool at the end of the selection process. Billy, picking up on the oft-repeated theme that the tempters were just "doing their job," lashed out at his girlfriend, Mandy: "Did you see that? Bad idea right there. That really pissed me off trying to get a rise out of me."[16] The show built on this cycle of provocation and reaction. Separated from each other and unable to communicate except via a few short video recordings, cast members were left to imagine what their partners were up to. The directors ensured their imaginations would be stimulated as much as possible by providing provocative glimpses of each cast member's date to his or her significant other.

The way in which this was done neatly emphasized the sadomasochistic play of voyeurism. In the early episodes, members of one group (either the men or the women) were given a choice: they could decide whether to view an excerpt from their partners' date, with the understanding that if they chose to see the excerpt, their partners would then have to watch an excerpt from their dates. The show's host, Mark Wahlberg, highlighted the logic of these rules when explaining to the women that the men had the first choice of whether to watch a "highlight" tape, adding that some of the men had decided not to watch their partners' dates: "Maybe they don't want to see what you did, maybe they don't want you to see what they did . . . sit with that for a moment." The decision of whether to adopt the position of voyeur by viewing the highlights of their partners' dates doubled as a decision regarding whether to take on the complementary role of exhibitionist (by forcing their partner to watch their own date). This double choice helped fuel tensions between couples, since a cast member who was angered by seeing his or her partner's date could "get even" by going on a particularly rambunctious date and then forcing the partner to watch it.

One of the show's central conflicts—that between Billy and his girlfriend Mandy—was driven by this circuit of voyeurism and exhibitionism. Mandy went on a particularly flirtatious date with one of the single men and then chose to watch the video of Billy's date, thereby forcing him to watch hers. At one point Billy told the host that he didn't want to see any more of the tape, saying he couldn't bear to watch (as she prepared to lick a drink off her date's belly). The host told him that he could close his eyes, but the rules were that the tape had to be played. So the other three male cast members watched as Billy looked away. But he couldn't escape the sound track of Mandy squealing in self-castigating delight: "Oh, no, Billy's going to kill me. . . . Oh, my God, Billy, I'm so sorry."[17] Billy, who was left to picture in his head the images that accompanied this soundtrack, was visibly troubled. Immediately after seeing the video, he described his reaction on camera: "Definitely trying to get the brain under control. . . . I mean. I heard her say, 'Billy's going to kill me.' Where did the date go from there? Did I see the worst part of the date, did I see the tamest part of the date? . . . That's the part that stings most."[18] From there, the situation continued to deteriorate. Billy, clearly deciding to "get back" at Mandy by cutting loose, performed a (partial) strip tease for the single women, thereby providing a highlight clip that was shown to Mandy when she was given the choice of viewing scenes from the "after-hours" partying in the men's compound. Her response as to whether she wanted to see the video was "Just play the tape. . . . I enjoy torturing myself to death."[19]

This self-stimulating and self-torturing cycle of a voyeurism that defaults to exhibitionism neatly recapitulates Lacan's description of the sadomasochistic logic of the scopic drive. Indeed, this default fulfills Lacan's assertion that "[i]f . . . the structure of the drive appears, it is really completed only in its reversed form, in its return form."[20] It is in this sense that the scopic drive—characterized by the pair voyeurism/exhibitionism—is not to be comprehended merely as the drive to see but rather as a form of "making oneself seen."[21] This claim is borne out by the example of *Temptation Island*, but how is it to be interpreted? Zizek relates it to the self-defeating (and self-stimulating) logic of perversion, arguing that the scopic drive "is neither a voyeuristic tendency to see nor the exhibitionistic tendency to be seen by another . . . but the 'middle voice,' the attitude of 'making oneself visible,' of deriving libidinal satisfaction from actively sustaining the scene of one's own passive submission."[22] It is this role of the "impotent master"—of actively staging one's passive submission—that characterizes the savvy attitude outlined above: taking pleasure in the impossibility of achieving one's goal—in the very act of repeatedly missing it. But recall wherein this pleasure resides: precisely in not being seen as a dupe—or to parallel Lacan's terminology, in *being seen* (making oneself seen) as not being a dupe. In short, the attitude is a staged one—a performance for the sake of what Lacan terms "the gaze," which he describes as "not a seen gaze, but a gaze imagined by me in the field of the other."[23]

Tellingly, the premise of *Temptation Island* invokes a certain form of savviness—of not being duped—as the show's guiding motif. The couples who appear on the show are doing so not for a cash prize or as part of a competition but ostensibly to test their relationships: to make sure that they have not been deceived about one another—that the person they are with is really "the one" for them. Thus, the show's host repeatedly emphasized that the couples had come to the island to learn the truth about themselves and their partners: to determine whether they had been duped by someone who, given two weeks in tropical paradise, would prove unfaithful. If, as Lacan puts it, the gaze is an imagined gaze in the field of the other, the "reality" format of *Temptation Island* realizes this gaze in the form of the audience: the voyeurs for whom the spectacle of courtship and temptation is staged. The audience gaze becomes that which "sees all," in contrast to the partial gaze of the cast members, who are left to imagine what their partners are up to. Furthermore, this imagined gaze—incarnated by the cameras that follow the cast members everywhere—serves as the guarantor of whether they are being duped. In the end, the cast members will know what went on "behind their backs"—it was all on national TV, thus allowing the imagined gaze in the field of the other to be realized in the form of the imagined audience. In this sense, *Temptation Island* enacts the fantasy of the gaze: that third-person position that legislates whether we have really been duped—which guarantees, in short, that reality that we ourselves cannot see. If the gaze serves as an elusive trace of the unsymbolized Real, the promise of a show like *Temptation Island* is to realize this trace—to assign it a place: that of the omnipresent gaze of the camera/audience.

This debilitating moment in which the voyeur's pleasure turns painful—and shameful—is central to the action on *Temptation Island*, which thrived on the reaction of the cast members to the images of their significant others. For example, one of the "highlights" pulled for the show's promotions featured Billy's reaction to the Mandy video: "Now the fun is over and I'm paying for it, and I hate to say it's a mistake, but now I'm in hell." As the show's critics rightly observed, the main focus of *Temptation Island* was on the emotional trauma resulting from the fact that the couples were split up and left to imagine the infidelities of their partners. What the show unleashed, via its selective use of video clips, was the power of the cast members to imagine the worst. The contestants were encouraged to fantasize the direst of outcomes—that their partners were falling in love with someone else. To stimulate this anxiety, the couples were repeatedly invited to share their anxieties about the fate of their relationships. In every case, the fear was that affections would stray and that the two-week *Temptation Island* experience would end up destroying a long-term relationship. In each case, these worst-case scenarios crystallized around an image—a brief glimpse—of the cast member's significant other. Billy, for example, responded to the videotaped image of Mandy about to kiss her date, while the cast member Valerie kept playing back in her mind her glimpse of Kaya on his first date ("I saw Kaya laughing, having a good time with this pretty girl—her hair blowing in the wind. . . . It just made me sick").[24]

The cast members—prompted by the show's host, repeatedly referred to the torment engendered by the image they couldn't get out of their heads. Billy, for example, was asked to reflect back on his decision to watch the infamous clip of Mandy and her date, Johnny: "At first I said, I've got to see it—I thought that would be best to do because my imagination runs free. But imagination is easier to deal with than reality."[25] More precisely, it is the reality of not knowing what Mandy is up to combined with the image of her flirtation that prompts him to imagine the worst. In this respect, it is the voyeuristic quality of the cast members' interactions—the fact that the only images they have to work with are stolen, fragmentary, out of context—that allows their imagination free rein.

Thus, *Temptation Island* neatly enacts Lacan's contention that in voyeurism, "What one looks at is what cannot be seen."[26] Valerie provides a literal example of this claim just prior to the final date, when by accident she encounters the group of temptresses who, because they have not been selected to go on the last date, are being sent home (the final date selections were not made in front of all of the cast members, so the cast members did not know whom their significant other had chosen). It is the *absence* of one of the temptresses from this group that bothers Valerie the most (that most stimulates her imagination). The missing woman is the one she feared Kaya would pick for his final date—the one that she felt he was most interested in, and hence the one who posed the biggest threat to their relationship. The absence of this woman from the group unnerved her and made her "rival" loom even larger in her imagination: "I have a visual in my head of who he's spending two days with, and I just didn't want to have that," she told the camera.[27] More generally, in each case, when the cast members viewed the clips of their significant others, they were trying to see what was left out—some indication as to whether their partners had been (un)faithful.

In the end, however, all of this anxiety was expressed to the cameras. The relationship of voyeurism to exhibitionism—of, for example, Mandy's grief upon getting a glimpse of Billy's strip-tease—clearly took place with an eye to the cameras that followed the cast members throughout the course of their two-week "holiday." In general, the cameras remained invisible, preserving the identification of the television viewers with the gaze of the camera, although given the beach attire appropriate to a tropical island vacation, it was possible to catch a glimpse from time to time of the radio microphones worn by the cast members. In one of the rare exceptions to the general invisibility of the production crew, Billy was shown attempting to escape the glare of the camera lights after his traumatic viewing of Mandy's highlight tape. "Turn it *off*," he yelled to the videographer chasing after him. "Seriously, this does not concern the show. It's my *life*." To which a disembodied voice—it was unclear whether it belonged to the videographer, the sound person, or a producer—replied, "Actually, your life *is* the show right now."[28]

The sound of this disembodied voice seemed uncannily out of place—an unwonted intrusion of the seemingly neutral gaze of the camera into the show's narrative content. It may sound odd to equate the sound of the voice with the gaze of the Other, but this is precisely the equation that Lacan, following Sartre, makes: "If you turn to Sartre's own text, you will see that, far from speaking of the emergence of the gaze as of something that concerns the organ of sight, he refers to the sound of rustling leaves, suddenly heard while out hunting, to a footstep heard in a corridor."[29] These sounds—heard exactly at the moment when the voyeur is "looking through the keyhole"—take the voyeur by surprise in the form of the sudden emergence of the gaze of the other. Similarly, the videographer's voice becomes the trace of the gaze that watches Billy as he watches Mandy. Billy's anger recoils back at the gaze in what comes across as an undecidable gesture: on the one hand, he seems to recognize the role of the show in stimulating the cycle of relationship transgression, on the other hand it's hard not to read each of *Temptation Island*'s emotional displays—Billy's included—as a self-conscious performance intended for that very gaze he ostensibly wants to elude. He *should* be outraged after seeing Mandy's video: it would look odd if he weren't. Moreover, he would, in some sense, be letting the producers down. In this respect, it is the presence of this gaze that provides the incitement to transgression that is central to the show's narrative tension.

This same cycle of transgression is central to the Lacanian version of perversion. Once Mandy makes the decision to see Billy's video—and thereby to force him to watch the highlights or her own date—the cycle begins. Apparently driven to distraction, Billy is seen disappearing into the cabana of one of the temptresses. Upon his disappearance, the other male cast members speculate that he is getting even by cheating on Mandy, which is what they say they'd do if they were in his place. Of course, the clip of this conversation is played for Mandy the same evening she chooses to watch the highlight video to "torture" herself. Her predictable reaction to the video is to imagine that Billy is willing to "throw away" their relationship—a fact that in turn frees her up to behave accordingly, and so the cycle continues.

Lacan's observation that the Freudian *Schaulust*—scopic drive—provides "the key" to an understanding of masochism is illustrated by this tension between Mandy and Billy.[30] For Lacan the sadomasochistic drive turns not on pain, per se, but on a violent act: "It is a question of a . . . violence done to what?—to something that is so unspeakable that Freud arrives at the conclusion, and at the same time recoils from it, that its first model . . . is to be found in a violence that the subject commits, with a view to mastery, upon himself."[31] This formulation suggests that the perverse role of the subject of the drive is per se sadomasochistic: it combines a violent act (inflicted on oneself) with passive acceptance of this act. In Zizek's terms, the drive is characterized by the derivation of libidinal satisfaction "from actively sustaining the scene of one's own passive submission."[32]

This formulation exactly describes the moment of resignation expressed by several of the cast members on *Temptation Island* in the face of anxiety about their partners' behavior: "If he or she wants to throw away our long-term relationship, so be it—it's out of my hands." Mandy, Valerie, and Andy all voice this sentiment, which rehearses the combination of activity and passivity described by Lacan: they are in the position of passively submitting to the violence that they have inflicted upon themselves. Billy's trip to the temptress's cabana enacts a similar logic: a resigned acceptance of the violence that he is inflicting on his own relationship—almost as if it's not of his own doing, as if it's beyond his control.

This sadomasochistic submission describes the paradigmatic subject position of late capitalism in which, oddly enough, those on both sides of the production process adopt the role of *victim* with respect to the big Other of the market. Producers remain "at the mercy" of the ever more volatile whims of consumers, while consumers end up having no other choice than what "the market" provides (just as workers are at the mercy of the unpredictable job market). This double submission occurs in both the narrative of *Temptation Island* (in which Mandy and Billy are at the mercy of the game itself—rather than each other) and in its critical reception. The series was roundly treated by pundits as one more example of the market making an appeal to the lowest common denominator (adopting the position that we, the viewers, are at the mercy of the market). At the same time, the show's producers described themselves as slaves to the market. Sandy Grushow, chairman of the Fox entertainment group, defended the show to the press, saying, according to one account, that the network would be negligent not to "pursue what is obviously an incredibly powerful trend in the industry": reality programming.[33] In Grushow's words, implicitly absolving the network from responsibility for the tastelessness of *Temptation Island*, the show was a result of Fox's "responsibility as network programmers to satisfy the tastes" of the audience.[34] The role of the market, in this case, is not naturalized by being relegated to the background. Instead, it is foregrounded—and bemoaned—in the passive gesture of the nonduped: yes, we are caught in a force larger than all of us, and it's time to face that fact. So be it.

This gesture enacts the "end-of-ideology" ideology of "late" capitalism. The market is no longer naturalized as the idealized, mystical invisible hand that will lead to the optimal outcome. Rather, its negative consequences are—to a significant extent—recognized and naturalized in this very fact of recognition. The disturbing consequence is that capitalism no longer need sustain itself on the basis of its promised benefits. Rather, the process of naturalization has been accomplished so thoroughly that even when the depredations of capital become evident, they attain the status of a natural disaster: tragic, but inevitable.

This naturalization is reflected in the co-optation of critique by popular culture and the entertainment industry, which, in the post–Cold War era, increasingly casts its villains as members of the capitalist elite: greedy captains of industry and corrupt politicians (and, of course, manipulative entertainment moguls). The "triumph" of neoliberalism in the 1990s has been accompanied not just by celebratory capitalist propaganda but also, tellingly, by a savvy critique of the breathless cheerleaders of the free market. From the standpoint of the savvy, the dupes are on both sides: on the one hand, those naïve enough to believe capitalism's propagandists; on the other, those naïve enough to still believe in the potential of progressive social change.

The problem faced by the social critic, then, is not the so-called false consciousness of an uninformed public but a complacent savviness that assumes it knows all too well. In other words, it's not that critical perspectives aren't being heard (e.g., the fact that Noam Chomsky can't get on *Nightline*), but rather that they have become a staple of popular culture—that Chomsky is more effectively glossed in a Hollywood product like *Bullworth* than in his own movie. Savviness works to inoculate capitalist culture by incorporating its self-critique into its self-propagation. It is in this respect that the savvy subject stages the scene of its submission as constitutive of its inner freedom: it attempts to avoid the fate of the duped, paradoxically, by accepting capitalism at its worst—by dispensing even with the promise of the benefits of the free market, a promise that might otherwise be enlisted to highlight societal contradictions.

Lest this capitulation appear too self-reflexive—as if the subject's "self-submission" is a purely internalized gesture—Lacan highlights the fact that the structure of the drive appears only "thanks to the introduction of the other." Translating this back into the example of *Temptation Island*, we might say that the self-proliferating voyeuristic drive enacted by the cast members (in watching video clips of their partners' dates) revolves around the vortex of the audience gaze—for which the entire spectacle is staged. The ostensible goal of each cast members' voyeurism is, precisely, to see from the position of the Other/audience: to discover the objective truth of the significant other's intentions (and thereby to see oneself as one is seen—to determine whether one is, in fact, a dupe). What is productive about this threefold relationship (between seer, seen, and gaze) is the disruption of the closed circuit of the intersubjective gaze between the two lovers by the intrusion of the camera: the "objective" gaze that epitomizes the trace of the real, the blind mechanism of the big Other/symbolic order. Thus, *Temptation Island* neatly highlights not just the sadomasochistic role of the scopic drive in the interplay between the cast members, but the socially complicit role played by the voyeurism of the audience. However—and

this is crucial to the format's fundamentally conservative (nonsubversive) perversion—*Temptation Island* avoids thematizing this complicity, allowing the
audience to *retain* the role of neutral observer, rather than highlighting the role
of its own desire in the sadomasochistic interplay.

PERVERSION 2: THE AUDIENCE

Temptation Island makes explicit one of the recurring questions of the reality-
based shows that document the day-to-day lives of a group of "real" people living
together: who is going to have sex with whom? One of the most publicized
"behind-the-scenes" details about the show was the fact that the production company ensured that all cast members—both the couples and their tempters and
temptresses—were tested for sexually transmitted diseases.[35] The repeated public
insistence of those associated with the show that *Temptation Island* wasn't about
sex—but rather about the dynamics of "serious relationships"—came across as
both obvious and disingenuous. Obvious, because given the conventions of prime-
time TV in the United States, there was no question of the show being any more
revealing than *Baywatch*; disingenuous, because the show—whose wardrobe was
not much different from that of *Baywatch*—revolved around the question of sexual fidelity. As a reality format, *Temptation Island* played like a version of *The
Real World* with all the parts that weren't about sex removed.[36] With respect to the
sexual drama/trauma staged by the series, the audience was ostensibly exempted:
viewers were offered the pleasure of watching the producers and the cast members
instigate anxiety, grief, and sexual tension. The format followed the conventions
of "objective" documentary to the extent that the action was presented as unfold-
ing before the neutral gaze of the camera/audience. These conventions typically
background the effect that the camera itself has on the action: that the entire scenario was staged for the camera's eye. The filmic conventions enlisted by *Temptation Island*—the invisibility of the production equipment, producers, and tech-
nicians documenting the show and the explicit claim to "reality"—encouraged the
audience to adopt the position described by Zizek as that of the "pure gaze":

> [W]hile we perceive ourselves as external bystanders stealing a furtive glance into
> some majestic Mystery which is indifferent to us, we are blinded to the fact that the
> entire spectacle of the Mystery is staged with *an eye to our gaze*: to attract and fas-
> cinate our gaze—here, the Other deceives us in so far as it induces us to believe that
> we were *not* chosen; here, it is the true addressee him/herself who mistakes his/her
> position for that of an accidental bystander.[37]

The position prepared for the viewer is, in the sense outlined by Lacan in his
essay "Kant with Sade," properly perverse, insofar as the audience is invited to
adopt the gaze of the object—of that which is not subjectively involved in the
scene, but before which the scene is staged. The audience realizes the position of

the gaze insofar as it adopts the position of what Lacan describes as the object cause which stimulates the closed loop of the scopic drive.[38] With this observation, the formal Lacanian structure of sadistic perversion comes into play: the sadist pervert is precisely the subject who takes on the role of the object. As Lacan puts it in Seminar XI: "The sadist himself occupies the place of the object, but without knowing it, to the benefit of another, for whose *jouissance* he exercises his action as sadistic pervert."[39]

The point here is not to enlist Lacanian theory to bring us back to our starting point: to write off the audience as a collection of perverted voyeurs who have hijacked entertainment television. Rather, it is to push the discussion of the audience one step further: to explicate its role in the economy that produces programming like *Temptation Island* by drawing on the relationship between the two aspects of Lacanian perversion: the subject position which "gets off" on the failure to reach its goal, and that which takes on the role of the object-instrument of the Other's pleasure. More specifically, the argument is that the subject position enacted in surveillance-based reality programming—that of the perverted subject in the throes of the scopic drive—neatly coincides with the subject position envisioned by flexible capitalism: that of the consumer committed to "making itself seen." The Lacanian claim that these two subject positions coincide seems particularly fruitful given the conjunction of the burgeoning reality TV trend with increasingly pervasive forms of private and state-sponsored surveillance.

Pursuing this argument requires a more detailed exposition of the Lacanian claim that the pervert occupies the position of the object instrument of the Other's desire. The audience, when it takes on the role of the objective gaze, simultaneously adopts the position of the sadistic pervert, whose desire is complicit in the action from which it is ostensibly removed. Translating this observation into the terms outlined earlier, we might note that the savvy subject—the voyeur exempted from the action—is the *ultimate dupe*, insofar as this exemption overlooks the complicit role of the ostensibly objective determination that "there is nothing to be done but understand the situation as it is."

How, then, is the position of the audience as pure gaze with respect to the onscreen action to be explicated? Insofar as the audience is positioned in the role of "pure gaze," it is allowed to suppress the desire at work in its ostensible neutrality, and thereby to background its complicity in the onscreen action. The truly subversive gesture to which the perversion of *Temptation Island* can be contrasted would be one that forced the audience to confront its own complicity—to recognize the way in which its own disavowed desire renders it the dupe of the entertainment industry itself, which takes on the role of the real other for whom the audience works. Such a gesture would demonstrate to the viewer who adopts the position of the other's instrument (objective arbiter of truth/audience commodity for sale) that this position is actually that of the victim—the unknowing exhibitionist in the closely monitored and tracked audience.

Temptation Island's socially "constructive" (nonsubversive) character is evidenced by the refusal of this route in favor of a conclusion that preserves the ostensibly objective role of the audience. The desire that stains the "pure" gaze of the audience (and gives the lie to its "objectivity") is the hope that infidelity will take place: that one member of a couple will have sex with one of the available singles. In the end, the audience is left with the sole satisfaction of the *failure* to realize its desire. Which raises the question of whether a truly subversive *Temptation Island* would confront the audience with the truth of the manipulation of its desire by actually *realizing* this desire in a culmination of infidelity and broken relationships. Such an outcome would surely be much more disturbing than the actual *Temptation Island* (although viewers would likely write it off as "not really" real, arguing that people who agree to participate in such a spectacle probably aren't in meaningful relationships in any case, and may well be faking the whole thing just to get on TV).

One might make a similar point with respect to the other controversial Fox reality spectacle: *Who Wants to Marry a Multimillionaire,* in which fifty women competed to marry a millionaire they had never met (and didn't even see until he had made his choice). The current analysis suggests that the more disturbing outcome would be one in which the marriage *worked out*—rather than being annulled shortly after the fact and written off as one more publicity stunt. As it turned out, the outcome served to underwrite the very values it ostensibly challenged: according to these values, such a marriage couldn't/shouldn't work out in reality. The import of the show's ostensible failure was that rather than being staged as the inherent transgression (obscene underside) of matrimony in capitalist modernity, the display of women as prizes for the millionaire (who, in the show, adopts the position of the gaze—the unseen "spot" which looks at the women "from all angles") is portrayed as marriage's fundamental violation—as its *non*inherent transgression. It is perhaps not insignificant that the network famous for its "tasteless" and perverse programming is owned by the notoriously conservative Rupert Murdoch. The complementary relationship between Murdoch's brand of conservatism and the perversity of a series like *Temptation Island* is highlighted by the network's decision to turn down an advertisement for female contraceptives, refusing to air it during *Temptation Island* because by the very nature of the product, the ad was deemed inappropriate for family viewers.[40]

THE SCOPIC DRIVE AND THE "AUDITED EYEBALL"

There is, in the end, nothing surprising about the fact that there is nothing subversive of the "moral order" in *Temptation Island*. What is perhaps more interesting is the way in which the show illustrated the socially constructive role of perverse transgression. In other words, it is the particular form of the *failure* of subversion (or, in positive terms, the form of *Temptation Island*'s complicity) that can perhaps shed some light on the current historical moment and its associated version of capitalism. Why the pervasive and growing emphasis on voyeurism and the role of the scopic drive in providing access to reality? Why now? The Lacanian explication of the relationship between voyeurism and the drive to "make oneself seen" provides some interesting approaches to these questions. Increasingly, an economy based on ever more sophisticated techniques for monitoring consumer behavior broadcasts the message that "making oneself seen" is a form of individuation and self-authentication. We are told that we can express ourselves through customized consumption—consumption that requires we make our preferences and habits known to producers. In this respect, we are invited to participate in the logic of the drive: we can attain our own "inner freedom" by submitting ourselves to ever more comprehensive forms of surveillance. This submission is portrayed not as a structural necessity of the proliferation of flexible capitalism—which requires proliferating consumption in response to enhanced productivity—but as the consumer's drive to express his or her authentic subjectivity, a subjectivity that has been stifled by the uniformity of mass society. In short, subjectification entails active submission to surveillance, which means that we don't just endure the monitoring gaze, we embrace the drive to make ourselves seen.

Getting real—attaining authenticity—means being seen. The corollary to this formulation is, of course, the guiding premise of the "reality-based" television format: we are told that we are being provided access to reality through surveillance, and are thereby invited to adopt the position of the "pure gaze." The audience response to reality shows including *Survivor*, *Big Brother*, and *The Real World* suggests that fans of the genre are drawn by the fact that the emotions of the cast members are real—that, for example, when a cast member is crying, he or she is not an actor playing someone who's crying but is *really* upset. As one respondent put it, "To me it's not staged or rehearsed, and that makes it real . . . the events and emotional tension the people have is real." Similarly, the winner of the American version of *Big Brother*, Eddie McGee, defended the "reality" of the show by referring to the pain of its participants: "When you saw Brittany crying, that was real. When you saw Mega's anger and frustration, that was real."[41] In short, the mark of authentic subjectivity was very often the pain that suggested the cast members weren't just acting, since they were really suffering. It is this equation that implicitly draws the interest of the audience, as is suggested by the exercise of trying to imagine whether anyone would watch *Temptation Island* if it proceeded exactly the same way except that the cast members were all professional actors playing the parts of anguished couples. The sadistic promise of the show, in short, was to provide access to the real suffering of real people, as opposed to the "faked" drama of fictional tragedy. The couples on *Temptation Island* were at their most real when they submitted their most painful moments to public scrutiny, as highlighted by Billy's attempts to elude the cameras with the claim that "this isn't about the show, it's my life"; in short, now that it hurts, this is no longer just a game—it's become real.

The fantasy of *Temptation Island* is that this suffering is a personal growth experience—that the audience is merely an incidental factor "added on" to the process whereby the couples learn about each other; or, put differently, that the cast members would have embarked on the experience even if it *weren't* televised. At no point does the show implicate the desire of the viewers to see the suffering of the couples, thereby ensuring that the purity of the audience gaze is left intact. Crucially, from a critical perspective, this implies that the audience is allowed to retain the position of the object instrument: the torment they witness is not staged for their delectation, so they remain accidental voyeurs, stumbling across the real trauma of others. Or, alternatively, their desire remains incidental to the action insofar as they are allowed to imagine the show wasn't staged specifically for them but rather for some other viewers—members of that elusive "lowest common denominator" to which the market caters.

In either case, if the more subversive move would be to highlight the reality of the role of the sadist as object-instrument—victim—of "the real Will-to-Enjoy . . . already at work in the state-bureaucratic apparatus," the complicit move of *Temptation Island* is to background the "other" for whom the viewer works.[42] The role of the *Temptation Island* viewer is that of the pervert who is not forced to confront the work he or she is doing for the real Sadist: Fox/Hollywood. Allowing the audience to retain the position of the pure gaze not only fails to implicate the audience desire in the "self-inflicted" torment of the cast members, it simultaneously backgrounds the perverse cycle of voyeurism within which the audience participates *as exhibitionist*.

Just as the voyeurism that takes place within the diegetic action of the series revolves around the vortex of the audience gaze, the voyeurism that takes place in the relation between viewer and spectacle similarly revolve around a third, excluded gaze: that which monitors and surveys the audience. Retaining the purity of the audience gaze—exempting it from the action, as it were—is the prerequisite for asserting the purity of this other gaze—that of the market. It is for this reason that Zizek suggests the ideological move par excellence is not that whereby we recognize our ideological interpellation as being specifically addressed to us (when we respond to the interpellation) but rather that whereby we are allowed to overlook the fact that "the entire spectacle of the Mystery is staged *with an eye to our gaze.*"[43]

The intermediate position of the audience voyeur, inserted between the gaze of the cast members (watching each other) and that of the marketers (monitoring the audience), is neatly summarized in the response of one advertiser to the question of whether he was put off by the racy premise of *Temptation Island*: "We buy audited eyeballs. . . . We don't care in the least about people pontificating about content."[44] The image of the audited eyeball tellingly evokes the Lacanian description of the gaze that manifests itself in auditory form: the rustling of the leaves that catches the voyeur by surprise in the act of making him- or herself seen (trying to catch a glimpse). At the same time, it highlights the role of the spectacle (of *Temptation Island*) in luring the viewer to make him- or herself visible via the system of audience surveillance upon which networks and advertisers rely. The constitutive capitalist fantasy is that this gaze is (like that of the accidental voyeur interpellated by *Temptation Island*) "pure"—that it serves as a neutral measure for tracking the behavior and preferences of consumers/viewers, without being in any way implicated in simultaneously fueling and thwarting that desire. In short, the preservation of the purity of this gaze coincides with the claim that consumers and producers are working for themselves—that the market serves merely as an efficient framework for allowing their own preferences to allocate resources.

What is perverse about *Temptation Island*, then, is not that it focuses on sexual infidelity (what television show doesn't these days?), not even that it displays the emotional suffering of others as a form of entertainment (what "serious" journalist doesn't?), but rather that it underwrites the purity of the monitoring gaze of the marketers. If the subversive strategy would be to let the narrative content of a show serve as an allegory for its process of enunciation (by demonstrating its own manipulative character), *Temptation Island* is complicit because it backgrounds the relationship between Fox and its public. Indeed, it stages the ideological version of this relationship: that the gaze of Fox is "pure" (just as is the gaze of the *Temptation Island* audience) insofar as it merely records and responds to audience preferences. This staging of the neutral gaze of the market might be understood as the allegorical version of the claim that "the market gives people what they want"—a claim that conspicuously disregards the role of the market not just in inducing demand and structuring/distorting market signaling, but in failing to provide those satisfactions it continuously promises and endlessly defers. The version of reality TV that enacts the drive to "make oneself seen" as a means of providing access to reality—whether this reality be that of one's own feelings, or the "truth" of one's romantic relationship—reinforces the ideological claim that we submit ourselves to the marketer's gaze for the sake of our "inner freedom" and self-expression.

In keeping with this logic, the finale of *Temptation Island* allowed the couples to portray their holiday not just as a reaffirmation of their relationships but—as in the case of the reality shows described above—as a therapeutic learning experience. In response to host Mark Wahlberg's question "The answers can be found; what have you discovered, what have you learned?" we hear, for example, from Mandy that "I realized that the best part of the trip was last night [her final date]. That's when I learned the most about myself. That's when I opened myself up the most to this game. That's when it stopped being a party and became a journey." All of the cast members in turn conclude with an assessment of what they have learned about themselves during the course of the show and how they have grown and changed. Valerie tells us, for example, that the "best part" about the show was "everything I learned about myself—things that I didn't expect to learn and feelings I didn't expect to feel." Her boyfriend, Kaya, who was caught on camera in heated embraces with two different "temptresses," concluded his segment of the show with the observation that "I took emotional chances. . . . I have no regrets for a single thing that I did here. . . . Every time I made a choice, I made the difficult choice because I knew that would be the way of growing and that would be my way of learning about myself and becoming who I am and learning about my individuality."[45]

The crucial aspect of these admissions was that they preceded any knowledge of what actually happened to their partners during the two weeks. The "learning experience" described by the cast members was associated not with what they saw, but with their own attempts to "make themselves seen." In other words, the failure of the scopic drive to attain its object—the failure that realizes the true reflexive character of the drive—provides the "experience." It is in this respect that *Temptation Island* neatly stages the logic of the scopic drive in the era of flexible capitalism: the failure of the drive to attain its goal—of consumption, for example, to serve an end other than its own propagation—rehearses the truth of the drive. The fantasy of *Temptation Island* is the same as that of the interactive economy: that submission serves as a form of empowerment.

NOTES

1. Slavoj Zizek, "How the Non-Duped Err," *Qui Parle* 4, no. 1 (1990): 2.

2. Ann Hodges, " 'Temptation Island' Gets Trashy," *Houston Chronicle*, 12 January 2001, 10; Hal Boedeker, "Viewers Deserve Blame for Success of Trash TV," *Orlando Sentinel*, 24 January 2001, E1; Matthew Gilbert, "A Perverse 'Fantasy Island,' " *Boston Globe*, 10 January 2001, F1.

3. Beverly Bartlett, "No Man Is an Island, but It's an Island That Tests Us," *Courier Journal* (Louisville, Ky.), 15 January 2001, 1F.

4. "Storm Hits Fox's New 'Temptation Island,' " *Atlanta Journal and Constitution*, 8 January 2001, 1A.

5. "Viewers Learn How Tempting Island Was," *Tampa Tribune*, 27 February 2001, Baylife, 4.

6. Bill Carter, "Some Sponsors Can't Accept Racy Reality," *New York Times*, 29 January 2001, C1.

7. Slavoj Zizek, *The Ticklish Subject* (London: Verso, 2000), 248.

8. Slavoj Zizek, "In His Bold Gaze My Ruin Is Writ Large," in *Everything You Always Wanted to Know about Lacan but Were Afraid to Ask Hitchcock*, ed. Slavoj Zizek (London: Verso, 1999), 291.

9. See, for example, John Fiske and John Hartley, *Reading Television* (London: Methuen, 1978); Michel De Certeau, *The Practice of Everyday Life* (Berkeley: University of California Press, 1988); Joshua Gamson, *Freaks Talk Back: Tabloid Talk Shows and Sexual Non-Conformity* (Chicago: University of Chicago Press, 1998).

10. Zizek, "In His Bold Gaze," 225.

11. Lisa De Moraes, "Fox Scrambles to Make Ratings Hay with an Extra 'Island,'" *Washington Post*, 2 February 2001, C5.

12. Zizek, "In His Bold Gaze," 248.

13. Zizek, "In His Bold Gaze," 304.

14. Zizek, "In His Bold Gaze," 291.

15. Todd Gitlin, "Blips, Bites, and Savvy Talk," *Dissent* (Winter 1990): 21.

16. *Temptation Island*, KDVR Denver, 22 February 2001.

17. *Temptation Island*, 12 March 2001.

18. *Temptation Island*, 12 March 2001.

19. *Temptation Island*, 12 March 2001.

20. Jacques Lacan, *The Four Fundamental Concepts of Psychoanalysis,* The Seminar of Jacques Lacan, Book 11 (New York: Norton, 1998), 183.

21. Lacan, *The Four Fundamental Concepts*, 195.

22. Zizek, "In His Bold Gaze," 284.

23. Zizek, "In His Bold Gaze."

24. *Temptation Island*, 22 March 2001.

25. *Temptation Island*, 1 March 2001.

26. Lacan, *The Four Fundamental Concepts*, 182.

27. *Temptation Island*, 18 January 2001.

28. *Temptation Island*, 22 February 2001.

29. Jacques Lacan, "Kant with Sade," *October* 51 (Winter 1989): 84.

30. Lacan, *The Four Fundamental Concepts*, 183.

31. Lacan, *The Four Fundamental Concepts*, 183.

32. Zizek, "In His Bold Gaze," 284.

33. Boedeker, "Viewers Deserve Blame."

34. Boedeker, "Viewers Deserve Blame," E1.

35. Jim Slotek, "Fox, Lead Us Not into Temptation" *Toronto Sun*, 15 January 2001, 47.

36. One of the interesting twists added by the media coverage was the widely circulated report, early on, that no one on the island had sex. The *Boston Herald*, for example, reported, "In an exclusive story posted on the Internet's WorldNetDaily.com, writer Paul Sperry claims that none of the couples had a fling and none split up at the end of 'Temptation Island.' According to a production source quoted by Sperry: 'Unfortunately no one had sex—unfortunately because, believe me, the producers wanted them to'" (Monica Collins, "A Deuce of Reality," *Boston Herald*, 11 January 2001, O41). The fact that media critics and viewers alike continued to speculate about who would have sex with whom highlights the perverse logic of the show's perception: getting off on missing "it"—the ostensible object of the voyeuristic gaze, the sex act itself.

37. Zizek, "In His Bold Gaze," 224–25.

38. In this example, the use of the term *object cause* is meant to designate the cause of the drive (the audience gaze around which the action turns) as distinct from its ostensible object (the object of the cast member's gaze: his or her significant other). The Lacanian point to be made with respect to this distinction is that what drives the cast member's voyeurism is not the attempt to make some kind of connection with his or her significant other but the drive to avoid being seen as a dupe—hence, the gaze of the other.

39. Lacan, *The Four Fundamental Concepts*, 185.

40. "Scene in Brief," *Boston Herald*, 2 February 2001, S04.

41. Eddie McGee, telephone interview with the author, 14 January 2001.

42. Zizek, "In His Bold Gaze," 221.

43. Zizek, "In His Bold Gaze," 225.

44. Bill Carter, "Some Sponsors Can't Accept Racy Reality," *New York Times*, 29 January 2001, C1.

45. *Temptation Island*, 1 March 2001.

Chapter Eight

Survivor and Uncanny Capitalism

Survivor is the most successful of the shows considered in this book and has become, perhaps, the "classic" format of the current generation of reality TV. Like several of the formats that emerged to capitalize on the new trend, *Survivor* was in part a game show and in part a reality TV spectacle that chronicled the exploits of sixteen people competing for $1 million as they lived a "back-to-basics" life on a tropical island in the South Pacific. The series, loosely based on a Swedish format called *Expedition: Robinson*, struck ratings gold during its first season, averaging over twenty million viewers per show and drawing more than fifty-two million viewers (almost half of the viewing public for the evening) for its finale, making it "the most watched summer broadcast since Nielsen started using electronic 'people meters' to collect TV ratings in 1987."[1]

The show's phenomenal success suggests its ability to navigate the inherent tension in reality programming between making an appeal to the "reality" of the spectacle and staging this spectacle so that it fulfills the expectations audiences have for prime-time drama: fast-paced action and complicated plot lines that provide both suspense and resolution during a one-hour time slot. Unlike *Big Brother*, which was roundly critiqued for being dull and poorly produced, *Survivor* offered the best of both worlds: "real" people and events that were neatly edited into one-hour segments, each of which ended with one of the contestants being voted off the island. One of the reasons for its success was thus the fact that unlike *Big Brother*, *Survivor* did not take place in real time—it was filmed in advance, providing ample time for sleek editing that complemented its relatively high production values.

Survivor also helped inaugurate the trend of reality shows that offer the promise of a return to a natural and implicitly more traditional (even, at times, tribal) environment. This was picked up on by shows ranging from *Temptation Island* to *Celebrity Mole Hawaii*. As noted earlier, one of the recurring themes of reality TV is the attempt to underwrite the authenticity of the interactions on the show by contriving a scenario that ostensibly fosters a return to a pre–mass (or perhaps a possible post–mass) environment. It is thus tempting to view a competition-based show like *Survivor* as an attempt to naturalize the (Darwinian) logic of contemporary economic competition by transporting it to an archetypal extrasocietal location. Such a reading invokes the standard model of ideology critique which uncovers the way in which human social relations are misrecognized and thereby portrayed as an inevitable consequence of unchangeable natural law. However, as the arguments in previous chapters have suggested, this version of ideology critique remains inadequate to a social context characterized by increasingly savvy viewers who derive pleasure in large part from debunking the ruse of naturalization.

Picking up where the previous chapter left off, the goal of my consideration of *Survivor* is to explore the role of self-reflexive naturalization rehearsed by the show and to differentiate its version of fetishization from the standard version of false consciousness associated with ideology critique. In so doing, I propose an analysis of the "uncanny" character of contemporary capitalism foreshadowed in the discussion of *Temptation Island*: the ability of the market to retain its autonomous force *even after it has been revealed as a social construction*. At stake is the question of the role of ideology in the era of what Ulrich Beck has dubbed "the risk society."[2] Classical notions of ideology critique break down in the reflexive era of the risk society, in which the critical character of demystifying rationality turns back upon itself—in which ideology critique becomes generalized. As we shall see, the question of ideology in an era of savvy reflexivity is closely related to reality TV's offer to expose the artifice behind the reality and present this revelation as the final frontier of the real. Such all-encompassing reflexivity undermines the modernist distinctions between nature and culture, facts and values, and, of course, reality and artifice—one more set of differentiations that face erosion in an increasingly dedifferentiated era.

PRODUCING REALITY

Survivor neatly epitomizes the paradox of reality TV by offering a "well-produced" version of reality, apparently more convincing than the transparently manipulative episodes of *Big Brother*. The seemingly self-contradictory tension in the notion of the "illusion of reality" recurs at several levels in the *Survivor* series. At the level of content, it is expressed in the juxtaposition of the back-to-basics "survivalist" premise and the cast members' self-conscious awareness that they were participating in a major media spectacle. At the level of production, the juxtaposition is highlighted by the contrast between the sparse quarters of the cast—a makeshift lean-to, furnished with logs and stumps—and the big-budget production crew, equipped with the latest in high-tech audiovideo gear. Making reality seem real, it turns out, requires the very latest in high-tech audio and video equipment. The production crew for *Survivor* numbered more than one hundred, including camera operators, medical staff, and transportation co-ordinators. Moreover, producers used "every format available" including 35mm, 16mm, and Super 8 film, as well as hidden surveillance cameras with night vision lenses, digital video, and aerial footage shot from a helicopter.[3] This high-budget production process perfectly summarizes the paradox of "manipulated authenticity": we can imagine a cast member, clad in a loincloth and clutching a hand-carved spear heading into the water to forage for dinner, followed by a gaggle of photographers and production assistants, shooting with hand-held cameras, dollies, and special underwater cameras to catch the action. The production crew never appeared in the versions of the show edited for broadcast but remained behind the scenes — allowing viewers to adopt the position of the voyeur catching the action in all its "immediate" authenticity.

The show's content reproduces the paradox of the illusion of the real at the level of "civilization" proper. The most cutting-edge form of commodified entertainment is provided by the regression of the cast members to a premodern ("precivilized") level of tribal culture. The language of tribalism and totemism is pervasive in the series, which divided the original sixteen contestants into two "tribes," each of which was assigned an indigenous name (that of the tribe's totemic animal) as they engaged in competitions for an "immunity idol" — a generic Hollywood pastiche of a tribal mask. *Survivor* was not the only reality format to invoke this appeal to tribal society (life in the *Big Brother* house was, on occasion, described in similar terms, as the small group in the house was isolated from the outside world and had to negotiate the intricacies of their own small community), but it certainly developed it more fully than any of the other formats.

It is this invocation of neotribalism — and in particular the deployment of the self-conscious parallels between such tribalism and the "jungle" of contemporary capitalism — that make it tempting to read *Survivor* as one more example of naturalization. However, such a reading fails to take into account the functioning of ideology in a reflexive era in which naturalization is itself debunked. As was suggested in chapter 3, the apparent striving for a trace of the real that ostensibly characterizes the promise of reality TV is coupled with an erosion of faith in representation itself — in the ability of mediated symbols to provide access to reality, rather than merely simulating it. The rise of surveillance-based reality television and the seeming obsession with "being watched" is, in other words, correlative to the advent of the risk society and the attendant decline of the metanarratives that underpinned the guarantee that any symbolic order — what Zizek calls a "Big Other" — could provide access to a real referent.[4] Beck outlines this decline in terms of scientific knowledge as the dominant metanarrative of modernization: "complete scientization . . . extends scientific skepticism to the inherent foundations and external consequences of science itself."[5] Zizek points out that the demystification occurs against the backdrop of the "spectral presence of Capital" as "the figure of the big Other which not only remains operative when all the traditional embodiments of the big Other disintegrate, but even directly causes this disintegration."[6] The formulation bears a marked resemblance to Jameson's assessment of postmodernism as "the cultural logic of late capitalism," but it goes a step further by arguing that the ostensible demise of Enlightenment metanarratives must be accompanied by compensatory formations if the mode of subjectivity they underwrote—that consonant with contemporary capitalism—is to sustain itself.[7]

In other words, the flaw of the hackneyed postmodern position critiqued by Terry Eagleton—that there are only appearances and no underlying realities—is the implicit attempt to have its cake and eat it, too: to dismantle the presuppositions of Enlightenment reason while conserving the emancipatory impulse and the associated form of autonomous subjectivity these presuppositions underwrote.[8] The attempt to disavow the Enlightenment while retaining the version of autonomy it generated fosters a unique form of the return of the repressed. Rather than freedom from the domination of power/knowledge, in the postmetaphysical era, we are subjected to/by the return of premodern forms of domination and their associated mythologies, not unrelated to the pop tribalism invoked by *Survivor*.

Beck makes a similar argument when he describes the consequences of the inability of scientific reason to assess the incalculable risks associated with industrial modernization: that of environmental degradation, invisible toxins, nuclear holocaust, and so forth.[9] The recognition that science cannot objectively calculate and counter such risks—that, on the contrary, the domination of nature facilitated by scientific progress has unleashed risks for which it cannot account—lies at the foundations of ostensibly postmodern skepticism. The result has been the return of the repressed specters of premodernity, animated by the instrumental reason that once promised to contain them: "Everywhere, pollutants and toxins laugh and play their tricks like devils in the Middle Ages. People are almost inescapably bound over to them. Breathing, eating, dwelling, wearing clothes—everything has been penetrated by them."[10]

None of which should be read in conservative terms as a devolution to premodern barbarity once the canon of Enlightenment rationality is discarded. This return of the repressed represents not regression but a particular moment in the development of capitalist society: that in which the exposed logic of the market supplants the Enlightenment metanarrative. In ideological terms, this development might be read through an analogy to the Marxist conception of the fettering model: the emergence of capitalism was reliant on the metanarratives associated with the Enlightenment (the principle of abstract, universal, reason, whose guarantee was to be found in the natural (divine) order, the universalization of bourgeois class interests). Once capitalist hegemony was secured in the post–Cold War era, these narratives served more and more as fetters; they highlighted the contradictions of capitalism and the failure of its promise. The conditions of capitalism's emergence came to serve as a hindrance, barring the way to a truly friction-free (contradiction-free) version of capitalism. The result might be described as a postmodernity that assimilates itself to premodernity: the free play of capital as a capricious arational force no longer constrained by Enlightenment presumptions of abstract universality, individual autonomy, and so on. As numerous authors have suggested, the postmodern critique of modernity and Enlightenment reason neatly assimilates itself to the logic of the market.[11] The decentered subject continually reinventing itself coincides with the ongoing self-transformation of the ideal consumer. Indeed, one of the downsides of the death of the metanarrative is the way in which it seems to foreclose alternatives to the naturalized version of capitalism.

By the same token, the hope that the very proclamation of this demise might undermine the hegemony of the market is, on the evidence, clearly overoptimistic. Instead of crumbling capitalist hegemony, undermined by the retreating faith in its central narratives, we are faced with the resurgence of the ultimate modernist force: the productive power of capital *qua* an irrational, undead automaton. The line between human artifice and uncanny force of nature has eroded. We are left with the scenario of *Survivor* in which the metaphor of premodernity is self-consciously enlisted to naturalize the contrived competition of the free market. Survival—as several fans interviewed for this chapter suggest—is hardly the point of *Survivor*. Rather, the series holds out the promise of "moving forward into the past." It enacts one version of friction-free capitalism: survival defined as an obsession with its own means, freed not only from the actual dictates of the search for sustenance within a hostile environment but also from those modernist narratives that might temper or modify this "freedom."

YOUR EYES VERSUS MY WORDS

The promise of reality TV takes on a specific significance within the context of Zizek's diagnosis of the "decline of the big Other"—a decline that undermines the efficacy of the symbolic order as such. Zizek uses the example of the Groucho Marx quip "Whom do you believe, your eyes or my words?" to suggest that the efficacy of the symbolic order relies on the subject's willingness to accept the symbolic claim (that of "my words") over ostensibly more direct sensory evidence.[12] He points out that this leap of faith is more common in daily life than one might imagine. We routinely rely on the efficacy of symbolic institutions rather than "immediate" sensory evidence—not just in the case of mediated versions of reality beyond the reach of our senses but also in the case of symbolic authority that is conferred on, for example, state officials. We know that presidents, generals, and so forth, may well be petty, mediocre humans, but, by virtue of occupying a particular position in the symbolic order, this recognition fades into the background.[13] Or did, at one time. The debunking of this symbolic authority is portrayed in the repeated accounts of how authority figures have been demystified by the attempt to bring the recognition of their fallible humanity to the fore. The familiar observation, for example, that the media's "respect" for the private lives of politicians has dissolved in the post-Fordist era rehearses this debunking of symbolic authority. Just as the exposure of embarrassing personal details undermines the mystique of officeholders, reality shows that expose the private lives of celebrities like Ozzy Osbourne and Anna Nicole Smith debunk celebrity aura.

The crucial aspect of the symbolic order lies not merely in its efficacy—that, in the case of the presidency, for example, the office is "more than the man"—but precisely in its disjunction from the "directly given." What the symbolic order allows is the possibility of thinking beyond the empirical facts. It provides the space for "the active will to disavow the actual state of things."[14] The centrality of the gap can be illustrated by the fact that the argument works in both directions: In a world in which change is still possible, not only must the symbolic order be irreducible to given experience, but experience must likewise be irreducible to the symbolic order (more precisely, the symbolic order, constituted around a central lack, can be understood to be insufficient *in itself*—to contain its own inherent limit). It is this gap or inconsistency—perceived as a disturbing inadequacy—that becomes the target of postmodern savviness, which seeks to eliminate it by ruling out anything external to the symbolic order itself (and thereby erasing its internal limit). The well-known result of this totalization of the symbolic (a facile reading of Jacques Derrida's claim *"il n'y a pas de hors-texte"*—there is nothing outside the text) is both the totalization and the debunking of the symbolic order.[15] The suppression of its inadequacy simultaneously deprives it of anything that could serve at its guarantor. The result of this suppression is a "return of the repressed" that reemerges (in one guise among others) in the form of the incalculable risks Beck associates with reflexive modernization.

Beck's formulation highlights the complicity of postmodern reductionism with scientific rationality. Both fail to address (and work to eradicate) the constitutive and constructive *inadequacy* of the symbolic order. Beck explores the consequences of this failure in the register of the technological rationality of industrial modernity. The ostensible objectivity of instrumental reason dead-ends with the recognition that, in the name of control, it generates incalculable risks of potentially uncontrollable magnitude. As Beck explains it, "Statements of hazard are never reducible to mere statements of fact" such as those, for example, that express the fact that the earth is round, or that it orbits the sun.[16] Rather, reflexive hazards—those that pose a threat to human life and habitat—necessarily incorporate a normative component, but this remains incompatible with the calculus of instrumental reason, as evidenced by the gruesome futility of weighing decisions according to a cost–benefit analysis of mortality, pestilence, and environmental degradation. What "value" is to be assigned a particular ecosystem or an individual life? Even if one could assign them a value (as economists incessantly do), the numbers appear nonsensical and the resulting calculations inane, especially in the context of multiplying cataclysmic possibilities ranging from the destruction of the ozone layer to bioterrorism and global warming. The result, as Beck puts it, is that "the sciences' monopoly on rationality is broken" (the grand narrative of industrial modernity stumbles).[17] We are left in a world in which current dangers are invisible and when they become visible, it may well be too late. All of which may help explain the apparently unquenchable appetite in the "postmodern"/risk society for the rehabilitation of a directly accessible, visible reality to break the spiral of self-referentiality. The consequent fantasy— one that reinforces the logic that generates it—is one of total visibility: if complete surveillance were possible, perhaps invisible risks could be visualized. The proposed antidote for the failure of instrumental reason is, disturbingly, to attempt to push it to its logical extreme. One result is the rehabilitation of total surveillance. In the wake of the 2001 terrorist attacks on the United States, for example, the government created an "Information Awareness Office" tasked with developing so-called total information awareness systems to counter the threat of terrorism by combining information from all available databases about the activities of all U.S. residents.[18] As Beck puts it, in response to the threat of a frustratingly incalculable risk, "the panorama of a *scientific and bureaucratic totalitarianism* is being laid out."[19] It is against this background that the appeal of the promise of reality TV—the hope that comprehensive surveillance might help rehabilitate access to a frustratingly elusive real—takes shape (and replicates the logic it supposedly supplants).

Reality TV similarly caters to the decline of the symbolic order by promising to restore direct access to the fullness of the real. The central paradox of the promise, however, lies in the futile attempt to attain immediacy by sidestepping the conventions of the symbolic order. The promise of total surveillance is that one needn't rely on the deceptive words of others if one could render the world fully, immediately visible. Thus, one might discern the symptoms of the decline in the faith in the symbolic order in the critical reactions of those fans who say they appreciate reality TV because it's not as predictable and contrived as fictional programming. The symbolic order of fiction has, for these fans, literally lost its efficacy; they are no longer interested in or satisfied by the attempt to make the leap of faith that would allow them to believe the symbolic drama rather than the "direct" knowledge that actors are mouthing words and fabricating their emotional responses. However, this savviness—like all the various forms of cynicism treated in this book—is unable to sidestep the symbolic order (and this very inability provides another manifestation of the ineluctable nature of the Lacanian Real): savvy "realism" reaches beyond the "direct sensory experience" provided by the cathode ray tube insofar as it depends upon a symbolic knowledge of the process of television production.[20] Nevertheless, the terms of the promise of reality TV are made directly to "your eyes" as opposed to "my words"—the symbolic creations of actors, scriptwriters, and so on. Some fans (although by no means all, as the discussion of *Big Brother* suggested) take this promise at face value. As one respondent put it, "To me shows like these are really interesting because it is not scripted; they are real people with real problems and everything, not just these beautiful Hollywood stars that are in normal sitcoms. You get to hear whatever they say and see what they do and even if it is not that exciting it is still interesting because it is like eavesdropping into their conversation."[21] Thus, in the face of the decline of the "big Other," the efficacy of the symbolic order is displaced by the desire for direct sensory evidence: for a direct experience of reality. This default from "my words" to "your eyes" provides another way of exploring the claim that postmodernist positivism offers a challenge to the abstraction of mass society. In the era of savvy cynicism, the injunction to television producers as well as to advertisers, politicians, and the entire cast of mediated characters is to get real.

THE RETURN OF THE REAL

Zizek describes this injunction to "get real" as a short-circuit between the imaginary (imagined alternatives to the given reality) and the real that results from the impasse of the symbolic order: "On the one hand, *symbolic* prohibitive norms are increasingly replaced by *imaginary* ideals (of social success, or bodily fitness . . .); on the other, the lack of symbolic prohibition is supplemented by the re-emergence of ferocious super-ego figures."[22] This formulation helps account for the correlation between the increasing popularity of gambling and the lottery ("all you need is a dollar and a *dream*") and the emergence of the new, corrupt, titans of industry. It is suggestive to consider the extent to which such figures have reemerged in the wake of the ostensible global triumph of capitalism in the post–Cold War era, and the attendant proclamations of the end of ideology (which relied on the symbolic order) and the end of history. Consider, for example, not just the tales of corporate villains that characterized the first years of the new millennium but also the emergence of the sinister and ferocious threat of the transnational terrorists alongside the proclaimed triumph of global capitalism.

Zizek's formulation is particularly fruitful for a consideration of the "tribalized" return of/to the real staged by *Survivor*. He anticipates the format's juxtaposition of the imaginary ideals of physical fitness (the contestants were supposed to be physically fit, despite the fact that their fate on the island was dependent more on mind games and scavenger hunts than survival skills) with the emergence of an "evil villain"/leader in the guise of the show's winner, a corporate consultant, who was routinely portrayed on the show and in the media as a devious master manipulator. Premodern "survival" skills (strength, stamina, coordination, etc.) are transposed into the context of a struggle that had more in common with office politics than jungle survival. As the show's producer, Mark Burnett, noted, "*Survivor* is based on real life. We've all met people like this.

We've all experienced workplace politics. We've all dealt with situations like this — people befriending you, people stabbing you in the back. It's duplicity and hardball. . . . We can identify."[23] Many viewers echoed Burnett's comparison of the *Survivor* scenario to "office politics." This comparison served to reinforce the recognition that the show was not at all about physical survival, an understanding bolstered by the fact that when it came down to the final two contestants, a river guide who consistently won the physical challenges and a pudgy corporate consultant who had distinguished himself as a master manipulator, it was the consultant who prevailed. Since physical survival wasn't the issue (as several viewers observed, CBS couldn't let any of the cast members starve), the physical ideals remained strictly on the level of image. When the producers saw that the cast members were having a hard time catching enough fish to eat, for example, they came up with other sources of protein for them (including, notoriously, rats). Periodically, they descended on the cast with tantalizing rewards of steak dinners, ice cream, and beer.

The ready interpretation of this juxtaposition of office politics with jungle survival skills is that it simply and straightforwardly naturalizes the condition of contemporary capitalism. This interpretation might well be applied to the tendency among viewers to echo Burnett's equation of survival in the jungle with survival in the office. The naturalization of the corporate jungle underwrites the claim that capitalism is merely an expression of human "nature," locked into the competitive, selfish, Darwinian struggle for survival. As one viewer put it, "The moral of the story is survival of the fittest."[24] This assessment was repeated verbatim by several other respondents, who tended to adopt the "realistic" stance that even though they may not like the competitive, Darwinist facet of human nature, that's the way it is: "Sometimes you must look past relationships [in order to look out for number one] when you are seeking a greater goal. . . . This happens every day both in nature and corporate America. Yes, I do at times find this abhorrent, but that's just how life is . . . as coldly Darwinian as that may sound."[25]

So are we left with the straightforward story of *Survivor* as one more alibi for the "jungle" of contemporary capitalism? Not quite: such a story fails to do justice to either the reflexive aspect of the viewers' "realist" attitude or to Zizek's assessment of the decline/impasse of the symbolic order. What is crucial to the viewer response is that the naturalization of workplace competition, selfishness, greed, and the like, is accompanied by the recognition of the *contrived* nature of this reality. Even as viewers rehearsed the equation of office politics with the Darwinian struggle for the survival of the fittest, they acknowledged the show's status as artifice. It is precisely at this level that the viewer response exhibits the characteristics of the decline of symbolic efficacy outlined earlier: viewers remain self-consciously aware of the contrived character of the concoction served to them as "reality."[26] This was a common refrain among the viewer responses, many of which included the observation that the show was not really real, and some of which expressed their suspicion that the reactions of the cast members were, at least to some degree, scripted. If, in other words, the equation of *Survivor* with daily office politics is to be taken seriously, it flows both ways, suggesting that the workplace is as contrived an environment as the ersatz jungle environment of *Survivor*. In other words, we might well discern a denaturalizing (or defetishizing) impulse at work in *Survivor*: it highlights the contrivance of what is taken as second nature: workplace competition and its associated "struggle for survival." Both are granted the "unnatural" status of human contrivance.

This alternative assessment of *Survivor* as a show that highlights the truth of the contrivance of the entertainment industry seems to stand in direct opposition to the interpretation that accuses it of naturalizing the "jungle" of the marketplace. In the latter case, *Survivor* is allied with straightforward fetishization; in the former, it allows for the thematization of fetishization itself. But this ostensible opposition assumes that the foregrounding of fetishization necessarily undermines it—that the fetish, if it is to retain its efficacy, must not be recognized as such. In the crudest terms we are faced with the opposition between naturalized ideology and the reality of human contrivance recognized as such. The standard assumption is that the process of fetishization—whereby a product of human activity is misrecognized as a force of nature—operates on the basis of this opposition. Against the background of the two standard stances toward the fetish (its uncritical acceptance as a natural "given" and the demystifying assertion that it is actually the product of human activity) a third stance emerges: the fetish is recognized as a product of human activity but nonetheless retains the status of a naturally uncontrollable given. This is the stance I have referred to in previous chapters as a conservative savviness that refuses to be duped by either the propagandist or the critical theorist. The savvy stance concedes the contrivance of reality, while nonetheless refusing to entertain the possibility that "things could be otherwise." We are left with the defining formulation of contemporary capitalism: the "jungle" of the marketplace is a human creation, but it is beyond human control.

It is important that this formulation be clearly distinguished from that of fetishism proper. The latter operates at the level of the symbolic order since its functioning is sustained by the *representation* of the product of human labor as an autonomous entity. It is no coincidence that Marx draws on religious terminology to describe the process of fetishization, which is reliant on the existence of some big Other—the gold standard, as it were, that underwrites the medium of symbolic exchange.[27] The commodity fetish only comes into being once it enters into exchange facilitated by a commonly accepted (symbolic) medium. It is, according to Marx, this medium which stands the ordinary table (the simple use-value) "on its head, and evolves out of its wooden brain grotesque ideas."[28]

The decline of the symbolic order—that which is sustained by the belief in something more than the evidence of "your eyes"—causes the fetish to default to the realm of the uncanny, the Freudian *unheimlich*. The disconcerting result is that even when, in the realm of the savvy, the fetish is seen through, we do not end up in a world of pure transparency, wherein humans can perfectly control the products of their collective activity. Rather, we find ourselves in the era of what might be called "uncanny capitalism." For Freud, the uncanny is famously that which is seemingly familiar, but disturbingly unfamiliar at the same time (an ambiguity captured by the German term *unheimlich*, which means homelike, familiar, as well as unhomelike). Freud offers the example of the automaton, the undead object, as the paradigmatic example of the uncanny: "We have heard that it is in the highest degree uncanny when an inanimate object—a picture or a doll—comes to life."[29] But as Freud points out, it is not just the animation of the object that is in itself uncanny, for the uncanny is characterized by the overlap of two opposed feelings: the feeling that an inanimate object might be alive accompanied by the doubt as to whether a seemingly animate object might actually be dead (the paradigmatic pop culture example invoked by Zizek is the ambiguous status of the undead corpses in *Night of the Living Dead*). As Freud points out, the animation of an object is not, in itself, uncanny; rather, it is the staple of children's nursery rhymes. What is truly uncanny is when the animate object reveals itself to be somehow not alive: when it reveals (by, perhaps, the blank automatism of its eyes and expression) that it partakes of the realm of the "undead." Zizek associates the stubborn emergence of the uncanny "undead" with the demise of the symbolic order and the reemergence of the unsymbolized drive: "The ultimate object of horror is the sudden emergence of this 'life beyond death,' the undead-indestructible object, Life deprived of support in the symbolic order."[30] It is this uncanny feeling that animates Beck's description of a society in which the demystifying force not only fails to domesticate the material world but reanimates it with incomprehensible risks or our own making, which nevertheless escape our control.

UNCANNY CAPITALISM

It is the figure of the automaton—the robotic undead product of human artifice—and not the fetish that best exemplifies the "post"-symbolic logic of contemporary capitalism. The fetish still lends itself to debunking within the symbolic order: what is naturalized can be shown to be the result of human activity. However, it is precisely the ostensible debunking of the symbolic order by the postmodern critique that renders the operation of defetishization (ideology critique) ineffective. Defetishization relies upon a certain symbolic efficacy not just to reveal the truth behind the fetish but also to inaugurate a different mode of collective action based on this revelation. Readjusting symbolic understandings can, on this account, allow for the possibility of thinking about the world differently and thus acting in it differently. Specifically, the hope is that once the social order is denaturalized and demystified, social actors can take responsibility for its reproduction, thereby gaining control over a seemingly autonomous process.

However, the truth of ideology critique within the contemporary context is that once denaturalization takes place (when, e.g., it becomes common knowledge that markets are not "natural"), the denaturalized process nevertheless retains its autonomy. The disturbing result is a complacent, canny, conservatism: "Yes, it's true that powerful elites run the market according to their interests, but there's nothing to be done—it couldn't be any other way, and the hope that things could change is merely naïve idealism." We are stuck with the impotent and unmediated juxtaposition of the imaginary (the illusion that things could be otherwise) with an implacably given reality. Beck captures the resulting, frustrating automatism in his description of reflexive modernization:

> [T]here is a general complicity, and the complicity is matched by a general lack of responsibility. Everyone is cause *and* effect, and thus *non*-cause. The cause dribbles away into a general amalgam of agents and conditions, reactions and counter-reactions, which brings social certainty and popularity to the concept of system. The generalized other—the system—acts within and through oneself.[31]

He might have added this action takes place seemingly against one's will.

It is the inadequacy of the symbolic order to capture and categorize risk—the fact that the symbolization process has itself become caught up in a general skepticism, debunking every formulation of the unseen for being compromised by particular interests—that underwrites the uncanny emergence of the system as subject. The example of global warming neatly exemplifies this process: for years the "expert" opinions were debunked by the political factions: political conservatives accused the scientists who sounded the alarm of "fuzzy science" and produced their own scientists who argued there was not enough evidence to justify action. Under a conservative president, the United States pulled out of the Kyoto Protocol. Shortly afterward, the Bush administration's Environmental Protection Agency (EPA) released a report in 2002 conceding that, indeed, human activity was responsible for climatic shifts but that it was too late to do anything about the changes. As a *New York Times* story put it, the EPA report "recommends adapting to inevitable changes. It does not recommend making rapid reductions in greenhouse gases to limit warming."[32] Rather, the report itself observes, "'Because of the momentum in the climate system and natural climate variability, adapting to a changing climate is inevitable. . . . The question is whether we adapt poorly or well.'"[33] In short, we can now recognize the slow climate shift as the result of our own actions—but this transparency doesn't provide any sort of control. We are left to adapt to the results of our own actions as if they were not our own, but external natural conditions foisted upon us. As Beck puts it, "It is as if one were acting while being personally absent."[34] The subject of uncanny capitalism defaults from autonomy to automatism.

The viewer response to *Survivor* neatly replicates this uncanny character of contemporary capitalism. A self-conscious awareness of the "truth" of the show—that it is contrived—coincides with an acceptance of its version of human *nature* as competitive, Darwinian, and so forth. This juxtaposition is correlative to the decline of the symbolic order, which, according to Zizek, results in the disintegration of practical, symbolic knowledge into "on the one hand, excessive 'irrational' violence with no ideologico-political foundation and, on the other, impotent external reflection that leaves the subject's acts intact."[35] In the register of reality TV, the savvy awareness of contrivance coincides with the brutal "reality" of survival at all costs. It is perhaps not coincidental that the current trend in reality television is increasingly toward various forms of borderline torture that guarantee the "reality" of the emotions portrayed. This tendency seems to bear out the assertion that the decline of the symbolic prohibition coincides with the reemergence of brutal "real" domination. Multiple examples from reality TV jump to mind: from the mildly sadomasochist tenor of *Chains of Love*, which chains several male suitors to one woman (or vice versa); to *Boot Camp*, which inflicts drill sergeant discipline on "real" people; to *Fear Factor*, which subjects contestants to various forms of torment, including jumping between speeding trucks and being covered with grublike worms. On the one hand, we know all this is contrived; on the other, we seem to demand more and more punishing contrivances in the hopes of squeezing out a bit of authenticity—of real emotion (fear, anxiety, pain, etc.). Tamer reality shows such as MTV's *Road Rules* and *The Real World* are also increasingly incorporating elements of competition and physical and psychological challenge into their formats.[36]

This pairing of cynical debunking with the emergence of ever more brutal forms of "reality" parallels the logic of uncanny capitalism outlined above. The "triumph" of capitalism in the post–Cold War era is accompanied by increasingly hostile portrayals of its character in popular culture. The standard villain is no longer the Russian-accented totalitarian but the megalomaniacal capitalist of *Anti-Trust*, *Wall Street*, or *The Pelican Brief*. The more generally accepted the fact of capitalism's unnatural brutality, the less able we are to exert any control over it. The explicitly critical portrayal, in other words, has no purchase on the brutal reality. We seem to be faced increasingly with what Zizek describes as external knowledge (about the workings of capital) that leaves the acts of the subject untouched.

The crucial point is that the ostensibly emancipatory move—the debunking of the metanarrative and the tyranny of the big Other—is ultimately unsuccessful. The hope seemed to be that if the symbolic order were caught up in the logic of domination—if discourse and power were inextricably intertwined—one way out might be to disable this order itself. Once we freed ourselves from the tyranny of the symbolic, we would be free to invent ourselves as we saw fit. However, it is the mediation of symbolic efficacy that provides the imaginary with purchase on the real. The debunking of the symbolic order (which is achieved paradoxically by its expansion to the point that there remains nothing for it to mediate) sacrifices the freedom it ostensibly secures. As Zizek suggests, the constellation of "postmetaphysical" positions cannot, as it were, shake the Enlightenment narrative: even as they critique the Enlightenment subject, they nevertheless retain an emancipatory project that conserves the version of a modern subject, "able to reason and reflect freely, to decide on and select his/her set of norms, and so on."[37] The attempt to cast off the bonds of subjectification by sacrificing the subject results in the uncanny return of subject *as* system.

In this respect, postmodernity must be considered an uncompleted (and uncompletable) project. Rumors of the death of the metanarrative have been grossly exaggerated, apparently in the name of emancipation from those forms of power and domination that saturate discursive regimes. Foucault clearly noted the difficulty of thinking beyond the horizon of the grand narrative, but the hope has nevertheless persisted that if the symbolic order is inherently oppressive, its decline might well be liberatory.[38] However, the decline of symbolic efficacy merely effects the short circuit between the impotent proliferation of imaginary ideals—versions of subjectivity and permutations of theory that rival the marketing industry in their slavish devotion to novelty—and the unchallenged hegemony of capitalism as the traumatic Real—an undead force beyond the control of the impotent, shifting strands of theory that mirror it.

The evidence of this short circuit is the savvy attitude that concedes the market is a human contrivance, but which nevertheless denies the possibility of controlling or changing it. It is crucial to recognize that this autonomy isn't accepted on the basis of the ostensible benefits of the market. The savvy attitude recognizes the brutality of the market and the falsity of the promise of optimal outcomes and natural efficiency but simultaneously concedes the "futility" of attempting to do anything about it. The split identified by Beck and embodied in the claim that "we know the market is not autonomous, we participate in reproducing its brutal logic, but there's nothing we can do about it" echoes the logic of the transgressive desire engendered by the superego prohibition ("the Law that generates its own transgression").[39] The desire that animates the "system" is experienced as of the subject, yet beyond its control.

Zizek draws on the writings of St. Paul to exemplify this vicious cycle of law and desire: the introduction of the prohibition coincides with the emergence of the desire to transgress: "Apart from the law sin lies dead. I was once alive apart from the law, but when the commandment came, sin revived and I died, and the very commandment that promised life proved to be death to me. For sin seizing an opportunity in the commandment, deceived me and through it killed me. . . . I do not understand my own actions. For I do not do what I want, but I do the very thing I hate."[40] The subject's desire appears transposed into the autonomous realm of the unconscious and appears foreign and uncontrollable to the subject. Desire appears in its uncanny form—as the undead automaton we can no longer even recognize as our own. By the same token, what we take to be our own "real" desire (to control or divert the autonomous system) is deadened. Isn't this the split that characterizes the savvy position from which subjects acknowledge the depredations of capital even as they continue to concede the inevitability of its reproduction, to participate in it, precisely because it is beyond their control, and to imagine otherwise would be to succumb to naïveté? Perhaps in this vicious circle of desire and the law the deadlock of liberalism can be discerned—on the one hand, the imaginary ideals of individual autonomy, of equal treatment, of universal freedom; on the other, their negation in the inexorable proliferation of capital.

POSTMODERN TROPICS

There is, in short, nothing natural about the second nature—the capitalist jungle—in which we struggle. This fact is, interestingly, thematized in the responses of the *Survivor* viewers surveyed for this chapter. One of their recurrent observations was that the show's title is a misnomer: if the people on the island really had to struggle for survival, there would be no room for the competition and manipulation that provided the storylines for the show. As one viewer put it, "In actual life, if any of us were placed in a true *Survivor*-type setting, real survival would depend on cooperating with each other, not deceiving and eventually betraying each other. . . . Each person would be essential in some way, and cooperation would be the key to survival."[41] The significance of this sentiment, which was echoed by several other respondents, is that the show itself can't be read through the lens of simple naturalization: it doesn't legitimate competition by situating it in a naturalized, tribal past, as if to say, "See—what takes place in the contemporary workplace is the result of human *nature* as evidenced by the fact that it manifests itself even when societal influences are removed." Rather, what *Survivor* enacts for viewers is the specific character of an unnatural, contrived system wherein survival and cooperation have all been subordinated to the profit motive: the $1 million prize awaiting the victor. The impetus to compete, to participate in instrumental manipulation and deceit in the service of personal gain is read not as the dirty truth of human nature but as a result of the contrived conditions to which the cast members are subjected. This reading is perhaps sustained by the admission of the show's winner, Richard Hatch, during the finale, that what viewers and other cast members saw was not his real personality but his game face—and that this image was part of his strategy. The reality format leads not back to some unmediated truth of human nature but to the reality of contrivance.

In keeping with the postmodern theme of generalized reflexivity, *Survivor*'s tropical island and tribal trimmings come to signify not some premodern Edenic scene of unsullied human nature but the artificiality of such a scene. Thus, any reading of the show as an example of classic ideology falls short of the mark. Rather, the show rehearses the impasse of generalized reflexivity itself—a reflexivity that ends up replicating the given reality not because it accepts it uncritically as second nature but because it recognizes it *as* contrivance while simultaneously foreclosing the possibility of anything beyond contrivance. From the perspective of the decline of the symbolic, the tribal scene cannot take on the guise it adopted in modernity, that of an idealized state predating the advent of civilization. Instead, it comes to stand as the truth of civilization when the narratives of modernity become indistinguishable from the myths they would supplant.

The promise of globalized reflexivity—of postmodern irony—is that it can recognize the contrived nature of all that is implicated in the symbolic order. *Survivor* enacts this promise insofar as its appeal to tribalism takes place not in the register of the new age rediscovery of hallowed premodern truths, but rather in the register of savvy reappropriation. The tribal myths invoked over the course of the show—stories about the beliefs of the tribes that inhabited the *Survivor* island and its environs—become tokens in the game, trivia that the cast members need to master in order to win competitive challenges and advance to the next stage. The same holds of the survival information that the players are asked to memorize. They are not put in situations in which they would actually *use* the information (e.g., by deciding what plant species might be used to treat a burn), but draw upon it only to answer questions and win points. Put in somewhat different terms, life on the island is not a back-to-basics, "survival"-level existence, but the deployment of imaginary knowledge about back-to-basics survival as a means of competing according to the stylized rules of a costly, exotic game show. The expert is not the practitioner but the winner of the trivia contest, the one who exhibits mastery of the *imaginary* ideal of the "survivor." The knowledge thus loses its practical character and is subordinated to the real goal: not survival as an end in itself, but the means to survival elevated to the status of an end in itself, to, in short, the accumulation of capital.

The obvious savvy objection to this line of argument is that the gap between the symbolic knowledge deployed within the context of survival and the reflexive appropriation of this knowledge is a mythic one underwritten by an already debunked metanarrative. What is the difference between the imaginary ideal of the survivor (the one who can answer the trivia questions about jungle survival most accurately) and a "real" survivor—someone who could "make it" in the jungle? The question itself demonstrates the short-circuit between the imaginary and the Real resulting from the decline of the symbolic order that sustained the gap between them. Paradoxically, this ultrasavvy question underwrites the "naïve" promise of reality TV: direct access to the real. Furthermore, it leaves us once again with a portrayal of contrivance not only as real, but as the *only* "reality"— a term it can recognize only in scare quotes. What disappears in this short-circuit is the very *inadequacy* of the symbolic order—an inadequacy that implicates that of the given (contrived) reality. The result of the ostensibly emancipatory debunking of the grand narratives that underwrote the gap between appearance and reality is, tellingly, a collapse into the inescapable, relentless reality of the given.[42] The inability to escape the reality of contrivance—the assertion that every contrivance is just as real as the next—is a short-circuit that secures the somewhat claustrophobic and complacent *adequacy* of the contrivance of reality served up to viewers by both television and the given social order. In other words, as Zizek argues, the realm of appearance *qua* appearance is itself sustained by the (inadequacy of the) symbolic order. The impasse of the demise of symbolic efficacy is that the debunking of its guarantee makes it impossible for appearance or contrivance to appear *as such* (if there is nothing *but* appearance, it disappears into its own background). Nevertheless, the savvy stance retains the notion of appearance even after ostensibly dismantling the conceptual apparatus that sustained it. The result is that appearance, deprived of its character as appearance, defaults to the register of real.

The result is fundamentally conservative with respect to the existing state of affairs. We are left confronting, on the one hand, the imaginary ideal (typified in popular culture by John Lennon's appropriately named song) and, on the other, its contribution—seemingly against its will ("imagine no possessions")—to the reproduction of the given ("Imagine" was Lennon's greatest post-Beatles economic success; even the piano on which it was written was auctioned off for millions of dollars[43]). The given state of affairs takes on the aura of the only possible state of affairs perhaps because it represents the status quo at the very point when the difference between contrivance and nature ostensibly disappeared. The emancipatory fantasy of the critique of the metanarrative was that if the imaginary and the real were to become indistinguishable, our freedom to control reality would be limited only by our imaginations. The actual outcome, however, was not the subsumption of reality to the control of the autonomous imagination but rather the emergence of an autonomous—and therefore impotent—imagination (one unable to have any purchase on reality) coupled with an inexorably autonomous reality. There is thus no contradiction in the assertion that the decline of symbolic efficacy leads to the collapse of the distinction between the imaginary and the real and the observation that this collapse equally underwrites their ostensible mutual autonomy. It is precisely the imagined autonomy from the real that leads the imaginary to continue to serve the reproduction of the given reality.

All of which sets the stage for the continuity between the decline of symbolic efficacy (the power of "my words" versus "your eyes") and the fascination of postmodern theory with the development of so-called virtual reality (VR). The fantasy of VR is that it can counter the subservience of the imaginary to the given reality (the continued co-optation of Utopian ideals by the inexorable logic of the market) by eliminating the resistant reminder of the physical world in which this reality is rooted. Material reality is the enemy—the obstacle to the free range of the imaginary that would exempt us for good from the deadlock of the symbolic order. Perhaps not coincidentally, the impulse to escape the constraints of material reality is similarly mobilized by the proponents of e-commerce, who see the Internet as a means of automating consumption—and thereby removing the "friction" of humans themselves.[44] Consider, for example, the fantasy of the corporate virtual work space that "virtualizes" work, thereby rendering labor markets perfectly fluid and flexible.[45] In a virtual world, the limits to capital—environmental, physical, and otherwise material—are overcome. The point not to be missed is the overlap of postmodern utopianism with neoliberalism, both of which converge on the ultimate fantasy of friction-free capital: the elimination of material constraints.

The fact that all attempts to expel material constraint from the realm of the utopian imaginary (capitalist, postmodern, or otherwise) results in the emergence of an inexorable automaton that counteracts these imaginary values is one more example of the operation of the Lacanian real.[46] The materialist point to be made with respect to the real is that its impasse is not to be located in a realm external to the realm of consciousness. Rather, it is the internal deadlock that makes consciousness possible. The realm of the imaginary is that of pure idealism characterized by the futile attempt to exempt consciousness from such a deadlock. This is the point of Adorno's (Hegelian-inflected) critique of identity thinking: that the condition of freedom is a heteronomous element: an unsubsumable kernel: the remainder of particularity over and above the determinations of the concept. It is this kernel that forms what Zizek terms the condition of (im)possibility of the symbolic order, insofar as it appears only negatively, as the impasse that cannot be shaken off. It is the deadlock in the symbolic order—its necessary inadequacy—that makes possible the emergence of appearance *qua* appearance.[47] It is the inconsistency that all forms of idealism attempt to smooth over and erase.

All of which suggests one way of interpreting the emergence of the current spate of reality programming—an emergence that corresponds to the triumph of the savvy subject, which arguably began in the Watergate era and subsequently flourished. Media sociologist Todd Gitlin argues that the reflexive savviness of both political public relations and mediated political coverage came into its own during the campaigns of the 1980s—a time line that parallels Zizek's discussion of the emergence of global reflexivity within the context of the theorists of the "risk" society.[48] The universalized skepticism associated with the various forms of the decline of symbolic efficacy is, despite itself, crucially reliant on the preservation of appearance *qua* appearance, contrivance *qua* contrivance. In other words, the unacknowledged support of global savvy reflexivity—of the recognition that reality is all *just* a contrivance—is the crucial remainder that makes possible the emphasis on the word *just*. Without some remainder in the real, the savvy import of the dismissive qualification evaporates.

The impasse of the savvy subject position is that, even as it collapses the imaginary into the real, it remains locked into the desperate search for some reality that would sustain its dismissal. Thus, it should come as no surprise that the obverse of the reign of savvy skepticism is the manic pursuit of an elusive real, reliant on ever more elaborate forms of torment to elicit its authentic trace. This search for the real that would underwrite the notion of appearance *qua* appearance is necessarily coupled with a rehabilitation of the efficacy of the symbolic order. Consider, for example, the case of a recent MTV reality series that invites viewers to reenact their favorite video. If selected, the viewers are flown to Hollywood, where they undergo makeovers to make them look like celebrities. They work with real video directors and sets to re-create the video and live, briefly, like rock stars, shuttling to and from the studio in chauffeured limousines. Like the spate of reality shows that explore the behind-the-scenes process whereby media commodities are created, the MTV series highlights the power of the symbolic order. The gap between the individual who occupies the place of celebrity and the symbolic network that creates the place itself is foregrounded: everyday people can be transformed into real celebrities thanks to the power of this network. This is certainly true in the case of *Survivor*, which turned several contestants into household names and eventually into celebrities in their own right.

What, then, are we to make of the case of *Survivor* and its popular reception in the terms outlined here? First, that it is crucial to recognize the invocation of tribalism that characterizes the show not as an example of fetishism—as the naturalization of social conditions—but rather as an invocation of the uncanny: a denaturalization that nevertheless endows these conditions with the disturbing independence of the automaton. The result is not the symbolic legitimation of competition, greed, and so on, as "natural," but rather the leveling of any possible distinction between human contrivance and reality. The net result is perhaps even more pernicious than fetishization precisely because it anticipates and co-opts the drive toward demystification. The process might almost be described as demystification taken too far—to the point that it turns on itself, in the ultimate gesture of reflexivity.[49] Second, the reflexivization of the turn to tribal imagery eviscerates even the critical potential of the return to "spiritualism." In other words, the ritual premodern knowledge of tribal peoples is presented neither as a transhistorical confirmation of the natural character of contemporary capitalism nor as an alternative to the current social order (one that would, e.g., point toward a more harmonious relationship with nature and one's fellow creatures), but as yet another species of artifice unable to escape the all-encompassing horizon of the contrived reality of capital.

In this respect, the functioning of *Survivor*'s tribal imagery bears a marked affinity to Zizek's discussion of the transformation of the "traditional cut"—the symbolic marking of the body—in the era of the decline of the symbolic. The significance of the cut—the symbolic tattoo and piercing—has reversed itself in postmodernity: "The traditional cut ran in the direction from the Real to the Symbolic, while the postmodern cut runs in the opposite direction, from the Symbolic to the Real. The aim of the traditional cut was . . . to 'gentrify' raw flesh, to mark its inclusion in the big Other . . . ; the aim of the postmodern sado-maso practices of bodily mutilation is, rather . . . to give access to the 'pain of existence,' the minimum of the bodily Real in the universe of symbolic simulacra."[50] Postmodern skepticism is coupled with the desperate search for some remainder that would sustain the status of contrivance as contrivance.

However, as is frequently the case with the Lacanian real, it is easier to find than the savvy postmodern subject might imagine: it manifests itself in the untranscendable horizon of the autonomous march of capital. The elevation of *Survivor*'s winner, Richard Hatch, to the status of the tyrannical master (underscored by his arrest during the show's run for accusations by his son that he was a tyrannical and abusive father) represents the return of the "big Other" in the register of the Real. This reemergence is a direct artifact of the default to uncanny capitalism enacted by the savvy debunking of symbolic efficacy. It addresses the need to explain the seemingly autonomous self-proliferation of capital: the fact that even though it is the result of our collective actions, it takes on an uncanny drive of its own. The postmodern, paranoid response is the resuscitation of the figure of the cruel master who pulls the strings behind the scenes. Symptomatic of this return is the 2001 movie *Anti-Trust* that features a Bill Gates character (down to the details of his house and haircut) who gains his monopoly power by secretly spying (Big Brother–style) on hackers around the world, stealing their inventions and brutally murdering them. The film suggests that the only way to explain the absurd level of power and wealth amassed by a figure like Bill Gates is to cede him the role of the cruel master, who, thanks to a fantastic spy network, is able to seize control not just of the computer industry, but of the global communication network. As in the case of the portrayal of *Survivor* winner Richard Hatch as a devious master manipulator, the ideological move is to personalize the autonomous logic of capital: to mask its disturbingly uncanny visage with the image of the evil master. Of course, in the *Survivor* postfinale show, the mask of the evil mastermind was revealed as a contrivance of the producers (participated in by Hatch). What was reestablished in this "behind-the-scenes" postscript was the remainder that sustains the appearance as appearance—and hence the efficacy of the symbolic order.

The image of the tyrannical master is imaginary in the sense that it precludes effective action. If we act on it, imagining that all we need to do is purge the system of the few villains who have seized control, we will discover that the autonomous movement of capital continues unchecked (as we may well find in the aftermath of the Enron and Tyco International trials). This autonomous movement is neither the result of a criminal mastermind nor of the blind functioning of a system turned subject. It is the disavowed collective practice of all those who concede the demise of symbolic efficiency—the split between knowledge and action that characterizes the savvy capitulation. All of which is not to dismiss the resistance of this congealed practice to social change. Rather, it is to recognize that the organization of seemingly autonomous capitalism provides direct evidence of symbolic efficacy. There is no way to counter it without rehabilitating the constructive power of the symbolic order and the recognition of the deadlock of the real that is inherent to it: a deadlock that makes it possible to imagine an alternative to the capitalist automaton.

CONCLUSION: THE REALITY OF PARTICIPATION

When the real world is transformed into mere images, mere images become real things.

—Guy DeBord

In her discussion of the changing nature of online work, Tiziana Terranova argues that, in the information economy, the commodity has lost the opacity associated with its fetish character: the hard shell that allowed it to appear independent from the human relations within which it is inscribed: "It is as if the acceleration of production has pushed to the point where commodities, literally, turn into translucent objects . . . showing throughout their reliance on the labor which produces and sustains them."[51] Perhaps reality TV can be read as one more example of this new translucency—an attempt to crack the glossy Hollywood veneer and peer into the messy public privacy of the Big Brother household, of the lovers' cabana on *Temptation Island* and the *Road Rules* Winnebago. As I have attempted to demonstrate in previous chapters, the promise of reality TV is not that of access to unmediated reality (the positivist promise) so much as it is the promise of access to the reality of mediation. This is particularly true of those formats that have incorporated game show elements—as is increasingly the case in the wake of *Survivor*'s phenomenal success. Even the new permutations of the *Road Rules/The Real World* challenge shows have been *Survivor*-ized: two teams compete for a cash prize as members are eliminated one by one from the competition. The hallmark of the reality TV commodity is its translucency—and in this respect it bears a certain affinity with the other "reality-based" trend that is proving increasingly successful: the behind-the-scenes feature, such as VH1's *Behind the Music* and MTV's *Making the Video*. In a similar vein, the additional storage capacity available on DVDs has allowed feature movies to be accompanied by "behind-the-scenes" or "the-making-of" features as part of the "added bonus" available to those who purchase or rent the movie.

The argument of much of this book has been that this new translucency ought to be read not as demystification but as a fetishization of mediation itself—the savvy reduction of reality to mediation with no remainder. The target of ideology critique—of critical theory generally—in this savvy era ought to be not the false mask that covers the obfuscated reality (already exposed by the behind-the-scenes features), but the function of the promise of access to this reality. As Zizek puts it, "The function of ideology is not to offer us a point of escape from our reality but to offer us the social reality itself as an escape."[52] Previous chapters have outlined the proposed lines of flight traced by the promise of access to the real: an alleged assault on the abstracted, hierarchical, homogenized character of mass society; the anticipated rehabilitation of participation and authentic experience; the decentralization of monitoring and control; and the ability of users not just to talk back but to "monitor back": to adopt the power position of the voyeur. However, the question that remains, from the perspective of ideology critique, is what precisely is the traumatic Real from which reality is offered as an escape? Zizek has repeatedly suggested class conflict—or rather the incommensurable drives of labor and capital—as the horizon of the Real: the unsymbolizable deadlock at the heart of "late" capitalism that renders incomplete any attempt to provide a comprehensive field upon which the contestants could come to some kind of "mutually beneficial agreement."

From this perspective, it is certainly telling that unprecedented merger activity has emerged alongside the promise of decentralization in the era of flexible capitalism. Narratives of the advantages of global capitalism as a means of uplifting the living standards of impoverished nations coincide with epic tales of corporate bag men. Increasingly, the shared characteristic of these juxtapositions is their transparency. Citizens in developed nations live in a world in which their reliance on the export of sweatshop labor and the casualization of the workforce comes to the fore. Most college students these days know that their running shoes and leisure wear were likely made in a third-world sweatshop. Uncanny capitalism is predicated not on the concealment of exploitation, but on its inevitability.

If the promise to expose the reality behind the artifice serves as a ruse of the inevitable *givenness* of the reality of artifice, what, if anything, remains to be salvaged from reality or reality TV? Paradoxically, it is the effort to maintain the notion of artifice qua artifice—to pry some minimal wedge between reality and appearance—that provides a seam in the smooth surface of the given. Similarly, it is the space that separates the promise of participation from its reality that provides a purchase point for the critique of the co-optation of interactivity. The closing sections of this chapter explore the way in which this critique emerges from the discussion of reality TV developed in previous chapters.

Democracy and Participation

I take the apparent failure of *Big Brother* (in the U.S. market) alongside the success of *Survivor* as offering some insight into the contradictions of the format, which were exacerbated by the producers' attempt to combine the interactive capability of the Internet with the one-way mass media format of television. Portraying the producers as the new incarnation of *Big Brother* by letting viewers see how the houseguests were manipulated catered to a sense of savvy realism to such an extent that the TV show itself apparently became a bit too transparent for the public's taste. The show was also hamstrung by its own promise of interactivity—one that allowed viewer input but offered little in the way of "customized" content in return. It might be possible to argue, based on the show's relatively poor showing, that the deployment of the promise of interactivity is an ineffective one. I don't take this to be the case, but suggest, rather, that the show was in some sense ahead of its time, anticipating a medium that will be more flexible and interactive than the current ad hoc combination of Internet and television. Perhaps when viewers can control the cameras and choose their camera angles (as may become the case in interactive broad-casts of professional sports), all the while providing information about themselves, their viewing habits, and their preferences, formats like *Big Brother* may come to eclipse the more spectacular, novelty formats that seem to be crowding the airwaves.

What is intriguing about the reality genre, and the phenomenon of Internet in-teractivity in the realm of e-commerce generally, is the portrayal of the relation-ship between surveillance and publicity. One way of reformulating the argument is to suggest that reality TV enacts the reality of the fate of publicity in the con-temporary era: its reduction not just to a form of manipulation but to the exposure of private, rather than public, life. The promise of democratization via interactiv-ity then becomes an invitation to mimic the contemporary version of publicity by submitting the details of one's daily life to comprehensive forms of monitoring. Reality TV provides a vantage point from which to consider the fate of publicity in a mass-customized society. Publicity emerges in the Enlightenment era in the form of a democratic promise of accountability and a testimony to the rational-critical abilities with which the Enlightenment theorists endow the Cartesian sub-ject. It thereby takes on its politically progressive guise, the one that, as Haber-mas notes, places it in opposition "to all domination."[53] Publicity as a form of public accountability, then, requires not just the open disclosure of the affairs of state to the public, but a mechanism whereby public opinion—that which legiti-mates authority—can be formed and made manifest. This mechanism might also be called a form of mutual monitoring, insofar as it requires a certain degree of self-disclosure on the part of both politicians and members of the public. State au-thority is, at least in theory, made accountable to its proper rulers—the members of the public—via the mechanism that makes public opinion manifest. There is a certain symmetry implied in this arrangement, one in which the ruled consent to be ruled by those who are, in turn, held accountable to them.

What we see taking place in the case of the deployment of interactivity is the assimilation of the promise of publicity to the deployment of surveillance. The equation is quite clear: producers are held "accountable" to consumers via a mech-anism that monitors consumer taste (which, taken to the limit of mass customiza-tion, are neither aggregated nor averaged but remain distinct and individualized). In return, the promise of a degree of transparency to consumers is held forth: the mechanism of production is made accessible insofar as the decision-making process is no longer conducted, as it were, behind closed doors. Of course, there is a patent falsity to this promise, insofar as the means of production remain pri-vately owned, and the promise of participation serves the same function as that of surveillance within the workplace: as a means of rationalizing production.

However, there is also a certain truth to the assimilation of surveillance to pub-licity, insofar as it amounts to a realistic assessment of how publicity itself has transformed. The process of "refeudalization" outlined by Habermas represents the process whereby the mechanism for the formation of public opinion becomes transformed into the mechanism for its rationalization. In this sense, publicity (of political events) comes increasingly to rely on surveillance (the monitoring and manipulation of public preferences). Correspondingly, the public transparency of the affairs of state tends toward its premodern equivalent: that of public display and spectacle.

Finally, the role of the "public" shifts toward that of the audience. The transformation of the deliberative-political role of publicity is accompanied by the evisceration of a meaningful conception of the public, which similarly destabilizes its boundary with the private. Thus, public accountability, in the bleakest assessment of it, devolves toward the public spectacle of the private lives of public figures, as recent events in the political realm so amply demonstrate. This is why Habermas's use of the term "refeudalization" falls short of the historical moment. The current form of the public spectacle of the ruler is not the controlled pomp of the feudal era; it is, rather, the unmasking of this pomp, to reveal the "real" person underneath. If publicity is eviscerated of politics, it turns into the accountability of the private—and the spectacle of politics merges with that of celebrity. The devolution of public accountability, in other words, goes hand-in-hand with the transformation of public opinion into a marketing tool. Thus, it is perhaps appropriate that Bill Clinton, famous for his reliance on extensive polling and "market testing" of his political agenda, should be the president most notorious for the public exposure of his private life.

The promise of reality TV gives the assimilation of publicity to surveillance one more twist: it democratizes public opinion in the register of the private. Every consumer is sovereign to the extent that he or she can partake of publicity via surveillance. Herein lies the logic of the inversion of the relationship between celebrity and public scrutiny: the fact that the latter makes the former possible in the era of "real" TV.

In an era characterized by the democratization of access to publicity *as* public relations, a critique of the notion of participation becomes central to the development of a critical theory of the media and of society. For it is precisely the equation of interactivity and participation that allows the celebrants of new media to herald the demise of what Habermas describes as "refeudalization." However, the interactivity they envision fails to live up to the rational-critical version of participatory publicity. It rehabilitates publicity as democratic via the offer of participation—an offer that fails to undo the reduction of publicity to public relations. If this is the case, it is nevertheless not a question of rejecting participation per se as a ruse of power but rather of embarking on an exploration of how an authentically democratic form of participation might be distinguished from that promoted by the interactive digital economy. This book highlights the necessity of making such a distinction within the social context of the development of "interactive" media. However, the attempt to develop a comprehensive critique of participation lies beyond the scope of the current investigation, which limits itself to exploring how interactive participation—portrayed as a means of overcoming abstracted social relations via access to "the real"—functions as a strategy of economic rationalization. The resources for such a critique lie, I believe, in the rich

theoretical debates that surround the notion of participatory democracy. I anticipate that the role played by interactive media in the coming years will highlight
the necessity of clarifying our conception of what counts as *democratic*—as distinguished from transactional—participation.

That the distinction between these two is not as obvious as we might hope—and
that it cannot simply be reduced to an unproblematic division between the properly "political" and the economic—is suggested by the readiness of some media
theorists and much of the popular public discourse to assimilate the promise of
new media interactivity to the potential revitalization of democratic participation.[54] Without a meaningful attempt to distinguish these two anticipated developments from each other, an even broader range of critical theory runs the danger of
serving as implicit legitimization for the equation of interactivity with democratic
participation and thus—in opposition to its stated intent—of the free market with
freedom. The book has focused primarily on the economic uses of interactivity because it is in the economic register that the promise of democratization is deployed
as a strategy of rationalization, a fact symptomatic of the reduction of democracy
to capitalism. Clearly, the resources of the new media provide certain organiza-
tional advantages to activists as well as to corporations. However, there are also—
as several theorists suggest—palpable disadvantages. Technology critic Kevin
Robins, for example, observes that the character of online community may well
lend itself more to economic rationalization than to political revitalization. In
keeping with the notion of the "thinning of experience" associated with the promise of the return of "authentic reality," Robins argues, "What virtual culture promises is an alternative space . . . where it will be possible, perhaps indefinitely, to go
on ignoring the erosion of the world's reality."[55] The resulting "depletion of the
real resources of life and life experience" can only facilitate the continuance of
what, following Simon Jarvis's work on Adorno, might be described as a deprac-
ticalized praxis—an instrumentalized politics that remains at the level of marketing and manipulation. Robins uses slightly different terminology to say much the
same thing: "With its well-intentioned belief in sharing, collaboration, mutuality
[and, one might add, "interactive participation"], virtual communitarianism is a
stultifying vision—an absolutely anti-social and anti-political vision."[56] Darin
Barney makes a similar point, arguing that the progressive potential of the new
media might be offset by their commercial deployment:

> To the extent that the surveillance function of networked computers in the work-
> place socializes people to accept their incapacity to exercise good judgment inde-
> pendent of omnipresent supervision, it is difficult to imagine how anyone could
> advocate letting these same people loose in the public sphere as genuine democratic
> citizens. In this context, it is also difficult to comprehend those who insist that net-
> work technologies constitute the infrastructure of a democratic renaissance.[57]

The prospect of mass-customized politics in an era of interactive monitoring lends
ironic truth to John Corner's assertion that one of the "classic" functions of documentary formats is to provide "publicity and propaganda for dominant versions of

citizenship."[58] Indeed, the form of civic participation modeled by reality TV is consonant with the emerging model of political participation facilitated by the perfection of voluntary self-disclosure via ever more extensive and intensive interactive polling processes. The promise of interactivity as power sharing threatens to reveal itself as a strategy for the rationalization of politics and the mass-customized engineering of consent.

The Illusion of an Elusive Real

Rather than ending on a terminally savvy assessment of the culture industry, I want to enlist one of the paradoxes of an Adorno-inflected account in order to explore the truth of the promise of reality discernable in the tension between the opposed interpretations of reality TV outlined above. This truth may well serve as a possible starting point for a critique of participation, insofar as the co-optation of participation cannot be unrelated to the withering of experience (and hence the "depracticalization" of practice) described by Adorno.

One possible reading of the promise of reality to resolve the shortcomings of the mass media would be to dismiss it as an utterly false reconciliation—a spurious resolution that amounts to complete reification, the hermetic and closed assimilation of given reality to the concept of reality. Such a closure would exemplify Hegel's description of the "unthinking inertia" that corresponds to the eradication of authentic experience.[59] Reading the promise of reality this way comes dangerously close to replicating the closure it describes. It amounts to the claim of total reification and a proclamation of the absolute triumph of constitutive subjectivity—one that Adorno scholars argue cannot be taken literally without foreclosing the possibility of dialectical thought.[60] Moreover, an unrelentingly negative reading would come dangerously close to countering giddy technological utopianism with a pessimistic determinism that echoes, for example, Barney's conclusion that "network technology is an instrument of democracy's continued impossibility in the modern world."[61]

Rather than jumping on either side's bandwagon, I am more inclined toward what Calabrese describes as an ambivalent attitude toward the "potential link between human emancipation and the means of communication."[62] Such ambivalence is warranted not just by the role of new media in forms of political mobilization described by scholars Jon Armitage and Doug Kellner, but also by the fact that, on the other hand, "innovative uses of the means of communication by mobile capital can work against such struggles."[63]

The goal of this extended discussion of reality TV is not to dismiss the promise of participation via interactivity as pure ideology but rather to note the importance of resituating the critical appeal of participation within the context of the era of mass customization. Despite his repeated and aggressive critiques of the culture industry, Adorno asserted an "element of truth in its fulfillment of a need that originates in the ever increasing renunciation demanded by society."[64] It would be hard to justify the time and energy that Adorno devoted to writing about the culture industry and its artifacts if not for the element of truth that could be discerned in them: the dialectical moment that famously related popular culture to high culture as "torn halves of an integral freedom to which, however, they do not add up."[65] In the same passage of this letter to Benjamin (responding to the latter's essay on the work of art in the age of mechanical reproduction), Adorno notes, "The reification of a great work of art is not just loss, any more than the reification of the cinema is all loss."[66] All of which is not to dismiss the very real tendency in Adorno's theory to privilege what he considered authentic art over the falsity of the culture industry—precisely because the former doesn't attempt to paper over the contradictions it invokes. However, Adorno's formulation allows for the possibility that one role for cultural criticism is to highlight the contradictions that popular culture attempts to resolve. In this sense, Fredric Jameson's critical approach in "Reification and Utopia in Mass Culture" remains true to the spirit of Adorno's work. Jameson argues that since "[b]oth modernism and mass culture entertain relations of repression with the fundamental social anxieties and concerns, hopes and blind spots . . . which are their raw material," what is needed is "a method capable of doing justice to both the ideological and the Utopian or transcendent functions of mass culture simultaneously."[67]

The discussion to this point has focused largely on the ideological function of the promise of reality as the naturalization of the given. The question remains as to how to characterize or discern what Jameson terms its "transcendent" moment. Gillian Rose's interpretation of Adorno's dialectic suggests one possible approach that I will invoke in closing. On her account, the method of negative dialectics works to portray the negative image of a (truly) rational dialectic by highlighting the inadequacy of identity thinking.[68] Put in slightly less abstruse terminology, the goal of Adorno's dialectic is to demonstrate repeatedly not just the inadequacy of the concept to its object in the sense that reality can never be reduced to abstract concepts, but also to highlight the critical moment in the concept: that, in contemporary ("damaged") society, it is never fulfilled by the reality which it subsumes. It is the inadequacy of the concept to the given reality that suggests the existence of a concept that could be something other than an alibi for the given. Or, put somewhat differently, this inadequacy points to a mode of experiencing the world that doesn't seek to reduce the object to an external concept. The hope of a negative dialectic then, would be to realize the "object's concept" via the subjective moment of interpretation, which is how I read Adorno's assertion in *Negative Dialectics* that "[t]heory . . . must transform the concepts which it, as it were, brings in from the outside into those which the object has by itself."[69]

The point of an interpretation of reality TV, then, would be to highlight the inadequacy of its conception of reality, which is enacted by the tension in the two accounts of its promise. Bringing out this tension means looking beyond the overlap between the accounts, and observing that positivism and postmodernism are not, *pace* Jameson, identical. The former attempts to sidestep mediation by subtracting the subjective moment, whereas the latter attempts to liquidate that which is mediated (thereby paradoxically providing immediate access to mediation itself). Each suggests (negatively) the inescapability of a dialectical approach through the resulting incoherence (and the slippage of each to its opposite extreme): Positivism becomes postmodern relativism insofar as the object retreats into the unknowable thing-in-itself in response to the subject's attempt to abstract itself out of the picture. Similarly, postmodernism becomes positivism insofar as it offers no escape from the irrevocable givenness of the depthless surface of reality. Each, in this sense, highlights the truth of the other's falsity, thereby, perhaps pointing beyond the choice between the two.

This dynamic can be observed in more concrete terms by the way each of the responses to *Big Brother*'s deployment of the promise of reality interact with each other. What I am calling the positivist response is engaged in the attempt to extract a bit of the real—the "truth" of human interaction isolated within the laboratory setting of the *Big Brother* house—from the meddlesome mediation of the entertainment industry, which keeps tampering with this truth to boost ratings. The savvy approach, on the other hand, salvages its piece of the real in the form of the "truth" that there is no reality behind the manufactured façade erected by the producers: the reality is that it's all about manipulation. Interestingly, each position enacts the desire to attain a frustratingly elusive real. If the positivist version laments that "we could really get to the real, if only we could eliminate the tampering of the biased subject," the postmodern version suggests that "if only we could eliminate the persistent fiction of objectivity, we would be in the real" (in other words, if only we could dispel the illusion that there is something other than the game, we could enjoy the game). At the same time, each side highlights the incoherence of the other: savviness highlights the truth on which positivism stumbles—the reality of mediation. Positivism, in its allegiance to an admittedly flawed conception of objectivity, points to the truth of mediation: that it is reliant on the object and collapses into incoherence in its absence.

Each, in other words, points to the inadequacy of the other's conception of the real, thereby tracing the negative image of a real that cannot be contained by such conceptions (and simultaneously rehabilitating the constitutive inadequacy of the symbolic). Moreover, and this is Rose's crucial point, the failure of the concept to coincide with its object (the real) highlights the inadequacy of given reality itself, or, to put it another way, this inadequacy points to the (negative image of a) possibility of something other than the merely given—the trace of an escape route beyond the dead end of hermetic positivism/postmodernism.[70] The possibility of this escape route can only be figured negatively, by the inadequacy of the versions of reality deployed in the two complementary approaches. Following Zizek, then, it is possible to locate the real in the inescapability of this inadequacy. If there were no real—to put it in crudely postmodern terms—then this inadequacy could be papered over—it would be merely contingent and eradicable. Interestingly, Zizek's version of (negative) materialism suggests that the real is not the incredibly elusive referent of postmodernity that recedes infinitely toward the horizon (like the "thing in itself"), but precisely the impasse that positivism and postmodernism can't elude, try as they might.[71]

Contra the Baudrillard-inflected suggestion that reality TV enacts the reality of the simulacra in the allegedly postmodern era, such programming stages not the *dissolution* of the real but the inescapably *real* inadequacy of the concept of reality upon which it relies.[72] To put it more generally, it stages the inadequacy of administered culture itself—and offers this inadequacy to viewers as the ultimate version of reality. Hence, the savvy appeal to viewers who watch the shows in order to deride them. As one online post discussing Fox's *Joe Millionaire* put it, "You know it's a good show when the only word we can use to describe watching it is 'ashamed'!"[73] As both the savvy and the positivist responses suggest, the inadequacy of the version of reality on offer corresponds to the contradictions of the society within which it functions: the rationalization of "real" experience in accordance with market logic. In keeping with the theme of the Utopian moment referred to by Jameson—one which, as Adorno's approach suggests, is literally Utopian in the sense that it can be located only in the inescapable character of its absence—it is perhaps noteworthy that the promise of reality deployed by a show like *Big Brother* is clearly perceived as inadequate and contradictory by its viewers. Moreover, the source of this inadequacy is, tellingly, located in the logic of the commodification of experience. The positivists repeatedly complain that the desire for ratings leads to tampering with reality, whereas the savvy viewers complain that it is the very promise of reality (the advertising appeal, as it were, of the genre) that is distorting, insofar as it distracts viewers and cast members from what counts—not the reality, but the entertainment value. In both cases, the commodification of experience is predicated on a promise that it can't make good. The inadequacy of commodified reality may not be the intended message of reality TV, but it is nevertheless what this book discerns in its interpretation of the genre. Perhaps, it is not going too far to assert that the recognition of this inadequacy is a prerequisite for the development of an elusive—but critically important—conception of what might count as real participation, or participation in reality.

NOTES

1. *Media Week*, "International Eye—Nastier Than Nasty Nick—and a Winner," 1 September 2000, 8.

2. Ulrich Beck, *The Risk Society* (London: Sage, 1992).

3. Sarah Woodward, "Surviving Survivor," *SHOOT*, 21 July 2000, 7.

4. The "incredulity" toward metanarratives is famously outlined in Jean Lyotard, *The Postmodern Condition: A Report on Knowledge* (Minneapolis: University of Minnesota Press, 1979).

5. Beck, *The Risk Society*, 155.

6. Slavoj Zizek, *The Ticklish Subject* (London: Verso, 1999).

7. Fredric Jameson, *Postmodernism, or the Cultural Logic of Late Capitalism* (Durham, N.C.: Duke University Press, 1991).

8. Terry Eagleton, *The Illusions of Postmodernism* (Oxford: Blackwell, 1996).

9. Beck, *The Risk Society*.

10. Beck, *The Risk Society*, 73. Beck couches his argument in terms of the environment, but the terms of his discussion, read against the background of the events of 11 September 2001, can hardly fail to invoke the specter of terrorism as a human manifestation of the ominous threats of the risk society. Terrorism cannot be accounted for by the political calculus of the nation-state associated with industrial modernization. Hence the temptation of some pundits and analysts to relegate it to a premodern era. However, the more we learn about the terrorists, the more this explanation seems untenable: some of the leaders were apparently highly educated, multilingual world travelers who relied on the most advanced of communication networks as well as some of the most traditional. They embodied not the precursor to globalization but its flip side—its internal risk. Indeed, the description of the new flexible, multinational organizations characteristic of the post-Fordist era neatly anticipates the description of the decentralized, multinational organization of terrorist cells that emerged in the wake of 11 September.

11. See, for example, Eagleton, *The Illusions of Postmodernism*; J. M. Bernstein, "The Causality of Fate: Modernity and Modernism in Habermas," *Praxis International* 8, no. 4 (1989): 407–25; Jameson, *Postmodernism*; Nicholas Garnham, *Capitalism and Communication: Global Culture and the Economics of Information* (London: Sage, 1990).

12. Zizek, *The Ticklish Subject*.

13. The election of George W. Bush provides a straightforward example: His handlers understood not only the crucial importance of ensuring that he occupied the symbolic role of president-elect before the votes were counted and the legal battles settled, but also that once he occupied this position, objections would fade. The symbolic power of office is underwritten by the mass media, as *New York Times* reporter R. W. Apple Jr. noted in his coverage of the Bush inauguration. Referring to the question of Bush's legitimacy, Apple observed that "the debate is likely to grow softer as the nation grows accustomed to pictures of Mr. Bush speaking from the Oval Office, boarding Air Force One, accompanied everywhere he goes by the strains of 'Ruffles and Flourishes' and 'Hail to the Chief.' In the television age, those images, more than anything else, confer the mantle of authority and legitimacy on a leader" (R. W. Apple Jr., "The Inauguration: News Analysis; Tradition and Legitimacy," *New York Times*, 21 January 2001, 1).

14. Zizek, *The Ticklish Subject*, 323.

15. Jacques Derrida, *Of Grammatology*, trans. Gayatri Spivak (Baltimore: Johns Hopkins University Press, 1976), 158.

16. Beck, *The Risk Society*, 26.

17. Beck, *The Risk Society*, 29.

18. Rob Morse, "Fighting Terror by Terrifying U.S. Citizens," *San Francisco Chronicle*, 20 November 2002, A2.

19. Beck, *The Risk Society*, 79; emphasis in original.

20. Which is not to argue for a default to the postmodern terminology of the simulacra. The notion of a "copy with no original" cannot, try as it might, dispense with the concept of originality. Were it to succeed, of course, the term *simulacra* would have no meaning; or, to put it somewhat differently, the simulacra would default to directly perceived reality—

we would have come full circle in order to arrive at positivist relativism: there is nothing other than sensory experience. In such a world, of course, the real disappears: there is no gap between the symbolic order and experience: between my words and your eyes. We become trapped in a world in which we can always only discern what we already know (and vice versa).

21. Anonymous, e-mail message to the author, 20 October 2000.

22. Zizek, *The Ticklish Subject*, 368.

23. Mike Sager, "What I've Learned: Mark Burnett," *Esquire* 136 (July 2001):1, at www.esquire.com/features/learned/010701_mwi_burnett.html (accessed 12 December 2002).

24. Anonymous, e-mail to the author, 27 October 2000.

25. Anonymous, e-mail to the author, 27 October 2000.

26. It may well be at this level that the real appeal of reality TV can be understood. In its very format, reality TV caters to the savvy awareness that reality itself is contrived. The recent phenomenal success of professional wrestling testifies to the power of this appeal. It highlights and concedes the contrived nature of sports as entertainment. Rather than inviting viewers to suspend their skepticism and lose themselves naïvely in the game, it frees them up to lose themselves in the action precisely because they don't have to drop their skepticism. This type of reflexivity seems increasingly prevalent, not just on television but in film and advertising. It thematizes and exploits the decline of the big Other by catering to the canny skepticism of the viewers and conceding that the symbolic order has lost its efficiency—that viewers are no longer duped by it—all the while suggesting the superfluity of this order: viewers can be entertained without having to make the leap of faith needed to believe what they are watching. Once again, we encounter what Zizek describes as the short-circuit between the imaginary and the Real: "To put it in Lacanian terms, . . . when the specific dimension of symbolic appearance starts to disintegrate, the Imaginary and the Real become more and more indistinguishable" (*The Ticklish Subject*, 195). Without the symbolic order, the simulacrum collapses into the real—if all is simulacrum, then the simulacrum is all there is to reality. Professional wrestling is, in such a world, just as authentic as "real" wrestling. This is the paradox of reality television, even as it promises access to the real, it facilitates the process of derealization.

One might also consider the recent success of the boy band 2Gether in these terms. Formed as a spoof of boy bands for a TV series that premiered on MTV, 2Gether highlighted (and satirized) the contrived commodification of such bands: how the members are selected according to rigid demographic formulas, how their songs and image are carefully manufactured to fit a mass-produced template. However, the commercial success of 2Gether as a band, one of whose albums outperformed the "real" boy band, *NSYNC, highlighted the proximity of the spoof to its real counterparts. Indeed, it is tempting to claim that boy bands themselves are already—as in the case of professional wrestling—self-conscious parodies. As contrived commodities—utterly "fake"—they represent the reality of the culture industry.

27. As Marx puts it, "In order, therefore, to find an analogy, we must have recourse to the mist-enveloped regions of the religious world. In that world the productions of the human brain appear as independent beings endowed with life, and entering into relation both with one another and the human race. This I call the fetishism which attaches itself to the products of human labour so soon as they are produced as commodities" (Karl Marx, *Capital: Volume 1. A Critical Analysis of Capitalist Production* [New York: International Publishers, 1992], 77).

28. Marx, *Capital: Volume 1*, 76.

29. Sigmund Freud, "The Uncanny," in *Psychological Writings and Letters*, ed. Sander Gilman (New York: Continuum, 1995), 147.

30. Zizek, *The Ticklish Subject*, 155.

31. Beck, *The Risk Society*, 33.

32. Andrew Revkin, "US Sees Problems in Climate Change," *New York Times*, 3 June 2002, A1.

33. Revkin, "US Sees Problems in Climate Change."

34. Beck, *The Risk Society*, 33.

35. Zizek, *The Ticklish Subject*, 203.

36. One of the most interesting recent developments along these lines is the MTV show *Tough Enough*, which combines elements of *The Real World* with professional wrestling. A group of young, would-be professional wrestlers live together while they are trained by members of the World Wrestling Federation in the ritualized art of fake wrestling. In light of the current argument, the marriage of these two formats seems particularly appropriate, since pro wrestling represents the culmination of the demise of symbolic efficacy: it thematizes cynical savviness by not even trying to make viewers believe the action is real. During the course of the show, one of the trainers, a professional wrestler, tells the show's cast that when he goes into the ring, he's a "storyteller" who uses not words (the symbolic order) but his body. Somewhere in this sentiment one might extract a Foucauldian strain: If the symbolic order is to be debunked as the ruse of power, the alternative we are left with is that of the body as the seat of subjective expression.

37. Zizek, *The Ticklish Subject*, 342.

38. Michel Foucault, *Power/Knowledge: Selected Interviews and Other Writings, 1972–1977*, ed. Colin Gordon (New York: Pantheon, 1989).

39. Foucault, *Power/Knowledge*, 148.

40. Foucault, *Power/Knowledge*.

41. Anonymous, e-mail sent to the author, 10 November 2000.

42. This same collapse is enacted in the ethical realm—which perhaps reveals its consequences most tellingly. The standard postmodern critique of Kantian ethics ends up turning back on the postmodern position itself (illustrating the genealogical connection between the two, both of which remain undialectic). The paradox of Kantian ethics is that it is predicated on incomplete knowledge of the truth: the hypothetical subject able to discern the proper course of action in every case—that course of action underwritten by the divine order—would lose the freedom to behave ethically, relegated to the role of automatically following a given blueprint of correct behavior. However, the attempt to remove the knowledge gap by debunking the ethical truth does not resolve the impasse. Consider the position of the subject facing an ethical decision with the savvy understanding that there are no grand narratives that can be used to evaluate whether the outcome is just or unjust, right or wrong. The conclusion to be drawn by this savvy subject is that the decision taken to be the just, right course of action cannot be contested. In other words the subject faces the same impasse as the hypothetical Kantian subject who has gained access to the noumenal realm. Both are unable to make a wrong decision; both thereby lose their status as ethical agents. Ethical behavior, on this account, entails both that the subject does not have any a priori guidebook that points out the correct application of the general principles of justice in every particular case, and that even though there is not an a priori guide to right behavior, the subject's choice can be wrong. Ethical behavior, then, entails the

struggle to take right action, knowing that even though the blueprint for action cannot be given in advance—that there is no transcendental guide as to the correct course of action—one can still be wrong. The same might be said for political action.

43. George Michael bought Lennon's piano for $2.1 million ("George Michael Purchases Lennon's Imagine Piano," MTV News Archive, at www.mtv.com/news/articles/1425505/20001018/story.jhtml [accessed 2 January 2003]).

44. Bill Gates imagines a world in which personalized computer programs come to know our wants and needs and then take over the consumption function for us: buying us what they know we want (Bill Gates, *The Road Ahead* [New York: Penguin, 1996]).

45. This example is taken from Steve Pruitt and Tom Barrett, "Corporate Virtual Workspace," in *Cyberspace: First Steps*, ed. Michael Benedikt (Cambridge, Mass.: MIT Press, 1991), 383–409.

46. Perhaps the neatest example of this "return of the real" in the realm of cyberfuturism is Ray Kurzweil's description of nanotechnology: the development of tiny molecular machines that can re-build matter by breaking it into its constituent subatomic particles and rebuilding it in any form desired (Ray Kurzweil, *The Age of Spiritual Machines: When Computers Exceed Human Intelligence* [New York: Viking, 1999]). This technology represents the ultimate dissolution of material reality and its subjugation to the imagination of the machine's controllers. However, Kurzweil's description of the liberating power of such technology is qualified by the recognition of the danger of such machines: that, should something go wrong, they could "digest" their creators with the blind automatism of an army of miniscule ants. In short, the potential threat posed by this ultimate freedom from reality is catastrophic; we would be dissolved by the technology of our own liberation. The dialectic of Enlightenment rebounds back on those who blindly disregard its logic.

47. Judith Butler, Ernesto Laclau, and Slavoj Zizek, *Contingency, Hegemony, Universality: Contemporary Dialogues on the Left* (London: Verso: 2000).

48. Todd Gitlin, "Blips, Bites and Savvy Talk: Television's Impact on American Politics," in *State of the Art: Issues in Contemporary Mass Communication*, ed. David Shimkin, Harold Stolerman, and Helen O'Connor (New York: St. Martin's, 1992), 213–22.

49. In Adorno's terms, we might describe this process of overshooting the mark—of demystifying even the process of demystification itself—as the self-eradication of reason characteristic of the dialectic of Enlightenment. Reason continues to show up the mythic character of all grand narratives, until it is left with nothing else to dismantle but itself.

50. Zizek, *The Ticklish Subject*, 372.

51. Tiziana Terranova, "Free Labor: Producing Culture for the Digital Economy," *Social Text* 63, no. 18 (2000): 2, 42.

52. Slavoj Zizek, "How Did Marx Invent the Sympton?" in *Mapping Ideology*, ed. Slavoj Zizek (London: Verso, 1994), 323.

53. Jürgen Habermas, *The Structural Transformation of the Public Sphere* (Cambridge, Mass.: MIT Press, 1991), 88.

54. Pateman, for example, makes the case that a concept of participatory democracy cannot be limited narrowly to the affairs of state, since the industrial sphere is not simply an economic one, but is also "a political system in its own right" (Carole Pateman, *Participation and Democratic Theory* [London: Cambridge University Press, 1970], 106).

55. Kevin Robins, "Against Virtual Community: For a Politics of Distance," *Angelaki* 4, no. 2 (1999): 167.

56. Simon Jarvis, *Adorno: A Critical Introduction* (New York: Routledge, 1998); Robins, "Against Virtual Community," 169.

57. Darin Barney, *Prometheus Wired: The Hope for Democracy in the Age of Network Technology* (Chicago: University of Chicago Press, 2000), 163.

58. John Corner, "Performing the Real," *Television and New Media* 3, no. 3 (August 2002): 259.

59. Brian O'Connor, "Introduction," in *The Adorno Reader*, ed. Brian O'Connor (Oxford: Blackwell, 2000), 12.

60. Gillian Rose, *The Melancholy Science: An Introduction to the Thought of Theodor W. Adorno* (London: Macmillan, 1978); Jarvis, *Adorno*; and Susan Buck-Morss, *The Origin of Negative Dialectics* (New York: Free Press, 1977).

61. Barney, *Prometheus Wired*.

62. Andrew Calabrese, "The Welfare State, the Information Society, and the Ambivalence of Social Movements," in *Communication, Citizenship, and Social Policy: Rethinking the Limits of the Welfare State* (Lanham, Md.: Rowman & Littlefield, 1999), 266 .

63. Jon Armitage, "Ontological Anarchy, The Temporary Autonomous Zone, and the Politics of Cyberculture: A Critique of Hakim Bey," *Angelaki* 4, no. 2 (1999): 115–28; Doug Kellner, "Globalisation from Below? Toward a Radical Democratic Technopolitics," *Angelaki* 4, no. 2 (1999): 101–13; Calabrese, "The Welfare State," 266.

64. Theodor Adorno, *Aesthetic Theory*, trans. Robert Hullot-Kentor (Minneapolis: University of Minnesota Press, 1997), 311.

65. Ernst Bloch, Georg Lukacs, Bertolt Brecht, Walter Benjamin, and Theodor Adorno, *Aesthetics and Politics* (London: NLB, 1977), 123.

66. Bloch et al., *Aesthetics and Politics*, 123.

67. Fredric Jameson, "Reification and Utopia in Mass Culture," in *Signatures of the Visible* (New York: Routledge, 1992), 25, 30.

68. Rose, *The Melancholy Science*.

69. Rose, *The Melancholy Science*, 44.

70. Again, it seems to me that the hardest part of interpreting this formulation is to do so without defaulting to the idealism that Adorno so persistently critiqued. Perhaps one approach is to argue that the contradictions of the given reality are of a piece with the current deployment of the concept as that to which particulars must be subsumed. Then the inadequacy of the concept to its object is the material consequence of the domination of identity thinking that characterizes it—it is the negative image of the material inadequacy of identity thinking. Which is not to say that the end of domination or capitalism would correspond to a state of affairs in which the concept was adequate to its object, but rather that the imperative to subsume the object to a concept would be eliminated. Reconciliation of concept and object does not mean that the latter finally becomes adequate to the former, but rather that it is able to incorporate the thought of its own inadequacy—of what Jarvis describes as its conditionedness (Jarvis, *Adorno*, 216).

71. Slavoj Zizek, *Looking Awry: An Introduction to Jacques Lacan through Popular Culture* (Cambridge, Mass.: MIT Press, 1997).

72. Jean Baudrillard, *Simulacra and Simulation* (Ann Arbor: University of Michigan Press, 1994).

73. "Joe Millionaire General Gabbery," at www.televisionwithoutpity.com/ijsbb/forum.cgi?cn=103 (accessed 7 January 2003).

Bibliography

"About DotComGuy." *DotComGuy*, at www.dotcomguy.com (accessed 14 September 2000).

Adorno, Theodor W. "The Actuality of Philosophy." In *The Adorno Reader*, ed. Brian O'Connor, 23–39. Oxford: Blackwell, 2000.

———. *Aesthetic Theory*. Trans. Robert Hullot-Kentor. Minneapolis: University of Minnesota Press, 1997.

———. "Cultural Criticism and Society." In *The Adorno Reader*, ed. Brian O'Connor, 195–210. Oxford: Blackwell, 2000.

———. *Kierkegaard: Construction of the Aesthetic*. Trans. Robert Hullot-Kentor. Minneapolis: University of Minnesota Press, 1989.

———. *Minima Moralia: Reflections from Damaged Life*. Trans. E. F. N. Jephcott. London: New Left Books, 1974.

———. *Negative Dialectics*. Trans. E. B. Ashton. New York: Seabury, 1973.

———. "Sociology and Empirical Research." In *The Adorno Reader*, ed. Brian O'Connor, 174–92. Oxford: Blackwell, 2000.

———. "Subject and Object." In *The Adorno Reader*, ed. Brian O'Connor, 137–52. Oxford: Blackwell, 2000.

Agre, Phil. "Wish List." *Network Observer* (May 1996), at dlis.gseis.ucla.edu/people/pagre/tno/may-1996.html (accessed 20 January 2003).

Alexander, Shana. "The Silence of the Louds." *Newsweek*, 22 January 1973, 28.

"American Candidate." *FX Network*, at www.fxnetwork.com/candidate (accessed 12 January 2003).

Andersen, Robin. *Consumer Culture and TV Programming*. Boulder, Colo.: Westview, 1995.

———. "Reality TV and Criminal Justice." *The Humanist*, 54, no. 5 (1994): 8–13.

Anderson, Ken. "Technology and Convergence of the Digerati." White paper, MediaOne Labs, June 1999.

Angulo, Sandra. "Race for $1 Trillion." *New York Post*, 18 November 1999, Business, 1.

Apple, R. W., Jr. "The Inauguration: News Analysis; Tradition and Legitimacy." *New York Times*, 21 January 2001, sec. A1.

Armitage, John. "Ontological Anarchy, the Temporary Autonomous Zone, and the Politics of Cyberculture: A Critique of Hakim Bey." *Angelaki* 4, no. 2 (1999): 115–28.

Ayres, Ian. "Lectures vs. Laptops." *New York Times*, 20 March 2001, sec. A20.

Bagdikian, Ben H. *The Effete Conspiracy and Other Crimes by the Press*. New York: Harper & Row, 1972.

———. *The Media Monopoly*. 5th ed. Boston: Beacon, 1997.

Bailey, Lee. "For Reality Stars, the Reality of a One-Time Payment." *New York Times*, 16 December 2001, sec. 2, 33.

Baldasty, Gerald J. "The Rise of News as a Commodity: Business Imperatives and the Press in the Nineteenth Century." In *Ruthless Criticism: New Perspectives in U.S. Communication History*, ed. William S. Solomon and Robert W. McChesney, 98–121. Minneapolis: University of Minnesota Press, 1993.

Barbash, Ilisa, and Lucien Taylor. *Cross-Cultural Filmmaking: A Handbook for Making Documentary and Ethnographic Films and Videos*. Berkeley: University of California Press, 1997.

Barlow, John Perry. "The Next Economy of Ideas." *Wired* (October 2000): 240–51.

Barney, Darin. *Prometheus Wired: The Hope for Democracy in the Age of Network Technology*. Chicago: University of Chicago Press, 2000.

Barsamian, David. *Stenographers to Power: Media and Propaganda*. Monroe, Maine: Common Courage Press, 1992.

Bartlett, Beverly. "No Man Is An Island, but It's an Island That Tests Us." *Courier Journal* (Louisville, Ky.), 15 January 2001, sec. 1F.

Baudrillard, Jean. *Simulacra and Simulation*. Trans. Sheila Faria Glaser. Ann Arbor: University of Michigan Press, 1994.

———. "The Virtual Illusion: Or the Automatic Writing of the World." *Theory, Culture & Society* 12 (1995): 97–107.

Beck, Ulrich. *Risk Society: Towards a New Modernity*. London: Sage, 1992.

Bedell, Doug. "FTC to Survey E-commerce Sites on How They Use Customers' Data." *Dallas Morning News*, 2 March 2000, 1F.

Bekken, Jon. "The Working-Class Press at the Turn of the Century." In *Ruthless Criticism: New Perspectives in U.S. Communication History*, ed. William S. Solomon and Robert W. McChesney, 151–75. Minneapolis: University of Minnesota Press, 1993.

Benjamin, Walter. "The Work of Art in the Age of Mechanical Reproduction." In *Illuminations*, ed. Hannah Arendt, 217–52. New York: Schocken, 1968.

Berger, John, Sven Blomberg, Chris Fox, Michael Dibb, and Richard Hollis. *Ways of Seeing*. London: British Broadcasting Corporation; Harmondsworth: Penguin, 1972.

Berman, Marshall. *All That Is Solid Melts into Air: The Experience of Modernity*. New York: Simon & Schuster, 1982.

Bernstein, Jay M. "The Causality of Fate: Modernity and Modernism in Habermas." *Praxis International* 8, no. 4 (January 1989): 407–25.

———. *The Fate of Art: Aesthetic Alienation from Kant to Derrida and Adorno*. University Park: Pennsylvania State University Press, 1992.

———. "Why Rescue Semblance? Metaphysical Experience and the Possibility of Ethics." In *The Semblance of Subjectivity: Essays in Adorno's Aesthetic Theory*, ed. Tom Huhn and Lambert Zuidervaart, 177–212. Cambridge, Mass.: MIT Press, 1997.

Bloch, Ernst, Georg Lukacs, Bertolt Brecht, Walter Benjamin, and Theodor Adorno. *Aesthetics and Politics*. London: NLB, 1977.

"The Boards." *Big Brother*, at BigBrother2000.com (accessed 18 August 2000). Boedeker, Hal. "Viewers Deserve Blame for Success of Trash TV." *Orlando Sentinel*, 24 January 2001, sec. E1.

Bourdieu, Pierre. *Distinction: A Social Critique of the Judgment of Taste*. Trans. Richard Nice. Cambridge, Mass.: Harvard University Press, 1984.

———. *The Logic of Practice*. Trans. Richard Nice. Stanford, Calif.: Stanford University Press, 1990.

Boyle, James. "Foucault in Cyberspace: Surveillance, Sovereignty and Hard-Wired Censors," at www.wcl.american.edu/pub/faculty/boyle/foucault/htm#iv (accessed 12 December 2001).

Brady, R. H. "The Idea in Nature: Rereading Goethe's Organics." In *Goethe's Way of Science: A Phenomenology of Nature*, ed. D. Seamon and A. Zajonc, 83–111. Albany: State University of New York Press, 1998.

Braverman, Harry. *Labor and Monopoly Capital: The Degradation of Work in the Twentieth Century*. New York: Monthly Review Press, 1974.

Bream, Joe. "Art around the Clock." *Minneapolis Star Tribune*, 22 September 1998, sec. 1E.

Brenkman, John. "Mass Media: From Collective Experience to the Culture of Privatization." *Social Text* 1 (1979): 94–109.

Brockes, Emma. "Welcome to Me TV." *The Guardian*, 10 December 1999, Features, 2.

Brownfield, Paul, and Brian Lowry. "As the Storm Clouds Gather." *New York Times*, 31 December 2000, Calendar, 9.

Bryan, Cathy, et al. "Electronic Democracy and the Civic Networking Movement in Context." In *Cyberdemocracy: Technology, Cities, and Civic Networks*, ed. Rosa Tsagarousianou, Damian Tambini, and Cathy Bryan, 1–17. London: Routledge, 1998.

Buck-Morss, Susan. *The Dialectics of Seeing: Walter Benjamin and the Arcades Project*. Cambridge, Mass.: MIT Press, 1995.

———. *The Origin of Negative Dialectics: Theodor W. Adorno, Walter Benjamin and the Frankfurt Institute*. New York: Free Press, 1977.

Burstein, Daniel, and David Klein. *Road Warriors: Dreams and Nightmares along the Information Superhighway*. New York: Dutton, 1995.

Butler, Judith. *Gender Trouble: Feminism and the Subversion of Identity*. New York: Routledge, 1990.

Calabrese, Andrew. "The Welfare State, the Information Society, and the Ambivalence of Social Movements." In *Rethinking the Limits of the Welfare State*, ed. Andrew Calabrese and J.-C. Burgelman, 259–77 (Lanham, Md.: Rowman & Littlefield, 1999).

Calabrese, Andrew, and Mark Borchert. "Prospects for Electronic Democracy in the United States: Re-thinking Communication and Social Policy." *Media, Culture and Society* 18, no. 2 (1996): 249–68.

Carey, James. "The Press, Public Opinion, and Public Discourse." In *Public Opinion and the Communication of Consent*, ed. Theodore L. Glasser and Charles T. Salmon, 373–402. New York: Guilford, 1995.

Carter, Bill. " 'Big Brother' Hopes to Engineer an Exit, Then Add a Face." *New York Times*, 4 September 2000, sec. E1.

———. "Fox Network Will End 'Multimillionaire' Marriage." *New York Times*, 22 February 2000, sec. C1.

———. "The Land Rush to Reality Island: Overcrowded? Yes, but Showing No Signs of Sinking." *New York Times*, 17 July 2001, sec. E1.

———. "Reality TV Alters the Way TV Does Business." *New York Times*, 25 January 2003, sec. A1.

———. "Some Sponsors Can't Accept Racy Reality." *New York Times*, 29 January 2001, sec. C1.

"Chat." *Big Brother*, at BigBrother2000.com (accessed 2 August 2000).

Clothier, Mike. "More Folks Watching Web Cameras and Waiting." *Chicago Tribune*, 7 October 1999, 7.

Collins, Monica. "A Deuce of Reality." *Boston Herald*, 11 January 2001, sec. O41.

"Computing's New Shape," *The Economist*, 23–29 November 2002, 11.

Copeland, Libby. "For DotComGuy, the End of the Online Line." *Washington Post*, 3 January 2001, sec. C2.

Corner, John. "Performing the Real." *Television and New Media* 3, no. 3 (August 2002): 255–70.

Couldry, Nick. *The Place of Media Power: Pilgrims and Witnesses of Media Age*. London; New York: Routledge, 2000.

Czitrom, Daniel J. *Media and the American Mind: From Morse to McLuhan*. Chapel Hill: University of North Carolina Press, 1982.

Davey, Steven. "Brother Not Big." *Now*, 21–27 September 2000, at www.nowtoronto. com/issues/2000-09-21/next.html (accessed 2 January 2002).

Davis, Jim, and Michael Stack. "The Digital Advantage." In *Cutting Edge Cutting Edge: Technology, Information, Capitalism and Social Revolution*, ed. Jim Davis, Thomas Hirschl, and Michel Stack, 121–44. London: Verso, 1997.

De Certeau, Michel. *The Practice of Everyday Life*. Berkeley: University of California Press, 1988.

Delaney, Kevin "'An American Family' Visits the Andy Warhol Museum" (1996), at members.aol.com/kdel691586/ love/amfamily.html (accessed 12 December 2000).

Deleuze, Gilles, "Postscript on the Societies of Control." *OCTOBER* 59 (Winter 1992): 3–7.

De Moraes, Lisa. "Fox Scrambles to Make Ratings Hay with an Extra 'Island.'" *Washington Post*, 2 February 2001, sec. C5.

Dovey, Jon. *Freakshow*. London: Pluto, 2000.

Dretzka, Gary. "He Got Game: Bill Gates Promotes Versatile Xbox," *Chicago Tribune*, 18 January 2001, sec. N4.

Eagleton, Terry. *The Illusions of Postmodernism*. Oxford: Blackwell, 1996.

———, ed. *Raymond Williams: Critical Perspectives*. Boston: Northeastern University Press, 1989.

Enzensberger, Hans Magnus. *Critical Essays*. Ed. Reinhold Grimm and Bruce Armstrong. New York: Continuum, 1982.

Epstein, Ilana. "Thanks a Million." *Jerusalem Post*, 1 February 2002, 9.

"Fantasy Music Tycoon." *MTV*, at www.mtv.com/bands/fantasy_music_tycoon/ (accessed 14 January 2003).

"FAQ." *DotComGuy*, at www.dotcomguy.com (accessed 14 September 2000).

"Farewell Seminal Coffee Can." *Wired*, at www.wired.com/news/culture/0,1284,42254,00. html (accessed 14 December 2002).

Farhi, Paul. "The Spin on 'Real World': Cast Members Say the MTV Show Adds Its Own Spice to a Duller Daily Life." *Washington Post*, 4 November 1999, C1.

Federal Trade Commission. "FTC Wraps Up Record Year in Anti-trust Enforcement with New Mix of Litigation and Guidance" (2000), at www.ftc.gov/opa/2000/10/ antitrustfy2000.htm (accessed 30 January 2001).

Fernback, Jan. "The Wired Community: An Exploration of the Cultural Practices of the Citizens of Cyberspace." Ph.D. diss., University of Colorado, Boulder, 1998.

Fetveit, Arild. "Reality TV in the Digital Era." *Media, Culture, & Society* 21 (1999): 787–804.

Fink, Bruce. *The Lacanian Subject: Between Language and Jouissance*. Princeton, N.J.: Princeton University Press, 1995.

Fiske, John. *Television Culture*. London: Metheun, 1987.

Fiske, John, and John Hartley. *Reading Television*. London: Methuen, 1978.

Flaim, Denise. "Body Scanners a Step toward Mass Customization." *Minneapolis Star Tribune*, 13 May 1999, sec. 7E.

Flynn, Laurie. "Compressed Data: Faltering TV Show Hits Stride on Web." *New York Times*, 18 September 2000, sec. C4.

Foucault, Michel. *The Archaeology of Knowledge*. New York: Pantheon, 1972.

———. *The Birth of the Clinic: An Archaeology of Medical Perception*. New York: Vintage, 1994.

———. *Discipline and Punish: The Birth of the Prison*. New York: Pantheon, 1977.

———. *The Foucault Reader*. Ed. Paul Rabinow. New York: Pantheon, 1984.

———. *The History of Sexuality, Volume I*. New York: Pantheon, 1978.

———. *The Order of Things: An Archaeology of the Human Sciences*. New York: Vintage, 1994.

———. *Power/Knowledge*. New York: Pantheon, 1972.

Frank, Manfred. *What Is Neostructuralism?* Trans. Sabine Wilke and Richard Gray. Minneapolis: University of Minnesota Press, 1989.

Fraser, Nancy. "Foucault's Body-Language: A Post-Humanist Political Rhetoric?" *Salmagundi* 61 (Fall 1983): 55–70.

———. "Rethinking the Public Sphere: A Contribution to the Critique of Actually Existing Democracy." In *Habermas and the Public Sphere*, ed. Craig Calhoun, 109–42. Cambridge, Mass.: MIT Press, 1991.

Freud, Sigmund. *Civilization and Its Discontents*. Trans. James Strachey. New York: Norton, 1961.

———. "The Uncanny." In *Psychological Writings and Letters*, ed. Sander Gilman, 120–53. Continuum: New York, 1995.

Gabler, Neal. *Life: The Movie; How Entertainment Conquered Reality*. New York: Knopf, 1998.

Galvin, Nick. "The Porn Star Next Door." *Sydney Morning Herald*, 10 January 2003, 27.

Gamson, Joshua. *Freaks Talk Back: Tabloid Talk Shows and Sexual Non-Conformity*. Chicago: University of Chicago Press, 1998.

Gandy, Oscar H. *The Panoptic Sort: A Political Economy of Personal Information*. Boulder, Colo.: Westview, 1993.

Gardyn, Rebecca. "The Tribe Has Spoken: Reality TV Is Here to Stay." *American Demographics*, at www2.realitytvfans.com/newspub/story.cfm?id=3335 (accessed 5 September 2001).

Garfinkel, Simon. *Database Nation: The Death of Privacy in the 21st Century*. Beijing: O'Reilly, 2000.

Garnham, Nicholas. *Capitalism and Communication: Global Culture and the Economics of Information* London: Sage, 1990.

Gates, Bill. *The Road Ahead*. 2d ed. New York: Penguin, 1996.

Giddens, Anthony. *A Contemporary Critique of Historical Materialism*. Berkeley: University of California Press, 1981.

Gilbert, Melissa. "A Perverse 'Fantasy Island.'" *Boston Globe*, 10 January 2001, sec. F1.

Gilder, George. *Life after Television: The Coming Transformation of Media and American Life*. New York: Norton, 1994.

Gimein, Mark. "The Greedy Bunch: You Bought, They Sold." *Fortune*, 11 August 2000.

Ginsberg, Benjamin. *The Captive Public: How Mass Opinion Promotes State Power*. New York: Basic Books, 1986.

Gitlin, Todd. "Blips, Bites and Savvy Talk: Television's Impact on American Politics." *Dissent* (Winter 1990): 18–26.

———. "Blips, Bites and Savvy Talk: Television's Impact on American Politics." In *State of the Art: Issues in Contemporary Mass Communication*, ed. David Shimkin, Harold Stolerman, and Helene O'Connor, 213–22. New York: St. Martin's, 1992.

Goffman, Erving. *Asylums: Essays on the Social Situation of Mental Patients and Other Inmates*. New York: Doubleday, 1961.

Gramsci, Antonio. *An Antonio Gramsci Reader: Selected Writings, 1916–1935*. Ed. David Forgacs. New York: Schocken, 1988.

Grossman, Wendy. "Shock of the New for Amazon Customers." *Daily Telegraph* (London), 26 October 2000, 70.

Habermas, Jürgen. *The Philosophical Discourse of Modernity: Twelve Lectures*. Cambridge, Mass.: MIT Press, 1996.

———. "The Public Sphere: An Encyclopedia Article." *New German Critique* 1, no. 3 (1974): 49–55.

———. *The Structural Transformation of the Public Sphere*. Cambridge, Mass.: MIT Press, 1991.

Harrington, Stephanie. "An American Family Lives Its Life on TV." *New York Times*, 7 January 1973, sec. 2, 19.

Harvey, David. *The Condition of Postmodernity: An Inquiry into the Origin of Cultural Change*. Cambridge, Mass.: Blackwell, 1990.

———. *Limits to Capital*. Oxford: Blackwell, 1982.

Heft, Richard. "Cues from the Real World." *Glasgow Herald*, 17 October 1998, 14.

Heim, Michael. *The Metaphysics of Virtual Reality*. New York: Oxford University Press, 1993.

Herman, Edward, and Noam Chomsky. *Manufacturing Consent: The Political Economy of the Mass Media*. New York: Pantheon, 1988.

Hodges, Ann. "'Temptation Island' Gets Trashy." *Houston Chronicle*, 12 January 2001, 10.

Hoffman, Nancy. "The Unity of Science and Art: Goethean Phenomenology as a New Ecological Discipline." In *Goethe's Way of Science: A Phenomenology of Nature*, ed. David Seamon and Arthur Zajonc, 120–75. Albany: State University of New York Press, 1998.

Holtzman, Steven. *Digital Mosaics: The Aesthetics of Cyberspace*. New York: Simon & Schuster, 1997.

Horkheimer, Max, and Theodor W. Adorno. *Dialectic of Enlightenment*. Trans. John Cumming. New York: Continuum, 1993.

Huxley, Aldous. *Brave New World*. London: Chatto & Windus, 1970.

Irwin, Louis. "Interactive Dateline Is #1." *Studio Briefing*, at studio@usa.net (accessed 14 July 1999).

Jameson, Fredric. *Late Marxism: Adorno, or, the Persistence of Dialectic*. London; New York: Verso, 1990.

——. *Postmodernism, or the Cultural Logic of Late Capitalism*. Durham, N.C.: Duke University Press, 1991.

——. "Reification and Utopia in Mass Culture." In *Signatures of the Visible*. New York: Routledge, 1992.

Jarvis, Simon. *Adorno: A Critical Introduction*. New York: Routledge, 1998.

Jay, Martin. "Mimesis and Mimetology." In *The Semblance of Subjectivity: Essays in Adorno's Aesthetic Theory*, ed. Tom Huhn and Lambert Zuidervaart, 29–53. Cambridge, Mass.: MIT Press, 1997.

Jhally, Sut, and Bill Livant. "Watching as Working: The Valorization of Audience Consciousness." *Journal of Communication* 36, no. 3 (1986): 124–43.

Jowett, Garth. "Dangling the Dream? The Presentation of Television to the American Public." *Historical Journal of Film, Radio, and Television* 14, no. 2 (1994): 121–45.

Jubera, Drew. "Entering the Real World." *Atlanta Journal and Constitution*, 2 June 2000, sec. 1C.

——. "Oh, 'Brother': Ratings Fall as Boredom Rules." *Atlanta Journal and Constitution*, 11 July 2000, sec. 4C.

Justin, Neal. "Reality Bits: The Most Compelling New TV Soaps Are All about the Ordinary Days of Our Lives." *Minneapolis Star Tribune*, 22 June 1998, 1E.

Kellner, Douglas. "Globalization from Below? Toward a Radical Democratic Technopolitics." *Angelaki* 4, no. 2 (1999): 101–13.

Kelly, Kevin. "What Would McLuhan Say? *Wired* 4, no. 10 (October 1996), at www.wired.com/wired/archive/ 4.10/dekerckhove.html (accessed 10 July 2001).

Kilborn, Richard. "'How Real Can You Get?': Recent Developments in 'Reality' Television." *European Journal of Communication* 9 (1994): 421–39.

Kissell, Ron. "Olympics Take Gold." *Variety*, 9 October 2000, 18.

Klass, Tim. "'Real' Spotlight Sometimes Glowed, Glared." *San Diego Union-Tribune*, 17 June 1998, E-1.

Kloer, Phil. "TV's Venture into Voyeur Vision." *Atlanta Journal and Constitution*, 23 March 2000, sec. 1G.

Krugman, Paul. "For Richer—How the Permissive Capitalism of the Boom Destroyed American Equality." *New York Times Magazine*, 20 October 2002, 66–78.

Kuczynski, Alex. "In Hollywood, Everyone Wants to Be Ozzy." *New York Times*, 19 May 2002, sec. 9, 1.

Kuptz, Jerome. "Independence Array." *Wired* (October 2000): 236–37.

Kurzweil, Ray. *The Age of Spiritual Machines: When Computers Exceed Human Intelligence*. New York: Viking, 1999.

Labaton, Stephen. "U.S. Is Said to Seek New Law to Bolster Privacy on Internet." *New York Times*, 20 May 2000, sec. A1.

Lacan, Jacques. *The Four Fundamental Concepts of Psychoanalysis*. The Seminar of Jacques Lacan, Book 11. New York: Norton, 1998.

——. "Seminar on 'The Purloined Letter.'" In *The Purloined Poe*, ed. Jon P. Muller and William J. Richardson, trans. Jeffrey Mehlman. Baltimore: Johns Hopkins University Press, 1956.

Lanham, Richard A. *The Electronic Word: Democracy, Technology, and the Arts*. Chicago: University of Chicago Press, 1993.

Larsen, Peter. "Spanish Were Watching as Big Brother Stole the Show." *Financial Times* (London), 18 March 2000, 10.

Lears, T. J. Jackson. "From Salvation to Self-Realization." In *The Culture of Consumption: Critical Essays in American History*, ed. Richard W. Fox and T. J. Jackson Lears, 1–38. New York: Pantheon, 1983.

Lefebvre, Henri. *The Production of Space*. Trans. Donald Nicholson-Smith. Oxford: Blackwell, 1991.

Leiss, William, Stephen Kline, and Sut Jhally. *Social Communication in Advertising: Persons, Products and Images of Well-Being*. Toronto: Metheun, 1990.

Lessig, Lawrence. *Code: and Other Laws of Cyberspace*. New York: Basic Books, 1999.

Lester, Toby. "The Reinvention of Privacy." *Atlantic Monthly* (March 2001): 27–39.

Lewis, Michael. "Boombox." *New York Times Magazine*, 13 August 2000, 36.

Lewis, Paul. "Making Television Searchable." *New York Times*, 22 April 1999, sec. G1.

Lipietz, Alain. *Towards a New Economic Order: Postfordism, Ecology and Democracy*. New York: Oxford University Press, 1992.

Lippman, Walter. *Public Opinion*. New York: Macmillan, 1922.

Lovejoy, Margot. *Postmodern Currents: Art and Artists in the Age of Electronic Media*. Upper Saddle River, N.J.: Prentice Hall, 1989.

Lowry, Brian. "Reality, in the Blinded Eye of the Beholders." *Los Angeles Times*, 29 August 2000, sec. F1.

——. "TV Viewers Call Up as 'Big Brother' Winds Down." *Milwaukee Journal Sentinel*, 25 September 2000, sec. 6B.

Lyon, David. *The Electronic Eye: The Rise of Surveillance Society*. Minneapolis: University of Minneapolis Press, 1994.

Lyotard, Jean François. *The Postmodern Condition: A Report on Knowledge*. Trans. Geoff Bennington and Brian Massumi. Minneapolis: University of Minnesota Press, 1993.

Marchand, Roland. *Advertising the American Dream: Making Way for Modernity, 1920–1940*. Berkeley: University of California Press, 1985.

Marx, Karl. *Capital: Volume 1. A Critical Analysis of Capitalist Production*. New York: International Publishers, 1992.

——. *The Economic and Philosophical Manuscripts of 1844*. New York: International Publishers, 1964.

Marx, Karl, and Friedrich Engels. *The Communist Manifesto*. Harmondsworth: Penguin, 1985.

Mathiesen, Thomas. "The Viewer Society: Michael Foucault's 'Panopticon' Revised." *Theoretical Criminology* 1, no. 2 (1997): 215–34.

McCarthy, Abigail. "An American Family & the Family of Man." *Atlantic Monthly* (July 1973): 72–76.

McChesney, Robert W. "Conflict, Not Consensus: The Debate over Broadcast Communication Policy, 1930–35." In *Ruthless Criticism: New Perspectives in U.S. Communication History*, ed. William S. Solomon and Robert W. McChesney, 222–58. Minneapolis: University of Minnesota Press, 1993.

McDaniel, Mike. "Oh Brother, at Last the End Is Near." *Houston Chronicle*, 28 September 2000, sec. H1.

McLellan, David. *Karl Marx: Selected Writings*. Oxford: Oxford University Press, 1977.

Meyer, Chris. "Hollywood Writers' Looming Walkout Could Hurt Films and TV and Lead Actors to Follow Suit." *San Francisco Chronicle*, 19 February 2001, sec. A1.

Meyrowitz, Joshua. "Mediating Communication: What Happens?" In *Questioning the Media: A Critical Introduction*, 2d ed., ed. John Downing et al., 39–53. London: Sage, 1995.

Miliband, Ralph. *The State in Capitalist Society*. New York: Basic Books, 1969.

Mills, C. Wright. *The Power Elite*. New York: Oxford University Press, 1957.

Morain, Dan. "Lotteries on a Roll." *Los Angeles Times*, 1 February 1987, sec. 1, 1.

Morley, David. *Television, Audiences, and Cultural Studies*. London: Routledge, 1992.

Mosco, Vincent. *The Political Economy of Communication: Rethinking and Renewal*. London: Sage, 1996.

Mougayar, Walid. *Opening Digital Markets: Battle Plans and Business Strategies for Internet Commerce*. New York: McGraw-Hill, 1998.

MSNBC Reports. "Look at Me! The Webcam Explosion." MSNBC, 29 August 2000.

Murray, Janet H. *Hamlet on the Holodeck: The Future of Narrative in Cyberspace*. New York: Free Press, 1997.

Myers, George, Jr. "As Seen on TV in Video Age, Everyone Wants to Get into the Act," *Columbus Dispatch*, 5 March 2000, sec. 1A.

Naughton, Keith. "CyberSlacking." *Newsweek*, 29 November 1999, 62.

NBC News Transcripts. "Death in the O.R." *Dateline NBC*, 13 July 1999, at www.lexis.com (accessed 28 August 1999).

Negroponte, Nicholas. *Being Digital*. New York: Knopf, 1995.

Negt, Oskar, and Alexander Kluge. *Public Sphere and Experience: Toward an Analysis of the Bourgeois and Proletarian Public Sphere*. Trans. Peter Labanyi, Jamie Owen Daniel, and Assenka Oksiloff. Minneapolis: University of Minnesota Press, 1993.

Nicholsen, Shierry Weber. *Exact Imagination, Late Work: On Adorno's Aesthetics*. Cambridge, Mass.: MIT Press, 1997.

Noble, David. *Force of Production: A Social History of Industrial Automation*. New York: Knopf, 1984.

Norris, Clive, and Gary Armstrong. *The Maximum Surveillance Society: The Rise of CCTV as Social Control*. Oxford: Berg, 1999.

"The Numbers." *The Numbers*, 19 August 2002, at www.the-numbers.com/movies/2001/OCEAN.html (accessed 12 January 2003).

O'Connell, Pamela. "Online Diary." *New York Times*, 10 October 2002, sec. G3.

O'Connor, Alan, and John Downing. "Culture and Communication." In *Questioning the Media: A Critical Introduction*, ed. John Downing, Ali Mohammadi, and Annabelle Sreberny-Mohammadi. Thousand Oaks, Calif.: Sage, 1995.

O'Connor, Brian. "Introduction." In *The Adorno Reader*, ed. Brian O'Connor, 1–20. Oxford: Blackwell, 2000.

Ostrow, Joanne. "Reality According to CBS." *Denver Post*, 10 January 2001, sec. G7.

Pateman, Carole. *Participation and Democratic Theory*. London: Cambridge University Press, 1970.

Peck, Janice. "The 'Oprah Effect': Texts, Readers, and the Dialectic of Signification." Unpublished manuscript, University of Colorado, 2001.

Perkins, Ken Parish. "Ratings Prove TV Viewers Want More and More Sleaze." *Fort Worth Star-Telegram*, 22 May 1999, 27.

Peters, J. D. "Distrust of Representation: Habermas on the Public Sphere." *Media, Culture and Society* 15 (1993): 541–71.

———. "Revising the 18th-Century Script." *Gannett Center Journal* 3, no. 2 (1989): 152–66.

Pine, B. Joseph. *Mass Customization: The New Frontier in Business Competition*. Boston: Harvard Business School Press, 1993.

Poniewozik, James. "We Like to Watch." *Time* 125 (26 June 2000): 26.

Poster, Mark. *The Mode of Information: Poststructuralism and Social Context*. Chicago: University of Chicago Press, 1990.

"Project Overview." *MIT Project Oxygen*, at oxygen.lcs.mit.edu/Overview.html (accessed 15 June 2002).

Pruitt, Steve, and Tom Barrett. "Corporate Virtual Workspace." In *Cyberspace: First Steps*, ed. Michael Benedikt, 383–409. Cambridge, Mass.: MIT Press, 1991.

Pulley, Brett. "Waiting for Riches." *New York Times*, 22 May 1999, sec. A1.

Revkin, Andrew. "US Sees Problems in Climate Change." *New York Times*, 3 June 2002, sec. A1.

Rheingold, Howard. *Smart Mobs: The Next Social Revolution*. Cambridge, Mass.: Perseus, 2002.

——. *Virtual Community*. Reading, Mass.: Addison-Wesley, 1993.

Rifkin, Jeremy. *The End of Work: The Decline of the Global Labor Force and the Dawn of the Post-market Era*. New York: Putnam's, 1995.

Robertson, Douglas S. *The New Renaissance: Computers and the Next Level of Civilization*. New York: Oxford University Press, 1998.

Robins, Kevin. "Against Virtual Community: For a Politics of Distance." *Angelaki* 4, no. 2 (1999): 163–70.

Robins, Kevin, and Frank Webster. "The Revolution of the Fixed Wheel: Information, Technology and Social Taylorism." In *Television in Transition*, ed. Phillip Drummond and Richard Paterson. London: British Film Institute, 1985.

——. *Times of the Technoculture: From the Information Society to the Virtual Life*. London: Routledge, 1999.

Rose, Gillian. *The Melancholy Science: An Introduction to the Thought of Theodor W. Adorno*. London: Macmillan, 1978.

Roseberry, William. *Anthropologies and Histories: Essays in Culture, History and Political Economy*. New Brunswick, N.J.: Rutgers University Press, 1989.

Ruoff, J. K. "'A Bastard Union of Several Forms': Style and Narrative in an American Family." In *Documenting the Documentary: Close Readings of Documentary Films and Videos*, ed. Berry Keith Grant and Jeannette Sloniowski, 286–301. Detroit, Mich.: Wayne State University Press, 1998.

Rutenberg, Jim. "Reality Shows Set Off Fight over Awards." *New York Times*, 12 February 2001, sec. C1.

Sager, Mike. "What I've Learned: Mark Burnett." *Esquire* (July 2001), at www.esquire.com/features/learned/010701_mwi_burnett.html (accessed 20 September 2001).

Schiesel, Seth. "New AT&T System Displays a 'Millionaire' Bonus." *New York Times*, 14 February 2000, sec. C4.

Schiller, Dan. *Digital Capitalism: Networking the Global Market System*. Cambridge, Mass.: MIT Press, 1999.

Schudson, Michael. *Discovering the News: A Social History of American Newspapers*. New York: Basic Books, 1978.

Sella, Marshall. "The Electronic Fishbowl." *New York Times Magazine*, 21 May 2000, 50–104.

——. "The Remote Controllers." *New York Times*, 20 October 2002, sec. 6, 68.

Serwer, Andy. "What Do These Guys Know about the Internet?" *Fortune*, 9 October 2000, 112.

"Share and Share Unalike." *The Economist*, 7 August 1999, 110.

Sharkey, Betsy. "Living in "The Real World"; Entering Its Sixth Season, MTV's Video-Verite Series Has Established Its Own Brand of Show." *Mediaweek*, 21 July 1997, 17.

Slack, Jennifer D. "The Information Revolution as Ideology." *Media, Culture and Society* 6 (1984): 247–56.

Slotek, Jim. "Fox, Lead Us Not into Temptation." *Toronto Sun*, 15 January 2001, 47.

Smythe, Dallas Walker. *Dependency Road: Communications, Capitalism, Consciousness, and Canada*. Toronto: Ablex, 1981.

Soja, Edward W. *Postmodern Geographies: The Reassertion of Space in Critical Social Theory*. London: Verso, 1989.

Soriano, Cesar G. "CBS, Tribe Speak Out on Lawsuit: 'Survivor' Not Rigged, They Say." *USA Today*, 8 February 2001, sec. 6D.

Souza, Josh. "The Big Brother Show." *JoshSouzaOnline* (2001), at joshsouzaonline.com/bigbrother.html (accessed 6 January 2002).

Stanley, Alessandra. "Forgotten Stars Never Die: They Show Up in Reality TV." *New York Times*, 18 January 2003, sec. A1.

Steiner, Linda. "Nineteenth-Century Suffrage Periodicals: Conceptions of Womanhood and the Press." In *Ruthless Criticism: New Perspectives in U.S. Communication History*, ed. William S. Solomon and Robert W. McChesney, 66–97. Minneapolis: University of Minnesota Press, 1993.

Storey, John. *An Introductory Guide to Cultural Theory and Popular Culture*. Athens: University of Georgia Press, 1993.

"The Story of the Wetlands." *The Wetlands*, at www.wetlands.net/Site01/index.html (accessed 12 November 2002).

Sunstein, Cass. *Republic.com*. Princeton, N.J.: Princeton University Press, 2002.

Teeple, Gary. *Globalization and the Decline of Social Reform*. Toronto: Garmond, 1995.

Terranova, Tiziana, "Free Labor: Producing Culture for the Digital Economy." *Social Text* 63, no. 18 (Summer 2000): 33–57.

Toffler, Alvin, and Heidi Toffler. *Creating a New Civilization: The Politics of the Third Wave*. Atlanta: Tower, 1995.

Tonnies, Ferdinand. *Community and Society*. Trans. and ed. Charles P. Loomis. New York: Harper & Row, 1957.

"The Trojan Room Coffee Machine." At www.cl.cam.ac.uk/coffee/coffee.html (accessed 12 December 2002).

Turkle, Sherry. *Life on the Screen: Identity in the Age of the Internet*. New York: Simon & Schuster, 1995.

Turner, Graeme. *British Cultural Studies: An Introduction*. Boston: Unwin Hyman, 1990.

"The Ultimate Soap Opera." *Time*, 22 January 1973, 36.

Weber, Max. "Science as a Vocation." In *From Max Weber: Essays in Sociology*, trans. and ed. H. H. Gerth and C. Wright Mills, 129–56. New York: Oxford University Press, 1946.

Webster, Frank, and Kevin Robins. *Information Technology: A Luddite Analysis*. Norwood, N.J.: Ablex, 1986.

Weingarten, Mark. "MTV Moves the 'Real' Fishbowl to Honolulu." *Los Angeles Times*, 14 June 1999, F2.

Weinraub, Bernard. "Sudden Explosion of Game Shows Threatens the Old TV Staples."
    New York Times, 9 February 2000, sec. E1

Whitaker, Reginald. *The End of Privacy: How Total Surveillance Is Becoming a Reality*.
    New York: New Press, 1999.

"The Will." *The Will*, at www.thewilltv.com/main.html (accessed 12 January 2003).

Williams, Raymond. *The Long Revolution*. New York: Columbia University Press, 1961.

———. *Marxism and Literature*. Oxford: Oxford University Press, 1977.

———. *Politics and Letters: Interviews with New Left Review*. New York: NLB, 1979.

———. *Television: Technology and Culture Form*. New York: Schocken, 1975.

Witkowski, Melissa. "Wearable Computing." Unpublished manuscript, Fairfield Univer-
    sity.

Woodward, Sarah. "Surviving Survivor." *SHOOT*, 21 July 2000, 7.

"The Works." *BitStreams*, at www.whitney.org/bitstreams/ (accessed 24 July 2001).

Wriston, Walter B. *The Twilight of Sovereignty: How the Information Revolution Is Trans-
    forming Our World*. New York: Maxwell Macmillan International, 1992.

Zizek, Slavoj. *The Fragile Absolute, or, Why Is the Christian Legacy Worth Fighting For?*
    London: Verso, 2000.

———. "How the Non-Duped Err." *Qui Parle: Literature, Philosophy, Visual Arts, History*
    4, no. 1 (1990): 1–20.

———. "In His Bold Gaze My Ruin Is Writ Large." *In Everything You Always Wanted to
    Know about Lacan but Were Afraid to Ask Hitchcock*, ed. Slavoj Zizek, 211–72. Lon-
    don: Verso, 1992.

———. *Looking Awry: An Introduction to Jacques Lacan through Popular Culture*. Cam-
    bridge, Mass.: MIT Press, 1997.

———. *The Plague of Fantasies*. London: Verso, 1997.

———. *The Ticklish Subject*. London: Verso, 1999.

———. *The Zizek Reader*. London: Blackwell, 1999.

Zurawik, David. "Real Deal: Clever Production, True Drama and Low Costs Make an
    Open-and-Shut Case for a New Breed of Network Reality Shows." *Baltimore Sun*, 4
    June 2002, sec. 1E.

Index

About the Author

Mark Andrejevic is assistant professor in the Department of Communication Studies at the University of Iowa where he teaches television and media studies. His articles on surveillance, new media, and reality TV have appeared in journals including *Space and Culture*, *New Media and Society*, and *Critical Studies in Media Communication*.